PRAI**O FREEDOM**

"The great strength of this book is that it is the story of people and not simply a repetition of dates and a listing of places and events. Put this book on your must-read list!"

— **JULIAN BOND,** chairman of the NAACP

"This book represents a rare opportunity to walk through the pages of history with a man who was there. A window to a not-so-distant past, it reveals the heart and soul of a movement that transformed America."

— **REP. JOHN LEWIS**

"This is totally engaging storytelling. . . . This book should be in the hands of all those who care about this history, but more important, it should be in the hands of all those who don't, at least not yet."

— **JUDY RICHARDSON,** series associate producer for *Eyes on the Prize*

"Brilliantly honors the struggles, the dreams, and the sacrifices of the past. *On the Road to Freedom* is must reading. Charlie Cobb reminds us that history is not some dead, long-ago series of events. As a veteran civil rights activist remembering and revisiting his journey, he guides us in rediscovering an important historical moment in our collective journey."

— **DANNY GLOVER**

"Cobb has written a well-researched and engaging book, enriched by his vivid tales of remarkable acts of resistance to injustice."

— **CLAYBORNE CARSON,** director of the Martin Luther King Jr. Research and Education Institute at Stanford University

D0059025

"Truly extraordinary. [Cobb] combines his personal knowledge, his knowledge of history, and his writer's ability to take us on a physical and emotional journey on the road to freedom."

—**CONSTANCE CURRY,** author of *Silver Rights*

"Geographer of an era and its battlegrounds, Cobb brings alive America's last good war and its many heroes, unsung as well as famous. From chapter to chapter, you are there."

—**HODDING CARTER III**

"This remarkable book is the product of a rare combination of historical analysis, insight, and personal acquaintance with some of the most important activists of our time. In the course of introducing us to the places of the movement, Cobb gives us a crash course in the people and personalities who made these places historically significant. We actually get to see how movement culture evolved. Time and again we are reminded of how many different kinds of people it took to make the movement. Time and again we are reminded that one never knows which spark will start the fire."

—**CHARLES PAYNE,** author of *I've Got the Light of Freedom*

"This essential book makes a major contribution to understanding the grassroots organizing that gave the Southern civil rights movement its strength."

—**WILLIAM RASPBERRY,** Pulitzer Prize–winning columnist

"*On the Road to Freedom* is a very important American story. . . . Cobb paints a brilliant picture of the civil rights movement, the people and communities that gave it texture. This journey down the long road of freedom is memorable and a must-read for everyone, especially our youth."

—**HARRY BELAFONTE**

ON THE ROAD TO FREEDOM

ON THE ROAD TO FREEDOM

*A Guided Tour of the
Civil Rights Trail*

BY CHARLES E. COBB JR.

ALGONQUIN BOOKS OF CHAPEL HILL 2008

Published by
Algonquin Books of Chapel Hill
Post Office Box 2225
Chapel Hill, North Carolina 27515-2225

a division of
Workman Publishing
225 Varick Street
New York, New York 10014

Published simultaneously in Canada by Thomas Allen & Son Limited.
Design by Charles Kreloff.
Photo research by Leora Khan.

For permission to reprint excerpts and photographs, grateful acknowledgment
is made to those mentioned on pp. 374–75, which constitute an extension of the
copyright page.

Library of Congress Cataloging-in-Publication Data
Cobb, Charles E., Jr.
    On the road to freedom : a guided tour of the civil rights trail /
Charles E. Cobb, Jr. — 1st ed.
        p. cm.
    Includes bibliographical references and index.
    ISBN-13: 978-1-56512-439-4
    1. African Americans — Civil rights — History — 20th century.   2. Civil
rights movements — United States — History — 20th century.   3. African
American civil rights workers — Biography.   4. African Americans — Homes
and haunts — Southern States.   5. Southern States — Description and
travel.   6. Southern States — History, Local.   7. Southern States —
Race relations — History — 20th century.   8. United States — Race
relations — History — 20th century.   I. Title.
    E185.61.C63 2008
    323.1196'073 — dc22   2007018842
10 9 8 7 6 5 4 3 2 1
First Edition

This book is dedicated to three great women, who took me by the hand and soul, and guided me until I learned the way: Mrs. Fannie Lou Hamer, Mrs. Annie Bell Robinson Devine, and Mrs. Victoria Gray Adams.

If there is no struggle, there is no progress. Those who profess to favor freedom, and yet depreciate agitation, are men who want crops without plowing up the ground. They want rain without thunder and lightning. They want the ocean without the awful roar of its many waters. This struggle may be a moral one; or it may be a physical one; or it may be both moral and physical; but it must be a struggle. Power concedes nothing without a demand. It never did and it never will. Find out just what a people will submit to, and you have found out the exact amount of injustice and wrong which will be imposed upon them; and these will continue till they are resisted with either words or blows, or with both. The limits of tyrants are prescribed by the endurance of those whom they oppress. Men may not get all they pay for in this world; but they must pay for all they get. If we ever get free from all the oppressions and wrongs heaped upon us, we must pay for their removal. We must do this by labor, by suffering, by sacrifice, and, if needs be, by our lives, and the lives of others.

—FREDERICK DOUGLASS, 1857

CONTENTS

ACKNOWLEDGMENTS

First, I must immediately acknowledge here all of the heroes and hero-ines across the South, and across the centuries of Afro-American life, who, through their organized resistance to slavery, segregation, and the racism that poisoned so much of their lives, made the story told in these pages possible. They have been, and remain, an inspiration to me and, just as important, my teachers. In many, many ways, this book is their book.

Love and gratitude to my wife, Ann, and daughter, Zora. They were tolerant and patient with my clutter, my moods, and the many days and hours I was lost in the book.

I have long struggled with what works and what does not work in conveying the events that are now grouped together as the civil rights movement, so special thanks to Dr. Anthony Bogues, chair of Brown University's Africana Studies Department. In inviting me to teach as a visiting professor at the university, he gave me an unexpected oppor-tunity to work on a storytelling language in the classroom with young students, for whom this era is a distant time. Significant portions of the Georgia, Alabama, and Mississippi chapters were drawn from lectures given in my undergraduate seminar at the university: The Organizing Tradition of the Southern Civil Rights Movement.

In much the same manner, during the three years I have been working on this book, Dr. Jeanne Middleton-Hairston, director of the Children's Defense Fund Freedom Schools National Training, has invited me to participate in their program, held at the Alex Haley farm in Clinton, Tennessee, every June. In conversations with and presenta-tions to the thousand or so mostly Afro-American young people who attend each year, I was also able to work on discovering language to tell this story effectively. I am grateful.

I began writing this book at the Blue Mountain Center, a writer's retreat in New York's Adirondack Mountains. I wish to express gratitude for the quiet and solitude their invitation gave me, enabling me to orga-nize my thoughts effectively and even get a few words down on paper.

This is not a history book in any academic sense but a story as I might tell it to you in face-to-face conversation — not the whole story or even most of the story — and I kept formal interviews to a mini-mum; but to Bernard Lafayette, Cleveland Sellers, John Lewis, Diane Nash, Chuck McDew, Reggie Robinson, Hank Thomas, Guy and Candie Carawan, Bob Mants, Unita Blackwell, Hollis Watkins, Joanne Bland, Gwen Patton, and Mattie Atkins, thank you for consenting to such sit-down interviews. Jean Wiley, Judy Richardson, Maria Varela,

Marilyn Lowen, Andy Young, Jack O'Dell, Julian Bond, David Dennis, Courtland Cox, Ruby Sales, Victoria Gray Adams, Ivanhoe Donaldson, Bill Strickland, and Reverend Jesse Jackson responded to my requests for specific pieces of information, and I want to acknowledge here the importance of their contributions to this book.

Parts of this book appeared in the September–October 2003 issue of *AARP: The Magazine*, as the article "Full Circle." I wish to acknowledge a debt to that publication, because its appearance attracted the attention of Algonquin Books' publisher, Elisabeth Scharlatt, and, from Algonquin, a commitment to this book. And here, I wish to acknowledge the inestimable value of my editor, the extraordinarily patient Andra Olenik, for her helpful guidance when I sometimes got lost in the thick tangle of events on my own trail.

This book has no bibliography, but a number of written works were a great help while writing it. In my background research I gave preference to books by movement veterans, and I always found something of great value in every one of such texts: *Coming of Age in Mississippi* by Anne Moody, James Forman's *The Making of Black Revolutionaries, Ready for Revolution* by Kwame Ture (Stokely Carmichael) and his earlier *Black Power*, Cleveland Sellers's *The River of No Return*, James Farmer's *Lay Bare the Heart*, Andrew Young's *An Easy Burden*, John Lewis's *Walking with the Wind*, Ralph David Abernathy's *And the Walls Came Tumbling Down*, H. Rap Brown's *Die Nigger Die!* Julius Lester's *Look Out, Whitey! Black Power's Gon' Get Your Mama!* Constance Curry's *Silver Rights*, Aaron Henry's *Aaron Henry: The Fire Ever Burning* (with Constance Curry), *Deep in Our Hearts* by Constance Curry, Penny Patch, et al., Len Holt's *The Summer That Didn't End*, Mary King's *Freedom Song*, Elizabeth Sutherland Martinez's *Letters from Mississippi, Barefootin': Life Lessons from the Road to Freedom* by Unita Blackwell and Joanne Prichard, *Lanterns: A Memoir of Mentors* by Marian Wright Edelman, and Robert Moses's *Radical Equations* (which I coauthored, I must say in the name of full disclosure). And let me acknowledge here some books that precede this 1960s focus but are organically connected to it: Jo Ann Robinson's *The Montgomery Bus Boycott and the Women Who Started It, Bridge Across Jordan* by Amelia Boynton, *Negroes with Guns* by Robert Williams, Septima Clark's *Echo in My Soul*, and *Rosa Parks: My Story* by Rosa Parks and Jim Haskins.

Four classics helped ground me in history: *From Slavery to Freedom* by John Hope Franklin, *The Negro in Our History* by Carter G. Woodson and Charles H. Wesley, *Before the Mayflower* by Lerone Bennett, and *There Is a River* by Vincent Harding.

There are also a handful of other books written by scholars whose usefulness to my effort I wish to acknowledge: Howard Zinn's *SNCC: The New Abolitionists;* John Dittmer's look at grassroots organizing in Mississippi, *Local People;* Charles Payne's *I've Got the Light of Freedom,* which I think gives the greatest insight into the tradition of community organizing that defined the movement; Harry G. Lefever's excellent *Undaunted by the Fight: Spelman College and the Civil Rights Movement, 1957–1967,* though focused on Atlanta, opens a window into campus, community, and the civil rights struggle; Richard Kluger's invaluable study of the people and events that led to the 1954 Supreme Court decision, *Simple Justice;* John D'Emilio's vivid *Lost Prophet: The Life and Times of Bayard Rustin,* portraying the only major movement figure who may be more ignored than Ella Baker; *Freedom Riders* by Raymond Arsenault, the definitive work on those historic journeys; Cynthia Fleming's look at the life of Ruby Doris Smith Robinson, *Soon We Will Not Cry;* Clayborne Carson's *In Struggle: SNCC and the Black Awakening of the 1960s;* Tom Dent's thoughtful *Southern Journey;* Barbara Ransby's *Ella Baker and the Black Freedom Movement,* as well as *Ella Baker: Freedom Bound* by Joanne Grant; the Taylor Branch trilogy on the King years; and David Garrow's detailed *Bearing the Cross.*

Unfortunately, civil rights veterans have written very few books, especially nonautobiographical books of reflection and analysis, which means both that the sensibility underlying the facts of what happened in the civil rights struggle is at risk of being lost and that the canon defining what the movement was is narrowly conceived. In this regard, I would like to acknowledge the people from the movement who are right now at work on books and in this last sentence offer my encouragement and announce my anticipation of being able to turn your pages.

—CHARLES E. COBB JR.

~ INTRODUCTION ~

We have Tomorrow
Bright before us
Like a flame

Yesterday, a night-gone thing
A sun-down name

And dawn today
Broad arch above the road we came

We march!
    —"Youth," LANGSTON HUGHES, 1925

The civil rights trail of Joanne Bland winds through time and place as she talks to a group of high school students from Milwaukee, Wisconsin, who are visiting the Voting Rights Museum and Institute in Selma, Alabama. Sometimes her words surprise them because they offer more than is usually offered to students, who, if they think of the civil rights movement, think of it in terms of the carefully crafted image of Dr. Martin Luther King Jr. and the mass protests he led. Joanne's words underline an important fact about that Alabama city, which was one of the most significant battlegrounds of southern civil rights struggle in the 1960s: ordinary local people who gave Selma's civil rights movement its extraordinary power have taken charge of telling their own story. Planned or unplanned encounters with people like Joanne Bland add immeasurable depth to the experience of anyone journeying civil rights trails.

"Y'all know Harriet Tubman?" she asks. Joanne is a tall, engaging woman, and with this question she is probing the

Milwaukee students to find out how much they know about the nineteenth century Afro-American abolitionist from Dorchester County, Maryland, who took black slaves out of the South via the Underground Railroad. This is something she constantly does when she talks to young people. With a look that can feel as though she's pinning your mind to her thinking, Joanne can command the complete attention of anyone when she focuses an idea on them. She can also knock you completely off balance with a volley of unexpected words. "Harriet carried a gun. Sounds like my kind of woman."

The small museum Joanne is guiding us through was established through local grassroots efforts in 1992 in the shadow of Selma's Edmund Pettus Bridge. The bridge, which arches across the muddy Alabama River, became an infamous site when, on March 7, 1965, state police troopers and a sheriff's posse opened fire with tear gas and then, swinging nightsticks, charged into and savagely beat civil rights marchers, most of whom were local people protesting the killing of farm laborer and civil rights activist Jimmy Lee Jackson. While participating in a protest against the denial of voting rights, Jackson had been shot by state police.

Joanne, who is the museum's director, offers us more than a history of local protest. "You know Charlotte Ray? First black woman to graduate from law school [Howard University in Washington, D.C., 1872]. Strong women have passed your way." Her eyes linger for a moment on a couple of the black girls in the Milwaukee group. They're hanging on Joanne's every word now.

While the museum pays tribute to civil rights struggles across the South, there is an emphasis on local heroes and heroines. "What about Annie Cooper? They didn't put her in your schoolbooks, but she's my *she-roe*! Moved back here from Kentucky in 1962; went to the courthouse [to register to vote] and they threw her out. Sheriff tried to beat her with that billy club. She took it and whipped him good!"

Ms. Cooper was still living in Selma when I last visited, and was well into her nineties. According to Joanne,

Ms. Cooper was also still driving her own car, "but not all that good." Furthermore, Ms. Cooper was living on Annie Cooper Avenue.

Annie Cooper Avenue! Could any of the civil rights marchers driven off Pettus Bridge on what is now called "Bloody Sunday" have imagined that Ms. Cooper would one day have a street named for her? In 1965, official Selma's violent resistance to civil rights horrified the nation, and soon thereafter, Congress passed the voting rights act.

"Oh Lord we've struggled so long, we must be free, we must be free," went the refrain of one of the freedom songs we used to sing. It has certainly been a long journey, and it is still unfinished. This book has two purposes: to tell some stories that are important to understanding the civil rights movement and to guide you to and through sites where significant events of the civil rights movement unfolded. Like Joanne Bland, we will wind through time and place. And let me emphasize here that this is a travel guide and narrative, not a history book, although history obviously forms its critical core.

This is also very much a book about Freedom. The idea of it and the pursuit of it are what we are actually following on the civil rights trail, and slavery is one of the crucial markers that will guide us. Slavery's stories are at once the same in every state and different in every state; they all color the white South's reaction to the modern civil rights movement. Moreover, this country—both its black people and its white people—has not yet come to grips with slavery's ugly and painful, but fundamental, place in U.S. history.

Primarily, however, this book focuses on the South and that intense period of civil rights struggle in the 1940s, 1950s, and 1960s. It is this period that produced new law, which changed racial practices that seemed entrenched and ineradicable. This period is remarkable not only for its political intensity but also for how much was accomplished in so short a time.

Part of what defines this era is that people and communities began speaking for themselves, making demands for the kind of society *they* wanted instead of standing aside silently while others, sympathetic advocates or white supremacists, spoke for them and of them. What the country began to hear clearly in the mid-twentieth century—or at least could no longer ignore—were insistent Afro-American voices from the grassroots. Through words and actions they refuted any idea that they were indifferent, apathetic, or willing to accede to the myth that they considered full citizenship rights "white folks' business." The public actions of ordinary black people across the South— among them sharecroppers, day workers, small farmers, factory workers, maids, and cooks—who found their own voices made the difference; they defeated Jim Crow. This period culminated with the passage and signing into law of the 1965 Voting Rights Act.

While admittedly this boundary of politics and time is a rough one, more often than not it is what people think of when they hear the phrase "civil rights movement." For that reason, it is a practical framework for this book. Indeed, many of the sites and markers, in cities and towns and along southern roads, memorializing the people and places of the civil rights movement focus on this era. Museums, as one might expect, offer a broader perspective, and the National Park Service's Register of Historic Places lists hundreds of Afro-American sites that reach back to the beginnings of black life in America. But if you are traveling with a specific interest in the civil rights movement, it is likely you are seeking a deeper understanding of the intense decades of the "modern" movement in the South that in a real way changed the face of America.

This is the movement of the Montgomery, Alabama, bus boycott that thrust Rosa Parks and Martin Luther King Jr. into national prominence; of the student sit-ins and Freedom Rides; of the Student Nonviolent Coordinating Committee (SNCC); the Congress of Racial Equality (CORE); and the Southern Christian Leadership Conference (SCLC); as well as the older NAACP. It includes both the growth of grassroots community organizing (around voter registration in particular) that took place throughout the black belt South and dramatically visible civil rights campaigns such as those that took place in Albany, Georgia, in 1962; Birmingham, Alabama, in 1963; the Mississippi Summer Project of 1964; and the Selma-to-Montgomery march in 1965. Some names will be familiar: Fannie Lou Hamer, Andrew Young, Julian Bond, John Lewis, Medgar Evers. Others, though crucial for understanding what took place and why, are virtually unknown: Ella Baker, who in important ways was the godmother of the modern movement; Septima Clark of Charleston, South Carolina, who led the way in establishing the link between reading-and-writing literacy and political literacy; Slater King of Albany, Georgia; Birmingham's Fred Shuttlesworth; or Jo Ann Robinson and E. D. Nixon of Montgomery Alabama; or C. C. Bryant, E. W. Steptoe, Annie Devine, Victoria Gray, and Amzie Moore, all of Mississippi. To know them even a little is to see some part of yourself in the makeup of their everyday lives, for they are mothers, fathers, aunts and uncles, grandparents and neighbors, who were driven not so much by politics or ideology but by the simple human desire for something better in their lives and the lives of their children. Their accomplishments help us recognize the too often obscured but important-to-know fact that you didn't have to be Martin Luther King to become meaningfully engaged with the civil rights movement. "Did we have a leader? Our leaders is we ourself," said Claudette Colvin in court testimony years ago. As a fifteen-year-old high school student, and nine months before Rosa Parks did the same thing in the same city, Claudette Colvin was arrested for refusing to surrender her bus seat to a white man.

There is much to see, but also much that is not readily evident. The gravesite of civil rights martyr Jimmy Lee Jackson on Highway 14 just outside Marion, Alabama, now the Martin Luther King Memorial Highway, is hardly noticeable. Today, thinking of the times that surrounded Jackson's murder reminds us of how far we have come. But Jackson's headstone is pockmarked from gunfire, and that reminds us there is still some distance to travel. Nonetheless, even in Marion, directly across from the county courthouse, there is a "Civil Rights Freedom Wall" that lists ninety-nine names as representing "a roll call of freedom fighters." The town's drowsiness today, its slightly decaying southern charm, gives no clue to how momentous a civil rights battle was fought on its streets. "People picketed the courthouse every day trying to get registered to vote," recalls Mattie Atkins, who though a young married woman with children in the 1960s was one of those picketers. Later, in 1978, she became the first Afro-American woman elected to the Perry County Board of Education. She has now retired as the purchasing agent for the Perry County Commission, where she had an office *inside* the courthouse.

Whether you're in a city like Selma, where civil rights struggle had high visibility, or in a tiny practically invisible town like Marion, behind ordinary outward appearances there is often something more. So, in part, this is an "insiders" guide. I know this trail. As a Student Nonviolent Coordinating Committee field secretary from 1962 until 1967, my work was concentrated in Mississippi, but that work plugged me into a civil rights network across the South. This network had been developed over many decades by a generation—indeed, generations—of people older than my nineteen-year-old self (my age when I first arrived in Mississippi), and this network offered sanctuary when needed, good advice, and political education, and, over time, passed the baton of civil rights struggle to us. "What they were is who we are now," says Bob Moses, a legendary figure in the civil rights movement, who first arrived in Mississippi in 1960 as a twenty-five-year-old schoolteacher from Harlem.

The key to understanding what the civil rights struggle means today is understanding that there is no single civil rights trail; after all, civil rights struggle unfolded everywhere. The sites in this book are places offering important lessons that help us understand the movement. Some choices

of sites reflect my personal and political preferences—
Washington, D.C., for example, which is not generally considered a part of the South (nor is its slave-market history
often highlighted). This book presents *a* civil rights trail,
not the *only* civil rights trail, and certainly it does not and
cannot discuss every single arena of civil rights struggle. I
have chosen not to chart specific, detailed itineraries, preferring instead to hone in on significant locations and offer
you their stories. And because this is very much my book,
the book of a former organizer, *people*, as much as place,
structure our journey. Many of them are not usually mentioned in the books that make up the civil rights canon.
But without meeting them it is impossible to clearly understand what civil rights struggle was.

Beginning in the U.S. Capital, the trail we will follow
takes us from the upper South into and through the heart
of the black belt, where we will retrace some of the significant civil rights events that took place in cities, towns, and
the countryside that surrounds them. Everywhere we will
go we will be able to hear local voices—voices like Joanne
Bland's in Selma—still echoing.

My movement experience is an organizer's experience:
entering small communities and learning to live in them
while assisting black people under fire from white terrorists to take control of their own lives. It was, despite all the
violence and intimidation directed at Afro-American communities, a time when the strength that broke the back of
white supremacy was drawn from deep wells of courage
throughout the South. Much of the organizing tradition
that shaped my movement experience—getting people
to voice a demand for the kind of society in which they
wanted to live—seems relevant today. So this book aims to
help you see and understand the stories in terms of how
people organized themselves to effect change. And, while
this is a book that I hope you, the reader, will curl up with
to enjoy the stories it tells, I hope, too, that you will find it
a meaningful and useful tool while traveling in general, or
in planning a trip with the specific intention of following a
civil rights trail.

AUTHOR'S NOTE

A note about the designations "black" and "Afro-American" as used in this book: I use "Afro-American" as a way of formally designating what I consider to be the *ethnic* group that over the past four hundred years has evolved in the United States from descendants of people from the African continent, many of whom were captured and brought to the Americas as slaves. "African-American" more properly describes any former citizen of an African nation who has chosen U.S. citizenship. I use "blacks" as a loose and broad racial designation without geographic specificity. Such wrestling with noun and adjective with regard to name is in many respects a writer's issue. But it is also cultural, related to an uncertainty that has always existed in the Afro-American community about who we are. After all, name and place were stripped from us by slavery. And if our place is now here in America, we still sometimes struggle with name because, collectively, we remain unsure of how much of the African part of our original selves we have retained or shed—or should.

ON THE ROAD TO FREEDOM

CHAPTER ONE

MY COUNTRY 'TIS OF THEE

Washington, D.C.

> 66 *As a colored woman I cannot visit the tomb of the Father of this country, which owes its very existence to the love of freedom in the human heart and which stands for equal opportunity to all, without being forced to sit in the Jim Crow section of an electric car which starts from the very heart of the city—midway between the Capitol and the White House. If I refuse thus to be humiliated, I am cast into jail and forced to pay a fine . . . [N]owhere in the world do oppression and persecution based solely on the color of the skin appear more hateful and hideous than in the capital of the United States, because the chasm between the principles upon which this Government was founded, in which it still professes to believe, and those which are daily practiced under the protection of the flag, yawns so wide and deep.* 99

—"ON BEING COLORED IN THE NATION'S CAPITAL,"
MARY CHURCH TERRELL, SPEAKING TO THE UNITED
WOMEN'S CLUB, OCTOBER 10, 1906

The trail begins in my hometown, Washington, D.C., because public demonstrations and protests that became hallmarks of the 1960s civil rights movement actually took place in the nation's Capital much earlier than that intense decade. In April 1943, for example, Howard University law student Pauli Murray led female students in a sit-in at the Little Palace cafeteria near Fourteenth and U Streets, NW, which in those days served only whites although it was just a few blocks away from the historically black Howard campus. Even earlier, in 1935, Kenneth Clark (who as a psychologist, along with his wife, Mamie Phipps Clark, would later play a crucial role in convincing the Supreme Court of segregation's damaging psychological effect on black children) was arrested while picketing the U.S. Capitol in protest of its restaurant's refusal to serve blacks. Like Pauli Murray, Clark attended Howard University; he was a student leader and agitator, editor of the school's newspaper. Twenty other students who walked the picket line with him were also arrested.

Demonstrations against racial discrimination first gained high national visibility in Washington, D.C., when in 1939 the Daughters of the American Revolution, who owned Constitution Hall, then the city's finest concert auditorium, denied the famed black contralto Marian Anderson permission to sing there. The District of Columbia Board of Education was then asked if Anderson could use the auditorium of the all-white **Central High School** (*13th and Clifton Streets, NW; now named* **Cardozo**

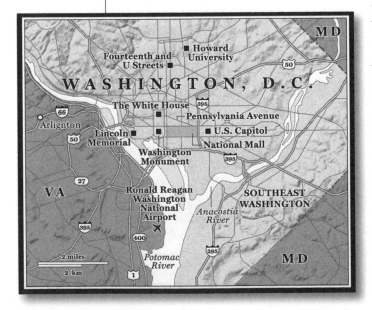

High School, an almost all-black inner-city school in a rapidly gentrifying neighborhood, but still standing on the same prominent northwest Washington ridge that offers one of the more splendid views of the city). The Board refused. Some of Central High's own students picketed the school board, protesting the denial. An incensed Eleanor Roosevelt resigned from the DAR. A Marian Anderson Citizens Committee formed, determined that Anderson would find appropriate recital space somewhere in the city. Supported by Mrs. Roosevelt, Secretary of the Interior Harold L. Ickes, who had once been president of Chicago's NAACP branch, offered the Lincoln Memorial for the concert.

Dr. Kenneth B. Clark, one of the most influential psychologists of the 20th century. In a 1984 interview, Clark told the New York Times *that he remained "bewildered" by the persistence of northern racism. "I believed in the 1950s that a significant percentage of Americans were looking for a way out of the morass of segregation. . . . It took me 10 to 15 years to realize that I seriously underestimated the depth and complexity of northern racism."*

Seventy-five thousand people attended that April 9 Easter Sunday concert—about a third of the number who would participate in the 1963 March on Washington so famously addressed by Martin Luther King, where once again Marian Anderson would sing at the Lincoln Memorial. My future father-in-law, Harold B. Chinn, rented a tuxedo for the occasion, a real sacrifice in that depression year, to show his respect and support; his wife, Louise, wore an evening gown she had made herself. The crowd, black and white, professional and working class, from artistic community and government bureaucracy, signaled an emerging national consensus, which would only grow stronger in coming decades, that white supremacy and racism could no longer be considered acceptable in either law or custom.

"My country tis of thee, sweet land of liberty, of thee I sing." The great voice of Marian Anderson opened with the song "America" to a crowd, some members in tears, that stretched from the memorial, around the reflecting pool, to the grounds of the Washington Monument across Seventeenth Street. Millions more across the country were listening via radio. *"From every mountainside let freedom ring."* The words warmed the chilly air. Anderson ended

with the spiritual "Nobody Knows the Trouble I've Seen," and the crowd rushed toward her like a great human tidal wave before she was whisked away. "It was a cold dreary day," recalled actor Ossie Davis years later. In 1939 Davis was a Howard University student. "Marian Anderson was on the front steps in her mink coat, as it were . . . But standing there listening to her all of a sudden I had a transformation that was almost of a religious nature. Something in her singing, something in her demeanor entered me, and opened me up, and made me a free man. And in a sense I never lost that. So she became a kind of angel of my redemption."

Eleanor Roosevelt

Eleanor Roosevelt may be the only first lady ever even to mildly, but directly and publicly, challenge racial segregation. In 1938 she visited Birmingham, Alabama, to speak at a meeting of the Southern Conference for Human Welfare. Mary McLeod Bethune, founder of Bethune-Cookman College in Florida and of the National Council of Negro Women, and the other blacks in attendance were required to sit in a segregated section. When the First Lady realized that, she placed her chair in the center aisle between the two designated areas

In 1939, Eleanor Roosevelt presents Marian Anderson with the NAACP's prestigious Spingarn medal, awarded for outstanding achievement by a black American.

and stayed there until she was called to speak. This put her in violation of a city ordinance requiring racial segregation, and though she was at least technically subject to arrest she was not apprehended—it's good to be the First Lady.

My grandmother, Ruby Kendrick, was also in that crowd, "just thrilled" to see "an accomplished colored woman" like Anderson singing on the federal mall before such a body of people, she said much later. My grandmother expressed no anger toward the DAR, I think because the sheer power of Marian Anderson in song on the steps of the Lincoln Memorial that day completely transformed the racial prejudice and discrimination that had forced her concert outdoors into an affirmation of the inevitability of change. It was as if Marian Anderson was supposed to be there, in the shadow of Lincoln, fated to stand before America in the embrace of Ossie Davis, my grandmother, my in-laws-to-be, and tens of thousands of other people, reflecting with the power of her voice and presence what would emerge as the anthem and central article of faith of the civil rights movement: "We Shall Overcome."

Marian Anderson performs on the steps of the Lincoln Memorial on Easter Sunday, April 9, 1939. Seventeen years earlier, some 3,500 invited guests, including President Warren G. Harding and Robert Todd Lincoln, the only surviving son of Abraham Lincoln, gathered here for the dedication of the memorial. Dr. Robert R. Moton, president of Alabama's renowned Tuskegee Institute, gave the keynote speech. But Dr. Moton was not allowed to sit on the speaker's platform; he had to find a seat in the roped off all-Negro section.

THE U.S. CAPITOL AND NATIONAL MALL

When it comes to Washington, D.C., most think only of the federal city, the nation's Capital. But there is also what some have called the "Secret City" and others the "Chocolate City" of neighborhoods and communities whose pace and lifestyle have little to do with the monuments and institutions so many visit to celebrate or protest. For much of its existence, *this* "city" was a small, thoroughly segregated southern town where Afro-Americans were second-class citizens.

> ## "So Much Power and Glory"
>
> A listener [comes] away from one of [Marian Anderson's] recitals uncertain whether he has enjoyed her aesthetic or a religious experience so completely fused are the two ideals in this great artist's own nature. When she sings she gives everything she has to God and He in His generosity gives it back to all the listeners within hearing. Her presence itself is compelling. Seemingly without making any conscious effort, she commands complete attention. Seldom, indeed, has such simplicity of manner, such peaceful bearing, been accompanied by so much power and glory.
>
> —FROM *KEEP A-INCHIN' ALONG: SELECTED WRITINGS OF CARL VAN VECHTEN ABOUT BLACK ARTS AND LETTERS*

Furthermore, this Washington, D.C., has always been bound to the old states of the southern Confederacy because until the late 1960s, the city's life was completely regulated by congressional legislators, many continually reelected to office in their home states because voting rights were denied to Afro-Americans. Therefore, we must, as we have already begun to realize through Marian Anderson and Kenneth Clark, do some traveling across the terrain of the federal government.

A bronze bust of Reverend Martin Luther King Jr. rests on a black granite base in the rotunda of the **U.S. Capitol**. King's face is solemn, dignified, and to me even spiritual in some indefinable way. It was installed January 16, 1986, to honor Dr. King's work and celebrate his birthday (January 15, 1929). During the weekend of October 29, 2005, the Capitol Rotunda became identified with another civil rights legend when, shortly after her death at the age of ninety-two, Rosa Parks, the "mother" of the modern civil rights movement, became the first woman to lie in state there for public viewing and tribute. Her image will soon join Martin Luther King's as a permanent presence in the

U.S. Capitol Artwork

Currently, Rev. King's sculpture is the only one of a black person in the rotunda, although elsewhere in the Capitol, Afro-Americans appear in some of the murals and paintings. On the Senate side of the Capitol just above the **Hugh Scott Room** *(S-120)*, Afro-American astronaut Ronald E. McNair is portrayed with his six *Challenger* colleagues, all of whom were killed in the 1986 space shuttle disaster. In the **west stairway of the House wing**, *Westward the Course of Empire Takes Its Way*, painted in 1862, shows a young Afro-American boy leading a mule on which are seated a woman and child. A fresco on the **north wall of the Senate Appropriations Committee Room** *(S-128)* depicting the 1770 Boston Massacre includes Crispus Attucks, the Afro-American who was the first man to die. A series of murals in the **Cox corridors of the House wing**, chronicling important events in U.S. history, includes vignettes of the cotton gin and the Emancipation Proclamation, both of which show some Afro-Americans. There are two of particular interest: "Civil Rights Bill Passes, 1866," found in the **eastern north-south corridor**, shows black abolitionist Henry Highland Garnet speaking with newspaper editor Horace Greeley, who supported this legislation that conferred citizenship on all persons born in the United States without regard to race, color, or previous condition; the other, titled "Lincoln's Second Inaugural, 1865," is located in the **central east-west corridor** *(Great Experiment Hall)* and includes an emancipated Afro-American casting a ballot. Additionally, outside the **entrance to visitors' seats overlooking the Senate chamber** there is a portrait of Blanche K. Bruce, from Mississippi, the first Afro-American to serve a full Senate term.

Capitol. On December 1, 2005, the fiftieth anniversary of Mrs. Parks's refusal to surrender her seat to a white man on a bus in Montgomery, Alabama, President George W. Bush signed into law a bill for the placement of a statue of her in the Capitol's Statuary Hall. The two-story semicircular room south of the rotunda is where all the states have statues of important figures from U.S. history. Mrs. Parks will be the first Afro-American honored there.

After introducing legislation every year since 1988, finally in 2003 Congressman John Lewis of Georgia— himself a civil rights legend—saw passed the "National Museum of African-American History and Culture Act." The museum will occupy a plot of land on the mall just off Constitution Avenue between Fourteenth and Fifteenth Streets, across the street from the National Museum of American History. There had been objections to putting another institution on the crowded National Mall; some still linger. However, insists Congressman Lewis, "The mall is one of the most visible places in the nation's capital. Hundreds, thousands of tourists come every year from all over the world. They see, they feel, they learn about our history. I don't think the full story of the country is told unless the full story of African Americans is told. With the museum we will have the opportunity to tell the story."

Also, on November 13, 2006, a groundbreaking ceremony was held for a **_Martin Luther King memorial_** on the mall—the first for an Afro-American there. It will be located on a four-acre plot at the northeastern edge of the Potomac River Tidal Basin between the Lincoln and Jefferson Memorials and will attempt to give physical and artistic expression to a line from Dr. King's "I Have a Dream" speech: "We will be able to hew out of the mountain of despair a stone of hope." A huge stone entryway opening onto grounds facing the tidal basin will symbolize the "mountain of despair," and the "stone of hope" will be a thirty-foot-high piece taken from the stone, cut with the likeness of King emerging from it. Twenty-four niches on an upper walkway will commemorate others who gave their lives to the movement.

A WASHINGTON, D.C., SLAVE TRAIL

One way to look at that bust of Reverend King and his memorial on the mall, and certainly the new museum Congress has approved, is by considering this: You cannot understand the United States without grappling with race and civil rights struggle. So, if the United States Capitol, with its elected House and Senate chambers, represents one of the finest expressions of democracy in the world, understanding the nature of this democracy becomes more complex and difficult when you consider that enslaved black people formed over half the labor force that built it. These slaves worked Virginia quarries, digging and transporting the stone for the Capitol. They baked bricks, dug ditches, hauled logs, and performed every task requiring strenuous manual labor, but their "owners" were paid for the work. Philip Reid, who oversaw the casting of the bronze figure atop the Capitol called the **Statue of Freedom**, was himself a slave, living and working on the outskirts of the city at the Clark Mills Foundry on what is now Bladensburg Road NE.

You will notice that the statue is a woman with her right hand resting on the hilt of a sheathed sword; her left hand holds a laurel wreath. She is wearing a helmet with an eagle's head adorned with feathers and talons. The sculptor, Thomas Crawford, who called the statue *Freedom Triumphant*, originally wanted her headdress to be the soft "liberty cap" worn by the freed slaves of ancient Rome, but deferred to the objections of Jefferson Davis, who, as secretary of war from 1853 to 1857, was in charge of much of the construction. Davis, a Mississippian, considered the liberty cap a way of protesting slavery and therefore unacceptable. "Why should not armed Liberty wear a helmet?" he wrote to the army corps engineer in charge of construction. On January 21, 1861, Davis, then a senator from Mississippi, announced his state's secession from the Union, resigned, and left Washington to become president of the Confederacy.

When I lived in Washington I passed the Capitol almost every day, often wondering—considering the eloquent brilliance of the U.S. Constitution and the Declaration of Independence—how the key figures behind the philosophy and protections of these documents could have been slaveholders. "We hold these truths to be self-evident," the

Declaration of Independence states, "that all men are created equal, that they are endowed by their Creator with certain inalienable Rights that among these are Life, Liberty, and the pursuit of Happiness." Thomas Jefferson, who became the third president of the nation, authored these now legendary words of human rights and human dignity, and felt that nothing he achieved was greater than having written them.

But Thomas Jefferson was also a Virginia slave owner. Thus, the question nags: How could a man who owned human beings as property, as *livestock*, and who considered it his right to own them, have penned the words we find in the Declaration? The original signed Declaration, along with the Constitution, Bill of Rights, and Abraham Lincoln's Emancipation Proclamation that freed slaves decades after those founding documents were written, are at the **National Archives** *(8th Street and Constitution Avenue NW)*.

Slaves were once auctioned just down the street from the National Archives. Slave trading in Washington, D.C., lasted until the Fugitive Slave Act banned it in 1850, but that act, signed by President Millard Fillmore, also made helping slaves escape or failure to assist in returning escapees to slavery a *federal* crime. The act hurt the business of the **St. Charles Hotel** *(northeast corner of Pennsylvania Avenue and 3rd Street, now John Marshall Square)*, which had opened its doors in 1820 and quickly become a favorite of buyers in town to purchase slaves. Its basement contained six thirty-foot-long arched holding cells that extended underneath Pennsylvania Avenue. Iron grates at street level provided air and a bit of sunlight. The hotel advertised the iron rings embedded in its walls and promised to reimburse guests the "full value" of any slave who managed to escape.

Except for government, slave trading was the city's largest industry. This combination of cruelty, pain, and privileged comfort is partially revealed just one block north of the White House at **Decatur House** *(748 Jackson Place NW)*. Now an elegant small museum, it was once the elegant home of a slave trader. Decatur House had a rear-courtyard auction block; slaves destined for auction were kept in an enclosed brick wing of the house running along H Street NW. Some slaves were chained in the attic. The permanent exhibit there today avoids the most brutal aspects of this house's slave history, but it does tell the story of Charlotte "Lottie" Dupuy, "owned" by Kentuckian Henry Clay, who was appointed secretary of state in 1824. Dupuy filed suit to stay in Washington when Clay left in 1828, arguing that she had an oral agreement with a former owner promising her freedom after a certain amount of time as a slave. She lost. Little else in the District offers much acknowledgment of its slave history, but you can always sit in Lafayette Park right in front of the White House—another federal structure built with slave labor—and imagine yourself being sold there.

CITY ON THE POTOMAC: REFUGE, CHALLENGE, AND RACE

On April 16, 1862, almost nine months before the Emancipation Proclamation was issued, the U.S. Congress freed the slaves in the District of Columbia. Throughout the Civil War and after, Washington's black population increased and flourished. While there was still plenty of poverty and racial discrimination, even before the Civil War ended, public schools for blacks were established, the first anywhere in the United States. A small black business community, which included banks and newspapers, took root and grew. Blacks voted in local elections. However, much of this progress would soon come under assault. After the federal government abandoned post–Civil War Reconstruction, the southern states quickly reclaimed their lost white power. Accompanying this restoration at the state and local level was growing power in the U.S. Congress, which governed the capital city.

So, as the nineteenth century spilled into the twentieth, segregation of public facilities became increasingly common. Jobs for Afro-Americans in the federal government steadily declined. When Woodrow Wilson, a Virginian and fan of the pro–Ku Klux Klan movie *Birth of a Nation*, became president, he began systematically demoting Afro-American civil servants, and, after his wife complained about seeing black men working in the same room with white women, ordered the racial segregation of government offices. The public galleries of the U.S. Senate and the lunchroom of the Library of Congress were segregated, and Washington, D.C.'s police and fire departments stopped hiring blacks. On September 8, 1913, my grandfather, Swan Kendrick, a federal government employee whose father had been born into slavery, wrote to the woman he would soon marry, Ruby Moyse, in Greenville, Mississippi: "I believe, the plain truth is that we are farther from Emancipation on this the 50th anniversary thereof, than we were when the Proclamation was signed."

During Wilson's second term, in the "Red Summer" of 1919, antiblack rioting erupted across the country. In the District, egged on by sensationalist and false reports in the *Washington Post* newspaper of assaults on white women by a "negro fiend," on July 19 whites ran amok, attacking some blacks right in front of the White House and at Center Market on Seventh Street NW. Blacks were also dragged off streetcars, and some whites attempted to invade Afro-American neighborhoods. But in some of those neighborhoods, black World War I veterans and merchants with businesses to protect fought back. Blacks manned barricades on New Jersey Avenue and on U Street; sharpshooters even placed themselves atop the **Howard Theater** (*620 T Street NW, now shuttered and deteriorating*). Highly organized self-defense, plus federal troops and heavy rain, finally ended five days of white mob violence. Of the Afro-American response, writer Peter Perl concluded in a 1999 *Washington Post* article: "Unlike virtually all the disturbances that preceded it—in which white-on-black violence dominated—the Washington riot of 1919 was distinguished by strong, organized

A 1902 parade of Ku Klux Klansmen just outside Washington, D.C. On August 18, 1925, Klansmen paraded down Pennsylvania Avenue. Klan parades in the District took place in 1926 and 1928, as well.

Woodrow Wilson and
Washington Segregation

O fficially sanctioned racial discrimination reentered institutions of the federal government during Woodrow Wilson's administration—thus reversing fifty years of integrated civil service. This policy was unexpected by the many blacks that had supported Wilson in the 1912 election, believing him to be a Progressive who would deal fairly with Negroes in promoting their interests in the country. But this period of social protest and economic reform was limited to the benefit of the white world at a time of pervasive Negro disfranchisement and all-out state sponsored discrimination. In writing on Wilsonian segregation, historian Nancy Weiss noted that "white America linked Progressive democracy and equality to greater separation from Negroes."

Wilson's stance with blacks suffered further when he and his cabinet attended a private viewing of *The Birth of a Nation* at the White House. In 1914, nationwide protests emerged over this controversial D. W. Griffith film depicting "vicious distortions of Negro activities during the Reconstruction era" that "infused new life into the Ku Klux Klan." In the summer of 1913, those working in federal departments were relegated to segregated toilets, lunchroom facilities, and work areas, and anyone applying for a federal job now had to add a photo to their application. In 1913 and 1914, blacks reacted. Civil rights advocate and federal employee Mary Church Terrell desegregated restrooms in her work area after threatening to go public with the arrangement. Likewise in 1914, a delegation of Negro leaders, led by William Monroe Trotter, met Wilson at the White House whereupon the group "detailed instances of continued segregation, charged certain officials with race prejudice, asked for investigation and redress by executive order, and predicted Negro opposition to the Democrats in 1916." Wilson asserted that segregation enforcement was "for the comfort and best interest of both races in order to overcome friction." The president abruptly ended the contentious meeting.

—FROM "CIVIL RIGHTS IN AMERICA THEME STUDY: RACIAL DESEGREGATION OF PUBLIC ACCOMMODATIONS," BY THE NATIONAL PARK SERVICE, DRAFT, FEBRUARY 2004

"The Spirit of Fight"

Within the last ten years there has come a change of attitude on our part which is bound to end in cultivating something we greatly need—the spirit of fight. We are beginning to see that things don't come right of themselves; that while laws are good, it takes active and persistent striving to get them enforced; that acceptance of oppression only breeds more of it; and that those "leaders" who counsel meekness and humility, and other such virtues do so either through ignorance or because paid to do it. We'll never have friends again like the Beechers, Garrisons, Birneys and others were shortly before and after the war. I doubt if that sort of friendship would be best. As the only way to learn how to swim is to get into the water, so I believe that the only way we will ever learn to fight our own battles is to start fighting them.

—LETTER FROM SWAN KENDRICK TO RUBY MOYSE,
OCTOBER 2, 1913

and armed black resistance, foreshadowing the civil rights struggles later in the century."

THE FIRST MARCH ON WASHINGTON FOR CIVIL RIGHTS

Until Mary Church Terrell's 1953 court victory that began the desegregation of restaurants, **Union Station** *(North Capitol Street and Massachusetts Avenue NW)*, Washington's handsomely restored railroad station, was one of the few downtown places where black people could eat. Directly across from **Gate D** at the station, there is a bust of A. Philip Randolph, first president of the Brotherhood of Sleeping Car Porters, a labor union that he helped organize in 1925. Twelve years later, after bitter battling with the powerful Pullman railway company, the brotherhood became the first Afro-American union recognized by a major corporation. On the base of the bust you will find these tough-minded words, so typical of Randolph, reflecting a militant "new Negro" and the modern civil rights movement that he played a major role in developing: "At the banquet table of nature there are no reserved seats. You get what you can take and you keep what you can hold. If you can't take anything, you won't get anything and if you can't hold anything, you won't keep anything. And you can't take anything without organization."

In 1941 Randolph organized the "March on Washington Movement" and threatened to bring thousands of blacks into the federal city to protest job discrimination in the defense industry. "This is the age of mass pressure, masses on the march," he said at a rally. "Discrimination against Negroes in employment will not cease until the President and the Congress of the United States see five thousand,

A. Philip Randolph's influence extended outside the United States, and was particularly felt in colonized nations. Here, Randolph (in profile, right) is meeting with officers and organizers of the Railway Workers Union in Rangoon, Burma.

WHY SHOULD WE MARCH?

What Are Our Immediate Goals?

1. To mobilize five million Negroes into one militant mass for pressure.

2. To assemble in Chicago the last week in May, 1943, for the celebration of

"WE ARE AMERICANS – TOO" WEEK

And to ponder the question of Non-Violent Civil Disobedience and Non-Cooperation, and a Mass March On Washington.

15.000 Negroes Assembled at St. Louis, Missouri
20.000 Negroes Assembled at Chicago, Illinois
23.500 Negroes Assembled at New York City
Millions of Negro Americans all Over This Great Land Claim the Right to be Free!

FREE FROM WANT!
FREE FROM FEAR!
FREE FROM JIM CROW!

"Winning Democracy for the Negro is Winning the War for Democracy!" — A. Philip Randolph

What Is The March On Washington Movement?

It is an all Negro Mass Organization to win the full benefits of democracy for the Negro people. It is pro-Negro but not anti-white nor anti-American.

What Has The Movement Done?

1. Won Executive Order No. 8802 from the President of the United States of America barring discrimination in war industries, government agencies and defense training because of race, creed, or national origin, the only such order issued since the Emancipation Proclamation.

2. Won the appointment of the Fair Employment Practices Committee to enforce this order.

3. Won thousands of jobs for Negroes in defense industries.

4. Brought together millions of Negroes in key cities all over the United States of America to protest against injustice and to demand redress of their grievances.

What Is Its Purpose?

1. To develop a disciplined and unified program of action for the masses of Negro people directed toward abolishing all social, economic and political discrimination.

2. To develop a strategy for non-violent struggle against jim crow and for the full integration of Negroes into every phase of American life.

3. To develop leadership from the mass of Negro people to struggle in their own behalf.

Who Can Belong?

Every Negro who believes in our purpose and who wants freedom so much that he is willing to struggle for his own liberation.

Where Can You Join?

There is a Branch of our Movement in your city. If there is not, you and your friends may start one by writing to the national office.

How Much Does It Cost?

The yearly membership fee is ten cents per person, five cents of which is to remain in your local treasury and five cents to be sent to the National office.

Who Are Its Officers?

A. Philip Randolph, National Director
B. F. McLaurin, National Secretary
E. Pauline Myers, National Executive Secretary

_____

I enclose my membership fee in the Cause For Freedom—ten cents (10c).

Name _____

Address _____

City _____ State _____

Mail to: E. Pauline Myers, March On Washington Movement, Hotel Theresa Building, 2084 Seventh Avenue, New York, N. Y.

Despite concessions from President Roosevelt, A. Philip Randolph continued his March on Washington Movement organization, and in the summer of 1942 huge rallies were held in New York, Chicago, and St. Louis.

ten thousand, twenty-five thousand Negroes standing on the lawn of the White House in protest." Apparently feeling the pressure, President Franklin Roosevelt invited Randolph, NAACP executive secretary Walter White, and T. Arnold Hill, acting executive director of the National Urban League, to the White House. There Roosevelt asked how many people could be put on the street. "One hundred thousand," Randolph replied immediately, and despite their doubts, the other two leaders nodded in agreement. One week later Roosevelt issued Executive Order 8802 banning racial discrimination in defense work. It was the first presidential order for civil rights since Reconstruction. And not long afterward the president created a federal Fair Employment Practices Committee. Presciently recognizing that the curtain was rising on a new era of civil rights struggle, Randolph, who can rightly be called the father of the modern movement for pioneering mass protest, urged civil disobedience against racial segregation, and on July 26, 1948, he founded the League for Nonviolent Civil Disobedience.

MISS MOLLIE'S DOWNTOWN CAMPAIGN

Every time I think about it, I find it amazing that one of the driving forces of the early phase of Washington's modern civil rights movement of pickets and boycotts was a woman who was born the year Abraham Lincoln issued the Emancipation Proclamation. On February 28, 1950, Mary Church Terrell, then eighty-six years old and affectionately known as "Miss Mollie," accompanied by three others, walked into the segregated **Thompson's Restaurant** (725 14th Street NW), a popular eatery that was once in the heart of downtown Washington. Mrs. Terrell, one of the founders of the NAACP, had long been arguing that segregation in the nation's capital should not be tolerated. "For fifteen years I have resided in Washington, and while it was far from paradise for colored people when I first touched these shores, it has been doing its

"Like a Leper"

As a colored woman I might enter Washington any night, a stranger in a strange land, and walk miles without finding a place to lay my head. Unless I happened to know colored people who live here or ran across a chance acquaintance who could recommend a colored boarding-house to me, I should be obliged to spend the entire night wandering about. Indians, Chinamen, Filipinos, Japanese and representatives of any other dark race can find hotel accommodations, if they can pay for them. The colored man alone is thrust out of the hotels of the national capital like a leper.

"As a colored woman I may walk from the Capitol to the White House, ravenously hungry and abundantly supplied with money with which to purchase a meal, without finding a single restaurant in which I would be permitted to take a morsel of food, if it was patronized by white people, unless I were willing to sit behind a screen . . .

"Unless I am willing to engage in a few menial occupations, in which the pay for my services would be very poor, there is no way for me to earn an honest living, if I am not a trained nurse or a dressmaker or can secure a position as teacher in the public schools, which is exceedingly difficult to do. It matters not what my intellectual attainments may be or how great is the need of the services of a competent person, if I try to enter many of the numerous vocations in which my white sisters are allowed to engage, the door is shut in my face."

—"ON BEING COLORED IN THE NATION'S CAPITAL,"
MARY CHURCH TERRELL, SPEECH, OCTOBER 10, 1906

level best since to make conditions for us intolerable," said the Memphis-born civil rights leader in a 1906 speech.

Though rarely enforced, "lost laws" dating back to 1872 were still on the District's books. These laws prohibited racial discrimination in restaurants and other public places. Notwithstanding, few places in downtown Washington served blacks. So Terrell, as head of a newly formed Coordinating Committee for the Enforcement of the D.C. Anti-Discrimination Laws, chose Thompson's Restaurant for a test case. Her group picked up trays, selected their food, then proceeded to the cashier. The manager came rushing up, explaining that the restaurant's policy was to not serve Negroes and refusing to take their money. "We can serve *you*," he said, pointing at the one white member of the quartet, "but not the rest." Terrell and her group left; that afternoon they went to court and charged the restaurant with violating the law. It took three years and a Supreme Court decision, but on June 8, 1953, in *District of Columbia v. John R. Thompson*, Justice William O. Douglas declared that the so-called lost laws were still valid and enforceable. Said the ninety-year-old Terrell when informed of the court's decision, "We will *not* permit these laws to become lost again."

Mary Church Terrell

Washington restaurants and other public facilities began desegregating. Some had removed racial barriers before the court decision. One of these was the city's oldest department store, **Hecht's** *(525 7th Street NW)*, seven blocks east of Thompson's. Although Hecht's desegregated in 1952, up to that point it maintained a strictly segregated cafeteria, despite placing a newspaper ad showing clasped black and white hands in celebration of World Brotherhood Week. The store had been one of the important targets of a "Dime Store Campaign" of picket lines and boycotts that Terrell pressed while the case against Thompson's slowly made its way through the courts.

Hecht's no longer exists, and at its old site on the corner of Seventh and F Streets a mixed-use development has been built. Named **Terrell Place** in 2004, the lobby of this complex houses a permanent exhibit celebrating Mrs. Terrell's life, including wall panels bearing excerpts from her writings, several photographs, two murals, and three dramatic bronze statues crafted by the renowned Afro-American artist and sculptor Elizabeth Catlett. "What delighted us so much about it," said John Donovan of CarrAmerica, the company that developed the property, "was a chance to honor [Terrell] where she was once unable to get a cup of coffee even. We also recognize that at the time she began this effort—and she was very elderly, at a time when most people would like to rest on their laurels—she could have walked from the White House to the Capitol and no place would have given her that cup of coffee."

PENNSYLVANIA AVENUE: TAXATION WITHOUT REPRESENTATION

The **District Building** (*14th Street and Pennsylvania Avenue NW*), now named the **Wilson Building** for the late City Council chairman John Wilson, is home to the District's city council. For city residents long denied voting rights, the building represents some ground gained on the continuing civil rights battlefield of "home rule." In 1963 the right to cast a ballot for a U.S. president and vice president was finally granted. In 1968 residents were permitted to elect a school board. Congress passed a Home Rule Act in 1973 allowing D.C. residents to elect a mayor and city council, although the Congress retained veto power over city laws and final say-so on the city's budget. Walter Washington became the city's first elected mayor in 1974 and took office in the District Building, as did a brand-new city council. The city now also elects a congressional representative who sits in the legislative body without the right to vote. It is one of the great ironies on a trail where you will encounter many ironies that residents of the city so many looked to for support of one of the civil rights movement's greatest issues and struggles—voting rights—are still denied those same rights by the U.S. Congress. And many of us think that the city does not have voting representation because, with Afro-Americans' comprising 57 percent of the city's population, it is too black a city; although like Mississippi and other southern states did in the 1960s, those denying us voting representation in the U.S. Congress say race has nothing to do with it.

The **National Council of Negro Women** *(633*

Pennsylvania Avenue NW) is the only Afro-American organization that owns property on the historic section of Pennsylvania Avenue, between the Capitol and the White House, known as the "Avenue of Presidents." On March 21, 2002, at the ninetieth birthday party of the organization's chair and president emerita, Dorothy Height, who has been called "the Uncommon Height," boxing promoter Don King stood up to speak. "Help me make Dorothy Height smile, as the Dorothy in the Wizard of Oz. Click your heels, Dorothy, and let's pay off the bill."

King then suddenly whipped out a check for $110,000 and turned to television superstar Oprah Winfrey. "Help me, Oprah."

And Winfrey responded by saying, "I came here to give two-point-five." Then she paused. "That's *millions*, should you wonder."

This started an avalanche of contributions from the entertainers, politicians, authors, and other well-heeled VIPs who were present. They ended one of Ms. Height's most worrying concerns in her semiretirement by coming up with $5 million to pay off the mortgage of the organization's Pennsylvania Avenue headquarters building. Says Ms. Height, frequently and emphatically, "No American president will be inaugurated without getting past *our* house!" Every year during the second week of September, the Council hosts a ***"Black Family Reunion"*** on the national mall. The two-day event celebrating traditional Afro-American family values attracts more than half a million people. Among a wide range of themed pavilions that are open all day are ones concerned with children, fathers, sons and brothers, health, economic empowerment, and spirituality. Ms. Height began holding this event in 1986 in response to what she felt was negative media portrayal of the black family.

UPTOWN TO HOWARD UNIVERSITY, THE "CAPSTONE" OF NEGRO EDUCATION

Despite its official Sixth Street address, **Howard University** (*2400 6th Street NW*) actually hovers over Georgia Avenue, which is mainly a strip of small businesses catering to university customers and a surrounding neighborhood on the cusp of gentrification. My earliest civil rights movement memories are here. In the spring of 1962 I had been on campus for only a few weeks when I was handed a leaflet calling for volunteers to join picket lines and take part in sit-ins in Baltimore, Maryland, and along Route 40. I decided to participate, perhaps because I was at that moment reading the first issue of the campus newspaper, the *Howard Hilltop*, which gave prominent space to a story about Howard students and the Freedom Rides. I had no idea that this decision was the first of a quick succession of steps that would lead me to Mississippi and to a deep involvement with its civil rights movement. But mine is a small story, and it replicates the story of other Howard students in those years. The larger point is that no civil rights trip to Washington, D.C., could be considered complete without visiting this historically black university.

Thurgood Marshall

The important role the school came to play in black intellectual and political life would not have seemed likely in its early years, despite the presence of dean Kelly Miller, who equaled W. E. B. Du Bois as one of the nation's great black public intellectuals. Howard was mismanaged, commanding virtually no respect as a university, and only its medical and dental schools were accredited. Then, in 1926, Mordecai W. Johnson, an iron-willed Baptist minister and educator from Tennessee, became at thirty-six years of age the first black president of the university. He began to attract some of the best and brightest, and soon the school was home to a pantheon of professors who would become some of black America's most influential voices: E. Franklin Frazier in sociology; Rayford Logan and John Hope Franklin in history; Dr. Charles R. Drew in medicine; poet Sterling Brown and writer Alain Locke, both professors of English; poet and dramatist Owen Dodson; future Nobel Prize winner Ralph Bunche in the political science department; and W. Leo Hansberry, the "father" of African studies. The university's law school—led by Charles Hamilton Houston and graduating students such as Thurgood Marshall—linked to the NAACP and became a legal laboratory where civil rights advocacy through legal challenge was practically invented. For their attacks on racial segregation and inequality, Howard lawyers gained renown as "Houston's Raiders."

In the early 1960s through the campus-based Nonviolent Action Group, a younger generation, including Stokely Carmichael and Cleveland Sellers, and strong, independent young women like Jean Wheeler, Muriel Tillinghast, and Cynthia Washington, would continue Howard University's prominent role in civil rights struggle. With sit-ins and picket lines, they challenged segregation in nearby Virginia and Maryland. Intellectual luminaries of the older generation were important to these younger activists, inviting them into their homes and offices for schooling in the lessons of life as they had lived it, stressing an obligation to "the redemption and vindication of the race." Of Sterling Brown, recalls Michael Thelwell, managing editor of the *Howard Hilltop* when I was a freshman: "Prof was my first close-up example of how a *committed* black intellectual could be in this world."

The significance of the campus's **Rankin Memorial Chapel** *(6th Street just inside the university's main gates)* is not usually recognized. One of the powerful intellects that Mordecai Johnson brought to the university in 1931 was theologian Howard Thurman. As professor of Christian theology and dean of the chapel, Thurman preached and taught a "social gospel" that racial discrimination and maltreatment of the poor betrayed both God and America. It was Thurman who first professed a philosophy of non-violent action for change. In the mid-1930s he took a group of black pastors to India for conversations with Mohandas Gandhi. Thurman had enormous influence with a whole generation of Afro-American Christian ministers, including Martin Luther King, who first encountered Thurman at the King family's Atlanta home (King's father and Thurman were Morehouse College classmates). They had more sustained contact at Boston University, where in 1953, as dean of BU's Marsh Chapel, Thurman became the first Afro-American academic dean at a predominantly white university. Love, not hate, is the crucial ingredient in the formula for change, Thurman taught: "To revile because one has been reviled—this is the real evil because it is the evil of the soul itself." His influence was "huge," says Jesse Jackson, whose phrase "I am somebody" was inspired by Thurman. During demonstrations Dr. King almost always kept nearby Thurman's *Jesus and the Disinherited*. "Fear, hypocrisy, and hatred are the three hounds of Hell . . . that track the trail of the disinherited," wrote Thurman in that slim 1949 volume about ancient Israel suffering under Roman oppression. Looking at the life of Jesus, Thurman wrote—and you can see Dr. King embracing these thoughts—that despite fear, "life under oppression provided no excuse for avoiding a path of courageous, creative integrity."

A CROSSROADS OF POLITICS AND ENTERTAINMENT: FOURTEENTH AND U STREETS NW

Two of black America's most historic streets—U and Fourteenth—are just a few blocks from Howard. Inexpensive property and new streetcar lines began attracting Afro-Americans here during the Civil War. Many black businesses thrived throughout the neighborhood. All the major civil rights organizations had offices here in the 1960s. And on the northwest corner of Fourteenth and U streets, a bottle thrown through the window of a **Peoples Drug Store** began the riot that erupted with the news of the assassination of Martin Luther King. A city government office building has now replaced the old store at this site.

The combination of desegregation in downtown Washington and the riots resulted in years of decline and neglect. SNCC's old office at 2208 Fourteenth Street is gone. So is the New School for Afro-American Thought that was across the street. Of the civil rights organizations that once inhabited the neighborhood, only the **Washington Urban League** *(2901 14th Street NW)* remains, having moved from its old 3501 Fourteenth Street address into the beautifully renovated Hines Funeral Home. The neighborhood is rapidly gentrifying, and today its streets hardly reveal the community's past as a thriving black political and commercial center. Starting at the **U Street/African American Civil War Memorial/Cardozo Metro station** *(Green Line)*, plaques placed along U Street facilitate access to the community's history via a self-guided heritage trail.

Former city councilman Frank Smith, who was a SNCC field secretary in Mississippi during the early 1960s, developed the **African American Civil War Memorial Museum** *(1200 U Street NW)*, for which the metro stop is named. It commemorates the more than 200,000 black soldiers who fought; 209,145 of their names are inscribed on a "Wall of Freedom," in front of which is a 9½-foot sculpture. The back of the piece shows a black family gathered around their uniformed son as he prepares to go off and fight. On the front are three infantrymen and a sailor. Photographs and a valuable computer data base visitors can use to find ancestors who were black civil war veterans are in the museum, which is housed two blocks away from the memorial, in the **True Reformer Building** *(1200 U Street NW)*, built in 1903. The Grand United Order of True Reformers was a benevolent society in Richmond, Virginia, that provided insurance to its Afro-American members who were denied insurance by white-owned firms. With conference rooms and a concert hall, the building has been a major center of social activity.

A few blocks farther is the nation's first black YMCA, the **Anthony Bowen YMCA** *(1816 12th Street NW)*, which was founded in 1853 as the Twelfth Street YMCA. Anthony Bowen had fled his slave life in nearby Prince Georges County, Maryland, and become a prominent black abolitionist whose home on E Street Southwest was a stop on the Underground Railroad. (That site, on what was then the 900 block of the street, is now part of the Southeast-Southwest Freeway). During the Civil War, Bowen met with President Lincoln and urged him to recruit black soldiers. The Bowen "Y," designed by W. Sidney Pittman (one of the first Afro-American architects in the United States and son-in-law of Booker T. Washington), moved to 1325 W Street NW in 1972; the renovated and restored five-story building at the original site is now the **Thurgood Marshall Center for Service and Heritage**. This was one of the meeting places where Marshall and other attorneys mapped out the legal strategy that resulted in the 1954 Supreme Court decision in *Brown v. Board of Education*. The center today provides services for at-risk children through a variety of changing exhibits and videos, and tries to expose neighborhood young people to the achievements of others, such as poet Langston Hughes; Dr. Charles Drew, the discoverer of blood plasma; and composer–orchestra leader Duke Ellington, who once lived in this community.

Looking at the multiethnic and multiracial mix on the sidewalks today, it is difficult to imagine that in 1933 one of the first "Don't Buy Where You Can't Work" campaigns took place down the street. When the white owners of the **Hamburger Grill** fired its black workers and hired an all-white staff, a Howard student named John Aubrey Davis, along with other students, quickly formed an organization called the **New Negro Alliance** *(NNA)*, and they began picketing. Just twenty-four hours after the campaign began, the grill rehired its black staff. Encouraged by this success, the NNA launched similar campaigns throughout the neighborhood. Picketers admonished blacks about to enter or just passing by stores that did not employ blacks, "Don't buy where you can't work." Store owners got a court injunction against the group. On March 5, 1938, however, setting an important precedent, the Supreme Court rendered a 6–2 decision in favor of the NNA, finding that "those having a direct or indirect interest in the employment of a group of people" had the right to "peacefully persuade others." By 1940 just about every store in the community had black employees on staff. The alliance's tactic of combining boycotts, picketing, and court action would be common in the 1960s, but it was a brand-new approach in the 1930s.

The **Association for the Study of African-American Life and History** *(525 Bryant Street)* is located in the C. B. Powell building on the Howard University campus. It was named the Association for the Study of Negro Life and History until 1972 and for years was housed on the second floor of a building a few blocks south of U Street at 1401 Fourteenth Street NW. In yet another sign of rapid gentrification in this neighborhood, the old building is now the site of an upscale furniture store with no marker indicating its historic importance to black America. The association was first headquartered in the Ninth Street home of its founder, **Carter G. Woodson** *(1538 9th Street NW)*, and Woodson continued to work there until his death in 1950. After languishing for years in disrepair, even after being declared a national historic site in 2003, the National Park Service bought the house in 2006 and promises to rehabilitate the home and its office "to look as they did during Woodson's heyday."

His is another of those astonishing stories of black achievement that are threaded through U.S. history. Woodson did not even begin high school until he was nineteen years old, yet he entered Harvard University and earned his Ph.D., becoming only the second Afro-American to earn a doctorate there (W. E. B. Du Bois was the first). Briefly (from 1919 to 1920) Woodson was Howard University's dean of academic affairs, but he left teaching to pursue what he determined to be his great mission in life: the recovery and presentation of black history.

"Let Us Banish Fear"

On January 28, 1915, Dr. Carter G. Woodson proposed in a letter to Washington's NAACP president, Archibald Grimke, a boycott or, as he put it, "diverting patronage from business establishments which do not treat races alike."

Grimke wasn't enthusiastic about the idea, and in a letter dated March 18, 1915, responding to what he considered insupportable fear, Dr. Woodson wrote back to Grimke, "I am not afraid of being sued by white businessmen. In fact, I should welcome such a law suit. It would do the cause much good. Let us banish fear. We have been in this mental state for three centuries. I am a radical. I am ready to act, if I can find brave men to help me."

Carter G. Woodson

"We have a wonderful history behind us," Woodson told a Hampton Institute (now Hampton University) audience in 1921. "[But] if you are unable to demonstrate to the world that you have this record, the world will say to you, 'You are not worthy to enjoy the blessings of democracy or anything else.'" He organized the association in 1915, and, using his own money, began publishing *The Journal of Negro History*, which the association continues to publish (in 2001 it became the *Journal of African American History*).

On February 7, 1926, Woodson initiated Negro History Week to bring formal recognition to the contributions and struggles of Afro-Americans. Negro History Week was expanded to the entire month of February and became Black History Month during the 1976 bicentennial celebrations of the United States. "With the power of cumulative fact [Woodson] moved back the barriers and broadened our visions of the world and the world's vision of us," said Mary McLeod Bethune, who founded the National Council of

Negro Women in 1932. There is a **Mary McLeod Bethume memorial** in Lincoln Park *(East Capital and 12th Streets NE)*. Engraved words on its base are taken from her will and directed at future generations: "I leave you love. I leave you hope."

SOUTHEAST WASHINGTON— CITY STEPCHILD

Perhaps no area offers more spectacular views of Washington than the southeast section of the city, on the far side of the Anacostia River. Gazing at the federal monuments on the mall from its hillsides is like viewing an enormous historical postcard. It makes you want to write some message of America.

Southeast Washington also contains some of the city's poorest and most neglected neighborhoods. The area is home to the city's greatest concentration of public housing and is frequently—and unfairly, in my view—written off as a neighborhood offering nothing but crime and danger. Dig deeper and you'll find there's more to it. For example, out of this neighborhood came an early shot aimed at segregation in public schools: *Bolling v. Sharpe.*

This 1950 challenge to all-white **John Philip Sousa Junior High School** *(3650 Ely Place SE)* was one of the five cases that ultimately led to *Brown v. Board of Education.* It was a carefully planned attempt crafted by Howard University law professor James Nabrit and a group of D.C. parents called the Consolidated Parents Group. The group was originally formed because of impatience and anger with "the whites, the highfalutin blacks, the Board of Education—everyone," said its organizer and leader, Gardner L. Bishop, owner of a U Street barbershop. Bishop had long been running afoul of the District's race laws. In the late 1930s he was arrested when his four-year-old daughter, Judine, sat down to swing at a whites-only playground. In December 1948 Bishop, whose daughter by that time was fourteen, had launched a boycott and begun picketing her school, **Browne Junior High School** *(850 26th Street NE)*, to protest overcrowding. Eighteen hundred students were in the school, which was designed for eight hundred. Overcrowding like this was typical in the city. The Dixiecrat-controlled Congress that governed voteless D.C. severely limited resources for the city's black schools; tiny per-pupil outlays for blacks as compared to whites were the norm. Before picketing, Bishop had shown up at one of the weekly city school board meetings with some forty students from Browne. The board let him speak about the condition of the school, Bishop said, years later, "but they sat there like a bunch of fools, not believing a word they heard." The next day almost all of Browne's students stayed at home in protest. They had been out of school for weeks when Bishop approached attorney Charles Houston and sought help. Houston asked Bishop how much money his group had in their treasury. About fourteen dollars, Bishop replied. "Well, you've got yourself a lawyer," responded the NAACP attorney. With this, the student strike ended and Houston began filing a battery of lawsuits aimed at equalizing teachers' salaries and improving school conditions.

But Houston was slowly dying of heart disease. From his deathbed at Howard University's Freedman's Hospital less than a year after the two men had met, Houston urged Bishop to get in touch with attorney James Nabrit at Howard. Expecting little, he met with Nabrit, who told him trying to equalize schools was shortsighted, but if Bishop and his group wanted to challenge the segregation of schools, he was willing to take on the case. So, in September 1950 Bishop brought twelve-year-old Spottsworth Bolling and ten other black students to what was then the brand-new Sousa Junior High School in Southeast Washington. The principal denied them admission and Bolling was forced to enroll in Shaw Junior High School, across town in Northwest Washington. The Shaw school, then forty-eight years old, had a playground that was too small for even a ball field, a welding shop that had been turned into a gym, and a science lab that had one Bunsen burner. And so

Frederick Douglass

young Bolling filed suit against Board of Education president Melvin Sharpe, beginning the process that would lead to *Bolling v. Sharpe.*

Also in Southeast Washington is the ***Anacostia Community Museum*** *(1901 Fort Place SE)*, which features a range of changing exhibits whose subjects have included black immigrants in Washington, the black church, black art in the 1920s, and Afro-American invention and innovation. The museum offers special programs for young people and is a repository of papers and other materials related to black life in Washington and elsewhere. Now part of the Smithsonian Institutions, the museum was established in

1967 as the Anacostia Neighborhood Museum in the old Carver Movie Theater on what is now Martin Luther King Avenue. In addition to what it offers on-site, much of what the museum has collected and preserved is available via an "On-line Academy." (http://anacostia.si.edu/Online_Academy/Academy/academy.htm).

Our final stop on the Washington, D.C., civil rights trail is the home of Frederick Douglass on *Cedar Hill (1411 W Street, SE)*, also in the historic old Anacostia section of the city. Douglass's home, shaded by oak, cedar, and magnolia trees, was acquired by the National Park Service on September 5, 1962, and became the first black national historic site. In a reception area adjacent to the home, a seventeen-minute film on the life of Douglass can be viewed. Limited park ranger–led tours of the home can be taken as well if reservations are made in advance.

Before Douglass bought Cedar Hill, it was forbidden for "any Negro mulatto or person of African blood" to buy land or a home in this neighborhood. So, in a sense we have come full circle with Douglass. From his roots as a slave, Douglass rose to prominence as an abolitionist and an eloquent spokesperson for his still-enslaved brethren. In Douglass, America was at long last hearing a clear, militant Afro-American voice, not just that of a sympathetic advocate. This distinction would prove crucial to the modern civil rights movement one hundred years later.

CHAPTER TWO

UP SOUTH

Annapolis, Cambridge, and Baltimore, Maryland

> 66 *At first it was these kids from out of state who were coming in to stir things up. I got to know them because of my daughter Donna's involvement . . . Before I knew it I was one of the leaders. There was something direct, real, about the way the kids waged nonviolent war. This was the first time I saw a vehicle I could work with.* 99
>
> —GLORIA RICHARDSON, *Newsweek*,
> AUGUST 5, 1963

Before heading south we are going to embark on three easy trips north and east of the District of Columbia to sites of civil rights struggle in Maryland. These areas are closely connected to Washington; in fact, one large chunk of the District was created on land sold to the newly independent American government by Maryland farmers. Although much of Maryland is above the Mason-Dixon Line, the symbolic line that delimits the South from the North, the state is southern in its disposition and has certainly produced civil rights leaders of note: Thurgood Marshall in Baltimore, the Mitchell and Jackson families also in Baltimore, and Gloria Richardson in Cambridge.

Maryland was a slave state, and one of the most militant black abolitionists, Henry Highland Garnet, who escaped from a Kent County, Maryland, plantation in 1824, attracted national attention when he called for all of America's four million black slaves to rise up in revolt. "You had far better all die—die immediately, than live slaves and entail your wretchedness upon your posterity," Garnet said, addressing the 1843 Negro National Convention, held in Buffalo, New York.

Frederick Douglass and Harriet Tubman were also escapees from Maryland plantations. Douglass is well known as a great abolitionist spokesman. Equally well known is Tubman, who became one of the preeminent conductors on the Underground Railroad, making nineteen dangerous trips back into Maryland to bring some three hundred slaves to freedom. Less well known than ei-

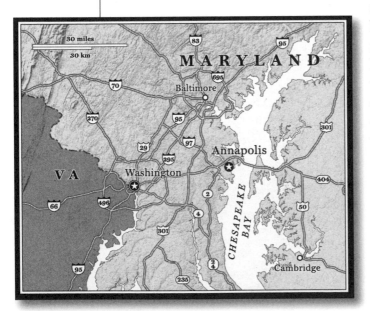

ther of them is Maryland native Benjamin Banneker, the self-taught Afro-American mathematician, who did much of the survey work in preparation for the establishment of Washington, D.C., as the nation's capital. When Pierre L'Enfant, the French-born engineer, architect, and urban planner chosen by George Washington to design the new American Capital, angrily quit the project in 1794, taking his plans with him, Banneker continued with it, recreating L'Enfant's plans from memory. Banneker also pressed Thomas Jefferson on slavery. In a 1791 letter to Jefferson, Banneker accused him and other Founding Fathers of hypocrisy, "in detaining by fraud and violence so numerous a part of my brethren under groaning captivity and cruel oppression, that you should at the Same time be found guilty of that most criminal act, which you professedly detested in others, with respect to yourselves." Today, another church stands on the site where Banneker worshipped and attended school, **Mount Gilboa Chapel** (*2312 Westchester Avenue*), about ten miles from downtown Baltimore in the town of Oella, and continues to serve the black community today. Near the church is the 142-acre **Benjamin Banneker Historical Park and Museum** (*300 Oella Avenue*). The museum chronicles Banneker's life and includes a living-history area portraying the farm life of the Banneker family. Surrounding the museum, a stream-laced valley offers walking trails.

Benjamin Banneker's
PENNSYLVANIA, DELAWARE, MARY-
LAND, AND VIRGINIA
A L M A N A C,
FOR THE
YEAR of our LORD 1795;
Being the Third after Leap-Year.

BANNAKER.

PHILADELPHIA:
Printed for WILLIAM GIBBONS, Cherry Street

A woodcut portrait of Benjamin Banneker on the cover of the almanac he published annually between 1792 and 1797. Along with scientific and mathematical content, the almanac also included political and social commentary.

During the Civil War, it was on Maryland soil that the great, bloody battle at **Antietam** (*5831 Dunker Church Road, Sharpsburg, MD. From Interstate 70, exit 29 onto Route 65 south; ten miles south on the left is the Visitor Center*) was fought; the battlefield today is a national park. Neither side can be said to have won or been defeated at Antietam, but Confederate General Robert E. Lee's withdrawal to Virginia afterward gave President Lincoln some necessary political leverage, a propitious moment to gain northern support for the Emancipation Proclamation. The proclamation freed slaves only in the breakaway Confederate states, but it encouraged thousands of Afro-Americans to enter military service on the Union side. "In giving freedom to the slave we assure freedom to the free," declared Lincoln.

Clarence Mitchell Jr., the "101st Senator"

One hundred years later on Capitol Hill, at the height of the modern civil rights movement, Clarence Mitchell of Baltimore was still seeking fulfillment of the promise embedded in Lincoln's proclamation. As director of the NAACP's Washington bureau for thirty years, Mitchell was the primary lobbyist for civil rights legislation. Minnesota Senator Hubert Humphrey, who later served as Lyndon Johnson's vice president, dubbed Mitchell the "101st Senator." Unquestionably, Mitchell shaped the 1964 and 1965 civil rights acts as much as anyone seated as an elected representative in the Congress. On March 8, 1985, Baltimore's main courthouse was renamed the ***Clarence M. Mitchell Jr. Courthouse*** *(corner of Calvert and Lexington Streets)*.

Although Mitchell emphasized law and legislation in his work, the streets of his hometown were far from quiet as protests burst from black college campuses in the 1960s. In Baltimore, the Civic Interest Group launched sit-ins that influenced students across the state and drew participants from as far away as Boston. Mitchell's wife, attorney Juanita Jackson Mitchell, among the first Afro-Americans to graduate from the University of Maryland Law School and the first black woman to practice law in Maryland, was one of the important adult "go-to" persons for arrested sit-in students campaigning to desegregate restaurants along old Route 40 and Maryland's Eastern Shore.

In Maryland, as in neighboring Washington, D.C.,

CORE-led protest in Baltimore

direct-action attacks on racial discrimination were not some new phenomenon that began in the 1960s. An interracial group of twenty-four people was arrested and jailed on July 11, 1948, while attempting to use the segregated clay tennis courts that were adjacent to the **Rawlings Conservatory** (*Druid Park Lake Drive and Gwynns Falls Parkway*) in Druid Hill Park. A marker lists the names of all twenty-four. And in February 1953 the Congress of Racial Equality (CORE) began sit-ins in Baltimore.

ANNAPOLIS

Maryland's capital city is just a thirty-minute drive from Washington, D.C., on Route 50. At the **Maryland State House Lawyers Mall** (*also known as State House Square*), on the site of the old Court of Appeals building, a statue of Thurgood Marshall honors this Baltimore native who became the first Afro-American Supreme

Alex Haley

Court Justice. Behind the statue are pillars with the inscription EQUAL JUSTICE UNDER LAW, and in front are two benches. On one is the figure of Donald Gaines Murray, whose admittance into the University of Maryland Law School gave Marshall his first significant civil rights victory. On the other bench are the figures of two children; they represent Marshall's achievement as lead attorney in the 1954 *Brown v. Board of Education* decision. Inside the State House (the oldest in the country still in legislative use) a plaque on the wall of the rotunda commemorates the accomplishment of Matthew Henson, who was a member of the 1909 arctic expedition of Admiral Robert E. Peary, and was the first man in the group to actually reach the North Pole. The memorial to this son of Maryland sharecroppers was the first state-sponsored memorial in Maryland honoring an Afro-American.

Anchoring past and present in Annapolis is the **Alex Haley Memorial**, at the entrance to **City Dock** (*1 Dock Street*), where a life-size bronze statue pays tribute to Haley, author of the celebrated book *Roots* that inspired the television miniseries. There are three statues nearby depicting children listening to Haley read from the book. It was at this colonial port, in 1767, that Haley's kidnapped African ancestor, Kunta Kinte, and ninety-seven other enslaved Africans are thought to have first entered the country on the slave ship *Lord Ligonier*. As a brass plaque next to the statue states, Haley's family story demonstrates that "the strength of the human spirit to overcome challenges" comes from maintaining strong family connections. This may be the only monument in the country where the African name of a slave is actually given. An annual commemoration ceremony is held at this site every year on September 29, and the city celebrates an annual Kunta Kinte Heritage Festival every August.

In downtown Annapolis the **Banneker-Douglass Museum** *(84 Franklin Street)* provides a useful view of Maryland's Afro-American history. It is located in the old **Mount Moriah AME (African Methodist Episcopal) Church**, which was built in 1874 and is the oldest Afro-American church in Annapolis. Renovation and expansion were completed in 2006, and the entire second floor now houses the museum's first permanent exhibit: Deep Roots, Rising Waters: A History of African Americans in Maryland. The museum contains memorabilia from Harriet Tubman as well as from Matthew Henson. Mount Moriah's lovely stained-glass windows are a visual bonus.

Reflecting more recent times, on the façade of the former **Greyhound bus terminal restaurant** *(126 West Street)*, which is now part of the Loews Annapolis Hotel, a marker commemorates five Annapolitans who led a November 1960 sit-in to desegregate the station's restaurant. And just a few minutes north of Annapolis, at **Anne Arundel Community College** *(101 College Parkway, Arnold, MD; from Annapolis take Route 50 east to exit 27, Route 2 north, Governor Ritchie Highway)*, a Martin Luther King Memorial statue was unveiled in 2006. It was designed by sculptor Ed Dwight, the first Afro-American trained as an astronaut, and also creator of Annapolis's Alex Haley memorial. The bronze sculpture is of Martin Luther King Jr. standing in front of a semicircular stone retaining wall, gesturing and holding a book. On the wall are five bronze plaques inscribed with quotations from Rev. King, as well as biographical information about the slain civil rights leader. Dwight has since agreed to incorporate Dr. King's wife, Coretta Scott King, in the memorial, which will make it the nation's first joint memorial to the couple.

❧ CAMBRIDGE ❧

Continuing east on Highway 50, after crossing the Chesapeake Bay Bridge you enter Maryland's Eastern Shore. There were sit-ins all along this route in the 1960s, especially in Salisbury, where Maryland State College students targeted local lunch counters. But it was in the town of Cambridge that one of the civil rights movement's most dramatic episodes unfolded.

The Maryland protests—part of the great wave of action by young people that swept across the South in 1960—grew in number and intensity: In 1961 African ambassadors complained to the Kennedy White House that while traveling on Route 40 between Washington, D.C., and the United Nations in New York they were denied service at restaurants. On March 9, Sierra Leone's chargé d'affaires, Dr. W. H. Fitzjohn, stopped at a Howard Johnson's restaurant and was told he could not eat there; on June 14, the ambassador from Niger was denied service at another highway restaurant. There were many incidents. Ambassador Malik Sow of Chad was not only refused service but was also assaulted. The owner explained, "He looked like just an ordinary nigra to me." The complaints from the African ambassadorial corps both embarrassed and worried the White House because it was trying to cultivate African cold-war allies by promoting U.S. "freedom."

The treatment of the ambassadors helped galvanize student activists who had already been protesting throughout the region for more than a year. All along Route 40 young activists—most from Maryland schools and Howard University but some coming down from Swarthmore College and historically black Lincoln University, in Pennsylvania—conducted sit-ins and mounted picket lines of protest. CORE organized Freedom Rides by car with people from all over the country, stopping at as many

"Tell Them to Fly"

Fearful that the refusal of restaurants on Route 40 to serve African diplomats would be exploited by the Soviet Union, President Kennedy established a Special Protocol Section of the State Department. Hospitality committees for black diplomats were also established because a State Department survey revealed that of two hundred rentable apartments considered suitable for diplomats, only eight were available to blacks, and Soviet diplomats were offering to rent housing for Africans. Harris Wofford, Chairman of the White House's Sub-cabinet Group on Civil Rights, recalled that Kennedy had an almost bizarre response to discrimination on Route 40.

"The African ambassadors would be insulted if they drove from New York to Washington. And Angie Biddle Duke, to whom all of this did not initially come naturally, who was made head of protocol in the State Department (which was the most unnatural place for civil rights to be advanced anywhere in government), he becomes head of protocol and it's suggested to him that [protocol] ought to be the place in the State Department that really works to help African ambassadors by integrating housing, roads, everything . . .

"So one day the newspaper tells about an African ambassador who got turned down for a drink of water or something on Route 40, at about quarter of eight in the morning, and it quoted Angie Biddle Duke saying something about what we're doing. Angie gets a call from the President. The President said, 'I just read that hell of a story about that ambassador not being able to drink on Route 40.' Angie says, 'Yes, Mr. President. We're working very actively. I've made six speeches up on Route 40. We know we haven't succeeded yet, but we think we're really making headway.' Duke was talking about all the progress he had made, and Kennedy said, 'Well that's not what I'm calling you about. I'm calling you to tell you to tell these African ambassadors to fly.' He said, 'You tell them I wouldn't think of driving from New York to Washington. It's a hell of a road, Route 40. I used to drive that years ago. Why the hell would anyone want to drive down on Route 40 when you can fly there today? Tell them to wake up to the world and fly.' And he hung up."

—KENNEDY LIBRARY ORAL HISTORY

"A Different Kind of Strength"

"Gloria was the first woman I'd ever seen—Black or white—who had that kind of strength. Now, I had seen other kinds of strength all through my growing up: smart, ingenious Black women like my mother, who kept their families together—no matter what. But this was a different kind of strength. It was a toughness revealed in my enduring image of Gloria: dressed in jeans and a pressed shirt, marching ramrod straight toward Gen. Gelston and rows of his Maryland National Guardmen (rifles drawn) with an attitude that said, 'No, I will not bend to your will.'

"Other images: Gloria standing before a mass meeting packed with local activists and college students, explaining the plans for the next day's demonstrations (which amazed me because, at the time, I couldn't talk to a room with more than three people). Or—Gloria and Reggie Robinson, SNCC's field secretary in Cambridge, after an exhausting day of demonstrations, working late into the night over Gloria's kitchen table . . . planning, always planning.

"She was a prodigious woman. And still is."

—JUDY RICHARDSON TO CHARLIE COBB

Gloria Richardson faces down National Guardsmen in Cambridge, 1964.

Maryland establishments as they could on Route 40 and sitting in when they were refused service.

These protests contributed to the formation of the Cambridge Nonviolent Action Committee (CNAC) in March 1962. Gloria Richardson, from one of the town's oldest and most prominent Afro-American families, whose cousin and daughter were among the young Cambridge activists, became CNAC's adult supervisor. Her role might seem surprising, given her social position as part of the traditionally cautious local black elite, who rarely engaged in any political protest. Her grandfather, H. Maynadier St. Clair, had served on the city council from 1912 until 1946. But in those days race always trumped any status a black person may have achieved. "The council had a banquet once a year," Richardson told a journalist in 1963. "They sent my grandfather's meal to his home by way of a police car."

When CNAC was formed, Gloria Richardson was managing her father's pharmacy. Perhaps because she was a college-educated professional woman and older than most of the civil rights activists, she recognized that there was more to civil rights struggle than getting a cup of coffee or sandwich at a lunch counter. She helped expand CNAC's agenda to include demands for health care and an end to discrimination in schools, housing, and the work force. Also assisting the Cambridge movement with "Project Eastern Shore" was the Northern Student Movement (NSM), a northern campus-based organization that had been formed to aid southern student civil rights efforts.

By 1963 local restaurants were targets of regular protests that were often met with violent white reaction. There were also protest demonstrations at city hall and the county courthouse. Race Street, which separated Cambridge's black and white communities, became a battle zone as racist white mobs clashed with demonstrators. For their part, state and local police, following the example of Birmingham, Alabama's public safety commissioner, Bull Connor, battered protesters with riot sticks and set police dogs to attack. The governor declared martial law and put national guardsmen—the entire Eastern Shore battalion of the guard—in

The Northern Student Movement

"The Northern Student Movement (NSM) was fundamentally the organizational and conceptual brainchild of Peter Countryman, a young white undergraduate at Yale who in 1961, inspired by the southern sit-ins, mobilized northern students to aid the southern student movement in general and SNCC (the Student Nonviolent Coordinating Committee) in particular.

"Countryman's initial efforts involved collecting thousands of books to send to southern black colleges and fundraising for SNCC. But he also recommended that a national committee be formed to coordinate civil rights activities on northern campuses.

"Combining protest against northern discrimination with their central focus of tutoring children in black communities, by the beginning of 1963, NSM had over twelve hundred members in nearly fifty campus chapters, and five thousand people associated with its tutorial program. But the more the NSMers tried to address the failures of the public school system, the more they began to feel that the system itself was dysfunctional and required basic change. Taking a leaf then from SNCC's strategy of community organizing, the NSMers redirected their energy to organizing local people to empower themselves.

"They worked on rent strikes in Harlem and school boycotts in New York and Boston. NSM collaborated with the Mississippi Freedom Democratic Party's (MFDP) Congresssional Challenge to the white Mississippi Congressmen who "won" their seats by depriving black Mississipians of their right to vote. NSM enlisted Malcolm X's support of the Challenge and arranged a meeting between him and Mrs. Fannie Lou Hamer, perhaps black Mississippi's most prominent leader, when Mrs. Hamer came to Harlem. Finally, in its later years, when the fact of American racism had become too apparent to ignore any longer, it was NSM's Detroit chapter which organized one of the most significant white antiracist groups in the country, PAR [People Against Racism]. This local transformation mirrored the transformation of NSM as a whole in the sense that, radicalized by its experience, it, like others, called for a new time and a New America."

—WILLIAM STRICKLAND TO CHARLIE COBB

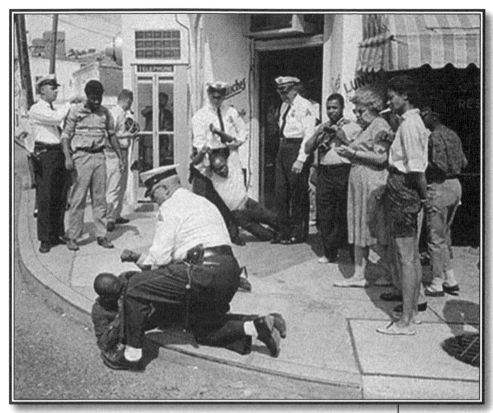

the streets. Court-ordered negotiations went nowhere; Richardson urged more protests and called for federal intervention as arrests and violence mounted. On the night of July 11, when carloads of armed whites went on a rampage through the black community, they were met with gunfire. Remarkably no one was killed, but the city seemed near civil war. Wrote Baltimore *Afro-American* newspaper reporter George Collins: "Only an act of God could have stayed the hand of death during the long night when bullets literally rained on the county seat of Dorchester County." And Gloria Richardson warned: "Unless something is achieved soon in Cambridge, then no one is going to be able to control these people who have been provoked by generations of segregation, by countless indignities—and now by uncontrollable white mobs in the streets."

Robert Kennedy, now alarmed and embarrassed by the televised violence so close to Washington, invited

After refusing to leave Cambridge's Dizzyland Restaurant on July 10, 1963, James Lewis (on the ground, center), Johnny Weeks (far left) and Dwight Campbell (back, at entrance) are placed under arrest as Gloria Richardson (right) watches.

Gloria Richardson and U.S. Attorney General Robert Kennedy announce the "treaty of Cambidge" at a Washington, D.C., press conference on July 23, 1963.

Richardson and town authorities to the capital city for talks on July 22, 1963. Kennedy also invited representatives of other civil rights organizations, hoping to moderate what he considered Richardson's abrasive militancy. For her part, Richardson made it clear to Kennedy that national leaders could not speak for the local movement. In this somewhat strained atmosphere a five-point "Treaty of Cambridge" was agreed to, committing the local government to desegregate schools and public facilities, provide low-income public housing, open job opportunities in the public sector to blacks, and establish a human rights commission. When they got back to Cambridge, however, city officials said that desegregation of public accommodations had to be approved by a referendum. Angered, Richardson and CNAC called for a boycott of the vote. Resisting pressure from Martin Luther King and other national civil rights leaders who urged her to mount a campaign to win

"A Renegade"

In the view of the national media, the government, and many civil rights leaders, it was Gloria Richardson's fault that little or no progress in race relations had been made in Cambridge. The recalcitrance of city officials came up for almost no discussion. Martin Luther King, the Urban League's Whitney Young, and Roy Wilkins accused Richardson of grandstanding. Noting that most of the civil rights leaders who criticized her had never been to Cambridge to see for themselves what was going on, Richardson was convinced that their attacks were made at the behest of the administration, that the Kennedys "wanted things quieted down, and so they told these people then to try to cut the ground from under the movement."

She was shunned as a renegade who did not hew to the traditional civil rights agenda, who claimed more for blacks than the right to vote and to use public accommodations. Her critics in the movement had no inkling that she was a harbinger of what the movement was to become.

—FROM *FREEDOM'S DAUGHTERS*, BY LYNNE OLSON

the referendum, Richardson stood firm on moral principle and insisted, "A first class citizen does not beg for freedom. A first class citizen does not plead to the white power structure to give him something that the whites have no power to give or take away." So, with 50 percent of eligible black voters not voting, the deal brokered in Kennedy's office lost by 274 votes.

Protest resumed but CNAC was weaker as many of the more conservative black leaders backed away from Richardson and her organization. Anger and frustration in the black community continued to deepen despite some concessions made by the city,

H. Rap Brown

Harriet Tubman was a nurse and spy for Union soldiers during the Civil War. After the war, she raised money to pay for the education of ex-slaves, for children's clothing, and to help pay for schools. During the last years of her life, she devoted her time to women's suffrage. She died in 1913.

and it was in Cambridge in 1967 that, standing atop an automobile, newly elected SNCC head H. Rap Brown declared, "If America don't come around, we're going to burn it down!" A few hours later a sniper, unidentified even today, shot Brown on Race Street. That same night, the black elementary school was set on fire and the uncontrolled blaze engulfed most of the nearby black businesses.

There is not a reference anywhere in Cambridge to these tumultuous events. Gloria Richardson simply does not exist in the city's official history. Harriet Tubman is very evident, however, perhaps because she is thought to belong to a different and distant time, and you will find on Cambridge's main downtown street the **Harriet Tubman Museum** *(424 Race Street)*. In fact, a whole tour devoted to this audacious Afro-American abolitionist is possible. About ten miles from downtown Cambridge, on Green Briar Road in **Bucktown** *(Route 397)*, is a historic marker in front of the former Brodess plantation that denotes Tubman's birthplace nearby; the exact spot is still unknown, and the farmland surrounding this marker is privately owned. But the **Bucktown Village Store** *(Bucktown and Greenbriar Roads)* is open to the public on request. Here she was hit in the head with a two-pound anvil hurled at her by an angry slave overseer because she refused to obey his order to hold down a runaway slave he wanted to whip. Just on the edge of Cambridge, the beautiful **Harriet Tubman Memorial Garden** *(Route 50, eastbound side at Washington Street)* is dedicated to the life of this fierce and fearless opponent of slavery and salutes the Underground Railroad routes that led away from Maryland's Eastern Shore. As well, Tubman's Underground Railroad path up the Transquaking River can be traced by kayak or canoe from the **Bestpitch boat ramp** *(off Bestpitch Ferry Road)*.

Even today, Harriet Tubman, from whom Gloria Richardson seems directly descended, feels palpably and powerfully present. She was a nineteenth-century harbinger of the crucial leadership role of women in the twentieth-century civil rights movement. In the twenty-first century we can still be inspired by her desire for freedom. "There are two things I got a right to," Tubman said of her own escape from slavery, "and these are death and liberty. One or the other I mean to have."

⁓ BALTIMORE ⁓

The Underground Railroad connects Harriet Tubman to **Orchard Street United Methodist Church** *(512 Orchard Street)*. It was an important stop on that escape route and is today home to the Greater Baltimore Urban League. Built in 1825, it is the oldest standing structure built by Afro-Americans in Baltimore. Tours, which include reenactments of Tubman leading slaves to freedom and the reading of excerpts from the speeches of Martin Luther King Jr., are available by appointment.

Baltimore's waterfront is where Frederick Douglass, the most influential abolitionist spokesperson of his time, learned to read as a boy. The restored **Frederick Douglass–Isaac Myers Historic Building** *(1417 Thames Street near Caroline Street, in the Fells Point neighborhood)* is where Douglass was employed as a caulker in the 1830s by Myers, a black businessman. The building now anchors a waterfront park that re-creates the nation's first black shipyard. A large bust of Douglass greets visitors at the park entrance.

In the 1960s the lunch counters and restaurants of Baltimore were targets of a sit-in movement that challenged segregation in every corner of the city. And the city resisted pressure to desegregate as stubbornly as any

"There's real, real power in numbers."

"Although we were Morgan State college students, at that moment we weren't thinking about jobs. It was opening facilities—I mean, everything was segregated in Baltimore. So it was the answer. For me personally it was the answer to 'You can't.' I grew up hearing 'You can't. You can't do this. You can't go to the symphony. You can't go to the library. You can't go to the swimming pool. You can't go to that park, no.' It became 'Oh, but I can do something about this. I don't have to wait for the legal route, which is moving too slowly anyway.' So in Baltimore, they started with the downtown area and the theaters, and especially one theater. It was just at the edge of the campus. The neighborhood around the campus was entirely white. This theater was the closest theater to—well, I mean, the black theaters were nowhere near, and the white theaters, of course, we couldn't go to anyway, downtown.

"The first time I heard of balconies was when I went to the Deep South. In Baltimore, you couldn't go to white theaters. There was this one theater, what was it? The North something. Northridge, North something. There it was on the edge of Morgan's campus—a totally black school and we couldn't go to it. Of course, that was a key target especially because people could get to it easily; they could join the picket line between classes, it was that close.

"I got arrested in Baltimore for sitting in and I was in jail when the Howard group sent word that they were on their way, en masse. Suddenly, the mayor woke up and even said on the radio that he wanted us out of jail. 'Just get them out. Forget procedure, just get them out of there.' And we got out. That was a real big, oh, boy, there's real, real power in numbers."

—JEAN WILEY TO CHARLIE COBB

Southern city. My own baptism into the sit-in movement began in Baltimore one spring weekend in 1962, when, after arriving in the city with a group of Howard University students, I went from a meeting at **Union Baptist Church** *(1219 Druid Hill Avenue)* into nonviolent action and arrest in Annapolis, at a restaurant called Antoinette's Pizza that was popular with naval academy midshipmen. This was unplanned on my part. At Union Baptist I had begun conversing with a group of experienced protesters, and when Juanita Jackson Mitchell sent them to Annapolis I went with them, thinking we were going to picket. Instead, we entered the restaurant, sat down, refused to leave when asked, were placed under arrest, and then went limp—a nonviolent tactic in which your body becomes dead weight, thus making it very difficult for police to drag you away and toss you into a paddy wagon. I had no training in nonviolence, but some sort of instinct kicked in and I clung to the biggest person in the group, thinking vaguely that maybe the police would give up since it seemed ridiculous that all of this was happening over an attempt to get some pizza. Instead, with this group, I spent several days in the Anne Arundel County Jail, where I began to hear stories of SNCC's organizing work in Albany, Georgia, and in Mississippi. I was eighteen years old.

On Baltimore's civil rights trail you can see significant working monuments to civil rights struggle, such as the **Afro-American Newspaper** *(2519 North Charles Street)*, the oldest black family-owned newspaper in the country. A former slave by the name of John H. Murphy founded the *Afro*, as it is often called, in his basement in 1892. Following his death in 1922, his five sons took it over. One of the sons, Carl, had graduated from Harvard University but because of his race had been denied admittance to the graduate school of Baltimore's Johns Hopkins University. He became the newspaper's editor and turned it into one of the most persistent and powerful national media voices of civil rights advocacy. At one time as many as thirteen editions were in circulation around the country. In the 1930s the newspaper's offices (then on Eutaw Street) also served as the NAACP's Baltimore branch headquarters.

As in neighboring Washington, D.C., a rich tapestry of black history drapes over the city. Much of this history is beyond the scope of this guide book, but some of it we should visit for the help we get in identifying what could be called the political foliage that both covers and surrounds the civil rights trail. In this regard, a place to start is the **Baltimore Black American Museum** *(1769 Carswell Street)*, which offers art and memorabilia from black culture and history. Also, the 82,000 square-foot **Reginald F. Lewis Museum of African American History and Culture** *(830 E. Pratt Street)*, which is the largest Afro-American museum on the east coast. The museum is named for the Marylander who owned TLC Beatrice Foods International and was the first Afro-American to own a Fortune 500 company.

I like (starting with its name) the **Great Blacks in Wax Museum** *(1601–03 East North Avenue)*. It is the first Afro-American wax museum in the country and, with more than one hundred wax figures, dramatically portrays the entire experience of Africans and African-descended people in the Americas. Part of its appeal is the visitor's opportunity to see lifelike figures in scenes that provide some historical context. Its replication of the horrible conditions on slave ships is bone-chilling. The museum also offers a "spirit tour" of historic Afro-American churches in the city.

Not to be overlooked is the **Baltimore and Ohio Railroad Museum** *(901 West Pratt Street)*, where you can step into a railroad dining car or sleeping car and listen to retired Afro-American railroad porters discuss their experiences. After their presentation they take questions.

While on Pratt Street, the **Thurgood Marshall Monument** *(outside the Edward A. Garmatz Federal Building and U.S. Courthouse, 101 West Lombard Street at Pratt Street)* is an excellent place to pause and ponder the tremendous Afro-American history found in this city. The monument pays tribute to the Baltimore native who gained such great fame for his civil rights work with the NAACP and even greater fame as the first Afro-American

Supreme Court Justice. But Marshall also accomplished much on the local level. As a young attorney starting out in his hometown, in 1936 he helped force the University of Maryland to open its doors to Donald Gaines Murray, thereby allowing Gaines to become the university's first Afro-American law student. Even less known is the fact that Marshall drafted the constitutions of the decolonizing African nations of Ghana and Tanzania.

You can hardly say Thurgood Marshall without saying NAACP, so it seems especially appropriate that past and present are connected by the **National Headquarters of the NAACP** *(4805 Mount Hope Drive)*, which moved from New York City to Baltimore in 1985. There is a tremendous wealth of material at the Henry Lee Moon Library and National Civil Rights Archives here, including every issue of *The Crisis* magazine since 1910, as well as fascinating

Delegates to the first Maryland state conference of NAACP branches stand in front of Baltimore's Sharp Street United Methodist Church (1206 Etting Street) in May 1941.

photographs from the organization's early days. Access is by appointment. I was puzzled that the graceful memorial garden here is named the ***Dorothy Parker Memorial Garden*** for the sharp-tongued writer who, with her satirical wit and intelligence, dominated the New York City Algonquin Writers Table. Naturally, there is a story. Parker died on June 7, 1967, leaving her literary estate to Martin Luther King Jr., although she had never met him. In the event of his death it was to go to the NAACP. So, after King's assas-

NAACP Appears Ready to Relocate to D.C.

BY NIKITA STEWART, STAFF WRITER, *THE WASHINGTON POST*, TUESDAY, DECEMBER 19, 2006

The NAACP is close to moving its headquarters to the District from Baltimore, Mayor Anthony A. Williams (D) said yesterday.

Williams said he expects to sign an agreement with the organization this week. The D.C. Council will vote today on emergency legislation that would give the NAACP a $3.5 million grant to help with land acquisition.

The headquarters could be an important anchor of the Anacostia Gateway, a development project city officials are hoping will spur revitalization along Martin Luther King Jr. Avenue SE.

NAACP Chairman Julian Bond said in May that the organization's board had voted to move to the District to have a presence in the nation's capital and was contemplating the change.

Williams said in a statement yesterday that he welcomed the possible relocation.

"There is no more appropriate place for the NAACP headquarters than Washington, D.C.," Williams said. "I am eager to help NAACP officials accomplish this move, and I look forward to working with them as they make our city their home."

The NAACP has been based in Baltimore since 1986, after the nation's oldest civil rights organization left New York, where it was founded in 1909.

sination, her estate was transferred to the NAACP. Parker was cremated, but for twenty-one years her ashes were mysteriously lost. When the NAACP discovered that for most of those years they had been sitting in a box in a New York attorney's file cabinet, the organization retrieved the ashes and created the garden in her name at their Baltimore headquarters. A plaque in the garden is "dedicated to her noble spirit which celebrated the oneness of humanity, and to the bonds of everlasting friendship between Black and Jewish people."

Anyone visiting Baltimore should pause at another monument that connects civil rights struggle to one of the deep streams of the Afro-American experience: ***The Black Soldier Statue*** *(Baltimore and Calvert Streets at Baltimore Monument Plaza)*. Erected in 1972, the tall bronze statue is dedicated to the memory of Afro-American soldiers who have fought and died in every American war, including the Revolutionary War that gave birth to this nation. Black military veterans such as Mississippi's Medgar Evers and Amzie Moore, or Savannah, Georgia's Hosea Williams (all soldiers in World War II) were especially important in the emergence of the modern civil rights movement, often taking on key leadership roles.

Baltimore's black leadership frequently met for strategy sessions at the home of Lillie Jackson. She was known as the "Mother of Freedom" and also as "Dr. Lillie" and "Ma Jackson," as well as "that NAACP lady." Her three-story Victorian townhouse became the ***Lillie Mae Carroll Jackson Museum*** *(1320 North Eutaw Place)*, which Morgan State University plans to reopen when they get enough money. After becoming president of the Baltimore branch of the NAACP in 1935, Mrs. Jackson breathed new life into the organization so that by the 1940s it had become the second-largest branch in the country. She led its six-year picketing of a whites-only movie theater until the management finally gave in. During her tenure as NAACP president, which lasted until 1970, Baltimore's black policemen received uniforms for the first time, and classrooms at the University of Maryland were opened to Afro-Americans.

"The Reg"

R eginald Robinson of Baltimore, or "the Reg," as he is widely known inside the Movement, may have traveled more widely and been involved in more projects than any single person in SNCC. He was the first to go to Selma, Alabama; was deeply involved with the struggle in Cambridge, Maryland; was one of two SNCC field secretaries to join Bob Moses in McComb, Mississippi, in 1961; was the first SNCC organizer to appear in Orangeburg, South Carolina; and was a SNCC fund-raiser who traveled on southern campuses as a recruiter for SNCC. He helped coordinate logistics in Atlantic City, New Jersey, during the challenge by the Mississippi Freedom Democratic Party (MFDP) to the all-white "regular" Mississippi delegation at the 1964 national Democratic political convention. And this is just the short version of his movement life. Like so many of us, in taking his first steps into the civil rights struggle, such extensive 24/7 commitment was not in his mind.

"I was a student at the Cortez W. Peters Business School when the Greensboro sit-ins broke out and I became involved with Baltimore's Civic Interest Group (CIG). Clarence Logan and Reverend Doug Sands really started that organization on the Morgan State campus. The dean of my school was Walter Dixon and he had been elected to Baltimore's City Council in 1955, and when the sit-ins in Maryland started he had already introduced a public accommodations bill. He called me in one day and told me to get to this statewide meeting of students involved with the CIG. I went and wound up being elected the group's treasurer. There was a lot of pressure from the NAACP folks—the Mitchells, Carl Murphy—who wanted to take over CIG and Clarence Mitchell III, who was our representative to SNCC, naturally went with his family. So, Clarence Logan sent me to a July 1961 SNCC meeting in Louisville, Kentucky, to represent Maryland. One of my assignments there was to get the next SNCC meeting to take place in Baltimore. As it happened, I had been hit in the eye—not during a sit-in, just an accident but everybody thought I had been attacked—and I was wearing a black patch over it. I think my appearance really helped add to the effect of my report, which said that over a three-month period we had registered some eight to ten thousand new black voters in Baltimore. They were impressed. And remember, SNCC was still having this argument about voter registration or direct action.

"During a break I was standing on Ann Braden's porch when this lady

Reggie Robinson attends to demonstrators in Cambridge who were gassed at a march.

came up and said, 'Come here, son; I want to talk to you because you look familiar. Where's your daddy from?' Smithfield, Virginia, I told her and she said, no that can't be it. 'Where's your mama from?' I told her Littleton, North Carolina and she asked, 'What was her maiden name?' I said Jenkins was her name; she's Leovester Jenkins. Then she said, 'You're McKinley!' and I said, 'Oh, that's my uncle.' And she said, 'You look just like him.' I was talking to Ella Baker and she had grown up in Littleton and knew my mother's people. The two of us went on and on—talking—through the night. That's what really helped get me over with Sherrod, McDew, and some of the other SNCC leaders there. And when I made my pitch for Baltimore, Ella Baker's interest in me surely helped with the decision to hold the next meeting in Baltimore. It took place the next month and that's actually where the decision was made to do voter registration projects. I joined SNCC's staff and became a field secretary at the end of that meeting."

—REGGIE ROBINSON TO CHARLIE COBB

It was in Lillie Jackson's living room that a "Don't Buy Where You Can't Work" campaign was launched against white-owned stores on downtown Baltimore's Pennsylvania Avenue that refused to hire black clerks. The stores sued the NAACP but lost their case. Mrs. Jackson, who believed that the NAACP was "God's workshop," played a pivotal role in getting NAACP branches organized all across Maryland. "God helps those who help themselves," she often said. "If you sit down on God you'll just sit." Her daughter, attorney Juanita Jackson Mitchell, who was my lawyer when I was arrested in Annapolis, carried on the tradition, although it wasn't always easy with militant young people challenging the black establishment as well as white power.

CHAPTER THREE

DON'T CARRY ME BACK

Arlington and Alexandria, Richmond, Hampton, Farmville, and Danville, Virginia

The judges declared in Washington town,
You white folks must take that old Jim Crow
sign down.
Hallelujah, I'm a-traveling
Hallelujah, ain't it fine
Hallelujah, I'm a-traveling
Down Freedom's main line.

—AS SUNG BY FREEDOM RIDERS,
SPRING AND SUMMER 1961

Now it's time to go south. Virginia lies just across the Potomac River from Washington, D.C. While it is not difficult to visit many Virginia sites by taking day trips from the nation's capital, travel through one of the most beautiful of the southern states has many rewards. Blacks have had some sort of contact with Virginia for more than four centuries. Well before the English settled Jamestown, Africans were in what is now Virginia as part of both Spanish exploration teams and French Jesuit missions. However, blacks were not a permanent presence until August 1619, when the captain of a Dutch man-of-war traded "twenty and odd" Africans for supplies at ***Fort Algernourne at Old Point Comfort*** (*now Fort Monroe; take I-64 to exit 268 to Mallory Street and follow signs to the fort*), which guarded the present-day city of Hampton. From there these Africans were sent up the James River to the Jamestown colony.

In one of the great historic ironies of the U.S. black experience, Fort Monroe, the oldest continuously operating military fort in the United States, has also become an important symbol of freedom. It happened this way. On the night of May 23, 1861, three runaway slaves belonging to Confederate colonel Charles Mallory swam across the Hampton Roads harbor from Sewell's Point in Norfolk and sought refuge at the fort, which was in Union army hands. The fort's commanding officer, Brigadier-General Benjamin Butler, sent a dispatch to the War Department, stating that despite the Fugitive Slave Act mandate that

escaped slaves were to be returned to their owners, he would not do so. Butler explained why in very practical, but consequential, terms. In seceding from the Union, Confederate Virginia was now a foreign country. "I find satisfactory evidence that these men would be taken to Carolina to aid secessionist forces there," wrote Butler. "I shall consider these people Contrabands

Union camp of General Benjamin Butler

of War." This set a precedent and accelerated the flight of southern black slaves to Union lines. It also had the perhaps unintended effect of defining the war as being about slavery instead of states' rights. On learning that the fort was a refuge for fugitive slaves, the Confederate army torched the town of Hampton, which burned to the ground. To this day, Fort Monroe carries the nickname "Freedom's Fortress." The **Casemate Museum** at the fort details this story; the screening of a black history film can also be arranged.

The first Afro-American child whose name is known was born in Jamestown: William Tucker, the child of Anthony and Isabella, two Angolans who had been among those twenty-some Africans traded for supplies at Old Point Comfort. Although his exact birth date is unknown, the boy's baptism was recorded as taking place on January 3, 1624. Neither his parents' European last names—if given at all—nor their African names are known; Tucker was the surname of the Dutch plantation owner who bought the couple.

Among the thirteen colonies of eighteenth-century America, Virginia—the home state of George Washington, Thomas Jefferson, James Madison, and George Mason— most strongly rivals Washington, D.C.'s importance in the birth of the United States. In its early years, Virginia had more slaves than any of the other colonies, yet arguably produced the most influential thinkers among the colonial leaders who developed the ideas and language that would define American democracy. Roger Wilkins, whose uncle, Roy Wilkins, was executive secretary of the NAACP, finds another great and sad irony in this. Slave labor freed plantation owners such as Jefferson to read and think. In *Jefferson's Pillow*, his contemplation of slavery and these four founding fathers, Wilkins writes: "It is odd that Jefferson, who started out as a real estate lawyer, would be best remembered as a romantic philosopher with a poetic touch. The transformation was made possible by the wealth in slaves he acquired on the death of his father-in-law, which gave him the leisure to study, to reflect, and to write."

So, as we did in Washington, in Virginia, too, we can see the early founding contradiction. In this regard, Jefferson's plantation, **Monticello** *(from Washington, take Constitution Avenue to Route 64 east, then exit 121A to Route 53)*, is worth a visit, although Jefferson considered blacks inferior and argued that this inferiority had caused their enslavement. More than two centuries later, in 1950, when an NAACP lawsuit resulted in the admission of Gregory Swanson as the University of Virginia's first Afro-American law student, the university's president, former Virginia governor Colgate Darden, actually argued that Swanson's admission violated "Jeffersonian ideals" on the inferiority of blacks.

Gregory H. Swanson, on September 15, 1950, consulting with assistant law dean Charles K. Woltz after becoming the first Afro-American to register for law school at the University of Virginia. Though admitted to the university, he was not allowed to live on campus. After completing his first year, Swanson withdrew because of "an overwhelming climate of racial hostility and harassment."

Yet, Jefferson's blood descendants are found among both Afro-Americans and Euro-Americans, perhaps making Jefferson and the state of Virginia near-perfect symbols of the great American contradiction of "race." At the Monticello plantation there are now both guided and self-guided tours of **Mulberry Row**, where in her childhood, Sally Hemings, the Afro-American mother of at least one of Jefferson's children, and other slaves lived.

The capture of Nat Turner

It is only fair to note that Jefferson recognized slavery as evil and worried aloud about the price his new nation would pay for it. Among the words etched on one of the marble panels inside Jefferson's tidal-basin memorial in Washington, D.C., are these: "Indeed I tremble for my country when I reflect that God is just, that his justice cannot sleep forever. Commerce between master and slave is despotism. Nothing is more certainly written in the book of fate than that these people are to be free." Nonetheless, Jefferson never freed his slaves.

Virginia is also where one of the fiercest of the nineteenth-century slave uprisings occurred. On August 21, 1819, some seventy slaves led by Nat Turner, a handyman and Christian preacher, moved along a meandering thirty-mile trek toward the county seat town of **Jerusalem** *(now the town of Courtland, on U.S. 58 in Southampton County),* killing dozens of people with swords and machetes. The rebellion was crushed in just two days, although it took more than two months to capture Turner. The panic this revolt set off across the South (where in some places blacks outnumbered whites two to one) generated bloody white retaliation. In Southampton alone, thirty blacks, including Turner, were hanged (Turner's body was also skinned and quartered). Virginia's governor, John Floyd, blamed the insurrection on northerners and on black preachers who taught reading in Sunday school, so he banned black churches. There are two **roadside markers** *(U.S. 58 at Quarter Road; Virginia Road 35 at Cross Keys Road near Boykins)* that relate to the rebellion, and the **Southampton County Historical Society** *(209 North Main Street, Franklin)* includes a Nat Turner pamphlet and videotape among its offerings.

FREEDOM RIDES, 1961

On May 4, 1961, two groups of Freedom Riders set out from Washington, D.C., one group boarding a Greyhound bus, the other a Trailways bus. They planned to ride all the way to New Orleans to test compliance with federally ordered desegregation of seating and terminals used for interstate travel. Organized by the Congress of Racial Equality (CORE), both groups were interracial and would upset traditional seating patterns: Blacks would sit in the front of the bus, whites in the back. Likewise, inside terminals black riders would use white-only facilities and white riders vice versa. It was assumed there would be arrests because much southern racial segregation was still deeply embedded in social custom and law.

The Freedom Riders skipped the Capital's immediate Virginia neighbors, Arlington and Alexandria. Though considered "moderate" on matters of race, about a year earlier (June 9, 1960) when a group of black students sat down at the Peoples Drug Store lunch counter in Arlington, the manager closed it rather than serve them. CORE's head, James Farmer, was anticipating worse when the riders reached Deep South states such as Alabama and Mississippi, and before leaving Washington, the riders had prepared in nonviolent workshops. "Intense role-playing sessions— sociodramas," was Farmer's description of them. "With some of the group playing the part of Freedom Riders . . . several played the role of white hoodlums coming in to beat up the Freedom Riders. Since the dramas were for survival not entertainment, the action was all too realistic. People were thrown out of bus seats and clubbed, knocked off lunch counter stools and stomped." The Freedom Riders pledged to stay in jail if arrested and to refuse bail, not only to generate publicity but also to fill up the jails, which would, said Farmer, "make the maintenance of segregation so expensive for the state and the city that they would come to the conclusion that they could no longer afford it."

Farmer modeled the 1961 Freedom Rides on a CORE-led 1947 ride, described then as a "Journey of Reconciliation." Sixteen riders— eight blacks and eight whites— traveled from Virginia through North Carolina and Tennessee to Louisville, Kentucky, testing court orders that desegregated interstate modes of transportation (basically, seating on buses).

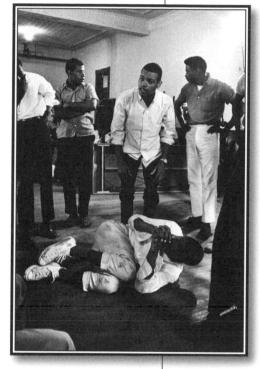

SNCC's Cordell Reagon conducts a nonviolence workshop in Danville. Here he explains how to curl up in order to avoid serious injury from blows to the midriff, groin, head, or neck.

However, while the law may have changed, custom remained firmly in place and most of the South ignored the Supreme Court's decision. Setting out from Washington, D.C., on April 9, 1947 (the day before Jackie Robinson became the first Afro-American to sign a major-league baseball contract), blacks sat in the front and whites in the back. The riders, all of them males, also challenged racial segregation inside bus terminals, which was an issue not resolved in law. On six separate occasions there were arrests, but for the most part there was not much interest in the ride.

This would not be the case with the 1961 Freedom Rides. Although they received very little press attention when they began, white mob violence changed that. By 1961 many white southerners felt that their way of life was under siege. Mounting resentment—as southern politicians put it,

Origin of the Freedom Rides

The origins of both the 1947 Journey of Reconciliation and the 1961 Freedom Rides lay with an earlier, now almost forgotten, challenge to Virginia bus segregation. On July 16, 1944, Irene Morgan, a twenty-seven-year-old mother of two, boarded a Greyhound bus at the Old Hayes Store Post Office in Gloucester County (nearby at Poropotank Creek, in what is known as the "Servants' Plot," black indentured servants once planned an early insurrection). Mrs. Morgan had been visiting her mother, who lived in this rural Tidewater community near Norfolk, and was headed back home to Baltimore, where her husband, a dock worker at the city's port, anxiously

New York supporters of the Freedom Rides en route to Washington, D.C., where some will join other riders for the journey into the deep south

awaited her return. She was still recuperating from a miscarriage earlier that summer, but she hoped to return to work at the Glenn L. Martin Bomber Plant, where she helped build B-26 Marauders, after getting a medical checkup. Mrs. Morgan sat down in the fourth row from the rear, in the "colored" section. A few miles down the road, the driver ordered her to get up so that a white couple who had just boarded could sit down. That meant Mrs. Morgan would have to stand on the crowded bus, and she refused. Not only that, she prevented the woman sitting next to her from surrendering her seat. That woman was holding a baby, and when she began to get up as ordered, Mrs. Morgan asked her: "Where do you think you're going with that baby in your arms?" The driver then drove to the town of Saluda and stopped in front of the jail, where a sheriff's deputy soon boarded with a warrant for Mrs. Morgan's arrest. She yanked it from him and tore it up. When the deputy then grabbed her arm to drag her off the bus, she kicked him, "in a very bad place," Mrs. Morgan said later. "He was blue and purple and turning all colors," she told a reporter. Finally she was thrown into jail.

At her trial three months later, representing herself, Mrs. Morgan pleaded guilty to resisting arrest and paid a $100 fine, but refused to plead guilty to violating the state's segregation laws, arguing that those laws were local and should not apply because she was traveling to another state. Ultimately, *Irene Morgan v. Commonwealth of Virginia*, an appeal taken on by the NAACP and handled by Virginia attorney Spottswood Robinson (one of Charles Hamilton Houston's freedom "Raiders" from Howard University School of Law), resulted in a landmark June 3, 1946, Supreme Court ruling striking down segregated seating in interstate travel. "It seems clear to us," the Supreme Court said, "that seating arrangements for the different races in interstate motor travel requires a single uniform rule to promote and protect national travel." The following year, riders on CORE's Journey of Reconciliation set out to explain the decision and test compliance with it. Bayard Rustin, who was on this journey—and who, in 1963, gained national fame as the key organizer of the March on Washington—even wrote a song: "On June the third the high court said, when you ride interstate, Jim Crow is dead. You don't have to ride Jim Crow!"

"Our Last Supper"

"I was, for the first time in my life, actually eating out.

"As we passed around the bright silver containers of food, someone joked that we should eat well and enjoy because this might be our Last Supper. Several in the group had actually written out wills in case they didn't come back from this trip. It was that serious. It was that real. As for me, just about all I owned was packed up in my suitcase. There was no need for me to make out a will. I had nothing to leave anyone."

—JOHN LEWIS, ON THE FREEDOM RIDERS' LAST NIGHT TOGETHER

of "the interposition and nullification" of states' rights by the federal government—left little doubt that at least in some places, reaction to the rides was likely to be fierce and ugly. Aware that their lives could be at risk, some of the Freedom Riders wrote their wills before leaving Washington; they also had a "Last Supper" at the Yenching Palace, a Chinese restaurant on upscale Connecticut Avenue that was a favorite of Louisiana's congressional delegation.

Still, violence and arrests were *local* responses to challenges to *local* law and custom; the federal government preferred, and often chose, not to intervene. Testing compliance with a *federal* order generated more pressure for protective federal intervention. As Jim Farmer put it, "Our intention was to provoke the southern authorities into arresting us and thereby prod the Justice Department into enforcing the law of the land." Desirous of avoiding rupture with its southern political allies over civil rights, the Kennedy administration tried to pretend the Freedom Ride was not happening. That became impossible after brutal attacks on the riders in Alabama, although Attorney General Robert Kennedy would claim he was unaware that before the Freedom Riders left Washington, CORE had sent a letter to him and to his brother John, the president, informing them of the group's dangerous itinerary. In short, not only was this Freedom Ride directly challenging the old southern way of life, it was also directly challenging the politically cozy tolerance at *federal* levels for that way of life.

❧ ARLINGTON ❧ AND ALEXANDRIA

W hen slavery finally propelled the country into civil war, Union forces established, mainly for "contraband" slaves, a *"Freedman's Village"* on land that once belonged to George Washington's adopted grandson, George Washington Parke Custis, and then to Robert E. Lee, and is now part of **Arlington National Cemetery** *(from Washington, across the Memorial Bridge to George Washington Memorial Parkway)*. During the Civil War this village was little more than a tent camp, but in 1865 the Freedman's Bureau developed permanent housing, schools, hospitals, and a training center aimed at producing skilled craftsmen. And the village's gardens grew produce to be sold in area markets. With the collapse of Reconstruction, the government turned the land over to the military, and villagers were given ninety days to clear out. The exact location of the village is unknown, but it is generally thought to have been in what is now the southeast section of Arlington cemetery. There is a replica of the village at **Arlington House**, inside the cemetery.

Some 3,800 Afro-Americans who lived in the village are buried in **Section 27** *(Ord and Weitzel Drives near the Memorial Amphitheater)*. Their headstones are marked with the words *Civilian* or *Citizen*, designations presumably distinguishing "contraband" from free blacks. Also buried in this section, as well as in **Section 23**, are about 1,500 of the black troops who fought for the Union; their headstones are marked U.S.C.T. (United States Colored Troops).

The assassinated Mississippi civil rights leader Medgar Evers, a World War II veteran, is buried in **Section 36**

Company F the Fourth Colored Infantry, stands before Fort Lincoln in 1865. This is one of their last photographs taken together.

(*36-1431, BB-40*) of Arlington Cemetery. Thurgood Marshall, who died of heart failure on January 24, 1993, lies in **Section 5** (*5-40-3, W36*). And interred in **Section 3** (*3-1377, LM19*) is former army Lt. Col. Lemuel A. Penn, the prominent Afro-American educator, who, on July 11, 1964, was shot and killed by three Ku Klux Klansmen while he was driving through Madison County, Georgia.

From 1920 until 1939, Washington, D.C., native Dr. Charles Richard Drew lived in Arlington. It was Dr. Drew who discovered that, for the purpose of blood transfusion, plasma could be used instead of whole blood, and that in storage, blood plasma would last longer and was less likely to become contaminated. His renown was such that, upon entering World War II, the U.S. government's medical director of the First Division for Blood Transfusion asked Dr. Drew to head the nation's blood drive. He accepted, but shortly resigned in protest when the War Department sent out orders to segregate blood according to race; "white" blood was to be provided to white soldiers only, "black" blood to Afro-Americans. On April 1, 1950, Dr. Drew died in an automobile accident near Burlington, North Carolina. He was only forty-five years old. A tale that has taken on mythic proportions, although it does not appear to be true, holds that Dr. Drew died after being denied treatment at the nearest hospital because he was black. **Dr. Drew's Arlington house** *(2505 1st Street South)* was designated a National Historic Landmark in 1976.

Like Washington, D.C., and Arlington, the historic city of Alexandria *(from Arlington, a short drive south along the George Washington Parkway)* was also largely built on the slave trade. An ironic remnant of this, linking the days of slavery with modern civil rights efforts, is the office of the **Northern Virginia Urban League** *(1315 Duke Street)*, located in what was once the notorious slave pen and headquarters of Virginia's biggest slave-trading firm, Franklin and Armfield. With offices in Natchez and New Orleans as well, Franklin and Armfield sold thousands into slavery on southern cotton and sugar plantations. "A lot of people who pass by think this is an old law firm," said league CEO Lavern J. Chatman, "but ten thousand slaves went through here." The league, which purchased the building in 1996, plans a basement museum "to preserve the historical and cultural significance of slavery's past and the continued struggle to eliminate bars to freedom."

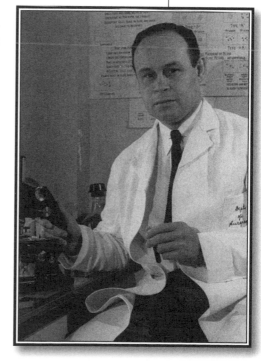

Dr. Charles Drew

Not far away, in another brick Federal-style building, **Bruin "Negro Jail"** *(1707 Duke Street)*, owned by slave dealer Joseph Bruin, is where the seventy-seven Washington, D.C., runaways on the schooner *Pearl* were jailed and ultimately sold farther south, most to New Orleans. On April 15, 1848, they had slipped away from their "masters" and in a light rain made their way aboard a fifty-four-ton schooner called the *Pearl* manned by abolitionists and docked at Whitehouse Wharf in downtown Washington. This was the largest recorded escape attempt by slaves in U.S. history.

According to abolitionist William Lloyd Garrison, one of the slaves on the *Pearl* worked in President James K. Polk's White House. Another led a relatively comfortable existence as the "property" of Dolly Madison. What slaves really wanted, as confirmed by this flight of men and women who could broadly be described as relatively comfortable "house Negroes," was not improved conditions or even wages, but freedom. Indeed, in my own family there are stories of Georgetown blacks standing on the banks of the Potomac River or in the windows of their "masters'" homes at night, waving lanterns to guide runaway slaves from Virginia into the relative freedom of Washington.

The runaways on the *Pearl* were quickly captured after seeking shelter from an unexpected storm, and an answer to the question of how they were discovered may lie with the ghosts that undoubtedly haunt the Bruin jail. Two sisters, Emily and Mary Edmundson, were among the escapees. As the story has been handed down in my family, Emily had turned down a marriage proposal, and so the angry, rejected suitor revealed how the escapees had slipped away and divulged the route they planned to take. In her *Key to Uncle Tom's Cabin*, Harriet Beecher Stowe says this jail was part of her background research for the book. The building now houses private business offices and is closed to the public.

Within a few hours of reaching New Orleans, the Edmondsons were lodged in a slave pen operated by J.M. Wilson, partner of Bruin and Hill. . . . The new arrivals were admonished to look happy or be beaten; selling contented slaves was serious business.

—FROM *THE PEARL, A FAILED SLAVE ESCAPE ON THE POTOMAC*, BY JOSEPHINE F. PACHECO

The **Alexandria Black History Museum** *(902 Wythe Street)* was originally established as a library in 1940 after five black men, led by lawyer and World War II veteran Samuel Tucker, were arrested for refusing to leave the whites-only Queen Street Library. As a result of this protest, the following year, Alexandria built the **Robert H. Robinson Library** for blacks, which is now the nucleus of the museum. Next door is the **Watson Reading Room**, named for Charles and Laura Watson, an

Afro-American couple who were early Alexandria landowners. It houses a collection of books, videos, documents, and periodicals about Afro-American life and culture. **African American Heritage Park** *(off Duke Street on Holland Lane)* is another satellite of this museum. Located on eight acres, part of the property was once a small nineteenth-century Afro-American cemetery, but few of the headstones exist now. A wetlands area provides homes for mallard ducks, turtles, beavers, and other small wildlife, but the focus of the park is a group of bronze trees sculpted by James Meadows, called *Truths That Rise from the Roots Remembered*, which acknowledges the contributions of Afro-Americans to the development of Alexandria. Other, smaller statues in the park pay tribute to black neighborhoods and to the unknown persons buried on the site.

Samuel W. Tucker (right), Henry L. Marsh III (center), and Frank D. Reeves (left), who waged legal battle to get Prince Edward County schools reopened. Marsh became the first Afro-American mayor of Richmond, and Reeves was the first Afro-American member of the Democratic National Committee.

🥀 RICHMOND 🥀
DOWN I-95

L ike the Freedom Riders, our first stop heading south from Alexandria is Fredericksburg. In 1961 **Robinson's Restaurant** *(corner of Canal and Princess Anne Streets)* was the only area restaurant that served Afro-Americans. Sit-ins had already broken out in town, and the following year, after an extended campaign, desegregation took place

fairly rapidly. By 1963, many of the city's public accommodations had desegregated.

Fredericksburg is a Rappahannock River port city, and in the eighteenth century, slavery was an important part of its thriving trade. You can still see the original ***slave auction block*** *(Williams and Charles Streets)* downtown—a rare preservation in the South today. On the south side of George Street, where it intersects with Barton and Liberty Streets, is ***Free Alley***, a path where slaves could walk freely to town without a pass.

James Monroe, before becoming Virginia governor and the fifth U.S. president, practiced law in Fredericksburg and was also a city councilman. Monroe was a founder of the American Colonization Society, which pressed for the return of African slaves to what is now the West African nation of Liberia; Monrovia, Liberia's capital, was named for him. There is a ***James Monroe Library*** *(908 Charles Street)*.

Interestingly, in the early nineteenth century, a free black family, the William De Baptistes, owned much of the east side of Charles Street: from William to Amelia Streets. In their home on the corner of Amelia and Charles, the family maintained a secret school for slaves. Since white southern authorities felt that educated slaves were dangerous, in order to fool suspicious town police, female students pretended to sew and the male students pretended they were making matches from sticks and sulphur.

The Shiloh New Site Baptist Church (214 Wolfe Street) is one of the many southern symbols of transition after the intense period of nonviolent civil rights activism of the early 1960s. In 1968, the minister, Reverend Lawrence Davies, stood up to angry black youths who wanted to sack downtown Fredericksburg after the assassination of Martin Luther King Jr. Afterward, with the support of the Chamber of Commerce, he organized a Boys Club and jobs program. Rev. Davies became Fredericksburg's first black mayor in 1976 and held the position until his death in 1996.

CORE's James Farmer taught to packed classrooms at Fredericksburg's Mary Washington College from 1985 until 1998, when illness forced his retirement; he died in 1999. A bronze bust of Farmer is on display at the college. In 1987, the college established a James Farmer Scholars Program to assist students, beginning in the seventh grade, to prepare to enroll in and attend any college of their choice. There is also a *James Farmer Multicultural Center (1301 College Avenue)*, which sponsors a multicultural fair every April.

James Farmer

The first national museum dedicated to slavery will open in Fredericksburg in 2008. Former Virginia governor Douglas Wilder, himself the grandson of a slave, has spearheaded the effort. Thirty-two acres overlooking the Rappahannock River have been acquired for a glass and stone building designed by architect Chen Chung Pei (son of the highly acclaimed I.M. Pei). The 290,000-square-foot museum will include a full-scale replica of a Portuguese slave ship in a glass-roofed atrium. "This is our Holocaust Museum," said actor

U.S. Slavery Museum Takes Uncensored Look

"HERITAGE TOURISM" A GROWING INDUSTRY, BY HEATHER GEHLERT,
LOS ANGELES TIMES, AUGUST 20, 2006

FREDERICKSBURG, VA.—Inferiority. Servitude. Racism. These are a few of the words that Vonita W. Foster uses when she travels to middle schools and high schools to teach students about slavery—a subject that, more than 140 years after its end, still makes some black students squirm.

"They're kind of uncomfortable," she said. "They're embarrassed that their ancestors were slaves, because they don't know the heritage."

Foster is on a mission to change that. She has become a driving force in creating the United States' first national museum dedicated to slavery.

With 290,000 square feet of space and a $200 million budget, the United States National Slavery Museum, scheduled to open in Fredericksburg in 2008, is a high-end example of a growing market trend, as the tourism industry realizes the popularity and profitability of opening and re-examining one of American history's ugliest scars.

Slavery studies has been growing as a field of interest in the past few decades, as people have sought the uncensored, unsanitized story of the trans-Atlantic slave trade—a topic that Foster, who will be the museum's executive director, says is glossed over in classrooms, textbooks, and movies.

"When you keep your citizens ignorant and you only share bits and pieces, people start to say: 'Wait a minute . . . why wasn't I told this in school? Why didn't I know this?'" she said.

What many don't know, she said, is the history of African-Americans sell-

Ben Vereen, who starred as "Chicken" George Moore in the television miniseries *Roots.*

From Fredericksburg it is only fifty-six miles to Richmond, where the first major slave revolt in the South took place: *The Gabriel Prosser rebellion (markers on Route 1 at Brook Ridge and at Bryan Park Avenue and Lakeside).* In the summer of 1800, Gabriel Prosser, a twenty-four-year-ing their own people, toddlers in shackles, and America, including the North, benefiting financially from slave labor.

"It's not as easy as 'Gone With the Wind' and 'Miss Scarlett' and all of that," Foster said. "There are so many variables."

Several smaller slavery museums and exhibits have opened across the South, particularly as the children and grandchildren of black people who migrated North in the 1930s and '40s trace their family histories.

"There's this demographic of baby boomer African-Americans with lots of leisure time and income returning to discover their roots," said Rich Harrill of the International Tourism Research Institute at the University of South Carolina.

The segment of the travel business known as "heritage tourism" encompasses many ethnic groups and allows travelers to see how they fit into a broader cultural history. It is the second-fastest-growing segment of tourism, behind nature-based excursions, Harrill said . . .

So far, the Fredericksburg museum has raised about $50 million from wealthy individuals, such as comedian Bill Cosby, and corporations including Wal-Mart and Wachovia Bank, but must raise another $50 million before construction can begin. The remaining $100 million in the budget is to furnish the building and establish an endowment for daily operations.

Plans call for 10 permanent exhibits, including a full-scale replica of a slave ship. About 6,000 artifacts have been collected, including deeds of sale, an 1840s census book with state-by-state slave listings, and torture devices, masks, and wooden instruments, known as specula oris, used to force-feed captives who refused to eat on the long sea passage from Africa.

The rise in slavery-themed attractions has met some resistance, particularly among blacks who are not eager to revisit the past. But, Foster said, "more people are embracing the project than are not."

In fact, the pain associated with slavery is now a main draw of many sites, with images that are graphic and tours that re-create the slave experience.

old blacksmith, organized several hundred slaves with the intention of taking over the city of Richmond by killing all whites except for Methodists, Quakers, and French, and creating in Virginia something akin to what his hero, Toussaint L'Ouverture, wanted to establish in Haiti. On the day of the planned insurrection, however, a sudden and unusually fierce thunderstorm swelled creeks and streams, making the anticipated launch from Brook Bridge impossible.

Prosser postponed the gathering, which gave time for informers to alert Governor Monroe. As a result, Prosser was captured and shortly hanged at Fifteenth and Broad Streets in Richmond. **Henrico County**, where this all took place, publishes a brochure in which key spots of the planned rebellion have been marked.

One hundred sixty years later, nonviolent civil rights struggle unfolded not far from here, when, on February 20, 1960, black students marched from the Virginia Union campus on Lombardy Street, down Chamberlayne Avenue, to **Woolworth's** on Broad Street in downtown Richmond. The students walked in, occupied all thirty-four seats at the lunch counter, and sought service. Management closed the store. And less than two weeks later, on February 22, thirty-five Virginia Union students were arrested at the lunch counter of **Thalhimer's Department Store** (*600 block of east Broad Street; closed, demolished, and now the site of the Virginia Performing Arts Center*). These were the first large-scale arrests connected with the surge of student-led protests that began in 1960.

Jackson Ward (*roughly bounded by Fifth, Marshall, and Gilmer Streets and the Richmond-Petersburg Turn-*

Virginia Union students sit in at Woolworth's department store on Broad Street on February 20, 1960.

pike) was once the center of black life in Richmond. Before being sliced and diced into depressing little pieces by the turnpike, this formerly vibrant community was known as "Little Africa," and until the 1960s more than 90 percent of the city's black community lived here. Jackson Ward resident Maggie Lena Walker, daughter of an Irish father and black mother, was the first female bank president in the United States. Her bank, the **St. Luke Penny Saving Bank** *(St. Luke Building, 900 St. James Street),* merged with Commercial Bank and Trust and the Second Street Savings Bank in 1931 to become the Consolidated Bank and Trust Company, which remains one of the oldest Afro-American–operated banks in the country. There is also a **Maggie Walker National Historic Site** *(600 North Second Street),* which has been restored to its 1930s appearance with original Walker family furnishings. The **Black History Museum and Cultural Center** *(00 Clay Street)* provides brochures for a walking tour through the community.

Arthur Ashe

Outside Jackson Ward, on the corner of Monument Avenue and Roseneath Road, there is a twelve-foot bronze statue of tennis great and native son **Arthur Ashe**. As a young man growing up in Richmond, Ashe could not play tennis on the city's whites-only courts. Now, depicted in warm-ups and tennis shoes, he stands among statues honoring Robert E. Lee and other uniformed Confederate heroes. Ashe holds a tennis racket in his left hand and books in his right hand. Four children gaze up at him, and inscribed on the granite base are words from the Book of Hebrews that capture the spirit of the civil rights movement and are still powerfully relevant today: "Since we are surrounded by so great a cloud of witnesses, let us lay aside every weight, and the sin which so easily ensnares us, and let us run with endurance the race that is set before us."

In addition to being the first Afro-American to win at both Wimbledon and the U.S. Open, Ashe was also active in campaigns against apartheid (the oppressive system of racial segregation in South Africa) as well as in civil rights campaigns at home. Pulitzer Prize–winning *Chicago Tribune* columnist Clarence Page compared Ashe to Jackie Robinson, who ended baseball's color line in 1947: "Arthur Ashe was a fellow who was not only appropriate to break the color barrier in his sport, but understood the larger significance of his achievement." On February 6, 1993, Ashe died at the age of fifty from AIDS-related pneumonia caused by a blood transfusion given him during heart surgery.

⊰ HAMPTON ⊱

According to civil rights canon, the southern student sit-in movement began February 1, 1960, in Greensboro, North Carolina, and then quickly spread across the state. On February 10, 1960, Hampton, Virginia, was one of the first cities outside North Carolina to experience sit-ins. Student activists on the campus of *Hampton Institute (now Hampton University, I-64 to exit 267)*, a private, historically black college, were the driving force behind these protests. Founded in 1868 as the Hampton Normal and Industrial Institute, one of the school's early students was Booker T. Washington, the young son of a freed slave. After graduating in 1875, Washington went on to found Tuskegee Institute in Alabama. Under a federally funded program, Hampton was also the first U.S. college to enroll Native Americans. However, some in Congress objected to a government-funded program for educating "Indians" at "expensive eastern schools" and federal funding stopped in 1912; Hampton's Indian Department shut down in 1923. Markers throughout the campus reflect the once-upon-a-time presence of this indigenous population. The large **Hampton University Museum** *(Huntington Building)* contains a truly fine collection of African, Afro-American, and Native-American art; it is the oldest Afro-American museum in the country. And downtown, the **Hampton History Museum and Visitor's Center** *(120 Old Hampton Lane)* covers four hundred years, bringing together, as few museums do, Native-American, Afro-American, and Euro-American history in this part of Virginia.

Booker T. Washington

The 204-acre campus overlooks the Hampton River and the northern edge of Hampton Roads harbor, and on this lovely campus you will find **Emancipation Oak** *(from I-64 to campus entrance on Tyler Street, then left onto Emancipation Drive)*, with a crown spread that is nearly one hundred feet wide. In 1863 slaves from the area gathered under this tree to hear the Emancipation Proclamation read to them—the first southern reading of Lincoln's proclamation. Before Hampton was even established, beneath this same tree, Mary S. Peake, a free black person, had long been secretly educating slaves in what may be the first organized effort to teach reading and writing to blacks in America. **Mary Peake Boulevard** in Hampton honors her. Her grave is at the **Elmerton Cemetery** *(Wine Street just north of Pembroke Avenue)*. The National Geographic Society designated Emancipation Oak one of the ten greatest trees in the world, and it is also a National Historic Landmark.

◆ FARMVILLE ◆
AN OPENING SHOT OF STUDENT PROTEST

One of the greatest but least-known stories of the modern civil rights movement unfolded in the tiny town of Farmville in the early 1950s. You can follow it at the **Robert Russa Moton Museum** *(Main Street and Griffin Boulevard)*. The museum was once the overcrowded Robert Moton High School. Built in 1939, the school was the first and only high school for blacks in Prince Edward County. It had been named for one of Farmville's most famous native sons, Dr. Robert Moton, who had succeeded Booker T. Washington as the head of Tuskegee Institute in Alabama. By 1950, however, Moton School was notorious for its overcrowded, dilapidated state: the roof leaked, forcing students to sit in classrooms holding umbrellas; students used discarded books purchased from the white high school; classrooms were heated by pot-bellied stoves or had no heat at all. The school was built to accommodate one hundred forty-five students, but in 1951 there were four-hundred fifty. To handle the overflow, three tarpaper shacks without insulation or electricity had been built on the grounds.

Parents had been complaining about the Moton School's condition for years, but the school board ignored them. Then one day Barbara Johns, a sixteen-year-old junior at Moton, missed her school bus. While pondering what to do, the bus carrying

An old stove in the back of a Moton School classroom offered little warmth on cold winter days.

white students to their school passed by, reminding her of the county's racial segregation and the horrible conditions of Moton School, especially compared to the school the white children were going to on their bus. "Right then and there I decided that indeed something had to be done about this inequality," she wrote years later in notes she planned to turn into a book. (Barbara Johns died young, of cancer, in 1991, but her unfinished memories can be read in a complete copy of her handwritten notebook on display at the Moton Museum.)

Her next steps put into motion an extraordinary chain of events. Johns called together the student council, and they met quietly on the bleachers of the athletic field. No definite plans were made, but the group decided to keep careful watch on the Moton PTA, as well as the county school board, to see if they would move on the long-standing request for a new and better building. Nothing happened and it quickly became clear that nothing would happen. In fact, after one February meeting attended by the Moton PTA, the school board told them that they needn't bother attending the monthly meetings anymore. When and if they decided to act on their request, the school board told the black parent organization, it would inform them. The student leaders decided to take action and formed a strike committee.

On the morning of April 23, 1951, an anonymous phone call was made to the school's principal, M. Boyd Jones, telling him that two Moton students had been fighting downtown at the Greyhound bus station and were about to be taken to jail. As the alarmed principal rushed out of the school, the same student leaders who'd been meeting with Barbara Johns delivered a forged notice to classrooms, announcing a short school assembly of all students that morning. At the assembly, the stage curtains opened and there were the student leaders. Ewilda Isaacs, who was an eighth-grader then, remembers the way Barbara Johns stepped forward and declared: "'We are tired of not having nothin'; we want a new school!' The teachers kept telling the students to go back to the classroom," recalls

Isaacs, chuckling quietly. "But Barbara asked the teachers to leave; a few of them objected to that demand but were booed by students." Finally, the teachers left. "Some [of the teachers] just stood in the hall to listen and see what was going on." Barbara Johns called on students to walk out of school and stay out until the school board responded to their demands. The Farmville jail was too small to hold them all if they acted together, said the young leader so remarkably ahead of the student protest movement that was still a decade away. Principal Jones returned while the assembly was still in session and pleaded with the students not to walk out. Progress was being made with the school board, he insisted. Johns asked him to return to his office and he did. Then the entire student body followed Johns out of the school. This was an extraordinary action for rural southwest Virginia in 1951, actually an extraordinary action for anywhere in the South in those days, just as important a harbinger as Marion Anderson's 1939 Lincoln Memorial concert had been.

The students not only walked out of Moton School, but picket signs had been made in advance and secreted away in the carpentry shop: WE ARE TIRED OF TAR PAPER SHACKS and WE WANT A NEW SCHOOL OR NONE AT ALL. Carrying these signs, the students marched into downtown Farmville. Johns and the strike committee sought a meeting with school board chairman Maurice Large, owner of a furniture-manufacturing company, but he refused to meet with them. They then went to the office of school superintendent T. J. McIlwaine, who did take the meeting. Among other things, they asked McIlwaine why they couldn't attend the white school. The superintendent said he had to obey Virginia law and told them to return to their classes at Moton.

Reverend Goodwin Douglass, pastor of Beulah AME Church in Farmville, leads a 1963 protest over the continued closure of Prince Edward County schools.

The students stayed out of the school for two weeks.

Two days after the walkout, students and parents met at **First Baptist Church** (100 South Main Street), the county's largest and oldest black church, which had served as a hospital for Union soldiers during the civil war. The pastor of the church, Reverend L. Francis Griffin, had served

Reverend L. Francis Griffin (right), NAACP executive secretary Roy Wilkins (center), and Oliver Hill (left), who was a lead attorney for the Moton School's desegregation case

in General George Patton's black tank corps during World War II. After returning home from the war in Europe, he had moved about the county encouraging action for social change and preached his "social gospel" at First Baptist. He now urged his congregants to begin planning a legal attack against segregated schools. "I offered my life for a decadent democracy and I'm willing to die rather than let these children down," Griffin told them. At the time of the Moton student walkout he was president of the local NAACP. A plaque in front of First Baptist, placed there after his death in 1980, has inscribed on it one of Rev. Griffin's favorite aphorisms, which plays on the title of *Reader's Digest* magazine's old humor section, "Grin and Bear It": "You May Have to Bear It, But You Don't Have to Grin."

Rev. Griffin put the students in touch with Spottswood Robinson, the head of the NAACP's legal office in Richmond. When Robinson asked the students what they would do if they did not get a new school, they replied that they would continue to stay out of school. Robinson urged them to demand an end to segregated schools, and about a month later, a legal challenge to segregated schools was filed. Later it became one of the five cases that led to the 1954 Supreme Court decision *Brown v. Board of Education*.

But the story doesn't end there. A new but still segregated school was built in 1953. Then, invoking states' rights when the Supreme Court ordered school desegregation in 1954,

*1963 protest by
Prince Edward
County
students*

Prince Edward County, where Farmville is located, led the way in fashioning a campaign of "massive resistance" and shut down schools for *five* years! A system of private "academies" was developed for whites, with funding available from the county government. The black community had to set up schools in churches and homes. National organizations, including the American Friends Service Committee, the National Council of Negro Women, and the NAACP, placed some students in homes and schools in other parts of the country, but many of the county's black students received no further schooling. "I never did go back," said Phil Walker, one of those students, speaking to me reluctantly and with great pain. "It's been more than fifty years and when you talk about it again, it hurts; it still hurts."

In 1964 the Supreme Court ordered the schools to reopen.

ᥱ DANVILLE ᥲ
A FIERCE AND BLOODY SUMMER IN THE LAST CAPITAL OF THE CONFEDERACY

Alexandria, Arlington, and Richmond began to desegregate almost as soon as the sit-ins of the 1960s began, but the tobacco and textile town of Danville dug in its heels and resisted. You wouldn't know it to look at its quiet streets today, but during the summer of 1963, as the nation focused its attention and alarm over Bull Connor and the fire hoses and dogs in Birmingham, an equally violent episode of the civil rights movement unfolded in Danville, Virginia.

The city was proud of its Confederate history and was known as the "Last Capital of the Confederacy" because after Union forces took Richmond, the Confederate government fled to Danville. The city's **Public Library** *(975 Main Street, now the Danville Museum of Fine Arts & History)* was where, on April 4, 1865, the Rebel cabinet held its last full meeting. It is also where, while eating dinner, Jefferson Davis received word of Robert E. Lee's surrender at Appomattox. When the civil rights movement erupted in Danville almost one hundred years later, the library was, in effect, a Confederate memorial.

High-school students protest on the steps of Danville's Municipal Building on Bloody Monday.

Protests targeting the public library led to a court order in 1960 requiring that the library desegregate. In response, it closed for several months and then reopened with all the seats removed—apparently indicating that unlike sitting together, standing together did not mean social interaction was taking place. The library campaign led to the formation of the Danville Christian Progressive Association, which was affiliated with Martin Luther King's SCLC and kept up pressure for desegregation. Municipal jobs were of special concern in this city where one third of the population was Afro-American, and on May 31, 1963, shortly after Rev. King had come to Danville to speak to the group, the association led a major march to the municipal building. Then, on June 10, 1963, now known as Bloody Monday, sixty high school students marched to the municipal building. Protest leaders were arrested while others were chased into a dead-end alley, where police turned high-pressure hoses

A follow-up workshop after Danville protests. Bandaged heads were not uncommon.

on them. Scores were injured as powerful streams of water slammed their bodies again the walls. The city also used a variety of legal weapons. Students were allowed to call their parents, who after arriving were arrested for contributing to the delinquency of minors. And even more noto-riously, leaders of the Bloody Monday protest were charged with a pre–Civil War stat-ute requiring the prosecution of "any person conspiring to incite the colored population to insurrection." This law had been passed after the Nat Turner rebellion and was used in 1859 to hang the abolitionist John Brown. When the protesters' attorney began arguing their case in court, he, too, was arrested. A uniformed black GI from nearby Fort Bragg joined a demonstration while on leave. He was arrested, and later he was reprimanded by the secretary of defense, Robert S. McNamara.

CHAPTER FOUR

MORE THAN A HAMBURGER

Greensboro, Raleigh, and Durham, North Carolina

The time was 1960, the place the U.S.A.
That February first became a history
*   making day*
From Greensboro all across the land
The news spread far and wide
That quietly and bravely youth
*   took a giant stride*
Heed the call
Americans all
Side by equal side
Brothers sit in dignity
Sisters sit in pride

—"BALLAD OF THE SIT-INS,"
BY GUY CARAWAN, EVE MERRIAM,
AND NORMAN CURTIS

While North Carolina is without question a "southern" state—a tradition of segregation being just one example—certain aspects of the state's history sometimes seem to set it apart from other southern states. Quakers operated Underground Railroad stops throughout the state and founded the town of Greensboro, where the student sit-in movement of the 1960s began. North Carolina was the last state to secede from the Union, and thousands of white North Carolinians enlisted with Union forces. Small independent farming is a strong tradition among whites and blacks alike. Reflecting on her life, Ella Baker, who was crucial to the founding of both the Southern Christian Leadership Conference (SCLC) and the Student Nonviolent Coordinating Committee (SNCC), would say that one of her important influences was her grandfather. After the Civil War the former slave worked land he had bought from his former "master" near Littleton, in the coastal and Tidewater area of North Carolina. In this coastal region, even before the Civil War, there was a high concentration of free blacks, and habits of fierce independence and rebellious plotting had taken root. Underground Railroad conductors ferried runaway slaves to freedom by water routes through the barrier islands that dot the coastline. During Reconstruction these coastal communities would elect three blacks to the U.S. Congress and seventy-seven to the state legislature.

Notwithstanding all of this, white racism was also deeply entrenched in the state—as deeply entrenched as any

place in the so-called deep South. Despite its reluctance to secede and its contribution of Union troops, North Carolina also provided the Confederacy with more soldiers than any southern state. And after the Civil War, state officials acted ruthlessly to restore white power. The only known coup d'etat in the United States occurred in North Carolina, when, on No-

Segregated bus station in Durham, 1940

vember 10, 1898, through force of arms, whites overthrew the elected black-controlled government in Wilmington, in the process destroying the presses of the city's influential Afro-American newspaper, the *Daily Record*, and burning down its office. The newspaper's editor, Alex Manly, fled *(you'll find an **Alex Manly historic marker** at the newspaper's site on Third Street between Nun and Church Streets)*. The subhead of the next day's front-page *Charlotte Observer* newspaper story read, "Manley [*sic*], the Defamer of White Womanhood escapes."

At that time in Wilmington, Afro-Americans were a majority of the population and represented the greatest concentration of black political power in North Carolina. The leader of the coup, Alfred Waddell, a former Confederate officer, took over as mayor and told his supporters that any black person found voting should be killed. Black government was intolerable, declared Waddell: "We intend to change it if we have to choke the Cape Fear River with carcasses." In 2005 a state commission found that what happened in 1898 has been wrongly called a "race riot," and what actually took place was a carefully planned "insurrection" by white supremacists.

Despite this kind of terror, the yearning and struggle for civil rights and full citizenship did not abate; instead, it

1898 Wilmington Race Riot

R ECONSTRUCTION: Wilmington's African-American population was a complex society in the 1870s and 1880s with cultural, social, educational, civic, business and political advances. They formed the foundation for development in the 1890s. In 1890, there were 11,324 blacks living in Wilmington and 8,731 whites. In 1900, there were 10,407 blacks in the city and 10,556 whites.

FORCES OF CHANGE: During the 1890s, African-Americans played a vital role in Wilmington's economic and political landscape. The city's black businesses grew at a faster pace than in any other North Carolina city, and black workers flocked to the city. In 1897, more than 1,000 blacks owned property here.

EVE OF DESTRUCTION: Despite intimidation from white Democrats, 2,965 blacks registered for the November 1898 election in Wilmington. There were 2,918 white voters registered. There wasn't any widespread violence on the Nov. 8 Election Day. Democrats won by a wide margin. Precinct workers at a majority African-American Republican precinct reported that 150 to 200 whites had entered the building or stood outside while votes were being tallied [and that during] a scuffle, the ballot boxes were stuffed to guarantee white victory.

RESOUNDING CHANGE: On Nov. 9 a large group of whites [passed] a series of resolutions . . . , forcing some blacks out of town. This included Alex Manly, editor of the city's only black newspaper, the "Record." A Committee of Twenty-Five was selected to implement the "White Declaration of Independence." The committee summoned black leaders—the Committee of Colored Citizens—to meet that night and prepare a response to its demands. The black committee sought to prevent violence, but its response was not delivered by the 7:30 a.m. Nov. 10 deadline.

RIOT ENSUES: Alfred M. Waddell, leader of the white committee, met a crowd of men at the Wilmington Light Infantry armory at 8 a.m. Nov. 10. Waddell led a march to the "Record" printing offices at the corner of Seventh and Nun Streets. A mob of almost 2,000 whites destroyed the offices by [arson]. Violence between groups of blacks and whites broke out shortly afterward at the corner of Fourth and Harnett streets. Several black men were identified as killed or wounded in sporadic fights. About 22 were reported dead. No official count exists because of a lack of records. No white casualties have been reported.

SHIFTING POWER: During the riot, Waddell's committee and others facilitated the coup d'etat to overthrow the Republican mayor, Board of Aldermen and police chief. By 4 p.m., the elected officials were resigning and replaced by men selected from the white committee. Waddell was elected mayor by the new board. All black municipal employees were fired. Prominent African-American leaders and businessmen, and white Republicans, were banned from the city starting the afternoon of Nov. 10. Families also left the city voluntarily during the following weeks.

DESTINY OF A RACE: State leaders did not respond to the violence in Wilmington. No state investigation was done. A federal investigation was opened; files were closed with no indictments in 1900. Waddell and the Board of Aldermen were officially elected in March 1899 with Republican resistance.

REBUILDING: African-Americans in Wilmington adjusted to the changes in society and redefined their position under the white supremacy movement and Jim Crow legislation. [The ones] who remained lost their political standing and suffered economic setbacks. No proof of white seizures of black property has been found. Wilmington's race riot marked a new epoch in the history of race relations. Several other high profile riots were modeled after it, including Atlanta in 1906, Tulsa in 1921, and Rosewood in 1923.

—FROM *1898 WILMINGTON RACE RIOT REPORT*,
WILMINGTON STAR-NEWS ONLINE TIME LINE ACCOMPANYING
DECEMBER 16, 2005, ARTICLE BY ANGELA MACK

went underground and stayed alive in households, schools, and churches, coming into public sight from time to time. As early as 1938, Greensboro blacks boycotted the city's movie theater. In many communities the effort to register to vote continued, and in 1947 an Afro-American was elected to the Winston-Salem city council. That city then passed an ordinance limiting city council representation to one black.

By the time the Freedom Riders passed through North Carolina, arrest as well as legislation had long been an important part of the state's white supremacist arsenal. In the college town of Chapel Hill during the 1947 Journey of Reconciliation, Bayard Rustin refused to sit in the back of the bus and, as a result, spent twenty-two days on the chain gang at the state prison camp in Roxboro. On that same journey, Jim Peck, who would be badly beaten on the 1961 Freedom Ride, encountered in an Ashville courtroom the most extreme manifestation of Jim Crow that he had ever come across: "Along the edges of one Bible had been printed in large letters the word 'white.' Along the page edges of the other bible was the word 'colored.' When a white person swore-in he simply raised his right hand while the clerk held the Bible. When a Negro swore-in, he had to raise his right hand while holding the colored Bible in his left hand. The white clerk could not touch the colored Bible."

In the summer of 1957, after a black youngster drowned in a swimming hole in Monroe, Union County NAACP president Robert Williams led efforts to integrate the city's tax-supported swimming pool—conducting several "stand-ins" at its gate, with young people who wore swimming suits and carried towels. The pool was finally filled with dirt and converted into a putting green. The following year what is known as the "Kissing Case" focused outraged attention on the city. After being kissed on their cheeks by a seven-year-old white girl, two black boys, aged eight and ten, were accused of rape, jailed for six days, and then sentenced to reform school until they reached the age of twenty-one. The national and international pressure Williams was able to bring on their behalf resulted in the charges being dropped, and the county NAACP chapter grew. "We ended

Winston-Salem to Asheville, North Carolina, 15th April

From Winston-Salem to Statesville the group traveled by Greyhound. [Wallace] Nelson [an Afro-American] was seated with [Ernest] Bromley [white] in the second seat from the front. Nothing was said. At Statesville, the group transferred to the Trailways [bus], with Nelson still in front. In a small town about ten miles from Statesville, the driver approached Nelson and told him he would have to move to the rear. When Nelson said that he was an interstate passenger, the driver said that the bus was not interstate. When Nelson explained that his ticket was interstate, the driver returned to his seat and drove on. The rest of the trip to Asheville was through mountainous country, and the bus stopped at many small towns. A soldier asked the driver why Nelson was not forced to move. The driver explained that there was a Supreme Court decision and that he could do nothing about it. He said, "If you want to do something about this, don't blame this man [Nelson]; kill those bastards up in Washington." The soldier explained to a rather large, vociferous man why Nelson was allowed to sit up front. The large man commented, "I wish I was the bus driver." Near Ashville the bus became very crowded, and there were women standing up. Two women spoke to the bus driver, asking him why Nelson was not moved. In each case the driver explained that the Supreme Court decision was responsible. Several white women took seats in the Jim Crow section in the rear.

—GEORGE HOUSER AND BAYARD RUSTIN
IN *FELLOWSHIP MAGAZINE*, APRIL 1947

up with a chapter that was unique in the whole NAACP because of [its] working class composition and a leadership that was not middle class. Most important, we had a strong representation of returned veterans who were very militant and didn't scare easy," Williams wrote later. On May 5, 1959, when a white man was acquitted of assaulting a young pregnant black woman, Williams exploded, speaking to reporters angrily: "We must meet violence with violence." The national NAACP disavowed Williams's stance and suspended him. Over the next two years, however, he remained at the center of civil rights struggle, and after giving refuge to a white couple who had taken a wrong turn and wound up in the black community one violent night in 1961, he was indicted by an all-white grand jury for kidnapping them. Williams fled the country and did not return until 1969. North Carolina eventually dropped all charges against him. He died of Hodgkin's disease October 15, 1996, in Grand Rapids, Michigan. The **Williams Gravesite** *(off U.S. 74 and Stafford Street)* is in Monroe. Speaking at his funeral, Rosa Parks said that during the bus boycott in Montgomery, Williams was much admired "for his courage and his commitment to freedom."

There is certainly no shortage of stories of racial injustice to be found in North Carolina, but the bottom line is that, undeniably and irreversibly, the times were changing as the 1950s wound down and the decade of the 1960s began. These changing times were defined not only by Robert Williams in Monroe or the 1954 Supreme Court decision, but also by protests in Montgomery and elsewhere, new nations emerging in Africa, and a new young president who seemed to be saying that he was willing to be a different kind of American leader in a changing world that required America to change, too. All of this undoubtedly helped ignite what, starting in Greensboro, North Carolina, would be a new phase of civil rights struggle.

ॐ GREENSBORO ॐ

You simply cannot tell when a spark will light a fire. The civil rights movement proves this over and over again, and the sit-in movement that caught fire in Greensboro is certainly one of the best examples. Late in the afternoon on February 1, 1960, four students from the campus

of **North Carolina Agricultural and Technical College** **(A&T)** *(1601 East Market Street)*—Ezell Blair Jr. (who has since changed his name to Jibreel Khazan), Franklin McCain, David Richmond, and Joseph McNeil—walked into Greensboro's **F. W. Woolworth Department Store** *(132 South Elm Street on the corner of what is now February One Place)*, bought a few things, then walked over to the store's lunch counter, sat down, and ordered sodas, coffee, and doughnuts. They were all eighteen years old and they were all college freshmen. "We don't serve Negroes here," said the waitress, who at first tried to ignore them by continuing to wipe the lunch counter; "Negroes get food at the other end," she said, pointing to a section of the counter where there were no seats and blacks seeking soft drinks or sandwiches were expected to carry out their order. After explaining that the store seemed to have no problem accepting their money for the various items they had just purchased, the four students sat until the store closed at 5:30 P.M.

Since the beginning of the school year, the four of them and others had been talking about some sort of challenge

The Woolworth lunch counter in Greensboro, February 2, 1960. The white woman to the students' left approached the counter intending to order lunch, but decided not to sit down and walked away without ordering. The three students shown here (27 students participated in all), Ronald Martin, Robert Patterson, and Mark Martin, sat in all day.

to racial segregation. In their dormitory, Scott Hall, there were regular "gripe sessions." A month earlier, Joseph McNeil, returning from a Christmas holiday visit to his hometown of Wilmington, had gotten off a Greyhound bus in Greensboro's Union Station and been refused service when he entered the station's restaurant seeking something to eat.

The Greensboro sit-in was not the first. In Durham, on June 23, 1957, Reverend Douglas Moore, a young Methodist minister, and six others were arrested when they sat down in the white section of the Royal Ice Cream Parlor. Washington, D.C., had seen sit-ins in the 1940s. There was a CORE-led sit-in campaign in St. Louis in 1949, and another in Baltimore in 1953. Negro Service Council leader Edward T. Graham led a "wade-in" at Miami Beach in 1945. And in the city of Miami, CORE began holding civil rights "action institutes" in 1958.

In Greensboro itself, in 1955, NAACP president Dr. George Simpkins, a dentist, and several of his friends were arrested and jailed after playing nine holes at the city-owned Gillespie Golf Course. They simply and unexpectedly walked onto the course and began playing. When the club pro ran out after the group and demanded that they leave, they continued playing. At the state superior court, recalled Simkins to author Tom Dent in *Southern Journey*, "the judge told us we had better not come out to *his* place trying to take over." A federal court finally ruled that the city's one-dollar lease was an artifice designed to pretend that the club was not city property. A date was set to open up the club, but then the clubhouse mysteriously burned down and was condemned, along with the golf course. So it was a logical next step, after sitting in that first day in February, for the students to solicit Dr. Simkins's backing. He pledged his support and then contacted CORE instead of his own national office for

Dr. George Simpkins, Greensboro NAACP president in 1960

assistance because, he said later, he'd been reading a CORE pamphlet about their Baltimore sit-in efforts and thought that they had more experience with direct action than the NAACP had.

Greensboro protest in 1963

No mass movement had ever sprung up around any of the earlier sit-ins. But in Greensboro, the very next day, twenty-seven students—twenty-three men and four women from **Bennett College** *(900 E. Washington Street)*, the historically black women's college just a few blocks away from A&T—went back to the Woolworth department store and sat in until it closed. And on February 3, sixty-three students sat-in, occupying almost every seat. On February 6, hundreds of students, including the entire A&T football team, descended on downtown Greensboro to sit in and picket in what is now known as Black Saturday. By the end of March, sit-ins had spread from Greensboro to seventy southern cities.

On July 25, 1960, the Greensboro Woolworth served its first black customer. It took three more *years* before all of the city's restaurants, movie theaters, and other public places opened their doors without regard to race. The continuing protests that led to this result were the stage upon which Reverend Jesse Jackson, then the A&T student council president, took his first steps into public life, leading protest marches in the spring of 1963; there were more than nine hundred arrests that spring. Greensboro's schools did not begin integration until 1971.

The Greensboro Woolworth closed in 1993. All four of the original sit-in students attended a final meal and management reverted to 1960 prices as part of the tribute (65¢ for a roast turkey dinner, 50¢ for a ham and cheese club sandwich, 5¢ or 10¢ for a "shop refilled" Coke, 10¢ for a hot coffee, 15¢ for pumpkin, apple, or cherry pie). The store had held a commemoration of the sit-in movement every five years. A vice president from the company would fly down from New York to speak—often about the company's commitment to "diversity." An eight-foot section of the original lunch counter can be viewed at the Smithsonian's **National Museum of American History** in Washington, D.C.

In Greensboro today, a sculpture of the four students is found in a quiet part of the A&T campus called **The Oaks**, which, as the name suggests, is shaded by live oak trees, as well as wax myrtles. A memorial tablet on the statue's granite base reads "These four A&T freshmen envisioned and carried out the lunch counter sit-in of February 1, 1960, in downtown Greensboro. Their courageous act against social injustice inspired similar protests across the nation and is remembered as a defining moment in the struggle for civil rights." Directly across from this statue, in the old Dudley Memorial classroom building and well worth a visit for its art collection, is the **Mattie Reed African Heritage Center.**

The statue on A&T's campus also represents something else we always need to keep in sight while on our civil rights trail: the challenges Afro-Americans presented to each other within the black community. When in 1958

Willa Player, 94,
Pioneer Black Educator, Dies

THE NEW YORK TIMES, AUGUST 30, 2003

GREENSBORO, N.C., Aug. 29 (AP)—Willa B. Player, a strong supporter of the civil rights movement and the first black woman to head a four-year college in the United States, died here on Wednesday. She was 94.

For 10 years beginning in 1956, Ms. Player was president of Bennett College here, a historically black institution for women. It was during her tenure that Bennett became one of the first black colleges to be accredited by the Southern Association of Colleges and Schools.

While president, Ms. Player organized an appearance on campus by the Rev. Dr. Martin Luther King Jr., at a time when no other group in Greensboro would welcome him. Dr. King's speech, at the college's Pfeiffer Chapel in 1958, planted a seed for many of the protests that followed in the city.

At the peak of downtown protests in support of desegregation, as many as 40 percent of Bennett's students were under arrest. Ms. Player backed those students, known as the Bennett Belles, visiting them daily and arranging for professors to hold classes for them and administer exams.

Ms. Player, a Mississippi native, graduated from Ohio Wesleyan University and received a master's degree from Oberlin College. She arrived at Bennett when she was 21, to teach Latin and French.

Martin Luther King asked to speak at A&T, the state school, fearful of being associated with the Montgomery civil rights hero, said no, as did every other potential venue in the Afro-American community. Only Bennett College (a private school, whose president, Dr. Willa Player, was a strong public advocate of civil rights) opened its doors, and King spoke on the campus at **Pfeiffer Chapel**. "I told them," recalled Player years later, "that this is a liberal arts college where freedom rings—so Martin Luther King can speak here." It was at this chapel, incidentally, that a group of "Bennett Belles," as the school's students are still sometimes called, met and planned the 1938 boycott of Greensboro movie theaters. The chapel was packed when King came to speak, and Ezell Blair, a high school student then, had to stand on the lawn, where King's voice reached him through loudspeakers. King's words "brought tears to my eyes," Blair said later. So, as much as sit-ins challenged the segregation at Woolworth and white supremacy in Greensboro, importantly, the action of Blair and his three classmates was also a challenge to the black community.

The attitude of the school's administration is now quite different. The university celebrates the Greensboro sit-in every year. And there is a different attitude about civil rights downtown, too. The art deco Woolworth building is under renovation, with plans for housing an *International Civil Rights Center & Museum*. The focal point of a street-level entrance will be yet another section of the whites-only lunch counter of the February 1 sit-in. Audiovisual aids will enable visitors to see and listen to reenactments of the dormitory conversations that led to the sit-in, as well as watch a reenactment of the sit-in itself, which will include the voice of Ezell Blair asking for a cup of coffee. After leaving the lunch-counter area, visitors will enter an area called The Battlegrounds, in which key civil rights events in Greensboro and elsewhere are to be showcased through videos, news clips, and film footage. The concluding exhibit will offer for exploration the idea of "freedom" as manifested in efforts across the world to eliminate discrimination by using the principles of "participatory democracy" and non-violent action. Outside at this location, along a *Walkway of History* that has embedded in it the bronzed footprints of protest leaders, scattered sidewalk markers chronicle various "chapters" of Afro-American history.

About ten miles east of Greensboro, in the town of Sedalia, black history that emphasizes education can be explored at the *Charlotte Hawkins Brown Museum at Historic Palmer Memorial Institute (6136 Burlington Road)*. The museum was the home of Palmer Memorial

Institute, an outstanding college preparatory school for Afro-Americans that Dr. Brown established in 1902. It is the first official historic site in the state to honor an Afro-American woman.

⁓ RALEIGH ⁓

A lthough sit-ins spread rapidly across the South, they were uncoordinated actions. While vaguely aware of one another, the Atlanta students did not know the Nashville students, who did not know the Baltimore students, who did not know the Charlotte students, and so forth. Ella Baker, the temporary executive director of SCLC when the sit-ins broke out, had two great insights in response to the widening student protests: that the sit-ins were an idea whose time had come, and that the student activists needed to come together to meet each other, to be encouraged to share ideas, and to begin thinking about coordinating their efforts. She discussed her desire to facilitate this with Martin Luther King and persuaded him to provide eight hundred dollars to convene the students at her alma mater, **Shaw University** *(188 East South Street)*.

Although SCLC staff chief Reverend Wyatt T. Walker wanted an SCLC student wing to come out of the meeting, Dr. King was amenable to Ella Baker's view that it was up to the students to decide how best to organize themselves. Speaking to reporters on April 11, just days before the gathering, King did express his hope that the students would "seriously consider training a group of volunteers who will willingly go to jail rather than pay bail or fines." Certainly King wanted a student arm of SCLC, and he probably could have gotten it at this Raleigh meeting if he had pressed for

Ella Baker on Leadership

Reverend Wyatt Walker, who in August 1960 replaced Ella Baker as executive director of SCLC, understood perhaps better than most in the organization that there was a basic incompatibility between this most experienced of civil rights organizers and the ministers he was now charged with fashioning into a coherent organization. But at least he could talk to them, had ministerial credentials himself, could fit into the organization in a way that Ms. Baker never would. "It just went against the grain of the kind of person she is and was," Walker explained once.

Ella Baker speaks. Behind her is a portrait of CORE field secretary Michael Schwerner, who was slain by Ku Klux Klansmen at the start of the 1964 Mississippi Summer Project.

One of the ways she was unlike many who were and would be prominent in the movement, was in her inclination to stay in the background:

"In government service and political life I have always felt it was a handicap for oppressed peoples to depend so largely upon a leader, because unfortunately in our culture, the charismatic leader usually becomes a leader because he has found a spot in the public limelight. It usually means he has been touted through the public media, which means that the media made him, and the media may undo him. There is also the danger in our culture that because a person is called upon to give public statements and is acclaimed by the establishment, such a person gets to the point of believing that he is the movement. Such people get so involved with playing the game of being important that they exhaust themselves and their time, and they don't do the work of actually organizing people."

—ELLA BAKER TO GERDA LERNER, DECEMBER 1970

it; he was esteemed by many of the participating students. But, for reasons that are still not clear, he did not. He might have been reluctant to take on Ella Baker over this; she was still formidable despite being on the way out of her position with his organization. James Forman, who would become SNCC's executive director, wrote that Ella Baker was determined to protect the young people gathered in Raleigh from SCLC's "leader-centered orientation" because she thought that SCLC was "depending too much on the press and on the promotion of Martin King, and was not developing enough indigenous leadership across the South."

Not enough can be said about **Ella Josephine Baker** of North Carolina. Over her lifetime (1903–1986) the remarkable Ms. Baker significantly influenced almost a half century of civil rights struggle. When she was the NAACP director of branches in the 1940s, Rosa Parks attended one of her leadership workshops. She was SCLC's first, albeit "temporary," executive director. Although she had been instrumental in getting the group organized, she took the position reluctantly, knowing that because she was a woman, her independence of mind, and willingness to speak it, would always rub SCLC's preachers the wrong way. And in 1960, when she was fifty-six years old, she brought the sit-in students to Shaw University. She thought that maybe a hundred might show up; about two hundred came.

The Shaw conference took place on Easter weekend of April 15–17 in 1960. In a convening speech, which she titled "More than a Hamburger," Ms. Baker urged participants to think beyond the immediate goals of getting cups of coffee, soft drinks, or sandwiches at lunch counters, and challenge the country's whole social structure. "She kept daring us to go further," recalled John Lewis. And with King, Wyatt Walker, and other adult civil rights leaders from CORE and the NAACP in the audience as observers, she declared, "The younger generation is challenging you and me; they are asking us to forget our laziness and doubt and fear . . ." During the conference Ms. Baker quietly but persistently encouraged the students to think of forming their own organization. Thus from this meeting emerged the Student Nonviolent Coordinating Committee (SNCC).

Most of the conference's early sessions were held at **Memorial Auditorium** *(Washington Street; now the BTI Performing Arts Center)*. There is a small marker on campus near **Greenleaf Hall** *(118 East South Street between Wilmington and Blount Streets)* commemorating the birth of SNCC, which for the nine years following its founding conference sent organizers ("field secretaries") into the

Bigger than a Hamburger

After SNCC's founding conference at Shaw University in Raleigh, NC, Ella Baker wrote the following article.

RALEIGH, N.C.—The Student Leadership Conference made it crystal clear that current sit-ins and other demonstrations are concerned with something much bigger than a hamburger or even a giant-sized Coke.

Whatever may be the difference in approach to their goal, the Negro and white students, North and South, are seeking to rid America of the scourge of racial segregation and discrimination—not only at lunch counters, but in every aspect of life.

In reports, casual conversations, discussion groups, and speeches, the sense and the spirit of the following statement that appeared in the initial newsletter of the students at Barber-Scotia College, Concord, N.C., were re-echoed time and again:

"We want the world to know that we no longer accept the inferior position of second-class citizenship. We are willing to go to jail, be ridiculed, spat upon and even suffer physical violence to obtain First Class Citizenship."

By and large, this feeling that they have a destined date with freedom, was not limited to a drive for personal freedom, or even freedom for the Negro in the South. Repeatedly it was emphasized that the movement was concerned with the moral implications of racial discrimination for the "whole world" and the "Human Race."

This universality of approach was linked with a perceptive recognition that "it is important to keep the movement democratic and to avoid struggles for personal leadership."

deepest, most difficult and dangerous parts of the black-belt South. I was one of them. Through us, Ms. Baker saw a way to pursue her commitment to organizing from the bottom up. Across the South she introduced us to the people who could teach us how to do this, warriors from the generations before ours who were still in the field; she plugged us into the network that she had built up over decades. But what Ms. Baker always made absolutely clear, while guiding us with intelligence, experience, and a gentle hand, was

---

It was further evident that desire for supportive cooperation from adult leaders and the adult community was also tempered by apprehension that adults might try to "capture" the student movement. The students showed willingness to be met on the basis of equality, but were intolerant of anything that smacked of manipulation or domination.

This inclination toward group-centered leadership, rather than toward a leader-centered group pattern of organization, was refreshing indeed to those of the older group who bear the scars of the battle, the frustrations and the disillusionment that come when the prophetic leader turns out to have heavy feet of clay.

However hopeful might be the signs in the direction of group-centeredness, the fact that many schools and communities, especially in the South, have not provided adequate experience for young Negroes to assume initiative and think and act independently accentuated the need for guarding the student movement against well-meaning, but nevertheless unhealthy, over-protectiveness.

Here is an opportunity for adult and youth to work together and provide genuine leadership—the development of the individual to his highest potential for the benefit of the group.

Many adults and youth characterized the Raleigh meeting as the greatest or most significant conference of our period.

Whether it lives up to this high evaluation or not will, in a large measure, be determined by the extent to which there is more effective training in and understanding of non-violent principles and practices, in group dynamics, and in the re-direction into creative channels of the normal frustrations and hostilities that result from second-class citizenship.

—"BIGGER THAN A HAMBURGER," BY ELLA BAKER,
THE SOUTHERN PATRIOT, MAY 1960

that this organization of young people, SNCC, was *ours* to build or destroy. And as SNCC's Bob Moses once remarked, "We did both."

Raleigh had a strong sit-in movement. Students, mainly from the Shaw and St. Augustine campuses, challenged segregation at Woolworth's, S. H. Kress, Walgreens, and other downtown stores. Walgreens desegregated first, in late February of 1960, removing the seats from its lunch counter to begin serving blacks and whites together—both standing. Generally, however, desegregation in any form was slow in the city. In 1963 protesters targeted theaters, the Sir Walter Raleigh Hotel, and other prominent sites, as well as the governor's Symphony Ball. Raleigh finally gave in to desegregation in 1964. Displays in a section of the **Raleigh City Museum** *(220 Fayetteville Street Mall)* called Let Us March On: Journey toward Civil Rights present the civil rights movement in Raleigh from the 1950s through the 1970s. And at the **North Carolina Museum of History** *(5 East Edenton Street)*, Ms. Baker's picture hangs in the Women's Exhibit Gallery; a short video summarizes her contributions.

There is a fountain of black stone with water running down it at the **Dr. Martin Luther King, Jr. Memorial Gardens** *(Martin Luther King Boulevard and Rock Quarry)*. It is open twenty-four hours a day. The garden is the first public park in the United States dedicated solely to the memory of the slain civil rights leader. A life-size statue of King, said by the gardens' publicists to be the world's only life-size statue of King in his doctorate clerical robe, is "intentionally designed to give young people the opportunity to touch and feel the sculpture." Another memorial in the garden recognizes local civil rights pioneers. Over five thousand trees, shrubs, and flowers add color and pleasure to sitting on the benches scattered about.

⚘ DURHAM ⚘

Hayti, the main commercial artery in Durham's black community before the Durham Expressway and "urban renewal" destroyed it, was one of the most prosperous examples of urban black enterprise in the United States. The **North Carolina Mutual Life Insurance Company** *(114–116 West Parrish Street)*, founded in 1898, is today a billion-dollar corporation and is the first black-owned company to achieve that status. Its West Parrish Street building is a national historical landmark and, as the National Park Service puts it, "one of the nation's most conspicuous landmarks of racial solidarity and self help."

Churches have always played an important role in civil rights struggle, and for that reason a good starting point in Durham is the renovated **St. Joseph's AME Church** *(804 Old Fayetteville Street, overlooking the Durham Freeway)* in the old Hayti neighborhood. It reflects a long heritage of struggle and accomplishment. St. Joseph's first minister, Reverend Edian Markham, was born into slavery in 1824 and escaped bondage via the Underground Railroad. He educated himself in New York and then chose Durham as his first missionary field. The church still offers an impressive sense of what black determination was able to build against all odds. After the congregation moved to a new location down the street in 1975, the old structure became headquarters for the **St. Joseph Historic Foundation**, with the mission of preserving the history of the Hayti community. It offers exhibit space to artists, meeting facilities, and a 415-seat performance hall. The foundation's aim is to "be an agent of social change with a long-term commitment to utilizing the arts as a tool to bring communities together and establishing common ground between the races." On the main street of a community so far-removed from its earlier prosperity, the church, with its tall steeples and twenty-four elegant stained-glass windows, is an unexpectedly grand structure to encounter.

As you travel, one way to think about the southern civil rights movement is in terms of networks, both old and new, enabling those of us involved in organizing for civil rights to move from place to place, effort to effort, finding sustenance and support. SNCC's Bob Moses describes the importance of networks this way: "Our young generation was dynamically linked to a rooted older generation who passed on wisdom, encouragement, and concrete aid when possible. This was empowering, enabling SNCC and CORE field secretaries to move from county to county across a network that provided different levels of support, a network made up of people offering whatever they could within their means."

Such a network meant that the Greensboro sit-in did not occur in a vacuum. The changing climate that enabled the student sit-in movement to take root and spread had been created by the earlier voices pioneering a new era: Doug Moore, attorney Floyd McKissick, *Carolina Times* newspaper editor Louis Austin in Durham, and Dr. George Simpkins in Greensboro. They kept the pressure on. After his attempt to play at the city's white golf club, for example, Dr. Simkins joined a suit to open up Greensboro's city swimming pool to blacks. He launched a very successful voter registration campaign and began pressing for school desegregation. He was also the primary litigant in a suit against the Moses Cone Hospital, challenging its refusal to permit black physicians and dentists to practice there although it received federal funds.

On that June day in 1957 when Doug Moore, then the young pastor of Durham's **Ashbury Temple United Methodist Church** (201 S. Alston Avenue at Angier Avenue), led a group into the **Royal Ice Cream Parlor** (corner of Roxboro and Dowd Streets, now a vacant lot), their action did not catch fire as the Greensboro sit-ins would three years later. But it is worthwhile following his trail for a bit so that we can see and learn something of civil rights networks, for Moore was part of an informal network of young ministers oriented toward social change in the South. I think this group still remains underappreciated, although you do not have to look hard or far to find them. Reverend C. E. Ward, the pastor of **First Baptist Church** *(101 S Wilmington Street)*, which played a prominent role in support of civil rights protest in Raleigh, went to school with Martin Luther King at Morehouse. After he graduated from the Atlanta school, King went on to Boston University for graduate studies where he and his classmate there, Durham's Douglass Moore, began discussing the idea of nonviolent struggle for civil rights. By then, King, after listening to a 1949 speech by Howard University president Mordecai Johnson about his trip to India, had already taken an interest in Mohandas Gandhi. My father also went to Boston University for graduate school. As a Durham native who had attended the New England university from our home in Springfield, Massachusetts, where he pastored a church, he was one of Moore's important mentors. Also in this circle of clergymen was my father's Boston University classmate and best friend Reverend Edwin Edmonds—to me "Uncle Ed"—who later became dean of students at Bennett College in Greensboro and was Dr. Simkins's predecessor as president of that city's NAACP. He was also involved with SCLC in its earliest days. And one of Rev. Edmonds's daughters—Karen—would, like me, wind up inside SNCC.

Douglass Moore, too, participated in the founding meetings of SCLC, but he was uncomfortable with the organization. Like Ella Baker, though, he was excited by the Greensboro student sit-ins and the speed with which they were spreading, and he, too, immediately recognized their significance. He called his friend James Lawson in Nashville, who in the fall of 1959 had begun training a group of Nashville students for nonviolent sit-ins. Moore urged Rev. Lawson to accelerate those plans. Moore also called Martin Luther King, who had just moved to Atlanta, asking him to come and speak to leaders of the North Carolina movement. King agreed, and upon his arrival, King, Reverend Ralph Abernathy (who flew in with King), Moore, and student activists picketed Woolworth's in downtown Durham. They might have held a sit-in there, too, except that the store's management had closed the lunch counter after sit-ins the

Martin Luther King at White Rock Baptist Church in Durham, on February 16, 1960. Seated behind King are Reverend Douglass Moore (right) and Reverend Ralph Abernathy (left).

week before. A portion of the counter of that Woolworth's is on display in the **William Jones Building** *(at North Carolina Central University, through university main gate to the right of the founder's statue).* That night, King spoke at a mass meeting held at the **White Rock Baptist Church** *(Fayetteville Street at Timothy Avenue).* More than one thousand people were in attendance, and for the first time King publicly made the call to fill up the jails: "Let us not fear going to jail if the officials threaten to arrest us for standing up for our rights," he said. "Maybe it will take this willingness to stay in jail to arouse the dozing conscience of our nation." As well, he publicly acknowledged the importance of young people. "What is new in your fight is the fact that it was initiated, fed, and sustained by students."

The church where King spoke is itself an important historic site. In 1913, in the basement of White Rock church, Dr. Aaron Moore started the second black library in North

1971—The Wilmington 10

A decade after the Freedom Rides, violence in the streets of downtown Wilmington once again made the city a combat zone. Wilmington had been racially tense for years; one of the largest riots after the assassination of Martin Luther King in 1968 occurred in this port city. School desegregation began in the 1969–70 school year when the city's main black high school, Williston High, was closed after students demanded that Martin Luther King be honored. They were bused to two white high schools, where they encountered hostility and violence. The black students announced a school boycott—actually a protest movement to demand the reopening of Williston. To assist the students, the Commission for Racial Justice of the United Church of Christ (which my father directed) sent in a young UCC minister, Benjamin Chavis (now Benjamin Muhammed, who for a brief time in the 1990s would controversially lead the NAACP). By this time the Ku Klux Klan and a new group called The Rights of White People were patrolling downtown, driving protesters away. On the night of February 6, 1971, a downtown store was firebombed and several other fires were set by unknown persons. Firemen arriving on the scene charged that snipers fired at them from the roof of Gregory Congregational Church (609 Nun Street), the movement center where Chavis had led students who had walked out of school in protest. Two people were found dead that night (a black teenager and a white man discovered shot to death in a pickup truck). No one knows who was responsible for either the fires or these killings, but Chavis and nine others (including one white woman who was a worker in the antipoverty program) were arrested, tried, and convicted of arson and conspiracy to fire on police and firemen. Now known as the Wilmington Ten, they remained in jail for almost five years, until a witness's confession to lying for the state resulted in their parole. In 1980 a federal court overturned their conviction.

Carolina. Three years later the library moved downtown and was renamed the **Durham Colored Library**. It is now the **Stanford L. Warren Library** *(1201 Fayetteville Street at Umstead Street)* and features the **Selena Warren Collection** of Afro-American culture, history, and literature. Dr. Augustus Shepard founded White Rock church. His son later founded what is now **North Carolina Central University** in Durham, where, if I may add one more link to this North Carolina network, my father began his college career.

CHAPTER FIVE

I'LL OVERCOME

Charleston, Columbia, Rock Hill, Orangeburg, and Clarendon County, South Carolina

This world is one great battlefield,
With forces all arrayed;
If in my heart I do not yield
I'll overcome some day.

Refrain: I'll overcome some day,
*   I'll overcome some day,*
*   If in my heart I do not yield,*
*   I'll overcome some day.*

—REVEREND CHARLES
ALBERT TINDLEY, 1901

I'll be all right, I'll be all right I'll be like him
   some day
I'll be all right some day
Deep in my heart, I do believe
I'll be all right some day

—"I'LL BE ALL RIGHT"
ADAPTATION (SOUTH CAROLINA TOBACCO
WORKERS, CIRCA 1945)

We shall overcome, we shall overcome
We shall overcome someday
Oh, Oh deep in my heart
I do believe
We shall overcome someday

—"WE SHALL OVERCOME"
ADAPTATION (CIVIL RIGHTS MOVEMENT,
CIRCA 1960)

T he civil rights movement often transformed traditional church hymns into songs of protest and determination to make change. When we get to Albany, Georgia, we will see how powerfully important that was. In South Carolina, though, the state that I consider the geographic and historical portal to the "deep" South, I find myself thinking not only of those songs but specifically of "We Shall Overcome." Undoubtedly the best-known of the movement's songs, its roots in protest go back to the mid-1940s in Charleston, South Carolina, when striking black female tobacco workers organized by the Congress of Industrial Organizations (CIO) embraced the turn-of-the-

Zilphia Horton
at Highlander

Highlander's 25th anniversary celebration in 1957: Martin Luther King; singer Pete Seeger; Charis Horton, daughter of Highlander founder Myles Horton; Rosa Parks; and Ralph Abernathy

century hymn "I'll Overcome" and refashioned it as "I'll Be All Right."

The women had walked off their jobs at the American Tobacco Company in the fall of 1945, sick of low pay and awful working conditions, especially of disrespectful and dictatorial foremen— white men inclined toward, or tolerant of, sexual exploi- tation. Many black hymns, of course, go back to the days of slavery's lash and were themselves songs that offered assurances of a bet- ter life to come. Long before Reverend Charles Albert Tindley's 1901 copyrighted lyrics, slaves sang versions of it in fields and in black churches or "praise houses," those often illegal sites that

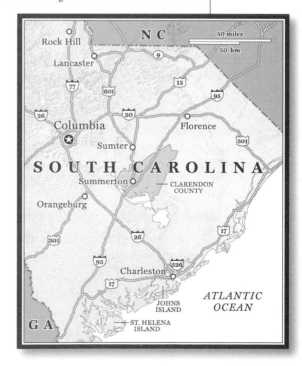

"The Anti-Communist Thing"

Jack O' Dell, who later would work with SCLC, in 1946 was a member and volunteer organizer for Operation Dixie with the National Maritime Union (NMU), a CIO union. He was kicked out of the union in Galveston, Texas, in 1950.

"Now, in the south . . . we were outnumbered because the anti-Communist thing became a banner—a tent under which . . . racist elements could assemble and cover their flanks. In Houston, Texas, they teamed up with the police, the Klan, and Union officials to run blacks out of the Union hall. It was almost like a Reconstruction thing you read about—how they overthrew the government, the blacks are forced to flee, and so forth. It was that kind of atmosphere they were able to create. I was expelled from NMU the day after the Korean War broke out—my Union book taken, June the 26th, 1950 and the Korean War broke out June the 25th. And so, from that point on within NMU we're in a cold war. Can you trust these guys to sail with you? These guys are pro-Soviet. Well, I sailed during World War II, and [so did] others like me, but now suddenly you wouldn't be trusted on the ship because you didn't support U.S. policy. And of course, the Communist thing was a brush that they would put on you. They didn't have to prove you were a communist. And how are you going to prove you weren't? But the basic assumption was that you were either a Communist dupe or a Communist front or you were a follower of the communists. You had to find jobs ashore. Well, fortunately, Marine Cooks and Stewards, which was a West Coast union, had a unit in New Orleans and so we could get port time and you could make a little light living on that. But you couldn't sail out, but you'd do port time. I did quite a bit of that."

—JACK O' DELL TO SAM SILLS

were centers of resistance to slavery. It was one of the songs secretly coded to encourage revolt, flight, and salvation.

Zilphia Horton, the wife of Myles Horton, who founded the Highlander Folk School in Monteagle, Tennessee, may have first heard the song "I'll Be All Right" when she joined a picket line of the striking tobacco workers in Charleston. However, the more commonly told story is that she learned the song from two of the striking workers who sang it to her during a labor rights workshop at Highlander. In addition to her other duties, Zilphia Horton was Highlander's music director. We do know that she heard the song somewhere within the context of that strike and taught it to folksinger Pete Seeger years later. There are various explanations of how "I" evolved into "We," but one of the South's great civil rights pioneers and heroines, South Carolina schoolteacher Septima Clark, is credited for replacing *will* with the more grammatically correct *shall*. A white California-born troubadour with family roots in North Carolina, Guy Carawan, picked up the song when he began working at Highlander in 1959. During an early April 1960 gathering of students at Highlander organized by Septima Clark, Carawan taught them the song, and through them, "We Shall Overcome," with the now familiar melody and time signature that we associate with it, passed into the civil rights movement.

Union organizing had less luck, although finally, after picketing for five months, enduring a cold and wet Charleston winter in which some of the women became disheartened and abandoned the effort, the tobacco workers did gain a contract giving them a slight pay increase. The strike had been one of the early efforts of an organizing drive called Operation Dixie conducted by the CIO in twelve southern states. But even as this organizing effort was getting under way, racism, Jim Crow laws, the Taft-Hartley Act, and the cold war "Red Scare" all combined to sabotage most union organizing efforts below the Mason-Dixon Line. And when the CIO merged with the more conservative American Federation of Labor (AFL) in 1955, the new union organization basically abandoned serious efforts to unionize black workers (and black and white workers together) in the South. It is unfortunate that as civil rights organizers we never quite figured out how to coalesce the common interests of white and black workers.

❧ CHARLESTON ❧

I f efforts to create an integrated southern labor union movement were on a steep decline by the mid-1950s, civil rights efforts, encouraged by both the 1954 Supreme Court decision in *Brown* and the 1955–56 Montgomery bus boycott, were surging. Clear signs of this began appearing in Charleston, where old racial mores rooted in slavery almost completely defined human relations. By 1770, 60 percent of South Carolina's population was enslaved Africans; in no other early American colony did blacks outnumber whites. Rice had made Africans the preferred people to enslave and exploit. With highly developed skills that they had long been using in the rice-growing regions of West Africa, they taught English settlers how to grow rice on South Carolina's wet coastal plain. Soon Charleston became the biggest slave port in America, selling about half the Africans brought into the American colonies. Addressing the Democratic Party's 1860 national convention held in Charleston, J. S. Preston, a South Carolinian who would later become chief of the Confederate Bureau of Conscription, spoke for Charleston and the slave South

54th Massachusetts Regiment at Battle of Fort Wagner in South Carolina 1863

with absolute clarity: "Slavery is our King. Slavery is our Truth. Slavery is our Divine Right."

The *Avery Museum for African-American Culture and History* *(66 George Street)* is a good primary source of information about both this period and the later civil rights struggle. You can also follow a ninety-mile historic *"Cotton Trail"* *(between I-95 and I-20; begins at exit 116 of I-20 at Bishopville)*, stopping at museums, homesteads, churches, cotton fields, and markets in Bishopville, Bennettsville, Hartsville, Society Hill, and Cheraw. Planning is under way for an *International African-American Museum* in Charleston. The proposed site for the museum is at the corner of Calhoun and Concord Streets, near the *Fort Sumter Visitor Education Center* *(downtown Charleston at the foot of Calhoun Street, on the Cooper River)*, which features exhibits that examine how the crisis over slavery led to the Civil War.

Liberty Square and downtown Charleston concentrate many marked and unmarked antebellum and Civil War sites. The square itself is a downtown green space with landscaped outdoor garden rooms near the Cooper River. It encourages reflection, and stone markers scattered throughout are inscribed with quotations tracing the evolution of liberty in America from the Constitutional Convention in 1787 to the civil rights movement of the twentieth century. From Liberty Square you can actually see *Sullivan's Island* *(from Charleston, U.S. 17 north, right on SC 703)*, where South Carolina's African slaves were kept in pens after being taken off the ships that had brought them across the Atlantic. A historic marker near the island's entrance highlights the horrendous conditions suffered by captured Africans during their Middle Passage voyage from Africa to America, and gives credit for the many contributions Afro-Americans have made to the development of the United States.

From the square you also see *Fort Wagner* on Morris Island. The June 18, 1863, attack on this Confederate fortification by the Fifty-fourth Massachusetts Regiment, which was comprised of black Union soldiers, has become

The Second *Battle of Fort Sumter, 1961*

On the approach of the Civil War Centennial, trouble stirred in Charleston, South Carolina, where reporters learned that a Negro delegate to the National Civil War Commission would not be permitted to stay in the hotel hosting the commemoration of the battle of Fort Sumter. When the legislature of New Jersey, home state of the Negro delegate, passed a resolution urging all states to boycott the opening ceremonies, President Kennedy bowed to pressure and wrote a letter to General Ulysses S. Grant III, chairman of the commission, stating that all delegates deserved equal treatment as officials of a government body. This venture earned him only scolding rejoinders from Southern delegates, who maintained that the President had no authority over the private affairs of South Carolina hotels.

The controversy escalated rapidly. General Grant supported the South against Kennedy, declaring through a spokesman that the commission's business was to commemorate the war and not to interfere in "racial matters." New York, California, and Illinois joined New Jersey in calling for a boycott. Administration officials, scrambling now that the authority of the President was at issue, eventually conceded that they could not force any suitable Charleston hotel to integrate for the occasion. To save face, they did muster the votes to move the ceremonial banquet out of the segregated hotel to a U.S. naval base three miles outside of Charleston, only to have Southerners gleefully notify reporters that the Navy still segregated its own personnel on the base. Then, on the eve of the Fort Sumter ceremony, a Southern delegate made a speech to the commission containing what Northern delegates called slurs on the ancestry of President Abraham Lincoln, racial and otherwise. After an escalating exchange of insults, the commission delegations acted out an upside-down parody of Civil War politics. Northeners called on President Kennedy to "relieve" General Grant [for] failing to preserve the honor of the federal government, while Southerners rallied to support the grandson of the man whose troops had mowed down their forebears from Shiloh to Appomattoc.

—FROM *PARTING THE WATERS*, BY TAYLOR BRANCH

famous. Although the attack was unsuccessful, the fighting was intense and established the worth of black soldiers, spurring recruitment of more blacks into the Union army. The story of the Fifty-fourth Regiment is told in the movie *Glory*, and is also recounted in nearby **Fort Sumter** *(ferry from Liberty Square)*, where the first shots of the Civil War were fired.

Nearby, on one of Charleston's few remaining cobblestone streets, is the **Old Slave Mart** *(6 Chalmers Street)*. Perhaps a quarter million shackled Africans were marched through its arched doorway and auctioned off in its large rooms. Miriam B. Wilson bought the Slave Mart in 1938 and turned it into Charleston's first Afro-American museum; it is now owned by the city and closed for renovations, after which, the city says, it will be reopened as a museum. A small plaque at the site indicates that it was placed on the National Register of Historic Places in 1973. **Emanuel AME Church** *(110 Calhoun Street)* is another short walk from Liberty Square. It is not only the oldest AME church in the South, but between the years 1818 and 1822, Denmark Vesey, who was one of the church's founders, held regular discussions here to plot insurrection. Emanuel Church was burned in retaliation after Vesey's attempted revolt and was rebuilt with Vesey's son, Robert, as its designer. Worship continued until 1834, the year all-black churches were outlawed. The congregation worshiped there in secret until 1865, when the members formally reorganized after the defeat of the Confederacy. The church was also an important staging area for nonviolent civil rights protests in the 1960s.

What can be considered Emanuel Church's institutional opposite is also found in downtown Charleston: the **Citadel** *(King and Calhoun Streets)* was built after Vesey's uprising, for the purpose of training a militia of white men prepared and able to quell any future slave uprisings. An imposing statue of South Carolina senator John C. Calhoun oversees Citadel grounds. Prior to the Civil War he was the leading advocate for slavery in the U.S. Congress, defending it as a "positive good."

With African slavery at the center of Charleston's early city life, it follows that the desire for freedom was at the center of black life in and around the city. On September 9, 1739, the first recorded slave revolt in the United States took place just outside Charleston. The Stono River rebellion began when an African named Jemmy (or Jemy), generally thought to be from Angola but who may have been from Congo, raided a weapons storehouse with a small group of men. Then, shouting "Liberty" and beating on drums, the size of the raiding party swelling as men and women joined the group, they marched with their captured weapons toward Spanish-controlled St. Augustine, Florida, where they had been promised land and freedom. After burning plantations and killing about twenty-five whites along the way, they were caught. Fourteen were shot resisting their capture by white militiamen, and their heads were placed on poles as a warning to other potentially rebellious African slaves. Forty were later captured and hanged. A "Negro Act" was quickly written, prohibiting group gatherings by slaves and forbidding both the teaching of writing (Jemmy was apparently literate) and the beating of drums. The new act also established slave patrols, or "paddyrollers," white male volunteer patrols with the duty of policing slaves to prevent new revolts from taking place. South Carolina also introduced a duty on the importation of new slaves that went into effect in 1741. The duty doubled the price of imported slaves in an effort to limit the number of Africans from the Continent who were brought into the colony—blacks born and raised in America were thought to be less rebellious. The starting point of Jemmy's rebellion, the **Stono River Slave Rebellion Site** (*about 20 miles southwest of Charleston, just off U.S. Route 17, on the west bank of the Wallace River before you enter Hollywood*) was designated a National Historic Landmark in 1974.

"The strong men keep a-comin' on . . . Gittin' stronger," wrote poet Sterling Brown. And almost three quarters of a century after the Stono River Rebellion, in 1821, Denmark Vesey, who had once been a slave in the Virgin Islands and had purchased his freedom for six hundred dollars after winning fifteen hundred dollars at the East Bay Street Lottery, settled in Charleston. *Vesey's Home (56 Bull Street)* is a National Historic Landmark. He also opened a carpentry shop, and began plotting rebellion. He

1830 illustration of the slave trade

circulated antislavery pamphlets and held meetings at his church and his home. The meetings were held on Sundays, a day when slaves were permitted to visit one another. He and other leaders of this highly organized plot were said to have recruited a secret army of thousands. A date was set for an uprising (July 14, 1822, a Sunday), but an informant tipped off authorities, resulting in more than three hundred arrests and thirty-five executions, including Vesey, who was hanged. On the day of Vesey's execution, state militia and federal troops were called to Charleston to quash a large demonstration by Vesey's supporters in the fairly sub-stantial community of free blacks in Charleston. Although blacks were beaten on the street for defiantly protesting the executions, many of the city's Afro-Americans nonetheless wore mourning black while witnessing the executions of Vesey and other black rebels. Their rebellion triggered such fear that there was even an attempt to destroy the trial records lest others be inspired by Vesey's dangerous idea of freedom.

It is, of course, an idea impossible to extinguish. Indeed, forty-three years later—when Vesey's insurrection was still within living memory of many participants—some four thousand black artisans and tradesmen, along with almost two thousand black schoolchildren, marched through the city pulling floats. One float showed an auction block with an auctioneer selling two women and their children; another featured a coffin labeled SLAVERY. This was, it must be said, a Charleston whose former ruling establishment was still staggering from defeat by the Union army—for blacks a celebratory time when both the immediate and long-term future seemed bright.

As elsewhere in the South after the Civil War, there was a

brief period during Reconstruction from 1866 to 1876 when Afro-Americans gained a measure of power and began a redesign of human relations and citizenship. Blacks were a majority of the state legislature, and they rewrote the state constitution, passing laws that guaranteed aid to public education and civil rights for all. In 1870 Joseph H. Rainey of South Carolina became the first black member of the U.S. House of Representatives. South Carolina sent eight Afro-Americans to serve in Congress—more than any other state ever has. But as was true across the South, in South Carolina, too, Confederate restoration did not take long. "Black codes" began restricting movement and association; new laws began establishing rigid rules of racial segregation.

Democrats campaigned for power and office as "Red Shirts," mocking the Republican Party campaign tactic of "waving the bloody shirt" to remind black voters especially of Union deaths and injuries during the Civil War. Red Shirts organized rifle clubs, threatened black voters, and stole elections. From the U.S. Senate floor in 1900, former South Carolina governor "Pitchfork Ben" Tillman proudly proclaimed, "We have done our level best [to prevent blacks from voting] . . . we have scratched our heads to find out how we could eliminate the last one of them. We stuffed ballot boxes. We shot them. We are not ashamed of it."

Thousands of Afro-Americans fled the state; whites became a majority of the population. Civil rights seemed crushed. Yet, at great risk, unheralded black voices pressed for changes that now seem moderate, but then were considered radical and revolutionary in the city and state. John H. Green, for instance, in 1941 founded the Cosmopolitan Civic League to increase the ranks of black voters—few of South Carolina's Afro-Americans had ever voted in the twentieth century. An Afro-American newspaper, *The Lighthouse*, pressed for equal pay for teachers. In 1944 this paper and another, *The Informer*, even proposed a parallel Democratic Party to be called the South Carolina Negro Democratic Party (SCNDP). Finally organized as the Progressive Democratic Party (PDP), it attracted some fourteen thousand members—mostly Afro-American.

There was at least one protest during the 1950s: the protest by South Carolina State students in Orangeburg in 1956. Sustained sit-ins began in April 1960 when twenty-four high school students surprised the entire city by entering the **Kress Five-and-Dime** *(281 King Street; the 75-year-old building houses various businesses today)*, took seats at the store's whites-only lunch counter, and asked for service. A hostile crowd of whites harassed them and the students were arrested. In general, Charleston's sit-in movement was not met with the dramatic public violence or the brutal arrests that occurred in some other South Carolina cities and towns. One day, for example, Ruby Pendergrass Cornwell, the wife of a black dentist, put on her hat, gloves, and a string of pearls, then rode in a limousine with friends to the posh **Fort Sumter Hotel** *(King Street on the Charleston Harbor waterfront; converted to offices and condominiums in 1974)*. After their arrival, they asked to be served lunch in the dining room. The group was arrested, and when the paddy wagon came to carry them away, the police captain in charge instructed his officers, "No funny stuff; these are respectable people." The elegantly militant Mrs. Cornwell, who was born in

A whites-only gas station in South Carolina, 1958

South Carolina State Remembers "Forgotten Protest"

BY CAROLYN CLICK, *THE (COLUMBIA, SC) STATE*, MARCH 2006

ORANGEBURG, S.C. (AP)—It was the civil rights protest history overlooked. In the spring of 1956—12 years before the Orangeburg Massacre— more than 1,200 South Carolina State College students went on strike to protest a legislative inquiry into the NAACP and alleged subversive activities on campus.

The April strike was the climax of a months long student boycott of Orangeburg businesses sympathetic to the white Citizens Council.

The segregationist council was resisting the National Association for the Advancement of Colored People's demand for school integration and was applying economic pressure to the black petitioners.

The students refused to go to class and, in the dining hall one day, after singing the blessing, they staged a walkout. They demanded Gov. George Bell Timmerman and lawmakers stop meddling in the college's affairs. They also called on then South Carolina State President Benner Turner to acknowledge the growing push to end segregation.

Turner and the white board of trustees immediately expelled student government president Fred Moore and suspended 14 others. None returned.

"Our boycott began before Rosa Parks sat on the seat on that bus and refused to move," said Rudolph A. Pyatt Jr., 73. "The Montgomery bus boycott followed after that, and it was five years later that the students from North Carolina A&T staged the sit-in in the Woolworth's dime store."

Always polite and immaculately dressed, the students staged demonstrations on the president's lawn and hung in effigy the governor, a state lawmaker and Turner.

Many faculty circulated a petition supporting the NAACP; a few resigned in protest or were fired.

Orangeburg was forgotten as places like Montgomery, Selma, Birmingham and Greensboro became touchstones for the civil rights movement.

"It was like it was swept off the map," said Alice Pyatt, a retired school administrator in Charleston who believes she was suspended because her older brother, affectionately known as "Rudy," was a campus leader.

"If it was not for the pictures that (photographer) Cecil Williams took and Fred Moore continuously talking about it, it would be as if it didn't happen."

For years, that collective amnesia puzzled William Hine, a white South Carolina State history professor who has made it his mission to understand the 1955–56 protest.

Hine scoured college and state archives and the presidential papers of Turner, a remote, Harvard-educated lawyer historians say was uncomfortable with the growing clamor for integration.

As this year's 50th anniversary of the April protest approached, Hine persuaded the administration to honor the forgotten protesters.

Alice Pyatt, now 70, simply hopes for closure to a devastating period that nonetheless fueled her lifelong drive for success.

The recipient of a four-year scholarship, she said she had been "part of the herd" during the protest. She received notice of her suspension several days after she returned home for the summer.

"The whole thing was unfair," said Pyatt, who transferred to Allen University in Columbia. "In all of our demonstrations, nobody was hurt. Nobody got in trouble. It was as quiet a march as you've ever seen. There were no arrests. I mean it was an organized, simple thing that was done to express the feeling of a campus."

Hine believes it is important to record the stories, if only to correct a popular belief that South Carolina moved quietly out of segregation.

"This notion that South Carolina eased itself so smoothly, and with such little rancor and acrimony, persists," he said. "And the only blot on South Carolina's splendid reputation in terms of the transition to a more equitable society is the (1968 Orangeburg) massacre. But that's not true."

There is still bitterness among the participants toward Turner, who retired in 1967 and died in the early 1990s, and the white authorities who ran South Carolina State, "and this has all been pretty much forgotten, and not talked about."

1898, lived to be 102 and said of herself, "I wasn't a product of the civil rights movement, I predated it."

Protests reached a peak in the summer of 1963 with an NAACP campaign demanding complete desegregation in the city. Demonstrations and picket lines focused on **King Street** and included sit-ins at hotel restaurants, lunch counters, theaters, and swimming pools; almost a thousand arrests resulted from these actions. In one demonstration that summer, when hundreds of protesters jammed the commercial intersection of King and Calhoun Streets (location of the Citadel), downtown traffic and business were brought to a complete standstill. A simultaneous voter registration campaign almost doubled the number of black registered voters.

Even though the city did not use the police dogs and fire hoses of Birmingham infamy, it clung to segregation with desperation and determination. As late as 1962, when NAACP president J. Arthur Brown went to court to enroll his daughter Millicent in the all-white Rivers High School, the city argued that a reason for segregating schools was that Afro-American children were degenerates, unstable, and infected with venereal disease.

South Carolina and Charleston have so many unsung heroes and heroines of civil rights struggle that any writer is handicapped by lack of space. Attorney Matthew J. Perry, Victoria DeLee, Bill Saunders, Mary Moultrie, and Gloria Blackwell come immediately to mind. But no discussion of civil rights would be complete without reference to federal judge Julius Waties Waring, who once threatened a sit-in inside his own courtroom. Waring was an eighth-generation white Charlestonian who rebelled against his culture, first by divorcing his wife of thirty-two years and marrying a liberal young woman from Connecticut. Probably encouraged by his new wife, Judge Waring began to challenge what he had always taken for granted—white racial privilege—by becoming a public advocate for civil rights. Waring is a genuine hero, and in my view anyway, the **Federal Courthouse** (*Meeting and Broad Streets*) should

The Last Campaign

—————

The last of SCLC's major campaigns in big southern cities took place in Charleston after a March 19, 1969, walkout of nurses' assistants and other low-level employees of the South Carolina Medical College Hospital. In addition to higher wages and improved working conditions, they were seeking recognition of the union they had formed the year before. Like the tobacco workers in 1945, these hospital workers were mostly women and mostly black. The strikers consciously linked their plight to the historical plight of blacks in South Carolina, and in addition to picketing the hospital, pickets went up around the Old Slave Mart. And the same recalcitrant posture that Charleston's white authorities took when the tobacco workers went on strike in the 1940s, and during the campaign for desegregation in the 1950s and early 1960s, they took once again. The medical college president told reporters that he was not going to "turn a twenty-five-million-dollar complex over to a bunch of people who don't have a grammar school education."

Martin Luther King had been assassinated in Memphis the year before, and his organization, SCLC, now headed by Reverend Ralph Abernathy, was invited to partner with the union. It was the first formal partnership between a civil rights organization and a union seeking recognition. In early April Abernathy flew to Charleston, where he addressed a mass meeting of some 1,500 at **Morris Brown AME Church** *(13 Morris Street)*, announcing, "I came to sock it to Charleston." SCLC used its resources to build national support for the strike, seeking, among other things, a nationwide boycott of South Carolina textile products and a sympathy strike by longshoremen in the Charleston port. Locally, after 113 days of picketing and arrests (Abernathy spent two weeks in jail), as well as a boycott of downtown stores, enough pressure was created to force the hospital to recognize the union and begin negotiating with it. "Charleston forged a unity between the community organizing techniques developed during the civil rights era of the Freedom Movement and the working class organizational techniques of strike action developed by the labor movement," SCLC staffer Jack O'Dell wrote later. "Sadly," however, notes Andrew Young, "Charleston was the first and last partnership of this type, and the last major campaign waged by SCLC."

*Judge Julius
Waties Waring*

really be named for him instead of Senator Fritz Hollings. Despite his bloodline, or perhaps because of it, Waring was soon a hated figure; only his wife was hated more by white Charleston. When outlawing the state's whites-only primary in 1948, he told the county registrars in his courtroom that he was prepared to sit in his courtroom all day finding them in contempt if they did not register blacks to vote. He forbade segregated seating in his courtroom, hired a black bailiff, eliminated racial designations from jury lists, and ruled in favor of equal pay for black and white teachers. It was Waring who pushed Thurgood Marshall and the NAACP to abandon argument for "separate but equal schools" and directly challenge the constitutionality of segregated schools. Shunned by the community in which he grew up, after retiring in 1952, Waring and his wife left Charleston and moved to New York. He died in 1968; at his Charleston funeral there were two hundred blacks and twelve whites.

Charleston also gave us the remarkable Septima Poinsette Clark. Indeed, any discussion of the southern civil rights movement must include this daughter of a former slave. Mrs. Clark was a schoolteacher. In 1916 Charleston would not hire black public-school teachers or principals, so she was forced to teach on Johns Island, one of the Gullah islands just off the coast. Her brief stint on the island would later have enormous consequences for the civil rights movement. When she did find work in Charleston, at the private Avery School established by the American Missionary Association, she almost immediately began agitating for the hiring of black public-school teachers and principals. In 1956, upon being named vice president of the Charleston NAACP, an "illegal" organization in the state then, she was fired and lost her pension (which was finally restored in 1976, along with eight years' back pay). By the time of her dismissal she had already begun an association with Highlander Folk School, conducting workshops there during the summers of 1954 and 1955. Rosa Parks participated in a Clark-directed leadership workshop four months before she refused to give up her bus seat in Montgomery, and the two women became close friends. Myles Horton hired Mrs. Clark as Highlander's director of workshops, and her strong belief in the connection between education and citizenship led to the creation of a program called Citizenship School. It focused on encouraging voter registration, emphasizing that ordinary people could address and solve issues through social activism at the grass roots. Her program set up schools that concentrated on un-

"Teaching People to Free Themselves"

"People learned new ways of functioning as they learned to think in different ways about each other. They owned the statement that it's supposed to be 'government by the people, for the people, of the People'—but only if you make it so. They could no longer sit back and let other people do it. The citizenship program was about teaching people to free themselves. One person said it helped black folks to unbrainwash themselves. Blacks in the south had been brainwashed to think they were less than other people, by subtle and not so subtle ways. That was the way the society was structured. I've always been angry about that. People would come to citizenship schools and express this anger, get it out, understand that they could learn ways to deal with it. To create something out of that energy.

"Miss Topsy Eubanks, from Macon, Georgia, said it another way, after a week of thinking about what it meant to be a citizen: 'I feel like I been born again.'

"Still another woman said, 'the cobwebs come just a-moving from my brain.' That's what the citizenship schools did. People had lived in this malaise, this air. They had succumbed to this notion that their place was at the low rung of the ladder. . . . Her son had been involved in demonstrations and she had tried to stop him. Then, after several days, she felt her opinion change. That's what the citizenship schools did. The cobwebs started to move from a lot of people's brains. They started to redefine themselves."

—DOROTHY COTTON TO HARRY BOYTE
OF THE HUMPHREY INSTITUTE, 1991

educated blacks, not only for the purpose of preparing them to pass the literacy tests required for voter registration in every southern state, but also to "educate" people to the idea that they could take control of their own lives. "The basic purpose of the Citizenship Schools is discovering local community leaders," she said. And when the state of Tennessee shut down Highlander in 1961, she took the program to the SCLC, where the dynamic Dorothy Cotton administered it.

In 1965 Clark became the first Afro-American ever elected to Charleston's school board, which had once fired her for her civil rights activities. Upon retiring from SCLC in 1970 at the age of seventy-two, she was reelected to the Charleston School Board. By then her citizenship education program had trained some ten thousand teachers who had taught more than one hundred thousand blacks to read and write. This bare-bones portrait of Septima Clark hardly does justice to her vital role. As Andrew Young puts it, the Citizenship Schools were "as much responsible for transforming the South as anything anybody did." While Rosa Parks is considered the mother of the civil rights movement, Septima Clark is often referred to as its grandmother. There is a **Septima Clark Memorial**, a fountain in her honor, in Charleston's Liberty Square. In front of the Fort Sumter Visitor Education Center, a marker is inscribed with some of her words: "Hating people, bearing hate in your heart, even though you may feel that you have been ill-treated, never accomplishes anything good . . . Hate is only a canker that destroys."

To really understand Mrs. Clark's work, our trail takes us to Johns Island, where in 1916 she began her teaching career. A bridge to the mainland was not built until 1929, and it could take eight hours to reach Charleston by boat. There were virtually no public services; many of the island's residents had not even completed elementary school, and there were enormous health problems. The islanders were Gullah, a culture in which there are strong African retentions in language and behavior that once made island life feel more akin to life in Sierra Leone or Nigeria than in nearby Charleston. Isolation contributed in part to their distinctiveness; the Africans and their descendants had

St. Helena Island

In the early days of the Civil War, the town of Beaufort and the outly-
ing sea islands were captured by Union forces. Plantation owners fled
and thousands of African slaves became free as "contraband." Inspired
by Treasury Secretary Salmon P. Chase, the Port Royal Experiment was
launched: a combined effort of the military, philanthropists, abolitionists,
and Quaker missionaries to create schools, draft blacks into the Union
army, and address a range of issues that arose with this newly freed population. As one historian put it, it was a "dress rehearsal for Reconstruction."

Among the thirty or so schools started during this experiment was
the **Penn Normal School**, now **Penn School Historic District and
Museum** (*Land's End Road, Frogmore*) on St. Helena Island. The
school was named for the founder of the Quaker-influenced state of
Pennsylvania, William Penn, and aimed to equip uneducated former
slaves to function as free people. In the beginning the Penn School
based its effort on what is now termed the Booker T. Washington model:
training in the trades and crafts that would enable the earning of a living, and with the ambition of making them, as Washington himself put
it, "so skilled in hand, so strong in head, so honest in heart, that the
Southern white man cannot do without [them]."

During the civil rights struggles of the 1960s, Penn Center was one of
Dr. Martin Luther King's places of quiet retreat. Gantt Cottage, the modest clapboard cottage where he stayed, can still be rented. It is said that in
this cottage King wrote a draft of the "I Have a Dream" speech he gave at
the 1963 March on Washington.

Much of the center's focus today is on preserving the unique Gullah culture of the Sea Islands; the center is particularly concerned with the surge
of tourism and the effects of the resulting resort and residential development in recent years. It has an extensive collection of preserved historical
manuscripts, oral histories, and musical recordings that offer an in-depth
view of Gullah culture and heritage unavailable anywhere else.

the partial resistance, imparted by sickle cell anemia, to
the malaria and yellow fever existing on these Sea Islands.
Their owners, however, had no immunity and retreated
from the coast, past the tidal marshes and saltwater creeks,

Septima Clark

to build their homes "off island." Gullah communities existed, and still exist, all along the South Carolina and Georgia coasts, although Gullah culture is rapidly losing out to seaside condominium culture and golf, as on Hilton Head Island.

On impoverished and isolated Johns Island, Septima Clark, only eighteen years old, began teaching at the one-room Promise Land school; she wrote out her lessons on paper bags because there was no blackboard. In the 1940s one of her former students, a farmer named Esau Jenkins, who gave lifts to people when he trucked his vegetables to the Charleston market, had been encouraging voter registration. Eventually he bought a bus and developed a regular bus service; he also typed up the voting procedures and began handing the information to passengers and suggesting that they register to vote. One of Jenkins's passengers, Alice Wine, an elderly woman who could not read, had someone read to her whole sections of South Carolina's constitution (the basic document used to test literacy when trying to register to vote). She memorized them and eventually became a registered voter. In 1955 while participating in one of her workshops at Highlander, Jenkins pressed Septima Clark and Highlander to consider setting up an adult reading class on Johns Island. It was urgent, Jenkins explained, because one result of his efforts was that officials were far less casual about literacy requirements for voter registration and were deliberately using them to prevent black registration; especially, said Jenkins, now that he had run for and almost won a seat on the local school board. Highlander agreed to sponsor a voter registration class, and Septima Clark's first citizenship school opened here, in the back of an island food co-op called the **Progressive Club** *(River Road at Royal Oak Drive; still standing but unused)*. Clark approached her cousin, Bernice Robinson, a beautician, to help. And this, too, reflected an approach that distinguished her effort from that of Charleston's traditional black leadership: In this project she wanted associates who could speak the language of ordinary people and were willing to do so. Fourteen people attended that first class; three could not read or write, but on this island testing ground, Septima Clark and Bernice Robinson slowly evolved effective ways and means to teach literacy skills, enabling islanders to tackle the voter registration test. More than one hundred passed it in the first year. By 1959 the two women were recruiting students and teachers from around the state.

Esau Jenkins died in 1972 and is buried at the *Wesley United Methodist Church (2726 River Road)*. His headstone reads LOVE IS PROGRESS. HATE IS EXPENSIVE. The *Esau Jenkins Memorial Bridge* over Church Creek connects Johns Island with Wadmalaw Island. The portion of U.S. 17 running through Charleston is now the *Septima Clark Expressway*.

COLUMBIA

Our stop in South Carolina's capital, Columbia, centers on the *State Capitol (Main and Gervais Streets)*, where grounds dominated by statuary dedicated to racists are also the site of the first memorial to Afro-American history on the grounds of any state capitol. The *African-American History Monument* consists of twelve large bronze panels sculpted by Ed Dwight, who also created the Alex Haley–Kunta Kinte memorial in Annapolis. Portraying the entire sweep of Afro-American history, the panels are grouped into two sections with a tall granite obelisk rising between them. At the base of the obelisk is an Atlantic Ocean Middle Passage map with engraved links to four rubbing stones from regions of Africa where great numbers of people were captured and carried off into

Modjeska Monteith Simkins, a leader in South Carolina's NAACP, fought to equalize teachers' salaries, health care, and education, and challenged segregated schools. Her association with individuals and organizations that were considered too leftist reduced her influence with the NAACP's national leadership.

slavery: Senegal, Sierra Leone, Republic of Congo, and Ghana. A tightly packed slave ship is depicted on the pavement directly in front of the monument.

I like this monument very much, beyond Dwight's artistry, because it is set in the midst of so much Confederate imagery. "Pitchfork Ben" Tillman is there, and so is an imposing statue to U.S. senator Strom Thurmond, who in 1947 called President Harry Truman's civil rights program a Communist plot, and who filibustered against the 1957 Civil Rights Act that established a civil rights division of the Justice Department. The capitol dome at Columbia once flew the Confederate battle flag, but an NAACP boycott forced its removal; it now flies in front of the building, and the boycott continues.

The first meeting of the Progressive Democratic Party (PDP), with one hundred fifty delegates representing thirty-eight of South Carolina's forty-six counties, took place on May 24, 1944, at the Masonic Temple on Washington Street. And, in a challenge at the national Democratic Party's convention in Chicago that year, strikingly similar to the challenge that would be made by the Mississippi Freedom Democratic Party (MFDP) in Atlantic City, New Jersey, twenty years later, the PDP sought to replace the all-white regular state party. Their challenge, too, was rejected.

The other important site in Columbia is the **Modjeska Monteith Simkins House** *(2025 Marion Street; now headquarters of the Collaborative for Community Trust, a nonprofit organization dedicated to social change).* In her home, the outspoken Modjeska Monteith Simkins (1899–1992), an NAACP leader, helped write the petition for *Briggs v. Elliot*, the first of the five cases the Supreme Court combined and considered in its 1954 decision outlawing racial segregation in public schools. "If I know a person has been mistreated, he's my friend," Mrs. Simkins once said. There are many Afro-American historic sites in and around Columbia. **Historic Columbia** *(1601 Richard Street)* publishes an Afro-American tour guide.

ᔰ ROCK HILL ᔰ

W hen CORE's Freedom Riders arrived in Rock Hill on May 9, 1961, after a fairly uneventful journey testing interstate bus terminals in Virginia and North Carolina, John Lewis and Albert Bigelow were attacked and beaten by a mob at the **Greyhound Bus Station** *(2915 Cherry Road)*. These attacks, says Lewis, drove home the realization that they had left the "border" South and were now on different, more violent terrain.

But Rock Hill had its own local movement and is another of the overlooked southern cities that, even before the Freedom Riders, had great impact on the 1960s civil rights movement. Students from **Friendship Junior College** were among the first outside North Carolina to respond to the Greensboro sit-ins with sit-ins of their own. On February 12, 1960, about one hundred students, mostly from Friendship, sat in at **McCrory's Department Store lunch counter** *(135 East Main Street)*. Protests continued

Students from Friendship College demonstrate in Rock Hill, March 1960.

after the McCrory sit-in, and about a month later some seventy students, the "Rock Hill Seventy," were arrested after sit-ins at restaurants and the bus station.

A year before the Greensboro protests, a boycott had been launched by the local Committee for the Promotion of Human Rights, and it put the segregated city bus line out of business. Rock Hill's black residents returned to that tactic in the spring of 1960, this time launching a boycott of downtown businesses that continued through the summer and fall. In a creative challenge of segregation, the wheelchair-bound Reverend Cecil Ivory, an NAACP leader who encouraged and built community support for these protests, rolled up to McCrory's lunch counter and asked for service. He was not violating the custom of racial segregation, argued Rev. Ivory, because he was not sitting in a lunch-counter seat. Nonetheless, he was denied service.

A year after the sit-in protests began, the city still hadn't budged: Some $17,000 in bail money had been spent, and just about all of Rock Hill remained segregated. A White Citizens Council had been formed immediately after protests began, and white violence had been pronounced; some protesters had even been attacked with ammonia bombs. So, on February 1, the first anniversary of the Greensboro

Protester Bunt Gill wiping his hat after being hit by an egg during a February 1960 demonstration in Rock Hill

sit-in, when ten students were arrested for sitting in at McCrory's, nine of them adopted a tactic that, though used by some of the protesting students in Nashville the year before, had mostly been talked about and debated by student activists—"Jail Without Bail." The nine chose thirty days on the chain gang when they were found guilty of trespassing. This caught the attention of the recently formed SNCC. Diane Nash, from the Fisk University campus in Nashville; Ruby Doris Smith, from Spelman's campus in Atlanta; Charles Sherrod, from Virginia Union College in Petersburg; and Charles Jones, from the Johnson C. Smith campus in nearby Charlotte were sent to Rock Hill by the newly formed organization. In making the decision to send them, SNCC was, for the first time, attempting more than exchange of information among student groups. It was taking its first step toward becoming an organization of organizers. These four would soon be among sixteen students who decided to drop out of college and commit themselves full-time to SNCC and the civil rights movement. SNCC's executive secretary, Ed King, issued a statement calling for others to join the initial four "at the lunch counters and in jail. Only by this type of action can we show that nonviolent movement against segregation is not a local issue for just the individual community, but rather a united movement of all those who believe in equality."

A day after their arrival in Rock Hill the four were arrested while sitting in and, like the nine before them, chose jail. They, too, were sentenced to thirty days' hard labor. Diane Nash and Ruby Doris Smith were then sent to the York

There are nine students serving thirty days on the York County Chain Gang for sitting at Lunch Counters and requesting service. Their sitting in shows their belief in the immorality of racial segregation and their choice to serve the sentence shows their unwillingness to participate in any part of a system that perpetuates injustice. Since we too share their beliefs and since many times during the past year we too have sat-in at lunch counters, we feel that in good conscience we have no alternative other than to join them.

—SNCC *Student Voice*
NEWSLETTER,
FEBRUARY 1961

> "The only thing they had to beat us over the head with was a threat of sending us to jail. So we disarmed them by using the only weapon we had left—jail without bail. It was the only practical thing we could do. It upset them quite a bit."
>
> —TOM GAITHER (OF CORE) ON ROCK HILL, TO THE *NEW YORK POST*

County Women's Detention Center; Sherrod and Jones joined the nine male students whose earlier arrests had triggered their arrival in Rock Hill. Protests continued. On February 12 about forty students from Nashville's A&I College arrived by bus for a weekend of picketing. On February 17 black female students picketed Winthrop College, a state school in Rock Hill for white women. Community support remained strong. Reverend Ivory told the local newspaper in a letter that neither he nor the NAACP had the "distinguished honor" of planning the students' protests or jailing. Friendship College dean Raymond Jackson said his school would not penalize students for cutting class to protest. Few, when arrested, chose jail without bail, however, and in that sense—only in that sense—the "jail-in" did not succeed. But something valuable emerged that would define all of SNCC's future work. As Charles Sherrod, who later that year would be directing SNCC's organizing efforts in Albany, Georgia, put it after his release, "You get ideas in jail. You talk with other young people you have never seen. Right away we recognize each other. People like yourself, getting out of the past. We're up all night, sharing creativity, planning action. You learn the truth in prison, you learn wholeness. You find out the difference between being dead and alive."

After serving her thirty-day prison sentence, Ruby Doris Smith flew home a heroine and was greeted at the Atlanta airport by a throng of students from the Atlanta University complex, who rushed to hug her as she descended onto the tarmac. Then they all joined hands and sang "We Shall Overcome."

✎ ORANGEBURG ✎

F ew people know of the Orangeburg Massacre of 1968. Two historically black institutions of higher education were at the center of the bloody events that unfolded: **South Carolina State College** *(now a university; 300 College Street NE)* and **Claflin University** *(400 Magnolia Street).* These schools differ in many respects—one is a state school; the other private, founded by the Methodists—but the graduates of both contribute to a higher-than-usual level of education in Orangeburg's black population. Events in the 1960s here, as elsewhere, would confirm the old fear of the slavers—that a black population educated to any significant degree is always a dangerous population.

Orangeburg was conservative and hostile to civil rights. In 1955 fifty-seven black parents petitioned for school desegregation, and many of them lost their jobs as a result.

Orangeburg protesters

"I Hadn't Done Anything Wrong"

"In 1959 I went to Sumter, South Carolina, with a classmate for Thanksgiving because South Carolina State where we went to school was closed, and Massillion, Ohio, where I'm from, was too far to go for only a few days. The night after Thanksgiving we went to a party, and because I didn't drink, I was the designated driver.

"On the way back home, a police car pulled me over. I wasn't worried; I knew I hadn't done anything wrong. I didn't feel any fear; no apprehension. I give him my driving license and as he takes it he asks, 'Where you from, boy?' Well! And I say, 'Ohio. You've got the license, can't you read?' He doesn't know what to make of me, and he asks, 'Don't you know how to say yes sir?' I can't figure him out either. 'You've got to be jiving,' I tell him.

"He hits me. Now I come from a tough, steel-mill town. Nobody could just hit you and you wouldn't hit them back. So I hit him. I was stomping on him. That was just instinct; my natural instinct and I was trying to stomp him unconscious. But his partner jumped in and the tide of battle turned. It wasn't long before they overcame me. And while they were beating me, I yelled to the guys in the car, 'I'm going to get you for this!' They were sitting there doing nothing. I didn't understand that it would be worth their lives to try and help me. They knew South Carolina and its cops.

South Carolina's first White Citizens Council was formed in Orangeburg to generate economic pressure on Afro-Americans who sought an end to all-white schools; and the organization prevented the delivery of goods to black-owned stores, restaurants, and gas stations after the school desegregation attempt. Other extremist and all-white groups, such as the John Birch Society, found a comfortable home in Orangeburg.

Blacks were not cowed, however, and in 1956 launched a boycott of twenty-three local white-owned businesses, as well as of Coca-Cola, Sunbeam bread, and Standard Oil. They also formed a relief fund to assist black businesses that were under Citizens Council pressure. And then

"They twisted my arm, broke my jaw, and put me in jail.

"My father sent money and got me out the next day. So now I catch the train to go back to Orangeburg; it was my first time on a train in the south. I didn't know the etiquette. The conductor says get back to the baggage car, boy. When the 'black' car was full they made you ride in the baggage car. I said no. Not even for my little bit of money am I going to ride with some mangy dogs. And I sit down in this 'white' car I'm standing in talking to this man. So, hours after getting out of jail that first time, I am back in jail.

"I got out of jail the next day and rode Jim Crow back to Orangeburg. I got off the train and decided to take a short cut through Edisto Park—a big garden in the middle of the city. I didn't know Edisto Park had a 'colored day'—coloreds, us, could go to a certain part of the park on Mondays. It wasn't Monday and I got busted again.

"Over the Christmas holidays my father said I could go to another school— up North—'Cause they gonna kill you down there.' And I was set to leave by the next semester. The closest I ever intended to be to the South again was Columbus, Ohio.

"Then, the sit-ins happened in Greensboro. A group of students planning them in Orangeburg came to me and asked if I would be the spokesman. I believe they thought, 'We've got this crazy Negro down here who will say anything to white folks.'

"At first I said no. After thinking about it I said yes."

—CHARLES "CHUCK" McDEW TO CHARLIE COBB

the sit-ins broke out. In 1960, almost immediately after Greensboro, the planning began in Orangeburg. By mid-February CORE's Tom Gaither was training students from Claflin and South Carolina State in nonviolent methods that included how to curl up protectively, covering eyes and head, when being assaulted. Hundreds of students took part in this training, and in late February they marched downtown to protest segregation. That time there were no arrests and no violence. But then, on March 14, when students marched downtown in bitterly cold weather that was unusual for that time of year, police used tear gas, dogs, and water hoses to break up the demonstration. There were more than five hundred arrests. The turreted **Orangeburg**

Picketing Kress in Orangeburg

County Jail *(44 St. John Street; unused since 1980, although you can still see the bars)* could not hold them, so most of the demonstrators were put in a big chicken coop that was fenced in with barbed wire. In a strange and still not-quite-explicable decision (perhaps because the March 14 demonstrators gathered at the gates of Claflin), after this demonstration South Carolina State decided to separate its students from neighboring Claflin and erected between the two campuses a barbed wire fence—which the students immediately dubbed the "Berlin Wall."

Picket lines and lunch-counter sit-ins at the Kress Department Store and other downtown facilities continued without much result. ***Trinity United Methodist Church*** *(185 Boulevard Street NE)* was the main staging area for protesters, as well as being a movement headquarters site and meeting place. Another downtown boycott was launched in 1963, but it was not until passage of the 1964 Civil Rights Act that white restaurants reluctantly began to desegregate.

For a time there was quiet. But there were holdouts to

desegregation, most prominently the ***All Star Bowling Lane*** *(559 East Russell Street NE)*. For years black bowlers had asked the owner, Harry Floyd, to let them bowl there; it was Orangeburg's only bowling alley, and because they were denied access to it, blacks had to drive forty miles to Columbia to bowl. Their initial request was modest: one night a week for black bowlers. Even though the city's Chamber of Commerce and the American Bowling Congress pressed him to desegregate, Floyd's response was to change his WHITES ONLY sign to one that read PRIVATELY OWNED. But the 1964 act that had opened restaurants in the city raised a new issue for Floyd's All Star Bowling Lane: It had a snack bar, and Floyd, it seemed, was legally bound to obey the new federal law and serve all. He refused. As they had in 1960, students picked up the issue and on February 5, 1968, showed up seeking entry to All Star. After the first student march, Floyd demanded police protection. The next night, when some three hundred students showed up, almost all of Orangeburg's police force was there, too. They arrested one student who tried to push his way inside. A series of protests and arrests culminated with a February 8 standoff between police and protesters near the colleges *(at Watson Street and College Avenue)*. The night before, frustrated, angry students, forced back from the bowling alley by police, had smashed store windows, scraped cars with rocks, and even thrown rocks at police. This chilly night, prevented by police from getting downtown, students built a bonfire in the middle of the street and sang both "We Shall Overcome" and "We Shall Not Be Moved." Four squads of highway patrolmen, as well as national guardsmen, moved forward as a fire department truck put out the bonfire. As the students retreated toward dormitories on State's campus, one of them threw part of a wooden banister taken from a vacant house, and it hit a policeman. A highway patrolman then fired a warning shot into the air. That gunshot, plus a rapidly spreading rumor that a policeman had been shot in the head, caused the police to open fire directly into the retreating crowd. The result was three dead students: Henry Smith, Delano Middleton, and Samuel Hammond

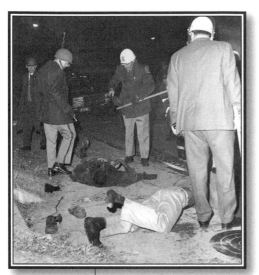

Aftermath of the Orangeburg Massacre

Jr. Twenty-seven students were wounded, almost all of them shot in the back. A ***Memorial Garden*** *(near the campus entrance)* honors those students. In addition, South Carolina State's main athletic stadium has been named for the three; their photographs and the story of their death are conspicuously displayed at the entrance. Every February 8 the university holds a memorial service.

Cleveland "Cleve" Sellers, SNCC's former program director, was present as these events unfolded and was shot in the arm that night. A native of nearby Denmark, South Carolina, he had begun working with students on the two campuses in October 1967. On State's campus, some students had formed a new organization, this one in response to Stokely Carmichael's 1966 call for Black Power—the Black Awareness Coordinating Committee (BACC; it was also a more militant campus alternative to the larger NAACP chapter). It was with this group that Sellers got involved. Neither BACC nor Sellers was particularly interested in desegregating the bowling lane. They were more interested in tackling a number of issues on the strict and paternalistic South Carolina State campus: male students were required to wear coats and ties on Sundays; and three white professors had been fired for encouraging students to question the absence of civil rights history from their courses. The latter resulted in a two-week student boycott of classes. The Afrocentric BACC, according to Sellers, considered integration "an irrelevant issue."

Despite his lack of enthusiasm for the protest, state-government fingers were quickly pointed at Cleve Sellers. On the night of February 8 the governor's office accused Sellers of being the "main man" behind the violence of some of the students that night. "He's the biggest nigger in the crowd," said Henry Lake, the governor's official spokesman.

"I Got Involved"

"I left SNCC in 1967 and returned to South Carolina in early October with the intention of enrolling in South Carolina State to complete my baccalaureate . . . and also, thinking back on it, to get off the front line of the struggle for a while. I didn't want to go back and live in my hometown, Denmark, at that time, but Orangeburg was near. Stokely even came down [at] Christmas, and we spent about a week or so with Esau Jenkins—he really liked Stokely—over on Johns Island. Stokely actually went to a Watch Night service [*a church service of thanks by Christian faithful held on New Year's Eve; it was on January 1, 1863, that slaves in the Confederacy were declared free by Abraham Lincoln's Emancipation Proclamation*] while we were there. There was no press.

"When I got back to Orangeburg, some students were already making plans to organize sit-ins at the bowling alley. And there was an anti–Vietnam war movement up the road in Columbia, white students from the University of South Carolina, and I got involved with some of them. There was a Captain Henry Levy who refused to go fight there and that made national news. Meanwhile, in Orangeburg students were organizing the Black Awareness Coordinating Committee (BACC)—a name designed to mirror SNCC's full name—and I was interested in bringing them and the white anti–Vietnam war students in Columbia together at least in terms of opposing the war.

"In BACC we really weren't interested in the bowling alley. Our focus was cultural. I wanted to talk to students about making a connection to the history of struggle that was all around them—Septima Clark, Esau Jenkins, Modjeska Simkins. It was the NAACP Youth Chapter that was talking about protesting at the bowling alley.

"In the days leading up to the massacre, there was escalating violence and escalating police provocation. And I began to see that whatever finally went down, they were going to make it look like I was behind it. On the morning of the day that turned out to be when the massacre took place, I called a press conference and said that the city was on a collision course with the protesting students. There was a need for some kind of intervention, I said. And I predicted that if anything happened, I would be the fall guy."

—CLEVELAND SELLERS TO CHARLIE COBB

Sellers was arrested while he was in the hospital emergency room getting his wound treated and taken to the state prison in Columbia, where he was placed in a cell on death row. A range of charges was lodged against him that, if he were found guilty of all, would have meant some seventy-eight years in jail. In 1970 he was found guilty of only one: refusal to disperse immediately when ordered to do so. He was given the maximum sentence, a $250 fine and a year in prison. Sellers lost his appeals, entered prison in 1974, and spent almost a year in jail.

Nine members of the highway patrol were indicted on a federal charge of denying protesters their rights. They were acquitted.

Cleve Sellers is now director of the African-American Studies program at the University of South Carolina in Columbia.

CLARENDON COUNTY

A short trip to **Summerton**, about thirty-five miles east of Orangeburg, is absolutely necessary. As with Barbara Johns at Moton School in Farmville, in this tiny village (just over one thousand people live in Summerton), an unexpected challenge brings us to another of the significant starting points of the modern civil rights movement. What seemed at first to be a modest and reasonable request by the parents of children attending **Scott's Branch School** (on *the western border of town just past where U.S. 15 and U.S. 301 intersect, on what is now Larry King Highway*) resulted in the Briggs-Elliott lawsuit—the first of the five cases that were combined into *Brown v. Board of Education.*

In 1947 the minister of *Liberty Hill AME Church* *(Liberty Hill Road)*, Reverend Joseph Armstrong DeLaine, who lived across the street from the school, where his wife taught, persuaded fourteen black parents, all members of his church, to ask for equal treatment from the school system. His effort had been triggered by the response of Clarendon County's school board chairman, R. W. Elliot (also a minister): When parents asked for a school bus, concerned that some children had to walk as far as ten miles to attend school, Rev. Elliott's reply was "We ain't got no money to buy a bus for your nigger children."

Thurgood Marshall took up their cause and transformed their initial request for a school bus into a direct challenge to segregation itself. Judge Julius Waties Waring, whom we met in Charleston, played a key role: In a 1950 pretrial hearing on the Briggs case, Judge Waring reminded the NAACP's lawyers that the real issue was segregation itself, not unequal facilities, and he dismissed the case without prejudice. The case came back before the U.S. District Court in 1951, and this time when the court upheld segregated education, Waring's powerful dissenting opinion provided the NAACP with important legal ammunition to argue against segregation before the U.S. Supreme Court.

But more than events in a courtroom make this site significant. It was at the Scott's Branch School that psychologist Kenneth Clark showed white dolls and black dolls to sixteen black students between the ages of six and nine and asked them which doll looked bad; eleven said the black dolls looked "bad." When asked to pick the doll most like them, seven picked the white one. This study at this site helped persuade the Supreme Court that racial segregation was inherently damaging and unconstitutional.

There was reprisal for the attack on segregation. Jobs were lost, credit was denied, homes were firebombed. Liberty Church was burned to the ground, and Rev. DeLaine's wife was fired from her teaching position, as were two of his sisters and a niece. Drive-by shooters fired into the DeLaine home, and the minister fired back to mark the car for later identification. As a result, *he* was charged with assault and

Reverend Joseph Armstrong DeLaine preaching at St. James AME church in Lakeside, South Carolina, just before he was forced to flee the state.

battery with intent to kill. Convinced that it would be impossible to get a fair trial, he fled the county and state. "I am not running from justice, but [from] injustice," Rev. DeLaine said later. The charge haunted him for the rest of his life, and he remained a fugitive—though not eagerly hunted once he was out of South Carolina. On October 10, 2000—more than twenty-five years after his death—Rev. DeLaine was finally cleared of the charges, and three years later was even posthumously awarded a Congressional Gold Medal for his commitment and heroism. There is a commemorative marker at the newer Scotts Branch High School, not far from the site of the old school. It lists the names of all the plaintiffs in the Briggs case. LET US SWEETLY LIVE is inscribed above these names. There is also a marker at the site of Liberty Church. The **Briggs-DeLaine-Pearson Foundation** *(1578 Gov. Richardson Road)* houses memorabilia in a community center and plans to place other commemorative markers in Clarendon County. Using volunteers, the foundation also provides a number of services to the economically distressed area.

CHAPTER SIX

...ON MY MIND

Atlanta, Albany, and Savannah, Georgia

> **"** *Not only is Georgia . . . the agricultural focus of our Negro population, but in many other respects, both now and yesterday, the Negro problems have seemed to be centered in this state. No other state in the Union can count a million Negroes among its citizens . . . no other state fought so long and strenuously to gather this host of Africans. Oglethorpe thought slavery against the law and gospel; but the circumstances which gave Georgia its first inhabitants were not calculated to furnish citizens over-nice in their ideas about rum and slaves.* **"**

—W. E. B. Du Bois, 1903

In Georgia, the last of America's original thirteen colonies to be settled, the civil rights trail is an intricate one.
From Atlanta, a self-proclaimed "City Too Busy to Hate,"
that encouraged a black bourgeoisie yet maintained a
strictly enforced code that no black person had rights
a white person need respect; to southwest Georgia and its
counties of pecans and peanuts that equaled Mississippi
and Alabama in their capacity for antiblack brutality; to
Savannah, where the cotton gin was invented and slavery
sank its earliest roots in the state, Georgia is a microcosm
of the entire South and hardly a place to be romanticized as
it is in *Gone With the Wind*. Indeed, to the extent that the
South of Rhett Butler and Scarlett O'Hara *is* gone with the
wind, that is to be praised as progress, and Georgia may be
one of the better examples of that, too.

On February 12, 1733, the *Anne*, which had left England almost three months earlier, pulled into Charleston, South Carolina. From there, in smaller boats, some
114 people headed south and pulled into Yamacraw Bluffs
near the mouth of the Savannah River where they disem-

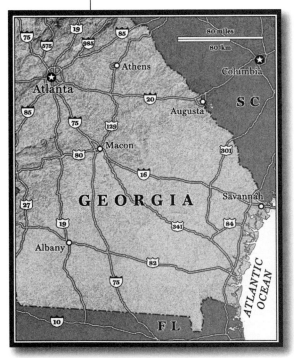

barked to set up a colony
at what is today the city of
Savannah. The colonists included laborers and tradesmen, as well as men who
had been released from
debtor's prison. In general,
however, the men who ar-
rived from England with
James Edward Oglethorpe
(he had received a charter
from King George II, for
whom the state is named)
seeking fortune in the "New
World" were not an espe-
cially savory bunch. Nevertheless, Oglethorpe planned
to establish in America a
kind of redemptive agrar-

ian Zion for the "worthy" poor—an "Asilum of the Unfortunate," he wrote—and in the colony's earliest days, slaves, rum, and lawyers were forbidden. In some respects, early Georgia was progressive and tolerant of diversity, offering sanctuary to Puritans, evangelical Lutherans, Quakers, and others who were being persecuted in Europe. Savannah's **Temple Mickve Israel** *(20 East Gordon Street)* is the oldest Jewish congregation in the South and the third oldest in the nation. "Everyone in this colony will be equal," declared the Oxford-educated Oglethorpe. Catholics, however, were not welcome.

Despite unusual receptiveness to persecuted religious congregations and the official ban on slavery, a leasing system was soon established permitting Georgia planters to rent African slaves from neighboring South Carolina. And it took only nineteen years for Georgia to legalize slavery, which it did on January 1, 1751. By the time Georgia joined the Continental Congress in 1775, slaves made up 45 percent of its population, and Oglethorpe had long since gone back to England (in 1743) to face what appear to be trumped-up charges brought by colonists unhappy with his bans on slavery and liquor. He never returned.

It was about seven miles west of Savannah that Connecticut schoolteacher Eli Whitney invented the cotton gin in 1793 at the **Mulberry Grove Plantation** *(burned to the ground by Union General William T. Sherman during his "march to the sea," but markers on Route 21 at the edge of the plantation site describe the invention's history).* Nothing but the civil rights movement—not even the Civil War—would have greater impact on the South than the cotton gin. It gave farmers the ability to quickly separate the locks (cotton fibers) from the seedpods and enabled

An early cotton gin. Small cotton gins were powered by hand, larger ones by horse.

the easy removal of the sticky seeds, thereby dramatically increasing the amount of cotton that could be processed. This technological breakthrough made it economically practicable to have a larger number of pickers in the field, rather than wasting laborers on the slow task of separating seeds from much smaller quantities of cotton.

The invention of the cotton gin accelerated the clearing of new lands (and the forced removal of Native Americans, notably the Cherokee; their "Trail of Tears" to Oklahoma begins in Georgia), and also drove an increasing number of African slaves across the south. In Georgia the slave population grew almost twentyfold, from 29,264 in 1790 to 462,198 in 1860, and Georgia's reputation as one of the cruelest slave territories grew, as well. In Savannah, a bronze **African American Monument** (*Rousakis Plaza, at River Street between the Savannah River and City Hall*) was unveiled in July 2002. It portrays a slave family embracing

A slave auction house in Atlanta, 1864

one another with broken shackles at their feet, undoubtedly wondering what the future holds for them. There is an inscription written by poet Maya Angelou: "We were stolen, sold and bought together from the African continent. We got on the slave ships together. We lay back to belly in the holds of the slave ships in each other's excrement and urine together, sometimes died together, and our lifeless bodies thrown overboard together. Today, we are standing up together, with faith and even some joy." Angelou added that last sentence to please a city council that found the words preceding it too bitter. It is the only monument to Afro-Americans in Savannah.

Almost immediately following the Civil War, a measure of black power began to emerge in Georgia. Nearly one hundred thousand Afro-American men registered to vote and thirty-three blacks were elected to the state legislature. Thirty-seven Afro-Americans were delegates to the 1867–68 constitutional convention, whose members rewrote the state constitution and, among other things, eliminated property qualifications for voting and granted property rights to women. But the Ku Klux Klan was also growing, and the assassination of black political leaders, combined with the retreat from Reconstruction by the federal government, steadily undermined post–Civil War gains. "The Negro is unfit to rule the State," an editorial in the *Atlanta Constitution* newspaper claimed. "The Democratic Party will protect him in every civil right. It is unwilling, however, to make him Congressman, Governor, and Judge." On September 3, 1868, Georgia's still mostly white General Assembly declared black legislators ineligible to hold office and expelled them. Leaving the assembly on that last day, one of those legislators, Henry McNeil Turner, when passing the Speaker's desk raised his foot and derisively brushed dust off his boot before walking out the door. "You may drive us out," Turner had warned the legislative body, "but you will light a torch never to be put out." There is a six-foot-tall bronze monument called ***Expelled Because of Their Color*** (*northeast corner of the state capitol grounds*) in downtown Atlanta. Its antebellum columns surrounded by bones represent the slave labor that was the foundation of Georgia's economy. Inscribed on the monument's base are the names of the expelled legislators. They were reinstated by court order the following year, but the course leading to the elimination of newly gained civil rights had been set, and by 1872, Georgia Democrats had regained complete power in the state. Later, as a prominent AME church leader, Turner, who was the Union Army's first black chaplain during the Civil War, would campaign for black emigration to Africa.

Movement for civil rights was not destroyed by this loss of black power, however. That became clear even as civil rights seemed crushed by legislation and lynch-mob lawlessness. Georgia was now a far distance from Oglethorpe's founding vision; the only state where more lynchings occurred was Mississippi. One of the most horrible of these murders took place in Newnan, Georgia, yet some of the roots of the NAACP are found in its aftermath. In an argument over wages on April 12, 1899, Samuel Wilkes, also known as Sam Hose, killed a wealthy white man, Alfred Cranford. A rumor spread that he had also raped Cranford's wife. "Determined mob after Hose; he will be lynched if caught," began an April 14 story in the *Atlanta Constitution*. On April 23 Hose was captured and handed over to a mob in Newnan who dismembered him and passed out his fingers, ears, and genitals as souvenirs. What remained of Hose—who was still alive—was then set on fire. "Oh, my God . . . Oh, Jesus!" the dying man managed to moan. When Hose finally did die, the mob cut out his heart and liver and took pieces of his charred skeleton and passed them out, too.

But just as white violence directed at civil rights protesters would do in the 1960s, this barbaric killing helped fuel black anger and organization both inside and outside the state. It greatly affected one man in Atlanta who would become, for much of the twentieth century, the leading public advocate of civil rights.

~ ATLANTA ~

“ *Perhaps Atlanta was not christened for the winged maiden of dull Bœtia; you know the tale—how swarthy Atalanta, tall and wild, would marry only him who outraced her; and how wily Hippomenes laid three apples of gold in the way. She fled like a shadow, paused, startled over the first apple, but even as he stretched his hand, fled again; hovered over the second, then, slipping from his hot grasp, flew over river, vale, and hill; but as she lingered over the third, his arms fell around her, and looking on each other, the blazing passion of their love profaned the sanctuary of Love, and they were cursed. If Atlanta was not named for Atalanta, she ought to have been.* **”**

—W. E. B. Du Bois, 1903

A week after the Sam Wilkes/Hose lynching, William Edward Burghardt Du Bois, then a professor of history and economics at Atlanta University, was downtown, walking to the offices of the *Atlanta Constitution*, bringing to the newspaper a commentary he had written about the murder. An acquaintance stopped him and told Du Bois that not far away a grocery store had in its window a jar of human knuckles that it was advertising as belonging to "the Negro fiend, Hose." That grisly display was the final whiplash of racism that tore Du Bois away from academia, hurling him into a lifetime of activism and advocacy—as he put it, the "red ray" that compelled him to begin focusing less on his scholarly work. In his third autobiography, *Dusk of Dawn*, Du Bois wrote that he had once been certain that America's race problem could be solved with knowledge and scientific investigation, but the lynching of Hose and others changed his mind. "One could not be a calm, cool, and detached scientist while Negroes were lynched, murdered and starved." And when in July 1905 he and a group of thirty-one other prominent Afro-Americans met on the Canadian side of Niagara Falls to discuss the challenges facing "people of color," lynching was high on the list of their concerns. The numbers still shock: Between 1880 and 1930 more than seven hundred whites and nearly five thousand blacks were lynched in the United States. Seeds that would, in less than four years, grow into the National Association for the Advancement of Colored People (NAACP) were planted at that Niagara Falls meeting. Du Bois became the editor of the NAACP's *Crisis* magazine and regularly railed against lynching; the organization fought for antilynching legislation for decades. But such legislation was never enacted by the U.S. Congress.

W. E. B. Du Bois

Atlanta seemed determined to drive blacks away in the beginning decades of the twentieth century. On Saturday, September 22, 1906, again inflamed by newspaper headlines alleging assaults on white women by black men, white mobs began attacking Afro-Americans on the street, by official count killing twenty-five people over several days. Part of what triggered that violence was growing fear of the potential competition of black and white labor. Also contributing was the success of black enterprise, which intensified fear that this success might bring with it black social and political power.

Atlanta was also emerging as a great center of black higher education. By the beginning of the twentieth century, its six black colleges represented the largest concentration of black institutions of higher learning in the country. On these campuses, younger voices, that of

*I*da B. Wells, *born into slavery and perhaps the most militant civil rights advocate of the late nineteenth and early twentieth centuries, was driven out of Memphis, Tennessee, for her antilynching crusade as editor of the* Memphis Free Speech *newspaper. In Chicago, she hired a detective to investigate the Wilkes/Hose lynching. Excerpts from the detective's report reveal that violence, early on, was deliberately instigated by business and economic powers determined to keep blacks subservient:*

"Was there a murder? That Wilkes killed Cranford there is no doubt, but under what circumstances can never be proven. I asked many white people . . . what was the motive. They considered it a useless question. A 'nigger' had killed a white man, and that was enough. Some said it was because the young 'niggers' did not know their places, others that they were getting too much education, while others declared that it was all due to the influence of the Northern 'niggers.' W. W. Jackson, of Newman, said: 'If I had my way about it I would lynch every Northern "nigger" that comes this way. They are at the bottom of this.'

"The burning of Wilkes was fully premeditated. It was no sudden outburst of a furious, maddened mob. . . . The Cranfords are an old, wealthy and aristocratic family, and it was intended to make an example of the Negro who killed him. . . . And it was not the irresponsible rabble that urged the burning, for it was openly advocated by some of the leading men. . . . E. D. Sharkey, Superintendent Atlanta Bagging Mills, was one of the most persistent advocates of the burning. . . .

"John Haas, President of the Capitol Bank, was [also] particularly prominent in advocating the burning. People doing business at his bank, and coming from Newman and Griffin, were urged to make an example of Sam by Burning him.

"W. A. Hemphill, President and business manager, and Clark Howell, editor of the Atlanta Constitution, contributed more to the burning than any other men and all other forces in Georgia. Through the columns of their paper they exaggerated every detail of the killing, invented and published inflammatory descriptions of a crime that was never committed. . . .

"I do not need to give the details of the burning. I mention only one fact, and that is the disappointment which the crowd felt when it could not make Wilkes beg for mercy."

—Louis P. Le Vin

W. E. B. Du Bois among them, were raising what Georgia's white leaders thought had been stamped out in the 1870s: the idea of equal rights. Earlier than in many southern cities, Atlanta's Afro-American leadership began mobilizing a black electorate to use the vote in the ongoing battle for social change. Especially important were churches that began to include, as part of their mission, teaching black people their rights as citizens.

It was a small electorate. At the turn of the century, Atlanta's black population was 30 percent of the city's total population, but most were not registered to vote. Still, as early as 1924, that electorate was able to force the city to build Atlanta's first black public secondary school, ***Booker T. Washington High School*** *(45 Whitehouse Drive SW, adjacent to Atlanta University on Atlanta's West End)*; Martin Luther King Jr. and singer-actress Lena Horne both graduated from the school. In 1927 an exact replica of the Booker T. Washington monument at Tuskegee University in Alabama was erected at the school's entrance. It is called ***Booker T. Washington Lifting the Veil of Ignorance***.

The inscription reads "He lifted the veil of ignorance from his people and pointed the way to progress through education and industry." The school is on the National Register of Historic Places.

By the middle of the 1940s, renewed black voting strength was evident, although white candidates tried to ignore it. Then in 1946 Helen Douglas Mankin, the only one of nineteen white candidates to actively seek Afro-American votes, won the midterm election for the Fifth Congressional District. Voting power bound Atlanta's black establishment to the white establishment, with consequences for the shape of civil rights struggle to follow. In 1948 the city hired its first Afro-American policemen, meanwhile denying them the right to arrest white suspects. Late in 1955 a group of black men were allowed to play golf on the public North Fulton course, but that same year the Georgia General Assembly ruled that any state or local official who spent tax money on an integrated school would be charged with a felony punishable by two years in prison. Throughout the 1950s Atlanta's city government muffled its segregationist preference while state government was stridently antiblack. In 1957, when members of the Spelman College Social Science Club sat down in the white section of the Georgia legislature, the speaker of the house, Marvin E. Moate, quickly strode to the microphone.

"You nigras move over to where you belong!" he thundered at the young women. "We got segregation in the state of Georgia!"

Black pressure for desegregation grew, however, especially after the success of the Montgomery, Alabama, bus boycott. In 1957, for example, six prominent ministers were arrested after sitting in whites' seats on city buses, launching what was called the Triple L Movement ("Love, Law, and Liberation"). The city began making small concessions. On May 22, 1959, Irene Dobbs Jackson (the mother of Maynard Jackson, who would become Atlanta's first Afro-American mayor) was issued a library card by the downtown *Carnegie Public Library (1 Margaret Mitchell Square at Forsyth Street and Carnegie Way; the handsome*

1902 beaux arts structure was torn down and replaced by a newer building that takes up the entire block). But some Atlantans had trouble getting used to even these modest concessions. One day there was an incident that now seems to have taken place in a galaxy far from Earth. A librarian became agitated and confused because blacks were permitted not only to check out books but to use other facilities in the downtown library, and called Atlanta's police chief insisting that policemen were urgently needed.

"Why?" asked the chief. "Are they destroying books?"

"No," the librarian replied.

"Are they tearing up the furniture?"

"No."

"Are they disturbing the peace?"

"No."

"Well, what are they doing?" asked the chief.

"They're looking in the card catalogue."

Atlanta had long been attracting rural Georgia blacks, who began settling around **Auburn Avenue.** Black businesses developed along the street, many concentrated on a dozen or so blocks just east of Peachtree Street and downtown Atlanta. The avenue acquired the nickname Sweet Auburn for its vibrant black life and commercial enterprise, and in 1952 *Forbes* magazine dubbed it the "richest Negro street in America." The **Auburn Avenue Research Library on African-American Culture and History** *(101 Auburn Avenue NE),* established in 1994, offers a comprehensive view of the street and the city, as well as the wider world of African people. Its archives division contains personal papers, photographs (many taken by Afro-American photographers in Atlanta and dating back as far as 1870), oral histories, and records of organizations and institutions, including over a million civil rights news clippings from 1940 to the 1970s. The library also has a substantial collection of artifacts that include slave shackles; medallions; commemorative coins, currencies, and stamps; and buttons depicting civil rights themes and political campaigns, slogans, and organizations.

Auburn Avenue is also Martin Luther King's old neighborhood, and the *"Sweet Auburn Historic District"* was designated a National Historic Landmark district in 1976. It is now part of the larger *Martin Luther King, Jr., Historic Site and Preservation District (bounded roughly by Courtland, Randolph, and Chamberlain Streets and Irwin Avenue)* that was established in 1980. Sites here concentrate on Dr. King's early life and legacy. *King's birthplace (501 Auburn Avenue)*, a modest Victorian two-story home, is open for free tours guided by National Park Service rangers who tell stories about the young King. In his post-Montgomery years as a national civil rights leader under constant pressure, Atlanta provided sanctuary for King in a way that no other city could; it was home. In his spare time, he usually rested, wrote, and sometimes preached at his father's church, *Ebenezer Baptist Church (407 Auburn Avenue)*, where he was copastor of the church, sharing ministerial duties with "Daddy" King.

A new, larger Ebenezer has been built across the street, but there is a grace to the old brick church that is lacking in the newer one. Fortunately, members of the Ebenezer congregation conduct informative brief tours of the original sanctuary. There are also annual events, such as the celebration of King's birthday, which attract large crowds peppered with civil rights–movement stalwarts. And despite the architectural shortcomings of the new sanctuary, visitors are always warmly welcomed at Sunday-morning services.

The *Martin Luther King, Jr., Center for Nonviolent Social Change (449 Auburn Avenue)* is just steps away from Ebenezer. In 1970 Dr. King's tomb was moved from a suburban Atlanta cemetery to this in-town site, where Coretta Scott King, committed to educating the public about her murdered husband's work and philosophy and feeling strongly that he would have wanted her to take on this mission, established a library, an archive, and a memorial. Today the center encourages study of Dr. King's use of nonviolence and the opportunity to join a "Beloved Community Network." A document collection contains field reports from SCLC and SNCC, as well as some of the papers of movement figures

Toddle House protest in Atlanta, December 1963. Right to left: *myself, Stokely Carmichael, Willie Ricks, Ivanhoe Donaldson (standing), James Forman. We'd heard that Jaramogi Oginga Odinga, vice president of newly independent Kenya, was in the U.S. on an official visit and was staying at the posh Peachtree Manor Hotel—a hotel we'd never known blacks to check into. A group of us decided to visit this "Mau Mau." We entered the hotel without incident and went up to his room. For about an hour he listened to us and talked to us about Kenya's independence struggle. As we were leaving, we decided to detour into the Toddle House coffee shop but were refused service. We refused to leave. What would Oginga Odinga think, after all? We were arrested and taken to jail.*

including Andrew Young, Ella Baker, Septima Clark, and of course, Dr. King. Sadly, however, maintenance of the center has been neglected for years, and a 2005 National Park Service report estimated that $11.5 million was needed for repairs. It is not clear at this writing whether or not the center will be sold; the family itself is divided over the issue. Notwithstanding these tensions, however, in the courtyard where Dr. King's crypt is slightly elevated above a shallow reflecting pool, there is a genuine feeling of tranquillity. Etched into its marble surface are the words Dr. King spoke concluding his 1963 March on Washington speech: FREE AT LAST, FREE AT LAST, THANK GOD ALMIGHTY I'M FREE AT LAST. When it is not too crowded, King feels very present at his final resting place.

Lamentably, not much from Auburn Avenue's glory days remains; the beautifully restored Ebenezer church, the King family home, and the King Center are among the few bright spots along a once-great black thoroughfare that is now depressed in so many places that it is difficult to imagine its former glitter and enterprise. Movement centers such as **B. B. Beamon's Restaurant** *(233 Auburn Avenue)* have vanished. Interstate 75 has cut the neighborhood in half, and even though there is prosperous black enterprise in the city, it has largely ignored Auburn Avenue, preferring, instead, suburban Atlanta. In its Trolley Theater, however, the **APEX Museum** *(African-American Panoramic Experience; 135 Auburn Avenue)* offers a video history of the old street that introduces visitors to businesses, personalities, and leading families. Nonetheless, for those who remember what it was like before, looking at the street today can be painful. Empty, boarded-up storefronts and squalid shotgun houses in some alleys stand as sad and ugly evidence that even with voting rights and racial desegregation, not all of Dr. King's dreams have been realized yet; nor, I suspect, will "Sweet Auburn" last much longer as a predominantly black street. Gentrification is accelerating in this neighborhood near downtown.

Urban, urbane Atlanta rivals Miami as the least "Southern" of southern cities today, although important chapters of civil rights history were written on its streets. The national headquarters of Dr. King's Southern Christian Leadership Conference remains in Atlanta. The organization's current address is 600 West Peachtree Street, but they were formerly headquartered in the old **Prince Hall Masonic Temple & Tabor Building** *(332–34 Auburn Avenue)*, which also once housed Atlanta's first black-owned radio station, **WERD**. When SCLC first moved in here, Dr. King would bang on the ceiling with a broomstick whenever he wanted to make a public statement, and in response the disc jockey upstairs lowered a microphone to his window. King would then pull the microphone in and make his statement. In 2006 SCLC announced plans to build a new office building on what is now a vacant lot next to the headquarters of **SCLC/W.O.M.E.N.** *(Women's Organizational Movement*

"It Was Too Scary"

"I was a field worker for the Young Christian Students (YCS) organizing Catholic students in the North to support freedom rides and sit-ins in the South. Casey Hayden wrote to ask if I would leave YCS and come down to Atlanta to work with her in SNCC's headquarters there. My gut said no. My mind was undecided.

"The demonstrations in the South were real-life illustrations of how Christians could involve themselves in action to dismantle segregation. Yet somehow I couldn't, when called, bring myself to answer. A few weeks later, I was lying in the bottom bunk of a dormitory at a Catholic college in Green Bay, Wisconsin, with Casey's letter in my suitcase and no decision made yet. I had to make one, and here I was still agonizing over what to do.

"It was too scary. Stories of people beaten, jailed, bombed, pursued by the KKK and sometimes killed were vivid in my mind. And . . . there were big cockroaches in the South. Some of them had wings. They could fly into your hair. I don't know what I was more afraid of . . . the bugs or the beatings. As I struggled with the pros and cons, it finally came down to 'How could I continue to persuade students to support fellow students in the South if I myself refused to go?' My conscience finally made up my mind. In the summer of 1963, I boarded a bus to Atlanta."

—MARIA VARELA TO CHARLIE COBB

for Equality Now; 328 Auburn Avenue) on the west side of the Tabor building.

Atlanta was also home base of the Student Nonviolent Coordinating Committee. Ella Baker gave the group a corner in Dr. King's SCLC headquarters, but in less than a year the organization rented its own space and established a **SNCC office** (first at 197 Auburn, then 135 Auburn; no markers) almost directly across the street from SCLC's first Atlanta headquarters at 208 Auburn Avenue.

Although some direct-action protest had taken place in the 1950s, it was after Greensboro that the Atlanta student movement launched a sustained series of sit-ins. This

Members of the Hungry Club Forum in front of the Butler Street YMCA in 1945

shifted the geography of local civil rights leadership for a time. The **Butler Street YMCA** *(20–24 Butler Street; Jesse Hill Street today)* near Auburn Avenue had long been a center of civil rights planning by Afro-American Atlanta's established leadership. Jesse Hill, the president of Atlanta Life Insurance Company, called the Butler Street Y the "Black City Hall of Atlanta." In the decades of the 1940s, 1950s, and early 1960s, it was an essential stopping point for anyone seeking to take the pulse of black Atlanta. The **Hungry Club Forum** started at the Y in 1942 as a meeting place where blacks and whites discussed civil rights. It was a secret organization at first. The club's motto was Food for Taste and Food for Thought for Those Who Hunger for Information and Association. Even today, the club holds luncheon meetings every Wednesday. But when the student sit-ins were launched from Atlanta's consortium of historically black schools—Clark College (now Clark Atlanta University), Atlanta University, Morehouse College, Spelman College, Morris Brown College, and the Interdenominational Theological Center—the west side of town became the movement's activist center. There is a large **Martin Luther King Statue** *(King Chapel Plaza, Westview Street at Morehouse College)* and behind it, inscribed on a brick wall of the complex's chapel (renamed in 1981 the *Martin Luther King International Chapel*) is King's famous "I Have a Dream" speech. In front of *Trevor Arnett Hall (223 James P. Brawley Drive)* on the quadrangle of Clark Atlanta University, there is a marker commemorating the powerful student movement that emerged from these campuses in 1960.

A valuable resource for exploring the Atlanta University consortium is the *Robert W. Woodruff Library (Atlanta University Center, 111 James P. Brawley Drive, SW)*. Here you can peruse movement handbills, correspondence, reports, photographs, and slides. In June 2006 a group of prominent Atlantans, led by Mayor Shirley Franklin and Andrew Young, rescued thousands of Dr. King's personal and political documents from being auctioned by Sotheby's in New York. Appraised at $32 million, they will now be housed at the library. A national advisory committee, which includes Harvard University's Henry Louis Gates and Stanford University's Clayborne Carson, will make recommendations on how the papers are to be accessed.

On the west side of town, the main drag, Hunter Street (now Martin Luther King Drive) was perhaps more of a "Movement street" than Auburn Avenue. The NAACP had headquarters on Hunter, as did movement attorney Howard Moore. In October 1962 SNCC moved its headquarters to the *Marx Building (8½ Raymond Street)* just off Hunter Street; there is a marker at this address. Ralph Abernathy's *West Hunter Street Baptist Church* was another movement center. The Pullman Porters Social Club and the movement-oriented *Atlanta Inquirer* newspaper (the *Atlanta Daily World* did not support sit-ins) were west Atlanta institutions. Black-owned eateries such as

HELP WANTED!!

Responsible position
2 hours Friday and
Saturday
PICKETING
DOWNTOWN
Immediate openings
Apply in person
Rush Memorial Church

—AD APPEARING IN THE
INTERCAMPUS VOICE,
JANUARY 7, 1961

"The Altanta Student Movement Had Begun"

"It began for me as it did for many more.

"About February 4, 1960, I was sitting in a cafe near my college campus in Atlanta, Georgia, a place where students went between or instead of classes.

"A student named Lonnie King approached me. He held up a copy of that day's *Atlanta Daily World*, Atlanta's daily black newspaper. The headline read 'Greensboro Students Sit-in for Third Day!'

Julian Bond

"The story told, in exact detail, how black college students from North Carolina A & T University in Greensboro had, for the third day in a row, entered a Woolworth's department store and asked for service at the whites-only lunch counter. It described their demeanor, their dress, and their determination to return the following day—and as many successive days as it took—if they were not served.

"'Have you seen this?' he demanded.

"'Yes, I have,' I replied.

"'What do you think about it?' he inquired.

"'I think it's great!'

"'Don't you think it ought to happen here?' he asked.

"'Oh, I'm sure it will happen here,' I responded. 'Surely someone here will do it.'

"Then to me, as it came to others in those early days in 1960, a query, an invitation, and a command:

"Why don't we make it happen here?

"He and I and Joe Pierce canvassed the cafe, talking to students, inviting them to discuss the Greensboro event and to duplicate it in Atlanta. The Atlanta student movement had begun."

—JULIAN BOND TO CHARLIE COBB

Paschals Restaurant & Coffee Shop (*830 West Hunter
Street; closed in 1996*) and **Frasier's Cafe Society** (*800
Hunter Street; also closed*) were regular meeting places for
discussions of strategy or just general relaxed conversation.
After the first arrested student protesters were released on
bond, Paschal's gave them free chicken dinners.

Like students across the South, Atlanta's young adults
were inspired by the February 1 Greensboro sit-ins, and
not long afterward Julian Bond, Marian Wright, Ruby
Doris Smith, Herschelle Sullivan, Lonnie King, and other
student leaders organized the Committee on Appeal for
Human Rights (COAHR) and began planning their own
lunch-counter sit-ins. But Atlanta's cautious and conservative civil rights old guard asked the students to hold off,
and the students instead placed a full-page advertisement
titled "Appeal for Human Rights" in the March 9 *Atlanta
Daily World*, *Atlanta Constitution*, and *Atlanta Journal*
newspapers. The "appeal" demanded an end to segregation in restaurants, movie theaters, and other places of
public accommodations. It also declared that they had run

out of patience. "Today's youth will not sit by submissively, while being denied all the rights, privileges and joys of life. . . . We do not intend to wait placidly for those rights which are already legally and morally ours to be meted out to us one at a time." The full text of the appeal can be viewed at the Robert W. Woodruff Library.

Because it was ignored by city officialdom, the appeal was soon followed by protest. On the morning of March 15, students staged highly organized sit-ins at ten lunch counters, including the railroad and bus stations, cafeterias in the Georgia Capitol, the county courthouse, and Atlanta City Hall. Of about two hundred students who participated, seventy-seven were arrested. The students then decided to hone in on Atlanta's premier downtown department store, **Rich's** *(61 Forsyth Street; closed in 1991, the building is now part of the Sam Nunn Atlanta Federal Center)*. The thinking was, as protest leader Julian Bond put it: "If Rich's went, so would everybody else."

And it was at Rich's that the student-led Atlanta movement literally changed the course of American politics. On October 19, 1960, the students persuaded Martin Luther King to join their sit-in at the department store's Magnolia Tea Room restaurant. He was arrested with them, and, like the students, he refused bail. Atlanta mayor William B. Hartsfield ordered the students released on October 24, but Dr. King was held for a hearing to decide whether participation in the protest put him in violation of probation on an earlier traffic conviction in nearby DeKalb County (for failure to switch his Alabama driving license to one from Georgia within the prescribed

> Close out your charge account with segregation; open up your account with freedom.
>
> —ATLANTA BOYCOTT SLOGAN

Picketing in support of the boycott

October 25, 1960, Martin Luther King is escorted from jail to the courthouse for a hearing on whether his arrest for participation in a student-led sit-in violated his probation on an earlier traffic violation.

time). At the hearing, Judge Oscar Mitchell, who had originally given King jail time for the traffic infraction, ruled that King had violated his probation. At 3:30 A.M. on October 26, the civil rights leader was rousted from bed in the county jail, shackled, and shipped off to the Georgia State Prison in Reidsville, 220 miles southeast of Atlanta, where he was to serve four months on a chain gang. A pregnant and very worried Mrs. King received a telephone call of sympathy from John F. Kennedy, who was running against Richard Nixon for the U.S. presidency. "I know this must be very hard for you," Mrs. King recalled the candidate saying. "I understand you are expecting a baby and I just wanted you to know that I was thinking about you and Dr. King. If there is anything I can do to help, please call me." The next day, Kennedy's brother, Robert, secretly negotiated King's release with Judge Mitchell and even got the charge dropped. At a celebratory mass meeting the evening of his son's release, a grateful Daddy King, who was a major Black Republican Party leader, pledged his support to Democratic Party candidate Kennedy. "Because this man was willing to wipe the tears from my daughter's eyes, I've got a suitcase of votes and I'm going to take them to Mr. Kennedy and dump them in his lap."

Flyers detailing the John Kennedy–Coretta King exchange were produced by the Kennedy campaign. Titled "The Case of Martin Luther King" and subtitled "'No Comment' Nixon versus a Candidate with a Heart, Senator Kennedy," the flyers, called the "blue bombs," for the color of their paper, were distributed only to Afro-American voters. This swung tens of thousands of black votes to Kennedy and was decisive in the senator's narrow victory (34,227,096 popular votes to Richard Nixon's 34,107,646). At the **Sam Nunn Atlanta Federal Center** *(the former site of Rich's)* on Forsyth Street, a 30- by 130-foot mural depicting significant events in the department store's history includes that October 19 sit-in. Drawing on a photograph that appeared in the *Atlanta Constitution*, a large mural of colored ceramic tiles, titled *Sitting Down at Rich's*, directly faces the main lobby. It shows Martin Luther King, Morehouse student leader Lonnie King, Spelman student leader Marilyn Pryce, and another Spelman student activist, Ida Rose McCree, who is carrying a sign that reads WE WANT TO SIT DOWN LIKE EVERYONE ELSE. There are also, on the wall of the corridor leading to the cafeteria, 8- by 10-inch ceramic tiles presenting other depictions of the October 19 sit-in. One shows Dr. King under arrest with three students.

Of course, civil rights struggle in Atlanta involved more than its students. Significant stops worth making on the city's civil rights trail include the **West Hunter Street Baptist Church** *(1040 Ralph David Abernathy Boulevard SW since 1973; the church was formerly at 775 Hunter Street)*, pastored by Rev. King's closest friend, Reverend Ralph David Abernathy. Both men had moved to Atlanta from Montgomery, where they had first met and emerged as key leaders of the bus boycott in that city. West

This letter comes to you at this time because of the resumption of activity... by students in the Atlanta University Center and the possible participation by your daughter who is enrolled at Spelman College. Demonstrations may include sit-ins, stand-ins, kneel-ins and related activities. Some, if not all of these activities could lead to arrest, and jail terms if bail is refused.

Spelman College sympathizes with the students in their goal to achieve full human rights. Although we shall continue to consult with and offer advice to the students, the decision whether or not to participate in demonstrations is one to be made by each individual student. Therefore, the institution cannot accept responsibility for your daughter's participation in any of these demonstrations and the possible consequences.

—LETTER TO PARENTS FROM DR. AUDREY MANLEY, PRESIDENT OF SPELMAN COLLEGE, OCTOBER 17, 1960

A lively civil rights discussion in Georgia. Our community meetings created an environment where all people felt they could speak.

Hunter Street's previous pastor, Reverend A. Franklin Fisher, was one of the six black clergymen arrested in the 1957 bus protest. Under Abernathy the church continued active advocacy of civil rights. Abernathy died April 17, 1990, and is buried at **Lincoln Cemetery** *(2275 Simpson Road NW)*. The inscription on his tombstone is I TRIED.

Other churches that played important movement roles are **Big Bethel AME** *(220 Auburn Avenue)*, for years the largest meeting space in Atlanta's Afro-American community; **Mount Moriah Baptist Church** *(200 Joseph E. Lowery Boulevard SW)*, where students met to plan their October sit-in at Rich's; and **Rush Memorial Congregational Church** *(150 James P. Brawley Drive SW)*, where training in nonviolent techniques of protest took place.

And when negotiations were concluded to end a three-month boycott of downtown white-owned Atlanta stores, the provision (signed by ten of the city's elder black leaders and the local Chamber of Commerce) only vaguely guaranteed desegregation, which in any case would begin no sooner than the following fall. Students denounced the agreement at a March 10, 1961, meeting at **Warren Memorial United**

Methodist Church *(181 Joseph E. Lowery Boulevard SW).*
Even Martin Luther King Sr. was upbraided for supporting
the deal, and it took pleas for unity from his late-arriving
son to calm students.

No reference to Atlanta's movement churches can
exclude the **Wheat Street Baptist Church** *(359 Auburn*
Avenue), which was presided over by Reverend William
Holmes Borders for fifty years. When the movie *Gone With*
the Wind premiered in Atlanta in 1939, Borders publicly
denounced it as a racist, false, romanticized depiction of
slavery. He also rebuked Daddy King for his decision to
allow the Ebenezer church choir, wearing bandanas, to
sing at the event. In 1946 Borders set up a fund to catch the
men who, in an infamous Georgia murder, shot two black
couples hundreds of times at the **Moore's Ford Bridge**
(roadside marker on U.S. 78, six miles east of Monroe, 60
miles east of Atlanta) following an argument with a white
farmer. It was also Rev. Borders who led black preachers
onto white seats in city buses in 1957. When he was a boy,
Martin Luther King Jr. sometimes sat enthralled in the
balcony of Borders's church.

Today's Atlanta, for all the unsettled issues of poverty
and poor public education that beset this city—as they do
cities across the nation—may be the clearest symbol of the
southern civil rights movement's accomplishment in the
political arena. SNCC's John Lewis is now the congressional
representative from the Fifth Congressional District. SCLC's
Andrew Young held the seat before Lewis and for two terms
was also the mayor of Atlanta. And Julian Bond, who served
several terms in the Georgia state legislature, is now board
chair of the NAACP. There continues to be a thriving class of
black entrepreneurs; among its members, CORE Freedom
Rider Hank Thomas, who wound up prospering in the city
as the owner of several McDonald's restaurants. Atlanta's
black bourgeoisie is in many respects "the establishment"
now, making the city attractive to kith and kin around the
United States. According to the Travel Industry Association
of America, Afro-American tourists choose Atlanta as their
favorite U.S. city to visit and account for about 25 percent of

the city's tourists each year. Every two years the **National Black Arts Festival** is held in Atlanta.

Still, for all this, there is unfinished business in Atlanta, symbolic—and real at the same time—of the business left undone everywhere as opportunities created by the movement were seized by some while others were left behind. The continuing high rate of poverty and huge deficiencies in the public education system remain especially visible as immense, seemingly intractable problems in need of solution. Dr. King had put these at the top of his list of priorities, but he was assassinated. Just how and when they will be successfully tackled remains unclear.

Ruby Doris

SNCC's real "boss"—or as many of us thought of her, the glue that held our organization together—Ruby Doris Smith Robinson died of cancer October 7, 1967, at the very young age of twenty-five. In many ways, SNCC died with her. This most heroic of Atlantans is buried in the city at the **South-View Cemetery** *(1990 Jonesboro Road, SE)*. Henry McNeil Turner is also buried there, as are Martin Luther King Jr.'s parents and Horace Mann Bond, the renowned educator and the father of Julian Bond. The epitaph on Ruby Doris's headstone aptly sums up our movement spirit and is worth carrying away from Atlanta with you: IF YOU THINK FREE, YOU ARE FREE.

Ruby Doris Smith Robinson

ALBANY

❝ *The first obstacle to remove . . . was the mental block in the minds of those who wanted to move but were unable for fear that we were not who we said we were. But when people began to hear us in churches, social meetings, on the streets, in the pool halls, lunchrooms, nightclubs, and other places where people gather, they began to open up a bit. We would tell them of how it feels to be in prison, what it means to be behind bars, in jail for the cause. We explained to them that we had stopped school because we felt compelled to do so since so many of us were in chains. We explained further that there were worse chains than jail and prison . . . We mocked the system that teaches men to be good Negroes instead of good men.* **❞**

—CHARLES SHERROD, 1961

Southwest Georgia would not concede to change as readily as Atlanta did. This resistance, as stiff as the region's red clay after a rain, reflects more than the difference between city and countryside. Southwest Georgia's landscape of peanuts, pecans, and corn makes it more akin to rural Alabama and Mississippi, where wealth and power are concentrated in white hands but are trumped by white poverty and the suppressed anger—often misdirected at blacks—that accompanies it. Far too often in these places, the large number of blacks relative to whites is considered a threat, and white violence is always close to the surface.

So, in October 1961, when SNCC's Charles Sherrod and Cordell Reagon arrived in Albany, 166 miles south of Atlanta and the largest city in the region, its black residents

SNCC
Southwest
Georgia
project director
Charles
Sherrod
visiting a
potential
registrant
in the rural
countryside.
SNCC field
secretary
Randy Battle
is seated on the
porch.

often crossed the street to avoid these "Freedom Riders." The two young men were not known, and the fear was that they would "start something," then leave when the inevitable reprisals came down on any local people associated with them. But the two SNCC field secretaries (later joined by Charles Jones from Charlotte, North Carolina) dug in, holding conversations to explain their purpose and get people used to their presence.

Albany was a kind of crossroads, a quiet town on the surface that could be considered moderate in its racial attitude when compared to the surrounding counties, which bore the nicknames "Terrible" Terrell, "Dogging" Douglas, "Unmitigated" Mitchell, "Lamentable" Lee, "Bad" Baker, and "Unworthy" Worth. Rooted in the slavers' belief in their right to keep blacks totally subjugated, all these counties had long been known for their vicious intolerance. The majority population of the region's counties was still black; but not that of Albany. When Sherrod and Reagon arrived in 1961, blacks represented 40 percent of the city's total population. A small area of successful black enterprise existed in a section of Albany commonly called Harlem, on the south side of Oglethorpe Boulevard (U.S. 82). That plus the existence of historically black Albany State College made the city a logical place to set up a home base, a place to take a first step in organizing work. In Albany, the organizers thought, it might be possible to set an inspirational standard for the difficult and far more dangerous work in the nearby rural counties where they planned to start working that winter.

Dissatisfaction was not difficult to find in Albany's black community. Many streets were unpaved, poverty was the rule, and police violence was a fact of life. As early as 1947, a Voters League had been organized, and by 1958 almost 20 percent of the black community had registered to vote. In 1959 an NAACP Youth Council was organized. Greensboro's impact was also felt in this Deep South city; in 1960 thirty-five high school students seated themselves in the white section of a movie house, leaving when the police arrived.

Just before Sherrod and Reagon came to town, a group of Afro-American ministers had written a letter asking the city government for a discussion of racial issues, stressing the need for paved roads and sewage lines. The city did not even bother to respond, although the local newspaper, the *Albany Herald*, denounced the ministers for making the request. The home of one member of this ministerial group was bombed shortly afterward. Despite all this, there was little expectation that one of the civil rights movement's most difficult early battles would take place in the streets of Albany, particularly because the main mission of Sherrod and Reagon was voter registration. But the cards that Fate sometimes deals are not necessarily for the game you expected to play. With "Freedom Riders" in town, Albany's students were impatient for action. And so, less than a month after the arrival of the SNCC organizers, nine students entered the white waiting room of the **Continental Trailways bus station** *(corner of East Oglethorpe Boulevard and Jackson Street)*. They left when asked, but filed affidavits with the Interstate Commerce Commission.

On November 17 the Albany Movement—a coalition of community groups that included the Ministerial Alliance, the NAACP Youth Council, the Negro Voters League, and the Federation of Women's Clubs—was born. Dr. William Anderson, an osteopath, became its president. Direct action accelerated. On November 22 three high school students from the NAACP Youth Council returned to the bus station and were arrested for refusing to leave the dining room. Later that afternoon, two Albany State College students, Bertha Gober and Blanton Hall, were also arrested after entering Trailways's white waiting room; unlike the three before them, Gober and Hall declined bail. The two were expelled from school, and, in protest, students marched on President William Dennis's campus home. On November 25 the first mass meeting was held at *Mount Zion Baptist Church (324 Whitney Avenue; it is now the Albany Civil Rights Museum)*. President Dennis, a member of the church, attended the meeting and defended his action.

For the next few weeks a string of protests continued to challenge segregation. On December 10, an integrated group of students from Atlanta rode into Albany. The five blacks entered the white side of the Central of Georgia Railroad Terminal, and the five whites entered the black side. They were all arrested. Two days later more than four hundred high school students marched downtown to protest these arrests and were arrested.

On December 15 Martin Luther King drove down from Atlanta. He had been invited to speak by Dr. Anderson, who had been one of his classmates at Morehouse. That night, speaking to a huge mass meeting at *Shiloh Baptist Church (325 Whitney Avenue at Jefferson)*, King enthusiastically embraced the Albany movement,

Rutha Harris of the Freedom Singers, the group formed in Sherrod's workshops, moved to the center of the platform and the din ceased abruptly, just in time for her overpowering contralto to switch songs:

I woke up this morning with my mind
... the crowd finished her line
SET ON FREEDOM
I woke up this morning with my mind
SET ON FREEDOM
Three times she led them in this call and response, and then they all raised the one-word chorus:
HALLELU—HALLELU—
HALLELUJAH!"

—TAYLOR BRANCH ON SINGING AT
THE DECEMBER 15 ALBANY MASS
MEETING AT SHILOH

pledging his support to joyous applause and amens. Author Taylor Branch was there and writes of the response to his entrance, "King was sighted on his way down to the pulpit [and] the sound exploded into cascades of rapture . . . FREE-DOM, FREE-DOM / Martin King says freedom / Martin King says freedom." A sign in front of the church today reads THE ALBANY CIVIL RIGHTS MOVEMENT STARTED HERE. Too many people had shown up for just one church, so when Rev. King finished speaking at Shiloh, he walked across the street to an equally enthusiastic crowd at an equally full Mount Zion Baptist Church.

The walls of both churches literally shook with the sound of powerful song. One of the unique characteristics of Albany's movement was the tremendous strength of its music. Even news reporters sometimes paused from taking notes, awed by the sound. Branch writes, "No one played the piano or organ for either the freedom songs or the church hymns . . . All sounds, from the soaring gospel descants of the soprano soloists to the thunderous handclapping of the congregation, were created by human flesh." Bernice Johnson Reagon, who years later would found

"Over My Head I See Freedom in the Air"

"I really did not know a lot about organizing. It mostly operated as breaking the rules and stepping out of line. There were many rules and many lines. If you grew up black in the south at that time, the people who love you lay out a path. To the extent that you stayed on that path—and it's not always up to you whether you can or not—you have a chance; not only of surviving, but of actually making a contribution to your people. And I was very much projected to be on that course. But when you start to do things that clash with what your parents think will keep you alive, you feel an incredible pressure from your community because there is the sense that you are inviting suicide. And there is nothing anybody can do to help you if you step [too far] out of line.

"One of the first indications internally for me that something had happened to me was when I did my first freedom song after the first march in Albany, Georgia. When we got back to the church, they say, 'Bernice, sing a song.' And I sing 'Over my head I see freedom in the air.' Now that's a spiritual. I know all the words to the spiritual and there's no 'freedom' in that spiritual. The first line I usually sing in that song is 'trouble.' But I knew we were in trouble. I didn't think that would help anybody. And so, as I sang the line I flipped the text [to 'freedom'] and watched everybody in the room resettle under the singing of that song, because they joined in the second line, which repeats—'Over my head, I see freedom in the air.' And in some way, I hadn't just stepped out of place; I'd crossed something that I was never going to go back into."

—BERNICE JOHNSON REAGON ON AN INSTITUTE
FOR POLICY STUDIES PANEL

the singing group Sweet Honey in the Rock, may be the best-known of Albany's movement voices, but the voices of Rutha Harris, her brother Emory, and Bertha Gober also inspired masses of sometimes uncertain and fearful people about to engage in protest that directly challenged white supremacy. In a 1961 field report to SNCC, Charles Sherrod vividly described young Bertha Gober's effect at the city's first civil rights mass meeting in November: "As Bertha, with her small frame and baby voice, told of spending Thanksgiving in jail along with other physical inconveniences, there was not a dry eye to be found. And when we rose to sing 'We shall Overcome,' nobody knew what kept the top of the church on its four walls. It was as if everyone had been lifted up on high." Bertha Gober's own haunting but affirmative "We'll Never Turn Back" rivals "We Shall Overcome" as a movement anthem. And few in the movement have forgotten the clear golden tenor of Cordell Reagon, just eighteen years old when he came to Albany from Nashville. It is almost impossible to recapture the powerful effect of music in Albany, but once a month at Mount Zion, a group of "freedom singers" sing and tell stories. Using newspaper clippings, photographs, and the memories of participants, the Mount Zion museum effectively conveys the intensity of those days and manages to present to visitors Albany's complex civil rights history.

One block away from the two churches, at **Charles Sherrod Civil Rights Park** (*Jackson and Highland Streets*), an inscription on a black granite memorial describes Albany's civil rights story. Footprints in the concrete sidewalk at the Jackson Street side of the park enable visitors to follow the route of protest marches (*north on Jackson Street past*

Martin Luther King and Ralph Abernathy being taken to jail in Albany

Oglethorpe Boulevard and Broad Street on to Pine Avenue). In those days the city jail faced Pine Avenue, too; marchers were herded into a side alley for processing. There were more than a thousand arrests at Albany's City Hall in the fall and early winter of 1961, so many that they had to be farmed out to jails in the surrounding counties.

The day after speaking at Shiloh and Mount Zion churches, Dr. King, Rev. Ralph Abernathy, and Dr. Anderson led a march of some 250 people to the county courthouse and were arrested. King refused bail. While they were in jail, talks between city officials and Albany Movement leaders resulted in a few small concessions: desegregation of train and bus facilities and a pledge to listen to blacks' concerns at the city's next business meeting. King posted bond and returned to Atlanta. The deal reached with city officials turned out to be worthless, and so the Albany Movement launched a bus boycott and a boycott of selected downtown businesses. In February King came back to Albany for trial; after his conviction for trespassing and disorderly conduct, the judge postponed sentencing.

A new wave of protests began in July when King and Abernathy were being sentenced. They were given the choice of paying a $178 fine or serving forty-five days in jail. They chose to serve time, but a mysterious "well-dressed Negro man" paid their fine two days later and they were released; Albany's police chief, Laurie Prichett, later admitted that he had arranged for the payment. "Frankly, it was a matter of strategy," he said. "I knew that if he [King] stayed in jail we'd continue to have problems." King promised to "turn Albany upside down," and for the next two weeks waves of protesters poured into the streets. When a federal injunction specifically naming King and other movement leaders banned further marches, King decided to obey it.

On July 21, though, a preacher by the name of Samuel B. Wells stood up during a mass meeting at Shiloh Baptist Church and declared that *he* was going to march. "I can hear the blood of Emmett Till coming from the ground!" said Wells, marching out the door. One hundred sixty people followed him. They were all arrested while King watched. Three days later the injunction was overturned on appeal and another march took place. And it was an angry march. Word had spread through the black community that Marion King, the pregnant wife of Albany Movement vice president Slater King, had been kicked in the stomach and knocked to the ground by two policemen when she attempted to bring food to friends being held in the Mitchell County jail in the town of Camilla. Mrs. King lost the baby. When police tried to halt them, the outraged marchers began throwing rocks and bottles. Chief Prichett called off his policemen but spoke to reporters, asking sarcastically, "Did you see those nonviolent rocks?" Rev. King halted the marches for one day, a Gandhian "day of penance," because the code of nonviolence had been broken, he said. Even though a day later he was arrested while leading a prayer vigil in front of City Hall and served his longest prison time ever (two weeks), the tension between his efforts and the local movement was evident and probably insurmountable. King left town and always thought of Albany as a failure: "The mistake I made there was to protest against segregation generally rather than against a single distinct

During a July 24, 1962, mass meeting in Albany, Georgia, participants chant "Freedom" and wave papers they have signed pledging to go to jail in the next day's protest.

Martin Luther King being arrested by Albany police chief Laurie Pritchett

facet of it. Our protest was so vague that we got nothing."

In Albany, Martin Luther King had come up against something he had never encountered before in leading protests: sophisticated police opposition. "I did research," said Laurie Prichett years later. "I found his method was nonviolence . . . to fill the jails, same as Gandhi in India. And once they filled the jails, we'd have no capacity to arrest and then we'd have to give in to his demands. I sat down and took a map. How many jails was in a fifteen-mile radius, how many was in a thirty-mile radius? And I contacted those authorities. They assured us that we could use their [jails]." In sight of news media, anyway, Prichett's methods were restrained; no police dogs or fire hoses in Albany. He ordered his officers to make arrests under laws protecting the public order, rather than under the more legally uncertain segregation laws. He also permitted King to hold staff meetings in jail.

In any case, Albany was hardly a failure. As Charles Sherrod put it, "Now I can't help how Dr. King might have felt, or . . . any of the rest of them in SCLC, NAACP, CORE, any of the groups, but as far as we were concerned, things moved on. We didn't skip one beat." A community of people standing with straighter backs emerged. Just two months after King left, successful voter registration efforts led to Afro-American businessman Thomas Chatmon's winning enough votes for a city commission seat to force a run-off election. In the spring of 1963 the city commission removed all the segregation statutes from its books. And Sherrod had been right: The work in Albany helped ease the way into the surrounding counties. But it did not decrease the danger. While Dr. King was in jail that last time, Sherrod and other SNCC workers were organizing outside the city.

On July 25 they were conducting a voter registration meeting at **Mount Olive Church** in Sasser, Georgia, a tiny town in "Terrible" Terrell County. Sheriff Zeke Matthews charged in with a dozen deputies who moved from pew to pew rubbing their pistols, slapping flashlights into the palms of their hands while staring at terrorized participants and saying "I know you." Matthews himself announced that whites were "fed up with this registering business." A few days later the church was bombed.

Charles Sherrod never left Albany, and he served on the city council from 1976 until 1990. Due to an influx from countryside to city, Afro-Americans now make up more than 50 percent of Albany's population. Ironically, something of the reverse is true in the rural counties that once had substantial black majorities; in most, nowadays, Afro-Americans are a minority. Sherrod now teaches at Albany State University, a school that once considered him a troublemaker. "They used to run me off that campus," says the civil rights veteran.

The Albany Movement was genuinely a local movement in which many heroes and heroines can be found. But on the

Albany protester Eddie Brown, a former gang leader, goes "limp" in nonviolent protest and has to be carried by police.

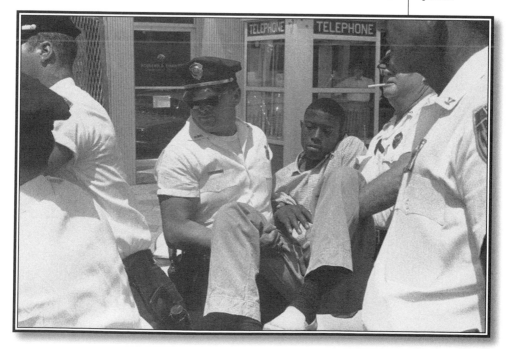

> "What did we win? We won our self-respect. It changed all my attitudes. This movement [in Albany] made me demand a semblance of first-class citizenship."
>
> —ANONYMOUS ALBANY BLACK CITIZEN

stage of civil rights struggle in Albany, perhaps no family deserves the spotlight more than the King family (no relation to the Atlanta Kings). I think of them standing at the *King family plot* in the *Oakview Cemetery (200 Cotton Avenue)*. Clennon Washington King founded Albany's NAACP. Chevene Bowers "C. B." King, one of the eldest of Clennon's seven children, was a graduate of Fisk and for a time the only black attorney in southwest Georgia. *Attorney King's office (221½ South Jackson Street, now part of the Ritz Cultural Center)* was the hub of legal defense for civil rights activists throughout the region. C. B.'s younger brother, Slater Hunter King, was one of the militant voices in Albany's movement and was arrested several times, and ultimately he replaced Dr. Anderson as head of that movement. He died tragically and young in a 1969 automobile accident in Dawson, Georgia. In 1961 another of the brothers, Preston King, fled the country after a racially motivated conviction for draft evasion. He had demanded that Albany's all-white draft board address him as "mister," and his student deferment was denied. Finally, the eldest of the King boys, Clennon Washington King Jr., applied to the University of Mississippi in 1958 (well before James Meredith's 1962 admission) and was declared insane and kept in a segregated Mississippi asylum until his brother C. B. secured his release. On the eve of the 1976 presidential election, this King attempted to join and integrate Jimmy Carter's all-white Maranatha Baptist Church in nearby Plains, Georgia.

❧ SAVANNAH ❧

---

*Three characteristic things one might have seen in
Sherman's raid through Georgia, which threw the
new situation in shadowy relief: the Conqueror,
the Conquered, and the Negro. Some see all
significance in the grim front of the destroyer, and
some in the bitter sufferers of the Lost Cause. But to
me neither soldier nor fugitive speaks with so deep
a meaning as that dark human cloud that clung
like remorse on the rear of those swift columns,
swelling at times to half their size, almost engulfing
and choking them. In vain were they ordered back,
in vain were bridges hewn from beneath their feet;
on they trudged and writhed and surged, until
they rolled into Savannah, a starved and naked
horde of tens of thousands. There too came the
characteristic military remedy: "The islands from
Charleston south, the abandoned rice-fields along
the rivers for thirty miles back from the sea, and
the country bordering the St. John's River, Florida,
are reserved and set apart for the settlement of
Negroes now made free by act of war." So read the
celebrated "Field-order Number Fifteen."*

—W. E. B. Du Bois, 1903

Forty acres and a mule, which was what field-order number fifteen promised, seems little to grant to former slaves after more than two hundred years of unrequited toil. It seems especially appropriate that it was announced at the birthplace of the cotton gin. After capturing the city with ease on December 22, 1864, William Tecumseh Sherman offered artillery and 25,000 bales of cotton to

President Abraham Lincoln as an early Christmas present: "I beg to present to you, as a Christmas gift, the city of Savannah, with 150 heavy guns and plenty of ammunition, and also about 25,000 bales of cotton," telegraphed the conquering general to the doomed president, who would be assassinated a few months later. Sherman issued his field order just four days after a January 12 meeting with twenty Afro-American leaders at his **Green-Meldrim House headquarters** *(Madison Square at 1 West Macon Street)* seeking their advice on what to do with the thousands of freed slaves following his troops. Lincoln had already approved the idea of granting land. One wonders what the South and the nation would be like today if Andrew Johnson had not reversed Sherman's field order when he became president after Lincoln's murder.

Those who visit this city of storied antebellum hauteur can approach it in terms of either the civil rights struggle or the slave trade that generated the city's wealth. The two, as we have seen all along our trail, are entwined. As you might expect, a range of tours focused on the Civil War or the antebellum era are available. To help balance that history, a visit to the city's **Laurel Grove-South Cemetery** *(2101 Kollock Street)* is an essential Savannah stop. In 1852 fifteen acres of the Laurel Grove Cemetery were set aside for the burial of "free persons of color and slaves." It was originally connected to the main cemetery, but the construction of Interstate 16 through downtown Savannah separates the burial grounds today. Studded with cypress trees, this site contains the largest number of free blacks of any cemetery in the state of Georgia. Among them is Andrew Bryan. Born into slavery, Bryan managed to purchase his freedom and was converted to the Baptist faith by Reverend George Leile, who in 1777 founded the First Colored Church, which in 1822 became the **First African Baptist Church** *(23 Montgomery Street on historic Franklin Square, where a fire brigade was manned by free and enslaved Afro-Americans in the 1820s; church tours can be arranged).* When the British were defeated by American revolutionists and evacuated Savannah in 1782, Leile left America with them and Bryan took over the church. In 1859 the congregation erected the first black-owned brick building in the state of Georgia, and for years thereafter First African Baptist was known as the "Brick Church." It served as a stop on the Underground Railroad, and beneath some of the wooden floorboards you can still see where runaway slaves were hidden. Another unique feature of the church is stained-glass windows depicting Afro-American subjects. There is also a small museum containing archives and memorabilia going back to the eighteenth century. Nearby, an **Andrew Bryan Marker** *(500 block of West Bryan Street, across from First Bryan Church, the church he set up before becoming the second pastor of First African Baptist)* credits him with being the father of black Baptists.

After his death on July 29, 2002, seventy-nine-year-old Westley Wallace "W. W." Law, a mailman who had been Savannah's NAACP president for twenty-six years, was buried at Laurel Grove-South. Because of his civil rights activities, Law was fired from his federal job in 1961, but pressure from the NAACP's national leadership forced his reinstatement. In his later years, Law, a historian and preservationist, crusaded to refurbish and replace damaged headstones in the cemetery. Inscriptions on many of the tombstones record Afro-American history not included in written histories of the region. Law also led the Yamacraw branch of Carter G. Woodson's Association for the Study of Negro Life and History and often said that his "biggest fear [is] for youth to forget and take for granted the time that was spent bringing diversity into our culture." Law founded Savannah's **Negro Heritage Trail Tour** *(502 E. Harris Street)*, a bus tour to sites of Savannah's rich Afro-American history.

As early as 1948, Savannah's racial segregation faced direct challenge when the Freedom Train carrying the original Declaration of Independence and United States Constitution came to the city. The NAACP Youth Council passed a resolution denouncing as "a shameful disgrace" the requirement of separate lines for whites and blacks who came to view the documents.

In later years, the February 1 Greensboro sit-in triggered sustained student protest in Savannah. On March 16, 1960, Joan Tyson, Carolyn Quilloin, and Ernest Robinson, of the NAACP Youth Council, entered *Levy's Department Store* (*201 East Broughton Street; now the site of the Savannah College of Art and Design library*), took seats in the Azalea Room, and were arrested. It was Savannah's first sit-in. Within days, black students began sit-ins at other downtown stores. There were also wade-ins on *Tybee Island*, a popular Savannah tourist destination then and now. (Incidentally, unnoticed by almost everyone, beneath some of that island's condominiums there are slave pens, one of the last remaining indicators of Savannah's important role as a slave port.) Shortly after these protests, the new movement called for a boycott of downtown stores until the owners abandoned segregation, hired blacks for more than menial labor, and addressed black adults courteously, as in, "May I help you, sir (or ma'am)?"

The city's response was to use whatever force it deemed necessary. Police violence, tear gas, police dogs, general harassment, and intimidation were all "necessary." In April 1960 the Savannah City Council forbade picketing of any business by two or more people. There were more "wade-ins" at nearby beaches, "kneel-ins" and "pray-ins" at all-white churches, "ride-ins" on the buses, and even what someone dubbed a "piss-in" at a segregated restroom. The boycott steadily squeezed downtown businesses, and several were forced to close. Finally, in June 1961, Savannah's bus company agreed to begin hiring blacks; in October desegregation of restaurants began and the boycott finally ended after fifteen months. No city, not even Montgomery with its 1955–56 bus boycott, has ever had a longer-lasting civil rights boycott.

Not every place desegregated, however, and some that had, backslid. Local movie theaters resegregated in June 1963. Large-scale marches and mass arrests resumed. Leading the campaign for desegregation was Hosea Williams. A research chemist at the U.S. Department of Agriculture in Savannah, Williams was one of the first federally employed Afro-American researchers in the South. He was also a World War II veteran. On the way home at the end of the war, Williams was badly beaten by a gang of whites in Americus, Georgia, when he tried to get a drink of water from a whites-only canteen in a segregated bus station. In 1957 he helped integrate the *Nancy Hanks II* passenger train, which ran from Savannah to Atlanta.

During his lunch hour, Williams sometimes stood atop **Tomochichi Rock** *(Wright Square, in front of the county courthouse),* urging sit-ins in nearby restaurants. (Tomochichi was a chief of the Yamacraws, part of the Creek nation, who assisted James Oglethorpe and his settlers when they first arrived. On the sixtieth anniversary of Tomochichi's death, a huge rock from Stone Mountain, Georgia, was brought to Savannah to mark his grave.) Hosea Williams spent sixty-five days in jail during these protests—no other civil rights leader spent that much continuous time in jail. Riots that followed his arrest resulted in the burning of Savannah's Sears and Firestone stores.

Using a "ballot bus," Williams also sought to increase Savannah's already high level of black voter registration.

In Savannah, demonstrators lie down on the sidewalk, awaiting arrest.

> I am going to do what I believe is right and Godly, irregardless what they say about me . . . My pay, my gratitude will come to me after death.
>
> —HOSEA WILLIAMS

Fifty-seven percent of eligible blacks were registered to vote in 1960 (about a third of all voters), and this influenced the political dynamic of the city. Williams's wife, Juanita, campaigned for election as superior court clerk in 1961. Although she lost, the political establishment took notice of this campaign—the day had arrived in which black voting strength could not be ignored. Savannah soon converted from an at-large system to a district or neighborhood system. In 1966 Bobby Hill became the first black state legislator from Savannah since Reconstruction. In 1995 Floyd Adams Jr. became Savannah's first black mayor. Martin Luther King credited Williams—who became one of SCLC's most militant organizers, accumulating more than one hundred arrests—with making Savannah "the most integrated city in the South." King's remark makes Andy Young's view that Savannah was a "failure" a bit puzzling. "In many ways, Savannah was a replay of Albany. The demonstrators had more enthusiasm than discipline," Young wrote in his autobiography. And in a sharp criticism of Hosea Williams that still raises important issues pertinent to black struggle, Young goes on to say, "Part of the failure in Savannah was due to the fact that Hosea didn't fully understand the principles of nonviolence. He had a genuine passion for justice [but] Hosea's goal was to win rather than transform the relationships between the races in Savannah so that everybody could maintain their dignity and self-respect."

Churches, of course, played an important role in Savannah's civil rights movement. ***Bolton Street Baptist Church*** *(821 Martin Luther King Jr. Boulevard)* is the site of the first mass meeting, which took place on Sunday, March 20, 1960. Those who attended voted unanimously to boycott downtown stores, some even throwing their department-store charge cards from the balcony. Savannah's second mass meeting took place down the street at ***St. Philip AME Church*** *(613 Martin Luther King Boulevard)*, and the First

African Baptist Church on Montgomery Street was also a regularly used launch pad for civil rights protesters in the 1960s. On the steps of **Second African Baptist Church** *(123 Houston Street)*, Gen. Sherman read the Emancipation Proclamation to Savannah citizens. Rev. King preached a version of his "I Have a Dream" sermon here, too, before delivering it in Washington, D.C., in 1963.

Our last stop on the Savannah trail could just as well have been our first. The **Ralph Mark Gilbert Civil Rights Museum** *(460 Martin Luther King Jr. Boulevard)* gives visitors a comprehensive presentation of Savannah's overlooked civil rights story. Along with Hosea Williams and W. W. Law, Ralph Gilbert, who arrived to pastor First African Baptist in 1936, was the third crucial movement leader molding Savannah's civil rights struggle. As president of Savannah's NAACP from 1942 until 1950, Rev. Gilbert breathed new life into the organization, boosting its membership from two hundred to three thousand, orga-

Hosea Williams, June 20, 1970. Now Southern Christian Leadership Conference vice president, he gives instructions to young people at the Florence, S.C., campaign headquarters of Dr. Claud L. Stephens, who is running against Rep. John L. McMillan in the 6th Congressional District.

Groups Pay Homage to Hosea Williams

THE GUARDIAN, TUESDAY, NOVEMBER 21, 2000

ATLANTA (AP)—Foot soldiers in the civil rights movement who marched alongside Hosea Williams had called him Little David.

And long after his time in Martin Luther King Jr.'s army for equality, Williams continued his attack on modern day Goliaths like racism, greed and indifference, friends of the late activist said at a memorial service Monday.

"Hosea wasn't afraid. In fact, I don't think there's anything he was scared of," said the Rev. Joseph Lowery, who in 1957 co-founded the Southern Christian Leadership Conference.

In 1965, Williams had been at the helm of the Bloody Sunday march across the Edmund Pettus bridge in Selma, Ala. Police with clubs, tear gas and dogs attacked peaceful protesters seeking voting rights.

Williams died Thursday from kidney cancer complications. He was 74.

During Monday's eight-hour viewing, thousands of mourners streamed through the International Chapel at Morehouse College to pay homage at a casket where Williams' body lay dressed in trademark denim overalls, red shirt and red sneakers.

nizing around the state, and leading a registration drive that brought in hundreds of new black registrants.

On three floors the museum offers black-and-white photographs that focus on key events and personalities of the civil rights era from 1954 to 1968. There are interactive exhibits and a fiber-optic map of eighty-seven significant civil rights sites and events. The first floor features a bronze bust of Gilbert, and also a re-creation of the Azalea Room of Levy's Department Store, where blacks could buy clothing but could not eat in the restaurant. The mezzanine houses a theater, which is a facsimile of an Afro-American church sanctuary. A visual montage of West Broad Street's people and its commerce gives visitors a feel for the street as a center of black enterprise and activity—what was once called Savannah's "Black Mecca" of trade and commerce. There

A funeral service was planned for Tuesday in Atlanta. Afterward, a mule-drawn pallbearing carriage was to lead a procession through downtown, along the same route marched after King was slain in 1968.

The assassination didn't defeat the sense of brotherhood or duty in Williams.

In 1970, he began serving holiday dinners to the poor. The growing tradition was expected to draw 30,000 this year to Turner Field at Thanksgiving and, again, at Christmas. Despite Williams' death, the dinners are slated to carry on, operated by daughter Elisabeth Williams-Omilami and funded by rapper Sean Puffy Combs.

"He was faithful," said Robert Winfrey, 72. "He was a man who didn't like to see people hungry. He believed in what he was doing and he was dedicated to it."

At the viewing, tributes to his courage included a gold medal inscribed with King's I have a dream motto, an American flag for military service rendered in Germany during World War II and hymns from the darkest days of the civil rights era, sung at the memorial's close.

"He was one of the last true activists," said Renee Dawson, who brought her 6-year-old daughter, Riana. "I wanted Riana to see him, and understand that because of him there's a lot of people better off."

are lecture halls, classrooms, a computer room, a video and reading room, and an Afro-American book collection for children. The physical structure of the museum itself is an example of the kind of preservation that W. W. Law encouraged. The building first housed the Wage Earners Savings and Loan, America's second-largest black-owned bank at the time. It became the home of the Savannah branch of the NAACP before falling into a period of neglect and disrepair. Law led a campaign of restoration, challenging Savannah as perhaps the whole South and, indeed, the entire nation, should be challenged: "If we are going to have an integrated society, then there has to be an appreciation of the contribution that *everybody* made . . . You see young people who have no idea how we got here and the sacrifices made."

CHAPTER SEVEN

LOOK BACKWARD, MOVE FORWARD

Montgomery, Selma, Lowndes County, Perry County, and Birmingham, Alabama

" There comes a time when people get tired of being trampled over by the iron feet of oppression. There comes a time, my friends, when people get tired of being plunged across the abyss of humiliation. "

—MARTIN LUTHER KING JR., 1955

The names and events associated with modern civil rights struggle in Alabama resonate with particular power: the Montgomery bus boycott and Rosa Parks; Governor George Wallace attempting to block court-ordered desegregation of the University of Alabama by standing in the schoolhouse door; the children's crusade in Birmingham and the dogs and fire hoses used against protesters; the Selma-to-Montgomery march and the fierce assault by state police on the Edmund Pettus Bridge; the bombing of the Freedom Rider bus in Anniston; the Sunday morning bombing that killed four children at the Sixteenth Street Baptist Church in Birmingham. All these events are burned into the national consciousness.

Alabama was one of the first southern states to recognize that there was value in marking civil rights sites to encourage tourism, and in many places acknowledgment of the wrongs found in its ugly racial history coexists with monuments to racism. So, for example, on a steel post at the back door of the ***Jackson County Courthouse*** *(102 Laurel Street, Scottsboro)*, where the nine black "Scottsboro Boys" were notoriously convicted of rape and sentenced to death in 1931, a plaque memorializes their long ordeal. At the end of a compressed history that even today gives no clue to what the county actually feels about the case, the marker concludes, "The U.S. Supreme Court ruled the defendants had not received equal protection under the law because Jackson County juror rolls excluded African Americans. Many consider the Scottsboro case and its aftermath one of the beginnings of the civil rights movement in America." An

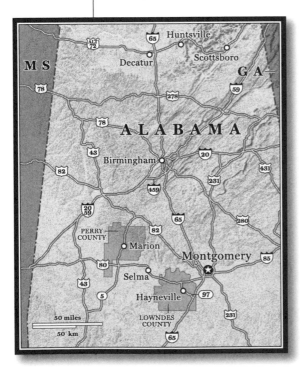

hour away in Decatur, carved into a tall memorial to the Confederacy at the **Morgan County Courthouse** (*302 Lee Street*), are these words: "Erected to the memory of those who offered their lives for a just cause, the defense of states rights."

Alabama thrust forward a notable set of civil rights leaders: from his Montgomery ministry, Reverend Martin Luther King Jr; also in that city, Reverend Ralph David Abernathy, who was Dr. King's best friend and

After the Alabama Supreme Court upheld the convictions of the nine Scottsboro boys, the well-known New York criminal defense attorney Samuel Leibowitz (center), took up the case. Although five of the men ultimately received long prison terms, even though the rape the men were accused of never occurred, the charges against these four were dropped. Leibowitz is credited with saving all nine from death.

SCLC colleague; Edgar Daniel "E. D." Nixon of Montgomery, one of A. Philip Randolph's union leaders and a former NAACP president; the heroic Reverend Fred Shuttlesworth in Birmingham; and from Troy, John Lewis, often bloodied as a young fighter for civil rights and now a Congressman. And though not native sons, Stokely Carmichael from New York and Bob Mants from Atlanta sank deep political roots in Lowndes County, where their work brought forth the Black Panther Party and Stokely's call for "Black Power." Notable women were not only the now revered Rosa Parks, but also Jo Anne Robinson, whose quickly composed leaflet of protest launched Montgomery's bus boycott in 1955; and Claudette Colvin, the fifteen-year-old who was arrested nine months before Rosa Parks for refusing to surrender her bus seat to a white man; Jean Childs Young, the wife of future Atlanta mayor Andrew Young; and Coretta Scott King, the wife of Martin Luther King Jr., both from Marion, a place of intense civil rights struggle and where the murder that triggered the Selma-to-Montgomery march in 1965 occurred. Less well known are SNCC's Annie Pearl Avery from Birmingham, and Gwen Patton, who led Tuskegee students in struggle. There's Montgomery's Johnnie Carr, whose words gave this chapter its title, and the powerful Amelia Boynton of Selma, who, along with her husband, Samuel W. Boynton, in 1936 breathed new life into the Dallas County Voters League that was founded in the 1920s.

The unique combination of heavy industry and agriculture, especially cotton, is at the root of much of the violence that has streaked Alabama's history. It began with the seizure by whites of Indian lands—largely Creek lands—to create a cotton kingdom. And that kingdom was heavily populated with slaves. Montgomery and Selma grew as slave markets where thousands of Africans were warehoused before and after their sale. Less than two months after Abraham Lincoln was sworn in as president of the United States, Alabama voted to secede from the Union. Montgomery became the capital of the newly established southern Confederacy, and it was from here that Jefferson Davis, as Confederate president, telegraphed the command to fire the first shots of the Civil War by ordering an attack on Fort Sumter in Charleston.

The city of Birmingham did not exist until two southern railroad lines intersected and the mining of nearby deposits of iron ore, limestone, and coal began. That was in 1871 and a great industry built around metal ore was born. By 1880 more than half of the city's industrial workers were Afro-Americans. With industry came efforts to unionize workers in coal fields and iron and steel mills. Ferocious battles bound to both race and economics erupted as companies, often using the Ku Klux Klan, sought to pit workers of different races and religions against one another. You would think that black workers and the just-as-exploited white workers would find common cause. In the end, however, the logic of action around the shared interests of workers was defeated by the hysteria of racial appeal that demonized Afro-American workers in particular and the Afro-American community in general. Klan violence, encouraged and supported by state and local government, grew as blacks in Birmingham and across the state, especially after the Montgomery bus boycott, sought civil rights with increasing public militancy.

✥ MONTGOMERY ✥

On December 1, 2005—the fiftieth anniversary of the arrest of Rosa Parks—I could not quite get a fix on my feelings while standing on the front lawn of the *Alabama State Capitol (600 Dexter Avenue).* The Capitol grounds are on a rise below which broad Dexter Avenue rolls into the heart of old downtown Montgomery. Part of the reason why I was fumbling for my feelings was because I remembered that everything around me was once hostile territory. To get to where I was now standing, I had walked along one side of the Capitol, where all of the Confederate flags, including the Confederate battle flag, were fluttering in the wind. The December air was crisp, and I shivered a little in my light jacket—perhaps not so much from the temperature as from the sight of some three thousand young people, black and white, marching down Dexter Avenue toward the building on a "Montgomery Children's Walk." They had begun at the corner of Montgomery and Lee Streets, where Mrs. Parks was arrested in 1955. Most were teenagers, some were younger, celebrating Mrs. Parks and the approaching anniversary of the bus boycott her arrest had triggered.

When they reached the Capitol, the young marchers began softly singing "We Shall Overcome" and were joined by many in the crowd of onlookers, and—strangely to me, only because some part of me was, once again in the 1960s—a couple of the city officials were singing, too. Policemen—they were white and black—had blocked the side streets feeding into Dexter Avenue, not to prevent marchers from reaching the Capitol building, but to create an unobstructed corridor for them. Some of them joined in singing the civil rights movement anthem, as well.

From a platform provided for speakers, a second grader—a white second grader—read aloud the leaflet written

In Montgom-ery, Rosa Parks is fin-gerprinted on February 22, 1956, two months after she refused to surrender her bus seat as ordered. She was among 156 people arrested for violating a 1921 law for-bidding the hindrance of a bus.

by Alabama State College (now University) English profes-sor Jo Ann Robinson calling for a boycott after Rosa Parks's arrest: "Negroes have rights too, for if Negroes did not ride buses, they could not operate ... please, children and grown-ups, don't ride the bus at all on Monday." Transformed by the young voice, these words of urgent appeal become a poi-gnant reminder that you can never tell where one defiant, righteous act will lead. From the opposite end of the age spectrum, ninety-five-year-old Johnnie Carr stepped for-ward to speak. A wise and tough voice from the past, and a good friend of Rosa Parks's, on this day Carr brought her considerable historical weight to bear on the future. "Look back but move forward," she declared. "I beg you, I admon-ish you to look around and see what has happened in the past but then march forward for the future." That ending phrase was taken up and briefly became a chant, a soul-ful voiced drumbeat from the crowd. "Look back, march forward!"

Could more than a half century have passed? I asked myself. It really didn't seem that long ago when, shortly

after boarding the Cleveland Avenue bus at *Court Square* (*a former site of slave auctions where Dexter Avenue converges with Commerce and Montgomery Streets*), Rosa Parks was arrested because she refused to surrender her seat to a white man. That was on December 1, 1955. The actual arrest took place a few blocks away, at the *Empire Theater bus stop* (*Montgomery Street between Lee and Moten, now the site of the Rosa Parks Museum*); there is a historic marker at this spot. Three black people as well as Mrs. Parks were sitting just behind the ten front seats reserved for white passengers. When more whites got on and filled those seats, the bus driver, James Blake, turned to the four and demanded, "Move y'all; I want those seats." No one moved and Blake threatened them, "Y'all better make it light on yourselves. I want those seats." At that point three of the black passengers (one man and two women) moved to the rear. Mrs. Parks moved over to the window and tried to ignore the driver by staring at the Empire Theater marquee, which displayed the title of the cowboy movie *A Man Alone*, starring Ray Milland.

Blake left his seat and approached Mrs. Parks. "Are you going to stand up?"

"No."

"Well, I'm going to have you arrested."

"You may do so."

Blake got off the bus and telephoned the police. As two white policemen, who reportedly seemed deeply embarrassed, led Mrs. Parks away, she said, "I paid my fare like everyone else."

Blake said years later, in an effort to defend his action: "I wasn't trying to do anything to that Parks woman except do my job. She was in violation of the city codes, so what was I supposed to do? That damn bus was full and she wouldn't move back. I had my orders."

Mrs. Parks's defiance ignited a decades-long fuse of dissatisfaction that a few days later set off an explosion—the Montgomery bus boycott. Black citizens initially united for a one-day boycott, then realized that victory would be neither easy nor quick, despite the fact that their demands were modest: courtesy; first-come, first-served seating; and black drivers in black areas. It took more than a day, indeed, more than a year—381 days—to end bus segregation in the city, because officials recognized the boycott for what it really was: the opening salvo of an organized assault on white supremacy. "What they are after is the destruction of our social order," declared Montgomery's mayor, William "Tacky" Gayle. And he was right. Nothing remained the same after the boycott, although the city and state bitterly resisted the inevitable for two more decades, fighting school desegregation and maintaining segregation in Montgomery's parks and pools (finally selling them when ordered by the courts to integrate). In a desperate effort to fend off change, on June 1, 1956, Alabama attorney general John Patterson (later governor) prohibited the NAACP from operating in Alabama and fined it $100,000, claiming that the organization was not properly registered because it refused to turn over its membership lists to the state. The ban lasted until 1964, when the Supreme Court unanimously ruled in the NAACP's favor. Before the decade was over, both Jo Ann Robinson and Rosa Parks had been driven from the state. And one of the Montgomery Improvement Association's earliest demands was not satis-

"My First Conscious Protest"

"In 1952 when I was nine years old, one Sunday my grandmother brought me into Liggett's Drug Store at Court Square right behind the fountain. The soda jerk called me a pickaninny. I knew that was a bad word and deliberately spilled water on the counter where I was standing. It was my first conscious protest. They knew at nine that I was going to be a militant, and by 1956 I was automatically dispatched to the Montgomery Improvement Association during the bus boycott. 'Go get me; go fetch me,' whatever the elders wanted. I wrote my eighth-grade paper on the Montgomery bus boycott—wish I still had that paper."

—GWENDOLYN PATTON TO CHARLIE COBB

fied until 1962, when the city bus company finally hired its first black drivers.

On September 3, 1958, Martin Luther King was arrested on the charge of loitering, which was later changed to "failure to obey an officer." His wife Coretta Scott King is here with him as he is being arrested. The day after pleading not guilty, he was convicted and fined. Over Rev. King's objections, the fine was almost immediately paid by the Montgomery police commissioner, Clyde C. Sellers.

As the decade of the 1960s began, student sit-ins broke out across Alabama. In Montgomery, just three weeks after Greensboro, on February 25, 1960, Alabama State College students sat in at the Capitol's segregated snack bar. They were arrested. The governor had the students expelled from the state school, but less than two weeks after these arrests and expulsions, on March 6, hundreds of protesting students filled the streets surrounding the Capitol. Perhaps because officials were still trying to recover from the negative image the city had gained during the bus boycott, scores of policemen separated the students from a raging white mob. On the other hand, the ***Freedom Rider Plaque*** *(210 S. Court Street)* erected in 1995 at what used to be the Greyhound bus station, reports that when the Freedom Riders arrived in Montgomery on May 20, 1961, "Their police escort disappeared and an angry mob of Klan supporters attacked and injured them at the Greyhound terminal."

Seated in the foreground of this bus carrying Freedom Riders, protected by national guardsmen, is David Dennis, then a student at Dillard University in New Orleans. Less than a year later, Dennis would be CORE's Mississippi project director. I always thought he'd been kicked out of school for taking this ride, but when I asked him about it, he said, "The dean of students called me in and sort of politely said maybe I ought to find some other school to finish up, and so I dropped out and began working with CORE full time."

From the Capitol grounds you can see the old **Dexter Avenue Baptist Church** just a block away *(now Dexter Avenue King Memorial Baptist Church, 454 Dexter Avenue at Decatur Street)* facing the Alabama Supreme Court. On June 3, 1974, the church was designated a national historic landmark. Across the street from the church, a marker informs you that Dexter Avenue is also part of 1965's "Historic Route of the Selma to Montgomery trail." At a meeting of about fifty people held in the church's basement on December 2, 1955, Rosa Parks first told the story of her arrest and the group decided to mount a bus boycott. What participants initially decided was to have a one-day boycott on Monday December 5, but because the boycott that day was so successful—roughly 70 percent of Montgomery's bus passengers were black, and most had stayed off the buses—discussion of continuing it began at a meeting afterward at the church. Many of the ministers were nervous about continuing boycott action, and former Montgomery NAACP president E. D. Nixon, a member of A. Philip Randolph's Brotherhood of Sleeping Car Porters, accused them of being cowards. Twenty-six-year-old Martin Luther King Jr., who the year before

---

"The Women's Political Council Was Born"

I n Montgomery, black women especially were regularly humiliated by the bus service. Years before her refusal to surrender her seat, Rosa Parks had paid her fare, then walked back through the front door of the bus to enter it through the rear door as custom required, and the bus pulled away without her. Jo Ann Robinson unthinkingly sat down in the white section of a city bus one day and was brought to tears by the bus driver, who cursed her out. Mary Fair Burkes founded the Woman's Political Council in 1946 partly in response to these indignities. The organization targeted Montgomery's small population of black middle-class women, many of whom were associated with historically black Alabama State College, encouraging their civic involvement and promoting voter registration. Even before Rosa Parks's defiant action, the group had been discussing the possibility of a bus boycott.

"Vernon Johns, pastor of Dexter Avenue Baptist Church, mounted one of his scathing attacks on the complacency of his affluent membership. I looked around and all I could see were either masks of indifference or scorn. Johns's attacks, his patched pants, and his Thoreauvian philosophy of plain living and high thinking did not endear him to his congregation. I was a feminist before I really knew what the word meant and so I dismissed the hard-faced men, but I felt that I could appeal to some of the women. I played bridge with them, but more important, I knew that they must suffer from the racial abuse and the indignity accorded to all blacks, even though they were somewhat insulated from it. Their outward indifference was a mask to protect both their psyche and their sanity. I believed that I could get enough such women together to address some of the glaring racial problems. Thus the idea of the Women's Political Council was born on that Sunday morning."

—MARY FAIR BURKS

had arrived to pastor at "Dexter," as local people called the church, stood up and said *he* was not a coward. That statement probably contributed significantly to King's being chosen to head a new organization formed at that meeting—the Montgomery Improvement Association (MIA), an umbrella organization that would coordinate a continuing boycott effort.

History cloaks you at once upon entering Dr. King's old church. Immediately greeting you is a large mural painted by Dexter member John W. Feagin depicting important moments in Montgomery's movement, and landmarks in King's life as a civil rights leader. The church has always figured prominently in the city's black life. It was built by former slaves, and worship in the redbrick sanctuary began on Thanksgiving Day 1889. The church itself was founded in 1877, when blacks began holding meetings in what was once a slave pen. White opposition to the church's location in the shadow of the Capitol and other state office buildings, and to its membership's being drawn from Montgomery's black elite, made it a symbol of racial redemption and respect even before the arrival of Martin Luther King. With bold sermons, King's predecessor, Vernon Johns (the uncle of, and a major influence on, Farmville's Barbara Johns) had been persistently challenging racism, posting on the bulletin board outside of Dexter Sunday sermon titles such as "It's Safe to Murder Negroes in Montgomery" after a lynching, "When the Rapist is White," and the sardonic "Segregation After Death."

In 1949 Johns walked into a white Montgomery restaurant and ordered a sandwich—an act that could easily have gotten him lynched instead of being ordered to leave. He also militantly challenged his own congregation, for they were conservative and cautious about risking what with great difficulty they had managed to carve out of a white supremacist society. Furthermore, if Johns's pronouncements on race sometimes made them nervous and his great literacy—he often laced his sermons with references drawn from the classical literature of Greece and Rome—earned him admiration, he also angered and embarrassed the

The Words of Vernon Johns

I know what the white man gets out of Negro education, but I have never been able to learn exactly what it is that Negroes are supposed to get out of it.

The Negro has a wheelbarrow income and Cadillac ambitions.

No man is fit to be alive until he has something for which he would die.

We Negroes need to resolve that we will not be forever hired out and forever sold out and forever bought out.

Two days from now my son's going to Korea, to fight, so many thousands miles away and yet he's fighting for those people for those things which he has been denied here. . . . I just as soon for him to die here as to die over there, and by dying here he will be dying for his own cause.

God never spoke about justifiable homicide. He said "Thou shalt not kill." He didn't say thou shalt not kill, unless you've got an excuse. He didn't say thou shalt not kill, unless you are a police officer. And he most assuredly did not say thou shalt not kill, unless you're white.

I'll tell you why it's safe to murder Negroes. Because Negroes stand by and let it happen. Do you know what occurred to me as I watched that cross burning in front of the church? When the Klan burns a cross it's a message. The next step is lynching.

As I watched that cross it occurred to me that what we call the crucifixion is just that—a lynching. Isn't it ironic? Everything we worship was made possible by a lynching. Because at that ultimate moment of death Jesus spoke the words that transformed a lynching into the crucifixion. That made Jesus the redeemer, not the condemner. Jesus said Father forgive them for they know not what they do. But you know what you do. And the white police officers who are free day after day to murder Negroes know what they do. And when you stand by and watch your brothers and sisters being lynched it's as if you stood by while Christ was being crucified.

congregation with his outspoken disdain for bourgeois pretensions. As a young man from a Prince Edward County family too poor to pay for his schooling, Johns was often seen plowing a field *and* reading. And to the mortification of many members, on some Sundays after church service

Johns would sell potatoes, vegetables, and watermelons in front of Dexter.

Just around the corner from the church is the **Civil Rights Memorial and Visitors Center** (*400 Washington Avenue*), where a circular black granite table designed by architect Maya Lin (designer of the Vietnam Wall in Washington, D.C.) lists the names of forty civil rights martyrs who died between 1954 and 1968 and presents a timeline of civil rights struggle. Water emerges from the table's center and flows over the top. Engraved on a curved wall behind the table are words from the Book of Amos that Martin Luther King used at the onset of the bus boycott: "Until justice rolls down like water and righteousness like a mighty stream." The origin of this memorial lies with the **Southern Poverty Law Center** (SPLC), which shares its address. The SPLC was founded in 1971 to generate money for civil rights lawsuits, to investigate radical right-wing organizations, and to produce a school-based Teaching Tolerance program. SPLC founder attorney Morris Dees had long been challenging racial segregation across Alabama, and in 1981, after the Ku Klux Klan lynched a young black man named Michael Donald in Mobile, Alabama, Dees sued the Klan on behalf of Donald's mother, winning a $7 million judgment that forced the Klan to sell its headquarters in order to pay her. The suit set a precedent, and other suits aimed at bankrupting white supremacists have been filed across the country. A film about Birmingham's civil rights struggle produced by the center, *Mighty Times: The Children's March*, won the 2005 Academy Award for documentary short subject.

With this background, it comes as no surprise that the SPLC has been a Ku Klux Klan target. When visitors enter the center, they will immediately encounter a clock stopped at the precise time in 1983 that the Klan set fire to the SPLC offices (4:17 A.M.). The main purpose of the center is to offer, through its exhibits and docents, an in-depth tour of civil rights struggle. A permanent "Here I Stand" exhibit details Montgomery's civil rights history. There is a sixty-seat auditorium where a video program briefs visitors. A "Wall of Tolerance" displays names of SPLC and civil rights movement supporters, and visitors can add their names by pledging to

Wives Were Key in Civil Rights Struggle

BY BILL TORPY *ATLANTA JOURNAL-CONSTITUTION*, FEBRUARY 2, 2006

The smoke-filled meetings often drifted into the wee hours as the young lions of the civil rights movement plotted their next moves during the Montgomery bus boycott.

Those meetings 50 years ago were sometimes at the home of the Rev. Martin Luther King Jr. More often, they were at the Rev. Ralph David Abernathy's parsonage.

"My house was like the headquarters and so I became known as the cook," Juanita Abernathy, the reverend's widow, recently recalled. She served up coffee, sandwiches and fried chicken. Her cooking wasn't first-rate, she joked. But her ideas were.

It was common during the brainstorming sessions for the wives to get in the thick of it.

"But you had to make them think the ideas were theirs; you know how chauvinistic men were," she said with a laugh. "There was a time when women were not allowed to be ourselves. We were in the shadows. Coretta and I were very vocal and opinionated. But it was always behind the scenes." Coretta Scott King's death Jan. 30 has brought to focus the role of women in that historic movement in a land and time far different from today. The men, as times dictated, were out in front. The women were often relegated to the back.

History has frozen the image of Coretta Scott King as the beautiful, grieving widow remaining stoic under a black veil.

But she, and countless other black women of that era, injected fortitude and wisdom into the effort while providing a steady hand for their husbands, allowing the men to throw themselves into their mission.

"Had it not been for the women and what they did, Dr. King and others couldn't have had the success they did," said Johnnie Carr, a 95-year-old Montgomery woman who was a close friend of Rosa Parks and active in the bus boycott. "Women weren't given the opportunity to be out in front. One of the focuses of the 50th anniversary (of the boycott last December) was to raise up the names of women who played a part."

Carr said black women were uniquely qualified to have key roles in the movement.

Slavery and decades of segregation had marginalized black men, who were viewed as a threat to white society and were often beaten down when they voiced protest to the inequities. Black women were not seen as such a threat.

"Black men could not speak out. They had to worry about being killed. We were able to speak out more," Carr said. Carr, a widow, said she was able to speak out more than others during the struggle because she worked for a black insurance firm and was not afraid she would be fired.

Abernathy, who chuckled while declining to give her age, said, "Black women have always been strong and have always had a certain amount of freedom that wasn't given to black males. Black women took care of the white bosses and their children and then had to go home and feed their own children.

"Women make a lot of sacrifices. It's who we are," she said.

Keeping the family intact during the struggles was a tightwire walk of faith, devotion and courage. The Abernathys' parsonage, like the Kings', was bombed. Abernathy, whose husband died in 1990, was alone with a baby daughter. Her husband was on the road when the bombing occurred. But they, like the Kings, were not deterred.

Wives of civil rights leaders were often de facto single mothers, with their husbands forever on the road.

Octavia Vivian, 77, the wife of the Rev. C. T. Vivian, a leader in the Freedom Rides and the Selma struggles, said, "The wives had to be father as well as mother. I was told the men would be out [traveling] a week and then back a week. But it was often out a month, in a week."

The Vivians, who live in Atlanta, had six children, all of them young during the early 1960s. They always were sad to see their father leave home and had a hard time understanding why.

"You had to explain what daddy was doing," said Vivian, who tried to keep her children from watching the TV news, fearing that the violence would frighten them. "If he was in jail, you had to explain why so they didn't lose respect for him. You had to explain to them about going to jail for the right reasons."

She knew she had succeeded when her youngest son went to day care one morning, cracked a huge smile at the teacher and proudly stated, "My daddy's in jail."

C. T. Vivian, now 81, said he and other civil rights leaders couldn't have done what they did without their wives.

"You never knew what was going to happen, we often were not there," said Vivian, who still calls his wife "Baby." "If our wives did not have the same vision we had, then things might have turned out differently. They could have turned our children against us if they didn't have the same vision."

The women also fought their own civil rights battles while their husbands traveled. Vivian said his wife arranged a protest when the principal of an Atlanta school that their children attended tried to resegregate the students.

"This was when I was not around," he said. "These were strong women."

Evelyn Lowery, wife of the Rev. Joseph Lowery, fought a similar battle when a daughter desegregated a Birmingham school in the mid-1960s.

The plan was for Evelyn to walk daughter Cheryl into the school by the hand while reciting a Bible verse. They decided the reverend would stay home, thinking the crowd would not get as angry at a mother and a small girl.

Evelyn Lowery said women were always "the foot-soldiers" of the movement, even if they weren't out front. In 1979, she founded the SCLC-Women Inc., saying "it was time for women to come out front." Many of the women who were active in the civil rights struggle have stayed active, trying to keep the movement alive as their numbers grow fewer. Lowery gets wistful as she ticks off the names of women of the movement who have died in the past few months: "Constance Motley, Dr. C. Dolores Tucker, Vivian Malone Jones, Idessa Redden, Rosa Parks and now Coretta."

For nearly 20 years, Lowery has organized the Evelyn Gibson Lowery Civil Rights heritage tour, which retraces the steps of the civil rights movement in Alabama. It is set to go again this March. The tour always visits Johnnie Carr, who still is the president of the Montgomery Improvement Association, the group that was founded in December 1955 to organize and sponsor the bus boycott.

Martin Luther King Jr. was its first leader. Carr was at the Smithsonian Institution in Washington last month at a forum in connection with the Martin Luther King Jr. holiday. Juanita Abernathy also was there. The women's comments and recollections were recorded for posterity.

Not to stop there, Carr is forever speaking of her life and had just come in from a talk at a high school this month when she picked up the phone to talk to a reporter.

What did she tell the students?

"I just told them that I was the end," she said. "I was the last."

Martin Luther King at the pulpit of Dexter Avenue Baptist Church

take a stand against hate, injustice, and intolerance.

Not very far away is the **Dexter Parsonage Museum (309 S. Jackson Street)**, which was once the home of the King family. The parsonage offers a rare view of Dr. King as a family man. Much of the original furniture remains. The Kodak Brownie camera on a bedroom dresser makes me wonder what the snapshots looked like. An Ethel Waters record album, *His Eye Is on the Sparrow*, lies next to an old phonograph. Of course, you are not far from the civil rights movement here, either. The parsonage study was where bus boycott leaders frequently met, and where, in the mornings, King worked on his Ph.D. dissertation and wrote his Sunday sermons. There is a portrait of Mohandas Gandhi on one of the walls. Organizing the Southern Christian Leadership Conference was first discussed around the parsonage's dining room table.

Still visible on the front porch of the parsonage and explained by a nearby marker is the ugly scar left from a dynamite blast while Coretta King, a friend, and the Kings' two-year-old daughter, Yolanda, were at home. The windows were shattered by the bomb, but mother, child, and friend were not hurt. King rushed home from a church mass meeting. An angry crowd of neighbors—many armed—had already gathered, but from the porch King asked them to return home with their guns. "He who lives by the sword will perish by the sword," he told them. But at this early point in his civil rights leadership, Rev. King himself was uncertain about his creed of nonviolence; he was a man of *southern* culture, after all, and, black or white, guns have always been an integral part of that way of life. Two days after this blast

King went to the sheriff's office and requested a gun permit. It was denied, but Bayard Rustin recalled that once when visiting the parsonage, he spotted a pistol on a chair—only for self-defense, explained King. The parsonage continued to be a target of racist whites, and despite the presence of round-the-clock armed watchmen and the installation of new spotlights on the roof, the King family frequently stayed with friends in other parts of Montgomery.

The backyard of the parsonage is now the **King-Johns Garden for Reflection**, where beneath shade trees visitors are encouraged to contemplate six principles: Equality, Forgiveness, Hope, Unity, Peace, and Understanding.

An **Interpretive Center** is now part of the parsonage. As the parsonage itself does in presenting King the family man, the Center presents another intimate dimension of Martin Luther King's life that is too often hidden by his iconic status as a great civil rights leader—Rev. King the pastor. Mounted on three panels are many photographs of King greeting and shaking hands with members of his Dexter fold and visitors; to ask about them is to learn something about King's relationship with his congregation. One photograph, for instance, is of a Mrs. Cleonia Taylor, an usher who often held baby Yolanda so Mrs. King could sing in the choir; and in a photo of the choir, there is Mrs. King, smiling broadly. There are warm photos of a surprise farewell tribute to King after he announced his resignation as pastor of the church. Many of the key participants in the bus boycott, including Jo Ann Robinson and E. D. Nixon, are also found in photographs here.

Much of Montgomery's bus-boycott story is power-fully told at the **Rosa Parks Library and Museum** *(252 Montgomery Street)*, where the Empire Theater once stood. Inside, on a reconstructed street corner you can enter a replica of the bus Mrs. Parks boarded. The museum also displays a copy of the leaflet that Jo Ann Robinson mim-eographed calling for a bus boycott, and visitors can have their photograph taken while seated next to a life-size bronze sculpture of Rosa Parks. A new children's wing, which opened in 2006, enables visitors to "go back in time" on the Cleveland Avenue Time Machine—another bus replica. On this journey, through a twenty-minute simulation that begins with the birth of the Jim Crow era, passengers experience eleven historical events depicting the struggle for civil rights. The idea, explained museum director Georgette Norman, is, for young people especially, "to discover that things just don't happen—people make things happen; that, they too, can make a difference."

E. D. Nixon, with Rosa Parks, to his right

Certain homes help us greatly in understanding Montgomery's movement. Although they all are occupied private homes, the simple fact of being in neighborhoods reinforces an essential element of what the movement was—one made by ordinary people, not gods of social change come down from the heavens. Markers in front of these homes offer important additional insight. Start with the **E. D. Nixon house** *(647 Clinton Avenue)*. If there was a single leader of Montgomery's black community, it was Nixon. By 1955 he had been president of both the state and local NAACP chapters. He founded the Montgomery Voters League in 1940, and in 1944 led almost eight hundred black men to the county courthouse, where they bravely attempted to register to vote. As a Pullman car porter traveling across the United States, however, Nixon could not give the new MIA his full attention, and this is also part of the reason Martin Luther King emerged—with Nixon's endorsement—to lead the new organization. Indisputably, E. D. Nixon remains one of the great heroes of Montgomery. He died in 1987 and is buried in the **Eastwood Memorial Gardens** *(7500 Wares Ferry Road)*.

Georgia Gilmore is not nearly as well known as E. D. Nixon, but stop for a moment at the **Gilmore house** *(453 Dericote Street)*, near the parsonage. Through Mrs. Gilmore we get some sense of the unsung heroes and heroines who formed the backbone of Montgomery's movement. Mrs. Gilmore had been a cafeteria worker, but she was fired for her involvement with the boycott. She organized women into the "Club from Nowhere," which sold cakes, cookies, and sweet potato and other pies on Montgomery's streets and in beauty salons to raise money for the boycott. At its peak the club was raising one hundred dollars a week. Mrs. Gilmore came up with a line that Reverend King would use often: "When they count the money, they do not know Negro money from white money." Her son Mark was arrested in 1958 for walking through whites-only **Oak Park** *(between Hall Street and Forrest Avenue)*. His case generated the lawsuit that ultimately resulted in the court-ordered desegregation of Montgomery's parks.

The **Rufus Lewis house** *(801 Bolivar Street)* was home to another now little-known community leader. In 1952 Rufus Lewis led the boycott of a grocery store whose owner had been accused of raping a young black baby-sitter when he drove her home. During the bus boycott, Lewis played the key role in organizing car pools. As coach of Alabama State's football team and a member of Dexter Avenue Baptist church, Lewis was part of the city's black elite. Yet, atypically, he was a militant civil rights activist, organizing voter registration campaigns not only in Montgomery but also in the surrounding counties that formed part of Alabama's black belt. His commitment equaled that of E. D. Nixon, with whom he was often compared. But in distinguishing the two men, it was said that "Mr. Nixon had the masses; Coach Lewis had the classes." Lewis, who was one of the important adult mentors of SNCC organizers when they began working in the state, ultimately became chairman of the Alabama Democratic Conference and was the first Afro-American to become a U.S. marshall in Alabama.

It is not a house, but nonetheless the four-story brick **Ben Moore Hotel** *(902 High Street)* is worth mentioning here. Located just two blocks away from the Dexter parsonage, in the Centennial Hill neighborhood, it was designed by black architect Mose B. Thomas and built by black contractors. These two facts alone make it one of Alabama's

Reverend Ralph David Abernathy being greeted by his parishioners after his release from jail in Montgomery on February 22, 1956. He and 155 others had been arrested under a 1921 law prohibiting the hindrance of a bus.

unique structures. When it opened in 1951 on what was then a thriving black commercial strip, the Ben Moore was the only hotel in Montgomery that catered to Afro-Americans. Its roof garden restaurant was a political center in the 1950s, especially during the bus boycott; city officials often met with black leaders there for negotiations. The hotel is now closed, although the building remains intact.

And there are the churches. As is true everywhere in black communities, churches exert a powerful influence. Two in particular, along with Rev. King's Dexter Avenue, represent the spiritual heartland of Montgomery's movement. **First Baptist Church** *(347 North Ripley Street)*, pastored by King's best friend, Reverend Ralph David Abernathy, was bombed several times because of its role in civil rights struggle. The church was formed in 1867, when blacks, mostly former slaves, who had held services in the basement of the white First Baptist Church, broke away and established what was the first institution organized

Bus Boycott Resolution

T*he December 5, 1955, one-day bus boycott was so successful that at the mass meeting held at Holt Street Baptist Church that night, the crowd overwhelmingly approved a resolution drawn up earlier by Dr. King, Reverend Abernathy, and other ministers to continue boycotting until the city agreed to desegregate its bus service.*

Whereas, there are thousands of Negroes in the city and county of Montgomery who ride buses owned and operated by the Montgomery City Lines, Incorporated, and

Whereas, said citizens have been riding buses owned and operated by said company over a number of years, and

Whereas, said citizens, over a number of years, and on many occasions, have been insulted, embarrassed (Yeah), and have been made to suffer great fear of bodily harm (That's right) by drivers of buses owned and operated by said bus company (Yeah), and

Whereas, the drivers of said buses have never requested a white passenger riding on any of its buses to relinquish his seat and to stand so that a Negro may take his seat; [Applause] however, said drivers have on many occasions, too numerous to mention, requested Negro passengers on said buses to relinquish their seats and to stand so that white passengers may take their seats, [Applause] and

Whereas, said citizens of Montgomery city and county pay their fares just as all other persons who are passengers on said buses (All right), and are entitled to fair and equal treatment (Yeah), [Applause], and

Whereas, there has been any number of arrests of Negroes caused by drivers of said buses, and they are constantly put in jail for refusing to give white passengers their seats and to stand. (All right) [Applause]

Whereas, in March of 1955, a committee of citizens did have a conference with one of the officials of the said bus line; at which time said officials arranged a meeting between attorneys representing the Negro citizens of this city and attorneys representing the Montgomery City Lines, Incorporated, and the city of Montgomery, and

Whereas, the official of the bus line promised that as a result of the meeting between said attorneys, he would issue a statement of policy clarifying the law with reference to the seating of Negro passengers on the buses, and

Whereas, said attorneys did have a meeting and did discuss the matter of clarifying the law, however, the official of said bus lines did not make public the statement as to its policy with reference to the seating of passengers on its buses, and

Whereas, since that time, at least two ladies have been arrested for an alleged violation of the city segregation law with reference to bus travel, and

Whereas, said citizens of Montgomery city and county believe that they have been grossly mistreated as passengers on the buses owned and operated by said bus company (All right) in spite of the fact that they are in the majority with reference to the number of passengers riding the said buses. [Applause]

In light of these observations, be it therefore resolved as follows:

Number One. That the citizens of Montgomery are requesting that every citizen in Montgomery, regardless of race, color or creed, to refrain from riding buses owned and operated in the city of Montgomery by the Montgomery Lines, Incorporated [Applause], until some arrangement has been worked out [Applause] between said citizens and the Montgomery City Lines, Incorporated.

Now I'm reading it slow and I want you to hear every word of it.

Number Two. That every person owning or who has access to an automobile will use their automobiles in assisting other persons to get to work without charge. [Applause]

by free Afro-Americans in Montgomery. For a while it was the largest black church in America, and the organization that would become the hugely influential National Baptist Convention was born here in 1880. First Baptist was literally built brick by brick by its congregation, for when the original wood church burned down, its pastor, Andrew Stokes, called on the congregation to each bring one brick every day for a new building.

Number Three. That the employees, I repeat, that the employers of persons whose employees live a great distance from them, as much as possible, afford transportation for your own employees. [Applause]

That the Negro citizens of Montgomery are ready and willing to send a delegation of citizens to the Montgomery City Lines, Incorporated, to discuss their grievances and to work out a solution for the same. (All right) [Applause]

Be it further resolved, that we have not, I said, we have not, we are not, and we have no intentions of using any unlawful means or any intimidation (Go ahead) to persuade persons not to ride the Montgomery City Lines buses. [Applause] However, we call upon your conscience, (All right) both moral and spiritual, to give your whole-hearted support (That's right) to this worthy undertaking. [Applause] We believe we have a just complaint and we are willing to discuss this matter with the proper authorities. (Yes) [Applause]

Thus ends the resolution. [Applause]

Dr. King, prayerfully, spiritually, sincerely, I wish to offer a motion. I move that this resolution shall be adopted.

DR. KING: I second the motion. [Applause]

KING: It has been moved, it has been moved, and seconded, that these recommendations and these resolutions would be accepted and adopted by the citizens of Montgomery. Are you ready for the question? (Thundering Yes)

All in favor, stand on your feet. [Enthusiastic applause] Opposers do likewise. Opposers do likewise. [Laughter] There is a prevailing majority.

—READ BY RALPH ABERNATHY [AT HOLT STREET BAPTIST CHURCH MASS MEETING DECEMBER 5, 1955] AND APPROVED BY VOICE VOTE

It was First Baptist pastor Ralph Abernathy whom E. D. Nixon first telephoned to discuss Rosa Parks's arrest, and Abernathy began contacting other Montgomery ministers to meet to decide how to respond. That meeting was held at the Dexter Avenue Baptist Church, but during the boycott many of the regular Monday-night mass meetings were held at First Baptist. King was speaking at one of these mass meetings when he got word that his house had been bombed.

First Baptist itself, along with Abernathy's home and three other churches, was bombed on January 10, 1957. And three years later, a mass meeting was held there regarding Freedom Riders who had been attacked at the Greyhound bus station and found refuge in First Baptist. While Rev. King was addressing the group, a white mob attacked the church. Alabama's governor declared martial law in the city as a result. This siege of First Baptist, plus violence targeting Freedom Riders at both the Greyhound and Trailways bus stations, led to a September 22, 1961, Interstate Commerce Commission order that all interstate bus stations be desegregated.

The other important movement church in Montgomery was the **Holt Street Baptist Church** *(903 South Holt Street at Jefferson Davis Avenue)*. It was here, concluding the initial day of the boycott, that King gave his first movement speech to some five thousand people, joyous and proud of the success of their one-day refusal to ride city buses. The excited crowd filled the pews, the balcony, and the surrounding sidewalks outside the church. King's speech, an excerpt of which opens this chapter, remains one of his most powerful. In her autobiography, Rosa Parks recalled her favorite passage from that night: "When the history books are written in the future somebody will have to say there lived a race of people, a black people, fleecy locks and black complexion, a people who had moral courage to stand up for their rights, and thereby they injected a new meaning in the veins of history."

SELMA

As the starting point of what is perhaps Alabama's most famous civil rights "moment," the 1965 Selma-to-Montgomery march, the city of Selma is one of the essential stops on our civil rights trail. From Montgomery, Selma is just fifty-four miles away via Highway 80. This entire stretch of *U.S. 80* is a National Historic Trail, and all along the way, blue signs erected by the National Park Service indicate significant sites, such as campsites that marchers used during their trek. Between mile markers 105 and 106 is a park service–operated *Voting Rights Trail Interpretive Center* displaying photographs and memorabilia from the march. This is also where in March 1966 a "tent city" sheltered forty black families after, because of their efforts to register to vote, white landowners kicked them off the land they worked as tenant farmers. The land here was owned by an independent black farmer, Matthew Jackson, whose son, John, became the first Afro-American mayor of nearby White Hall in notorious "bloody Lowndes" County. There are plans for two more centers on this Alabama trail.

Selma was once Alabama's cotton capital—a heartland of slavery and oppressive antiblack codes. Yet for a time after the Civil War, Selma also represented burgeoning black power. During the Reconstruction era, Selma had black city councilmen, congressmen, and judges, as well as some prosperous black businessmen. The Interlink Cotton Gin Company was one of the few black-owned cotton gins in the state, and in 1867 the first black policeman ever hired in Alabama was hired in Selma. In 1872 Jeremiah Haralson, a former slave, defeated Confederate hero Edmund Pettus in the election for a seat in the state legislature. Benjamin Sterling Turner, who before the Civil War ran the *St. James Hotel* (*on Water Street*) for his "owner," was Selma's first black city councilman. Turner was also Dallas County's first black tax collector and was elected to the U.S. Congress in 1870—the first black Alabamian to be elected to that office. Turner's gravesite and those of other Afro-American notables can be found amid the graves of Confederate generals at the *Old Live Oak Cemetery* (*Alabama Highway 22, southwest from U.S. 80*).

Two institutions of higher education serving blacks are located in Selma: Selma University, a Baptist college founded in 1878; and Payne University, founded by the AME church in 1899. These two schools made Selma known—in a startling characterization for those of us who retain the horrific images of Bloody Sunday in our minds—as the "Athens of Black Alabama."

As in Montgomery, in Selma, too, my feelings are mixed when after almost four decades I find myself in this city. Times have changed, however. A Chamber of Commerce representative gives me a big smile and a bag full of brochures and tells me that the city's unofficial motto is now "From Civil War to Civil Rights"—a phrase you will encounter frequently in cities from Washington, D.C., to Jackson, Mississippi. Selma's civil rights history is an important tourist draw. Civil War buffs are the other big tourist bloc. During the Battle of Selma in 1865, Union forces under General J. H. Wilson seized control of the city arsenal (nearly half the munitions used by the Confederacy were manufactured in Selma), and this signaled the rapidly approaching defeat of the Confederacy as a secessionist nation. Nathan Bedford Forrest, who would later lead the Ku Klux Klan, led Confederate cavalry against Wilson's troops. I wonder what he would think now of Selma's Afro-American mayor. Or of me—a black man—eating lunch on the riverfront at the charmingly renovated *St. James Hotel (1200 Water Avenue)*, which was so popular with slaveholders before the Civil War and may have been a familiar place to Mr. Howell Rose who "owned" and worked my great-great-grandfather on a plantation just outside of Wetumpka, a small town on the Coosa River minutes away from Montgomery. And what might Mr. Rose, or for that matter, Nathan Bedford Forrest, think of the ironic fact that in Selma, the city's self-guided civil rights walking tour begins at the intersection of *Martin Luther King Jr. Street (changed from Sylvan Street in 1976 by a six-to-five city council vote)* and *Jefferson Davis Avenue*? On the walk southeast along Martin Luther King Jr. Street from that avenue named for the Confederate leader to to the one named for the city itself, there are twenty memorials. Together they are a very effective beginning for any visitor seeking understanding of Selma's civil rights movement. It is strange to find, however, that some of the markers praise Selma's 1965 mayor, Joseph T. Smitherman, and even the chief of police, both of whom resisted civil rights movement–generated change.

The gateway into Selma is the **Edmund Pettus Bridge** *(Highway 80 at Broad Street and Water Avenue)*, named for Confederate brigadier-general Edmund Winston Pettus, who eventually became a U.S. senator. The bridge had been a part of Confederate culture since its construction in 1940. Then, on February 26, 1965, when Jimmie Lee Jackson died of the gunshot wounds he suffered while trying to protect his mother from police assault in nearby Marion, a decision was made to march from Selma to Montgomery. What happened as a result of that decision has fixed the bridge in most minds today in a manner that its designers and earlier Chambers of Commerce could not have imagined.

The Selma-to-Montgomery march passes over the Edmund Pettus Bridge on March 21, 1965.

Although there was much white antagonism to voter registration and other civil rights efforts in Selma, the marchers did not seem to be expecting much violence. Some of the six hundred or so people lining up behind SNCC's John Lewis and SCLC's Hosea Williams, in defiance of a ban that was placed on civil rights marches by Governor George Wallace, were dressed in their Sunday best; some carried bedrolls, toothbrushes, and knapsacks for the long journey. Jail was almost certainly in the minds of some, but other than that no plans had been made for where to stay overnight during the fifty-four-mile trip. March 7 was a chilly and overcast day. It was a Sunday, so downtown Selma was quiet. When the marchers stepped onto Pettus

March 7, 1965, John Lewis on the first attempted Selma-to-Montgomery march. Just behind him is 19-year-old Doris Wilson, who lost her $12 a week lunchroom job and was later jailed while protesting the denial of voting rights.

Bridge, they could see about fifty or so state troopers wearing blue helmets and standing shoulder-to-shoulder across Highway 80 at the other end. And behind this wall of police was a posse of another fifty or so white men recruited by the Dallas County Sheriff, Jim Clark; a number of them were on horseback. City of Selma policemen do not seem to have been present. As the marchers approached this massed force, Major John Cloud of the state police, holding a small bullhorn to his mouth, spoke to them:

"You have two minutes to disperse."

"May we have a word with you, Major?" asked Hosea Williams.

"There is no word to be had," shot back Major Cloud.

No sooner had he finished the reply than his troopers began putting on gas masks and Cloud suddenly called out, "Troopers forward."

The marchers began kneeling to pray, but within seconds, troopers charged into their ranks and chaos erupted—the marchers scattered, chased by Cloud's men, who now opened fire with tear gas and used billy clubs to beat anyone they could reach, among them John Lewis, who was clubbed unconscious. Possemen joined the police, letting loose with rebel yells while beaten and choking marchers screamed. Those able to stand were chased back across the bridge into town. Although no one was killed, this brutal event, which still stains Selma's image, has become known as "Bloody Sunday."

Today you can hardly feel this terror in the quiet **Voting Rights Memorial Park**, tucked beneath the bridge. This small park commemorates those who campaigned for voting rights. There are murals and monuments to Hosea Williams and John Lewis, and a short, winding walking trail through the park features many plaques recognizing heroes of the movement who are not as well known.

After the police riot on the bridge, many marchers fled to the **Brown Chapel AME Church** *(410 Martin Luther King Jr. Street)*, just six blocks away, on what was then Sylvan Street. This was where they had begun their march. The dramatic Romanesque Revival style of the structure, with its high-reaching twin towers, almost forces you to feel the powerful and important role of the church in civil rights struggle. Inside, sunlight is filtered by beautiful rose-colored stained-glass windows. SCLC maintained its headquarters here during the three-month campaign for voting rights in 1965. The church, founded in 1867, was the first AME church in Alabama, and it has long had a prominent role in the community. On February 4, 1965, about three weeks before he was assassinated and just after having spoken to students at Tuskegee, Malcolm X spoke at Brown Chapel. Martin Luther King was in jail at the time, and Malcolm X explained to anxious civil rights leaders that by speaking he was making it easier for whites to accept what King wanted.

Richie Jean Jackson, a retired schoolteacher who conducts tours of the church today, wants to stress the kind

On the Pettus Bridge, police and white possemen break up the March 7 march. In the foreground, John Lewis is being beaten unconscious. The day becomes known as "Bloody Sunday."

of strength that ultimately defeated racism and white supremacy, not only in Selma, but across the South. In the weeks that led up to Bloody Sunday, she explains, the downstairs Sunday-school room was a meeting place for strategy sessions. Often church women made sandwiches in the basement. She recalls a gathering led by Rev. King at the church two days after Bloody Sunday. "Close your eyes," she says as she sits with me in the quiet chapel. "Feel the magic, feel this sanctuary. Can you feel nine hundred to twelve hundred people sitting as tight as they can, sometimes having to raise their heads just to get a little breath of air? Picture Dr. King preaching, teaching, calming; feel him in your mind's eye." Still the teacher, Mrs. Jackson, I realize, has a lesson for me, a lesson basic to understanding the southern civil rights movement of that momentous and deadly year: Look at what these local people reached inside themselves and found—look at what my friends and neighbors found. We live better because of it. Not perfectly, but better.

A marker in front of Brown Chapel commemorates four martyrs of that momentous and deadly year: Jimmie Lee Jackson, whose murder triggered the Selma-to-Montgomery march; Reverend James Reeb, a Unitarian minister who died from a savage attack by a white gang in Selma while walking home after finishing dinner in a black restaurant; Viola Liuzzo, a thirty-nine-year-old Detroit housewife gunned down on Highway 80 on March 25 after participating in the third and largest march following Bloody Sunday; and Jonathan Daniels, a young Episcopal minister who was murdered in the rural Lowndes County town of Hayneville, where a voter registration campaign was under way. Next to this marker, another plaque beneath a bas relief of Martin Luther King reports that after passage of the 1965 Voting Rights Act, the number of Afro-Americans registered to vote grew from 1,400,000 to 3,800,000. With some seven thousand new black registrants in Selma and Dallas County, Sheriff Jim Clark lost his job in 1966; he wound up selling mobile homes. In 1978 Clark pled guilty to smuggling marijuana from South America and was sent to prison.

A great deal of the planning for the Selma-to-Montgomery march also took place just two blocks down the street, at *First Baptist Church (709 Martin Luther King Jr. Street)*. (Selma, like many southern cities, has two First Baptist churches.) Organized in the 1840s, the church began its existence sharing space with a white congregation, but in 1894 a new building was finally built on what was then Sylvan Street. Constructed in the Gothic Revival style by local black architect Dave Benjamin West, First Baptist is considered one of the most architecturally significant late-nineteenth-century black churches in the state. When SNCC and the Dallas County Voters League began nonviolent-action and voter-registration workshops in 1963, First Baptist was one of the first of Selma's churches to permit use of its sanctuary for those sessions. SNCC established its march headquarters here in 1965, and Martin Luther King frequently spoke at mass meetings. Both Brown Chapel and First Baptist are on the National Register of Historic Places.

After the assault on the Pettus Bridge, Martin Luther King, who had been in Selma just before the march, returned and called for another march to be held two days later. However, there was now a federal court order forbidding

The King family on the March 21-24 Selma-to-Montgomery march. Center: *Coretta Scott King and Martin Luther King. Ralph Bunche is next to Mrs. King, and John Lewis is next to Bunche. In front of them are the three King children:* left to right: *Bernice King, Dexter King, and Yolanda King.*

a second march, and there was intense debate over whether to defy it; King had never yet disobeyed a federal court order. Finally, in a secret compromise with federal and local authorities, King decided to lead marchers up to the site where the Bloody Sunday marchers had been attacked and then turn around after kneeling in prayer. This demonstration, which took place March 9, was later called "Turnaround Tuesday" by angry civil rights activists who had not been told of the deal. And though there was no police violence on the bridge that day, there was tragedy in town that night. Reverend James Reeb, a young white Unitarian-Universalist minister from Boston, was bludgeoned outside a tough Ku Klux Klan hangout, the **Silver Moon Cafe** *(34 Washington Street)* after finishing dinner with two other ministers at nearby **Walker's Cafe** *(118 Washington Street, now Strong's #2 Restaurant)*, a black restaurant. He died as a result. Three men were indicted for Reeb's murder, but they were acquitted. There is a statue honoring Reeb on the grounds of Selma's **Old Depot Museum** *(4 Martin Luther King Jr. Street)*. This restored former L&N railroad station also has a Black History room featuring 1965 campaign memorabilia that

October 7, 1963, demonstrators at Selma Federal Building hold placards urging voter registration. They would soon be arrested.

include a newspaper announcement for the first mass meeting at Tabernacle Baptist Church. The museum also has a very good, and rare, collection of photographs of turn-of-the-century rural black life.

Because he was white and from the North, Reverend Reeb's death caused a much greater outcry than Jimmie Lee Jackson's murder had two weeks before. President Lyndon Johnson flew Reeb's wife to Selma on a government jet; telegrams poured in to the White House and Congress. With this death occurring just days after the televised images of Bloody Sunday, legislation for a voting rights act was introduced in the U.S. Congress, where it passed easily and was signed into law before the end of the summer. "It's part of the story of civil rights, and the tragedy of civil rights, that it was the death of a white minister that was the final impetus to the passage of the Voting Rights Act," said Reverend Clark Olsen, who was one of the two ministers accompanying Reeb that night and who also had been attacked. "The deaths of any number of blacks had not received anywhere the amount of attention that a white minister's did."

The third important movement church in Selma is **Tabernacle Baptist Church** *(1431 Broad Street)*. When in 1963 SNCC organizer Bernard "Little Gandhi" Lafayette and his wife, Colia, rolled into Selma in a battered old 1948 Chevrolet, only two hundred of Dallas county's fifteen thousand voting-age blacks were registered to vote. The Lafayettes checked into the black-owned **Torch Motel** *(1802 Vine Street; now closed and in disrepair)*. Shortly, the Lafayettes began to hold quiet meetings about citizenship and voter registration in private homes. They also attempted to recruit Selma University students, although more often than not they were run off campus by school officials. The Lafayettes established SNCC's first Alabama headquarters at **Boynton's Insurance and Real Estate office** *(21 Franklin Street)*. The **Boynton home** *(1315 Lapsley Street)*, though always a target in the crosshairs of racists, was also sanctuary for SNCC and SCLC movement organizers.

Bernard and Colia dug in and began holding workshops on nonviolent protest with high school students in the basement of Tabernacle Baptist. The civil rights commitment of the church's pastor, Reverend Lewis Lloyd Anderson, often put him at odds with his board of deacons. From the time he began his Selma ministry, Anderson had been challenging racism in his sermons and preaching that because blacks had contributed so much to Selma's development, they deserved much more from the white power structure. He pressed voter registration, sometimes accompanying blacks who wanted to register at the county courthouse. With the support of Rev. Anderson, who fended off fearful church elders, SNCC's Bernard Lafayette was able to conduct Selma's first modern movement–mass meeting here on May 14, 1963. Anderson had threatened to hold the meeting *outside* and use a loudspeaker to tell the crowd that his deacons were too afraid to hold a meeting inside the church. The meeting was officially a memorial service for Samuel Boynton, who had died earlier that month. Given Boynton's history, no one doubted that this "memorial" was going to be a civil rights meeting. In fact, the leaflet handed out for the meeting read "A memorial service for Mr. Sam Boynton and voter registration."

The Boynton family was arguably Selma's most political black family. The son, Bruce Carver Boynton, was the plaintiff in *Boynton v. Virginia*, which had led to the 1960 Supreme Court decision ordering the desegregation of interstate train and bus terminals. Returning home from Howard Law School in December 1958, Bruce had attempted to get a sandwich and a cup of tea at the cafe inside the Richmond bus station and was refused service.

Police cars with flashing lights surrounded Tabernacle Baptist at the memorial service–meeting. A group of young white thugs, brandishing long newly lathed table legs taken from a furniture shop, threatened arriving participants. The taillights and windshields of some autos were smashed by these youths—and also by some policemen, it was reported. Before the meeting started, Dallas County sheriff Jim Clark burst into the church with some of his armed deputies. After showing a court order from Judge James Hare, a circuit judge, authorizing him to enter the sanctuary to prevent "insurrection," Clark stationed his deputies in the back of the church. Despite all this, the meeting went on, at least partly because Samuel Boynton was held in such high

James Forman at a SNCC meeting in Atlanta. Just behind him in the trench coat is Marion Barry, future Washington, D.C., mayor.

regard. SNCC's James Forman was the featured speaker, and he called his remarks "The High Cost of Freedom." Pointing at Clark and his deputies that night, Forman said it might be a good thing that they had entered the church: Blacks had to realize that freedom would not come easily or cheaply, and if they agreed with Sam Boynton's efforts to get them to register to vote, they should say so in front of Clark. Forman urged blacks to go to the county courthouse en masse. This was in many respects the beginning of the campaign of grassroots organizing and mass protest that climaxed with the Selma-to-Montgomery march.

Just a few blocks away from Tabernacle Baptist, the **National Voting Rights Museum and Institute** *(1012 Water Avenue)* stands in the shadow of the Pettus bridge, occupying a modest storefront building that was once used by Selma's White Citizens Council. What I especially like about this museum, aside from the dynamic personality of its director, Joanne Bland, who was eleven years old on Bloody Sunday and was arrested in subsequent protests, is its collection of messages on an "I Was There Wall" from participants in Selma's various voter registration marches. There are also black-and-white photographs that were taken by the Alabama Department of Public Safety on Bloody Sunday. The museum was originally organized to honor those who marched on that day and to provide a place where local volunteers could recount the struggle for voting rights to visitors. Today, however, the museum also offers a much broader view of civil rights struggle. An entire room is devoted to blacks elected to Congress during Reconstruction. "We put the collections and exhibits together ourselves," says Joanne. "Maybe it's not as fancy as some museums, but many people tell us that they feel the people more here.

"Yeah, Selma Was Dangerous"

"Everybody thought Selma was too tough, too difficult. Reggie Robinson had already been there—he was the first SNCC person to go there, I think. And he reported back that people in Selma were just too afraid of white folks. But Jim Forman said if you want to go there and try and do something there's money and you can go try. I told Jim, 'I'll take Selma; I don't have to *try* and do anything there; I'll do something there.'

"I'd actually heard about Selma before this. It was during the Freedom Rides when, after leaving Birmingham, the bus I was riding to Montgomery was stopped by state police who said it needed to take another route to Montgomery because there was a white mob waiting in Selma and they couldn't protect us. I'm saying to myself, 'Oh, Lord—even the state troopers are scared of that city.'

"But even remembering that, I decide I'm going to work in Selma . . . and get married. Colia [Lidell] who I married was not afraid of anything. And we married. Our honeymoon was going to be Selma.

"But before going there we decided to do some serious research. Jack Minnis had already done some for us in Atlanta and in about half a day he taught me how to use Tuskegee Institute's library, which had all kinds of subscriptions to magazines and newspapers, including one to the White Citizen's Council newsletter. That's when I discovered that eight families controlled Selma and that's how Jim Clark had become sheriff—he was [former Alabama governor] Jim Folsom's nephew. When he was made sheriff he'd just gotten out of jail on a bad check charge, I think.

"By the time I left Tuskegee I had written a fifty-page paper about Selma— don't know where it is now; wish I did.

"Before going on to Selma I stopped in Montgomery and spent about four days with Rufus Lewis. He was widowed and we'd eat at Georgia Gilmore's. Rufus Lewis told me I should go into Selma quietly; not to have too much visibility or make too much noise. I took his advice.

This is real history of the local people." Nearby is the ***Slavery and Civil War Museum*** *(1410 Water Avenue).*

The ***Dallas County Courthouse*** *(105 Lauderdale Street)* is Selma's tallest building. It seems the sleepy center of a sleepy town today, but in the 1960s it was the

"Another reason for going into Selma was because it was the county seat of Dallas County. The Justice Department had already filed a suit alleging discrimination in voter registration and intimidation. SNCC, though, was split over voter registration. In fact, I was one of the direct-action people, more interested in that than voting drives. But it was becoming clear to me that in places like Selma, voter registration *was* direct action.

"When I first got to Selma I introduced myself to Sheriff Jim Clark in his office. It was a professional thing. I gave him my telephone number, then asked him for his. He looked up at the ceiling, then down at the floor and finally said, 'It would be best if you just contacted me here.' Guess what. That's where he slept; in his office. His wife had put him out, so he slept in a holding cell right there.

"I never brought one single person down to the courthouse to register. My position was if they can go and register their car or whatever, they could go themselves to register to vote. I was encouraging local leadership and I became a staff person for the voters league that the Boyntons led.

"Of course there was harassment. After that first mass meeting at Tabernacle I got stopped going back home. Now, I always checked my taillights and things like that before driving my car so I couldn't get stopped or arrested for some petty violation. After moving back to Atlanta Dr. King got sentenced to a chain gang because he forgot to change his Alabama driving license to one from Georgia. This policeman looked at my license for a long time thinking he had me, but he didn't—I had an Alabama license; one of the first things I did in Selma. But he decided to arrest me anyway. He charged me with vagrancy.

"Yeah, Selma was dangerous, but you've got to overcome a fear of death if you're going to live. Part of what makes people fearful is they think they are alone, so one of the things our mass meetings did was show them that they were not alone. Jim Forman spoke at the first one at Tabernacle. Lois Reeves from Tuskegee was the second speaker; she headed the YWCA on campus. Ella Baker was the speaker at our third mass meeting."

—BERNARD LAFAYETTE TO CHARLIE COBB

regular target of voter registration efforts by groups sometimes numbering in the hundreds. On Saturday, March 6,
1965, just a day before Bloody Sunday, Reverend Joseph
Ellwanger, a white Lutheran minister, led about seventy
members of a group called the Concerned White Citizens
of Alabama (a newly formed offshoot of the Birmingham-
based Alabama Council on Human Relations) in a march to
the courthouse protesting voter registration discrimination
against black citizens. A riot almost broke out as segregationists standing nearby sang "Dixie" and Ellwanger and
the CWCA responded with "America the Beautiful." Black
bystanders sang "We Shall Overcome."

Inside was the Dallas County office of voter registration,
which was open twice a month. Blacks who entered that
office with the idea of registering to vote always found themselves confronted with arcane questions, almost impossible
to answer to the satisfaction of registrars who claimed that
they were merely trying to determine literacy. In her autobiography, *Bridge Across Jordan*, Amelia Boynton recalled
one woman's attempt: "The registrar read a half-page [of
the U.S. Constitution] to her and then told her to leave the
room and stand outside. She was there for more than fifteen minutes. Not knowing what to do, she was about to
leave when the door opened and the man called her back.
He then told her to write what he had read to her before
she left the room." With obstacles of this kind, people made
little headway. Although large crowds began appearing at
the courthouse and formed long lines to wait for a chance
to try and register, they faced continuous harassment from
Sheriff Jim Clark and his posse. Then Circuit Judge James
Hare—the same judge who had empowered the sheriff
to prevent "insurrection" at the May 14, 1963, Tabernacle
Baptist Church mass meeting—banned any public gathering of more than three people to discuss civil rights,
effectively prohibiting church mass meetings and meetings
of the Voters League. It was then that the league decided to
ratchet up its effort by inviting Martin Luther King, who
had just won the Nobel Peace Prize.

King arrived in early January 1965 and preached a

potent sermon to a full house at Brown Chapel. "We will seek to arouse the federal government by marching by the thousands [to the courthouse]," he said. "When we get the right to vote, we will send to the statehouse not men who will stand in the doorways of universities to keep Negroes out, but men who will uphold the cause of Justice. Give us the Ballot!"

After protesting outside the Dallas County Courthouse in Selma, about 500 schoolchildren were arrested and then led by police to a detention facility. Because they had cut classes to protest, they were charged with juvenile delinquency.

A few days later, King and SNCC's John Lewis led hundreds of potential registrants from Brown Chapel to the courthouse.

Selma continued to heat up as black protest and voter registration efforts intensified. On January 22 about one hundred teachers staged a silent protest in front of the courthouse. Marches continued, with Sheriff Clark responding with cattle prods, truncheons, and arrests up until the March 7 attempt to march to Montgomery. More than three thousand people had been arrested in Selma by then; hundreds of them were schoolchildren like Joanne Bland.

❧ LOWNDES COUNTY ❧

In the mind of SNCC's Stokely Carmichael, who came to Alabama shortly after Bloody Sunday, the Selma-to-Montgomery march seemed likely to help with the early efforts to gain a foothold in nearby rural areas. "We could see who from the counties was participating in the march and these would be the strong people we could work with," Carmichael told me shortly before his death in 1998. And in his autobiography, *Ready for Revolution*, Carmichael (who in the 1970s changed his name to Kwame Ture) elaborated:

"[W]e trailed that march. Every time local folks came out, we'd sit and talk with them, get their names, find out where they lived, their addresses, what church, who their ministers were, like that. So all the information, *everything*, you'd need to organize, we got."

Carmichael honed in on Lowndes County, a nearby majority-black county. On Highway 80 between Montgomery and Selma, most of the land on both sides of the road is Lowndes County, 81 percent black in 1965 but feared as a county of white terror. Not one Afro-American was registered to vote when he and a small group of SNCC organizers began working there. Just four days before the Selma-to-Montgomery march, John Hulett (who in 1970 would become sheriff of the county) and a blind preacher, Reverend J. C. Lawson, became the first Lowndes County blacks registered to vote in the twentieth century.

On August 14, 1965, a small group of black teenagers began picketing stores in the tiny town of Fort Deposit. Soon hostile whites surrounded them, some driving up in cars with bumper stickers that read OPEN SEASON. Joining the protesters were a young Episcopal seminarian from New Hampshire, Jonathan Daniels, and Father Richard Morisroe, a Catholic priest, both of whom had participated in the Selma-to-Montgomery march and had chosen to stay in Alabama. The picketers were arrested—for their own protection, claimed the sheriff, who put them in the county jail in Hayneville, the county seat. They were held until August 20, when they were suddenly released without explanation or transportation. Some of the teenagers went to find a telephone while Daniels, Father Morrisroe, and two others walked to a nearby grocery store, ***Varner's Cash Store*** *(Hayneville near the intersection of Routes 21 and 97)* to buy soft drinks. Blacks customarily patronized the white-owned store with its big Coke sign. When they entered the store, however, Tom Coleman, an unemployed highway construction worker, pointed a twelve-gauge shotgun at them and ordered them

Stokely Carmichael in Sardis, Mississippi, continuing the James Meredith March Against Fear. Meredith had been shot not far from where Stokely is standing. A few days later, Stokely would call out, "Black power!" He was 25 years old.

"Things Happened So Fast"

"They let us out of jail, and there was no one there to meet us. It was one of those hot, southern, sticky days when you can look down and see little waves coming up from the pavement.

"We were hot. We were thirsty. There was a little store on the corner, a store that we had gone in many times. So someone decided that Jonathan Daniels, Father Morrisroe, Joyce Bailey, and myself should go and get the sodas for the group. We started over to get the sodas, and for a moment we hesitated, but we continued and got to the door, and there was Tom Coleman, standing there with a shotgun, threatening, first of all, 'Bitch, I'll blow your brains out,' because I was in front and Jonathan was behind me. Things happened so fast. The next thing I know, there was a pull and I fell back. The next thing, there was a shotgun blast and then another shotgun blast, and I heard Father Morrisroe moaning for water. And I thought to myself, This is what dead is. I'm dead."

—RUBY SALES

out. "Get off this property or I'll blow your goddamn heads off!" yelled Coleman, who was also a deputy sheriff. Then he opened fire, apparently aiming at sixteen-year-old Ruby Sales, who was standing in front of Daniels. The young minister had pulled her out of the way while Coleman spoke, and the shot intended for Sales hit Daniels in the chest, killing him instantly. Ruby Sales lay still beneath Daniels, covered with his blood, pretending to be dead. The others fled and Coleman fired again, this time hitting Father Morrisroe in the back. Coleman then went to **Lowndes County Courthouse Square** *(1 Washington Street)* and turned himself in. Daniels lay dead on the store's concrete porch; Father Morrisroe, alive, lay in the dirt road. Despite admitting to the killing during a defense that took less than an hour, Coleman was acquitted by an all-white jury.

The Lowndes County courthouse is also where Collie Leroy Wilkins was tried for the killing of Viola Liuzzo on Highway 80 during the Selma-to-Montgomery march. In that case, the jury deadlocked and a mistrial was declared. The courthouse had three bathrooms then: WHITE MEN, WHITE WOMEN, and COLORED.

With passage of the 1965 Voting Rights Act and with SNCC's organizing work, the county became one of the symbols of a great, still largely unacknowledged political success: In only one year, registered black voters outnumbered registered white voters. With its new empowering voting numbers, in April 1966 Lowndes County's black community formed a political party called the Lowndes County Freedom Organization (LCFO). Because of Alabama's high rate of illiteracy, state law mandated that a political party have a visual symbol and LCFO chose a panther, a black panther (the Democratic Party's symbol was a white rooster; the "white cock party," Stokely used to call it). Mark Comfort, a volunteer from Oakland, California, working with SNCC in Lowndes County, took that panther symbol back home, where it became both impetus and symbol for the Black Panther Party, which was formed and led by Huey P. Newton. In Lowndes County, one of the most creative campaigns for black political power took hold. Comic books were designed and distributed explaining the duties of all county offices. One comic book tracks the growing political awareness of a "Mr. Blackman," who, in the end, registers to vote and becomes sheriff. It is here that we see the roots of Carmichael's call for Black Power.

Mount Gilliard Baptist Church *(Trickem Fork, off Highway 80 at Route 17)* is the site of the first mass meet-

In 1966, blacks in rural Wilcox County, just south of Selma, line up to vote at a general store. The passage of the voting rights act the year before resulted in registered black voters' outnumbering white voters in this county.

ing held in Lowndes County. Viola Liuzzo had been killed a few days earlier, but despite the fear of murder and reprisal hanging over the region, more than a hundred people showed up, including a few teachers, important signals that ground was being gained in the civil rights campaign. In fact, two teachers who were movement stalwarts—Dorothy Hinson and Sarah Lou Logan—were fired from their jobs for their activism. Their successful suit for reinstatement established the precedent for teacher tenure in the state of Alabama.

First Baptist Church (Pine Street, Hayneville) first opened its doors to the movement for a memorial service for Johnathan Daniels. It was also the first polling place for blacks in Lowndes County. This breakthrough, too, was unintentionally aided by Alabama law, which required nominations for local offices to take place at or near the courthouse. Blacks were hardly going to enter the intimidating territory of the courthouse in large numbers, but the law gave them an option. First Baptist, just a few blocks away, was their choice. On May 3, 1966, some nine hundred new black voters met outside the church to nominate an LCFO slate for county offices. This was remarkable (even though the slate lost), considering that only a year before, *no* blacks had even been registered to vote.

⊷ PERRY COUNTY ⊶

While SNCC was tackling Lowndes County, Martin Luther King's SCLC was deeply involved in campaigning and organizing for voting rights in another mostly black county near Selma—Perry County. Coretta Scott grew up here, about twelve miles from Marion, the county seat. And Jean Childs, the wife of Rev. King's close associate Andrew Young, was from the town of Marion and met Young in 1952 when he was a student pastor there.

"Freedom Folks" Museum for Lowndes County, Alabama

The civil rights marchers who walked from Selma to Montgomery in 1965 camped on various black-owned farms, and signs along Highway 80 point out the locations. But it's not Selma that defines this trail, it's Lowndes County. Forty-three of the fifty-four miles of what the National Park Service now designates a "freedom trail" passes through Lowndes County.

The county is as rural now as it was forty years ago. It also remains one of Alabama's poorest. There are still people living without sewers or septic tanks; a third of the county's 13,500 residents live in mobile homes. One of the important figures in the county's civil rights movement is Bob Mants, an Atlanta native who dropped out of Morehouse College, joined SNCC, and worked in Americus, Georgia, before coming to Alabama. He came with John Lewis and was with Lewis on the bridge on Selma's Bloody Sunday. Bob puts on one of the several hats he wears today—this one, chair of the "Friends of the Trail"—to talk to me for a while. The organization, he points out, has been around for sixteen years. "We began doing this long before the park service's Selma-to-Montgomery trail." In our conversation Bob elaborated on his ideas for local tourism. It's not just about civil rights movement history, he says. "Everything is here for tourists from civil rights history to Civil War history to wonderful bird-watching.

"People who just think of Selma and Montgomery need to know there is a long, rich history here, going back to Native Americans, Hernando Desoto, who passed through the area, and Jesse James, who hid out here for a while.

Not long after SCLC's efforts had begun, the killing of Jimmie Lee Jackson during a nighttime protest in Marion would trigger the Selma-to-Montgomery march. This protest began the evening of February 18, 1965, at **Zion United Methodist Church** (*corner of Pickens Street and Martin Luther King Drive, adjacent to Marion's town square*). Reverend C. T. Vivian of SCLC gave a stirring speech that was followed by some five hundred people spilling out of the church and heading for the **Perry County Jail** (*206 Pickens Street*) half a block away, where SCLC's lead

Booker T. Washington helped establish the county's first black public school. The Southern Tenant Farmers Union was active here in the 1930s and the civil rights movement during the 1960s, of course. This is where the Black Panther Party in Oakland got their panther and the idea for their party—Eldridge [Cleaver] was out here working on an article about our panther party for the old *Ramparts* magazine. History could very well be our economic lifeline."

The civil rights history projected by the park service skips over Lowndes County, Bob feels; or as he puts it, "does not capture the true flavor of Lowndes County's civil rights legacy." From the campgrounds that civil rights marchers once used, Bob Mants envisions historic tours, hiking and exercise trails, and produce markets for local farmers. He wants to rehabilitate sites of historic importance, including the old Hayneville jailhouse and the **SNCC "freedom house"** *(625 Freedom Road, in White Hall)*, where civil rights workers stayed. He also wants to bring attention to churches like **First Baptist Church** in Hayneville, "where people voted for the first time under the black panther emblem," and **Gillard Church** in White Hall, an important base of civil rights support—and even do something with the county courthouse.

And he is looking for money for a permanent local "Freedom Folks Museum" reflecting "those who bore the burden in the heat of the day," such as people who spent two years in the tent city on Highway 80. He's prepared to help get it started with his own extensive collection of material: leaflets, photographs, "even my W2s from SNCC."

Bob never left the county and has no plans to retire and move somewhere else. "This is a lifelong mission for me," he says. "The work didn't stop with the civil rights movement, and I'll be doing it until the day I die. It's part of the whole unfinished question of justice."

organizer in the county, James Orange, was the latest of hundreds who had been jailed. The week before, protesting students had been arrested and placed in a stockade where they drank water from livestock troughs. When their parents protested these conditions, they were arrested, too. On this night the marchers intended to sing freedom songs and then return to the church.

Even before all the marchers had left the church, those in front found their way blocked by state troopers, sheriff's deputies, and local police. Reverend James Dobynes, a

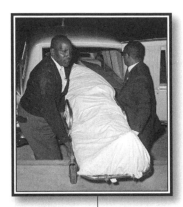

Jimmie Lee Jackson's body is removed from a Selma hospital on February 26, 1965. Jackson's murder by a state policeman in nearby Marion triggered the Selma-to-Montgomery March.

local leader, knelt to pray and was clubbed in the head, then dragged off to the jail. Suddenly, the streetlights went out and lawmen moved into the protesters' ranks, swinging billy clubs at anyone who seemed associated with the march (NBC correspondent Richard Valeriani was beaten with an axe handle). State troopers chased marchers in all directions; Jimmie Lee Jackson and his grandfather, eighty-two-year-old Cager Lee, slipped into *Mack's Café (226 East Jefferson Street; now Lee and Rollins Funeral Home)* just behind the church. Jimmy Lee's mother, Viola Jackson, worked there. Troopers stormed into the cafe after them, knocking over tables, clubbing Cager Lee and then attacking his daughter when she tried to protect him. When Jackson tried to help his mother, he was shot in the stomach. Eight days later Jimmie Lee Jackson died in a Selma hospital. While Jackson was still hovering between life and death in the hospital, the head of Alabama's state troopers, Colonel Al Lingo, served him with an arrest warrant. The Atlanta-based SCLC Women, Inc., has placed historic markers at Zion Methodist and the jail. There is also a marker with a likeness of Jackson in the parking lot of the nearby *Lee and Rollins Funeral Home.* Just across from the county courthouse, a *"Civil Rights Freedom Wall"* has been erected, with ninety-nine names representing "a roll call of freedom fighters."

Speaking at Jackson's funeral at Zion Methodist, Martin Luther King attributed Jackson's murder to "the irresponsibility of every politician from governors on down who has fed his constituents the stale bread of hatred and the spoiled meat of racism." After the service, a crowd numbering in the hundreds walked behind the hearse in the rain to the *Jimmie Lee Jackson Gravesite (Heard Cemetery, off Highway 14, renamed the Martin Luther King Memorial Parkway).* The inscription on Jackson's headstone reads HE DIED FOR MAN'S FREEDOM. It is pocked by shotgun blasts, presumably fired by racist vandals. SCLC holds a memorial service at the site every February.

BIRMINGHAM

B irmingham (dubbed "Magic City" because of its rapid, almost astonishing growth after the Great Depression) is Alabama's biggest, most industrialized city. Although Afro-American workers played a key role in establishing the CIO union, city laws mandating segregation and the power of Ku Klux Klansmen undermined any lasting interracial unity in the struggle for good wages and better working conditions.

Racial separateness—American apartheid—was deeply ingrained in every aspect of city life. In downtown Birmingham, even the parking lots were segregated, and physical partitions segregated eating places, which were required by law to have separate entrances for blacks and whites. There was even a city law making it illegal for white and black children to play together, and a book that showed white rabbits and black rabbits frolicking together was banned from the public schools. Violation of Birmingham's segregation laws was punishable with a $100 fine or six months in jail or both.

Official violence by city authorities and private violence assisted by those same authorities was used regularly to enforce segregation. There were *five* Klan organizations in Birmingham, as well as the National States Rights Party and the White Citizens Council. Mere days after the Montgomery bus boycott ended, singer Nat King Cole was attacked and beaten by whites while performing on the stage of Birmingham's municipal auditorium because, his attackers said, he was singing love songs to white women. In 1957, as part of an initiation rite, four Klansmen chose at random, abducted, and, using a razor blade, castrated black handyman Edward Aaron. Anger over the 1954 Supreme Court decision, the success of the Montgomery boycott, and its spillover effect in black Birmingham resulted in numerous bombings in the 1950s; the city acquired the nickname "Bombingham."

Such savage white conduct fueled intensifying efforts

Reverend Fred Shuttlesworth preaching at Bethel Baptist Church shortly after the September 15, 1963, bombing of the 16th Street Baptist Church in Birmingham. Many considered Shuttlesworth the most fearless of the southern leaders.

to bring about change. As early as the 1930s, attorney Arthur Shores began determined legal challenges to segregation. In the 1940s the militant Southern Negro Youth Congress was headquartered in Birmingham. On June 1, 1956, when Alabama's state government secured a court order outlawing the NAACP, Reverend Fred Shuttlesworth, the president of the Birmingham chapter and pastor of **Bethel Baptist Church** *(3233 Twenty-ninth Avenue North)*, brought together four ministers—N. H. Smith Jr., G. E. Pruitt, T. L. Lane, and R. L. Alford—to discuss starting a new organization. A few days later, to a packed mass meeting at **Sardis Baptist Church** *(1240 Fourth Street North; a New Sardis is now located at 1615 Fourth Court West)*, they announced the formation of the **Alabama Christian Movement for Human Rights** *(ACMHR)* and declared that by deliberately breaking segregation laws ACMHR would, through both direct action and legal test cases, challenge those laws.

Following the December 13, 1956, Supreme Court ruling making segregated seating in city buses illegal (as a result of the 1955–56 Montgomery bus boycott), ACMHR members began trying to "ride integrated." The Klan responded with violence, and on Christmas Eve Shuttlesworth's house was bombed and completely destroyed. The next day, however, Shuttlesworth led some fifty blacks to **Second and Third Avenues North at Nineteenth and Twentieth streets** in downtown Birmingham, where they boarded city buses; twenty-one of the riders, including Shuttlesworth, were arrested after surprised police tracked them down later in the day. When Shuttlesworth attempted to register two of his children at **Phillips High School** *(2316 Seventh Avenue North)*, a white mob beat him mercilessly with brass knuckles and chains. His wife, Ruby, who had accompanied him, was stabbed in the buttocks. (She later told her doctor that her only regret was that modesty prevented her from showing off her wound at the next mass meeting.)

By the time the Freedom Riders arrived in Birmingham in 1961, the ACMHR had paid almost fifty thousand dollars in bail bonds and fines, and eighteen black homes and churches and one synagogue had been bombed. So in 1962 Rev. Shuttlesworth invited Martin Luther King and SCLC to come to Birmingham. King himself, depressed by what he believed was defeat in Albany, was looking for a place to wage a civil rights campaign and win a clear victory. Birmingham seemed obvious now, if only because in addition to its total segregation, there was also a lightning rod of racist wrong in the person of Police Commissioner Theophilus Eugene "Bull" Connor.

Planning began on "Project C" (for Confrontation). The thinking was, defeat segregation in Birmingham and it would signal the end of segregation everywhere. At the heart of the effort would be a campaign of picketing, sit-ins, and boycotts of downtown stores during the Easter season of 1963. Broadly speaking, the campaign would aim to jeopardize the ability of white business owners to make money.

The campaign began on the morning of April 3, 1963, when twenty-four Miles College students sat in at four downtown lunch counters: **Kress**, **Woolworth's**, **Pizitz**, and **Loveman's**. The stores all closed in response. Two days later, on Palm Sunday, protesters on the way to city hall were arrested. The following week black ministers appeared in their pulpits wearing blue jeans, calling on their congregations to refrain from buying new clothes for Easter and calling for a boycott of downtown

Following his arrest during a downtown Birmingham protest, Reverend Martin Luther King is held by his belt as a policeman steers him to a waiting paddy wagon. Three days later, while still imprisoned, King wrote "Letter from a Birmingham Jail."

stores. But the protests were still small; only about fifty people joined Martin Luther King and Ralph Abernathy—both of them wearing crisp new dungarees—when they marched on Good Friday. Bull Connor arrested the two ministers downtown at a police roadblock on Fifth Avenue North, and while in jail, King penned his powerful "Letter from a Birmingham Jail" in response to local white ministers who denounced the protests. King was kept in a harsh solitary confinement and later wrote that his time there was "the longest, most frustrating and bewildering hours I have lived." After eight days in jail with the city still not budging, King came out and agreed to the controversial strategy of using children in protest marches. On May 2 hundreds of singing black schoolchildren poured out of the **Sixteenth Street Baptist Church** to protest; five hundred were arrested. The next day hundreds more repeated the action, but this time were met by Bull Connor and policemen holding leashed, snarling German shepherd dogs. The fire department was also present, with fire hoses at the ready. And when the firemen turned them on, powerful blasts of water slammed students against walls and sent them rolling uncontrollably down the street as the dogs lunged and tore at their flesh. Nightstick-wielding policemen moved in and attacked with all their might as hundreds of whites lining the sidewalks cheered and urged even more brutal police action. Still the young people continued to protest. On May 7, in a "freedom dash," students raced out of Kelly Ingram Park, then immediately scattered in all directions before converging on Twentieth Street, the heart of Birmingham's business district. There, they sat in or, more accurately, squatted in various shops and on the streets. Fire hoses and dogs were used again, but even as they fled, the students pledged to come back with an even larger force of young people. Altogether over these few days some twenty-five hundred people

Police dogs in Birmingham. The use of dogs against nonviolent protesters outraged the nation.

Excerpt from Letter from a Birmingham Jail

Perhaps it is easy for those who have never felt the stinging dark of segregation to say, "Wait." But when you have seen vicious mobs lynch your mothers and fathers at will and drown your sisters and brothers at whim; when you have seen hate-filled policemen curse, kick and even kill your black brothers and sisters; when you see the vast majority of your twenty million Negro brothers smothering in an airtight cage of poverty in the midst of an affluent society; when you suddenly find your tongue twisted and your speech stammering as you seek to explain to your six-year-old daughter why she can't go to the public amusement park that has just been advertised on television, and see tears welling up in her eyes when she is told that Funtown is closed to colored children, and see ominous clouds of inferiority beginning to form in her little mental sky, and see her beginning to distort her personality by developing an unconscious bitterness toward white people; when you have to concoct an answer for a five-year-old son who is asking: "Daddy, why do white people treat colored people so mean?"; when you take a cross-county drive and find it necessary to sleep night after night in the uncomfortable corners of your automobile because no motel will accept you; when you are humiliated day in and day out by nagging signs reading "white" and "colored"; when your first name becomes "nigger," your middle name becomes "boy" (however old you are) and your last name becomes "John," and your wife and mother are never given the respected title "Mrs."; when you are harried by day and haunted by night by the fact that you are a Negro, living constantly at tiptoe stance, never quite knowing what to expect next, and are plagued with inner fears and outer resentments; when you are forever fighting a degenerating sense of "nobodiness"—then you will understand why we find it difficult to wait. There comes a time when the cup of endurance runs over, and men are no longer willing to be plunged into the abyss of despair. I hope, sirs, you can understand our legitimate and unavoidable impatience.

—MARTIN LUTHER KING JR.,
APRIL 16, 1963

were arrested, and it was this "Children's Crusade" that finally forced negotiations. On May 8—over Shuttlesworth's objections—King announced a twenty-four-hour truce. The next day a settlement was announced in the courtyard of the **Gaston Motel** *(1501 Fifth Avenue North; now the A. G. Gaston Gardens)*. It called for the commitment of business leaders to desegregate stores and begin hiring blacks, the release on bond or personal recognizance of those who had been arrested, and the creation of a biracial committee for sustained discussion of desegregation.

In May of 1961, the Freedom Riders were crossing into Alabama from Atlanta, following U.S. 78 en route to Birmingham and plunging into some of the South's most dangerous territory. The riders met with Martin Luther King in Atlanta shortly before their departure, and he pulled aside *Jet* magazine's Simeon Booker, who was traveling with the group, warning the reporter sotto voce: "You will never make it through Alabama." King could well offer prophecy about the state where he had emerged as a civil rights leader, and when Freedom Riders arrived at the Greyhound terminal in Anniston, their bus was surrounded by a white mob of more than one hundred men carrying pipes, bats, knives, and bricks. They slashed the tires and pursued the bus as it sped from town. When flat tires finally forced the limping bus to stop near Forsyth and Son grocery on Route 202 six miles southwest of town, a firebomb was thrown through its smashed back window. As black smoke and flames engulfed the interior, the attackers pressed against the door to prevent the Freedom Riders from exit-

High-pressure fire hoses rolled young protesters down the street, sometimes slamming their bodies against brick and concrete walls. Calling the use of dogs and fire hoses against demonstrators "shameful," President Kennedy said the scene was "so much more eloquently reported by the news cameras than by any number of explanatory words."

Jailed high-school students held in Birmingham Stadium, which had been converted into a prison compound

ing. A few riders slipped through an open back window. Most, however, were trapped. "Burn them alive!" shouted the mob. "Fry the goddamn niggers!" Then the fuel tank exploded and the mob scattered, and the rest of the riders escaped. "That's how we got out," recalled Hank Thomas, one of those riders whom I looked up in Atlanta. The locals, however, quickly regrouped and resumed their attack. Thomas was struck in the head with a baseball bat. Finally, the police intervened, firing a few warning shots in the air, and the mob withdrew. A second explosion inclined the mob to stay away.

There is no marker along the highway where this took place, just a scattering of fast food restaurants. When the Freedom Riders retraced their route in 2001, on the fortieth anniversary of this Freedom Ride, the mayor of Anniston and a cheering crowd greeted them. "I was overcome with emotion," says Thomas. "I was thinking, look, they're cheering us, and forty years ago they wanted to kill us."

At Birmingham's **Continental Trailways Bus Station** (*Nineteenth Street and Fourth Avenue North*), Freedom Riders were also attacked by a white mob, but this time they were attacked after they had disembarked. James Peck was beaten with an iron pipe and required fifty-two stitches to close his head wounds. William Barbee wound up paralyzed for life. There was no police intervention; in fact, there was police collaboration with the Klan mob. Bull Connor, who knew of the plans in advance, excused the absence of police by saying that much of his force was off duty celebrating Mother's Day. There is a marker at the Trailways site.

A replica of the Greyhound bus that was burned in Anniston can be viewed at the **Birmingham Civil Rights Institute** *(520 Sixteenth Street North)*, which offers a self-directed tour of the exhibits that completely engulfs you in Alabama's civil rights movement of the 1950s and 1960s. You can watch a brief film tracing Birmingham's early history or explore the Barriers Gallery, which describes life for blacks in a separate

The bombed and flaming Freedom Rider bus in Anniston, May 1961

but unequal society. The Confrontation Gallery features a photographic image of an eighteen-foot-tall burning Klu Klux Klan cross. There are examples of "white" and "colored" drinking fountains and a replica of the jail cell where Rev. King wrote his "Letter from a Birmingham Jail" on the margins of a local newspaper in which local white ministers had criticized him. King's famous letter explains "creative tension" and urges passive religious leaders to recognize the need to challenge segregation with direct action against it. **Birmingham City Jail** *(417 Sixth Avenue South)* is now a police department administrative building; the bars from the old jail have been used in the institute's replica. Finally you join the Selma-to-Montgomery voting-rights march and move through a Processional Gallery into the Milestones Gallery, where steel obelisks commemorate the dates of significant civil rights events. The institute offered, I felt, one of the best multimedia presentations of the civil rights movement that I had encountered. Move through it slowly.

The institute anchors a six-block Civil Rights District

that includes the redbrick **Sixteenth Street Baptist Church** (*1530 Sixth Avenue North; groups by appointment only*), Birmingham's first black church, where on September 15, 1963, four young girls were killed in a bomb blast set off by Ku Klux Klansmen. The church was designed by the Afro-American architect Wallace Ryfield and built by an Afro-American contractor. The terrible September bombing that killed eleven-year-old Denise McNair, fourteen-year-old Addie Mae Collins, fourteen-year-old Carole Robinson, and fourteen-year-old Cynthia Wesley has made the church—initially reluctant to become deeply involved with the Birmingham campaign—a tragic symbol of the bloody price paid to secure civil rights. A Memorial Nook in the church basement contains photographs and other reminders of what happened

> "I don't think I was scared . . . I felt my idea was more powerful than the mob's. Theirs was white supremacy; mine was equality under law for all men. . . .
>
> I was hit over the head with a club. Even now my chest hurts and I almost conk out every time I climb a few steps. But I'm ready to volunteer for another ride. Sure. Any time."
>
> —HANK THOMAS, 1961

The four little girls murdered at the 16th Street Baptist Church bombing (left to right): Denise McNair, 11; Carole Robertson, 14; Addie Mae Collins, 14; and Cynthia Wesley, 14. Carolyn McKinstry, who was also 14 then and Cynthia's best friend, calls the bombing "a pivotal moment in America's history" and, she tells me, devastating to her. "At first we didn't know anyone was killed. My father came to the church, found me, and took me home. My two little brothers had run away from the church and he found them later. Carole's mother called to see if she was with us. Then, around 4:30 in the afternoon we got the call that they were dead, Cynthia, Carole . . . I was sick inside; I was afraid. And then I was just numb. For the next week I remember going to school and just being there. Even in Birmingham I had always felt secure—I had four big brothers, big brothers, and I always had the sense of being protected. Now, all of a sudden, I wasn't."

on that Sunday. In the balcony there is a stained-glass window of a crucified black Jesus and the words "You do it unto me." Every year the church holds a memorial service on the anniversary of the bombing. McNair is buried at the **Shadow Lawn Cemetery** *(120 Summit Parkway, Homewood),* where her headstone reads, SHE LOVED ALL, BUT A MAD BOMBER HATED HER KIND. The other three girls are buried at **Greenwood Cemetery** *(Airport Boulevard and Aviation Drive).*

In the spring of 1963, black demonstrators—mostly schoolchildren—gathered at **Kelly Ingram Park** *(across from the church and the institute)* and marched on City Hall and downtown businesses to protest racial discrimination and segregation. A statue of Martin Luther King greets you at the entrance facing the Sixteenth Street church. He feels welcoming here, encouraging you to take the "freedom walk" amid the park's magnolia trees, where there are scattered bronze sculptures that include leaping police dogs on the attack, children in jail, police cannons aimed at protesters, and three kneeling ministers in prayer. The park was appropriately described as a "place of revolution and reconciliation" by Birmingham's first Afro-American mayor, Richard Arrington.

One last meaningful stop born of the bloody tragedy in 1963 is the **Chris McNair Studio and Art Gallery** *(45 Sixth Avenue South).* Eighty-year-old Chris McNair, a prominent photographer when Birmingham's civil rights movement unfolded, and the father of Denise McNair, opens his studio to the public on the third Sunday of every month for a buffet breakfast prepared by his daughter Kimberly. For years Mr. McNair refused to talk about the church bombing that killed his eleven-year-old child, but when he realized that many young Afro-Americans in Birmingham knew little or nothing about the civil rights movement, he created memorial space dedicated to Denise that contains vivid black-and-white photographs of Birmingham's civil rights struggle. Sometimes Spike Lee's profoundly moving Academy Award–nominated documentary film *Four Little Girls* is also shown.

CHAPTER EIGHT

DON'T KNOW HOW WE WERE SO BRAVE

Jackson, Philadelphia, McComb, Greenwood, and Ruleville, Mississippi

> *When you're in Mississippi, the rest of America doesn't seem real. And when you're in the rest of America, Mississippi doesn't seem real.*
>
> —BOB MOSES

During a panel discussion at Jackson State University's Fannie Lou Hamer Institute, Judge Mamie Chinn from Canton, Mississippi, a site of great civil rights effort in the 1960s, sighed and then mused wonderingly, looking back on antiblack terrorism that occurred when she was a young girl involved in the movement. "I don't know how we were so brave." As Judge Chinn spoke, her words reminded me of the Mississippi I imagined before arriving in the state in the summer of 1962, and soon I was thinking back to my first days there. More than any of the other places we have visited in this book, my own civil rights trail winds through Mississippi.

The **Greyhound bus station** *(219 South Lamar Street)* in Jackson, where scores of Freedom Riders were arrested in 1961 and where I first set foot in Mississippi, now houses an architectural firm. The building's handsomely restored arte moderne architecture makes the site more attractive than I remember, but the design and color of buildings was hardly on my mind when I stepped off the bus. This was, after all, Mississippi; a state that dominated my nineteen-year-old consciousness as the place where fourteen-year-old Emmett Till had been brutally murdered just a few years earlier. On August 24, 1955, two white men, Roy Bryant and his half-brother, J. W. Milam, believing that Till had insulted Bryant's wife, snatched Till from his uncle's house in the middle of the night. They then beat the teenager, shot him in the head, and finally strapped him with barbed wire to a seventy-five-pound cotton-gin wheel and threw him into the Tallahatchie River. Six days later a fisherman

found his bloated body. His mother, Mamie, had insisted on an open-casket funeral, and the gruesome photograph of Till that appeared in *Jet* magazine confirmed to black America—especially to my generation of then teenaged males—that no state was more dangerous to a black person than the state of Mississippi.

I was not a Freedom Rider, but because I had been involved with the sit-in movement in the Washington, D.C., area, CORE had invited me to participate in a civil rights leadership-training workshop for young people in Houston. I decided to use the invitation as a way to see the deep South and purchased a bus ticket that would carry me from Washington, D.C., through Virginia, the Carolinas, Georgia, Alabama, Mississippi, Louisiana, and finally into Texas.

I only got as far as Mississippi. Upon leaving the bus station, I had made my way to **SNCC's Lynch Street office (1104 Lynch Street)**, which it shared with CORE. There had been sit-ins in Jackson over the past year, and one of the students involved in those protests—Lawrence Guyot, who later became chair of the Mississippi Freedom Democratic Party—challenged me when I explained that I was just

Getting through Alabama did not end the woes of the Freedom Riders. In Jackson, most who protested at the bus terminal were arrested and charged with either disorderly conduct or disturbing the peace.

Emmett Till and his mother, Mamie Bradley, in 1950

passing through on the way to a civil rights workshop in Texas.

"Civil rights workshop *in Texas!*" Guyot sneered, giving me a hard look. Guyot is a big guy and he hovered over me, forceful, disdainful.

"Tell me, just what's the point of going to Texas for a workshop on civil rights when you're standing right here in Mississippi?"

His challenge was clear: You can chatter about civil rights in meetings or you can *do* something to get those rights. If you want to *do* something, then the thing to do is join our effort here in Mississippi.

That idea had been nowhere in my mind when I left the capital. Now that I was confronted with it, I found myself wrestling with whether or not to commit to the work in Mississippi, and decided to stay over in Jackson for a few more days to at least learn what was going on. I felt connected to these young Mississippians I was meeting the same way I had felt connected on first encountering Freedom Riders and sit-in students at Howard University. My friend and movement comrade Bob Moses describes a similar feeling upon first seeing, in New York City newspapers, photographs of students sitting in at southern lunch counters: "They looked like I felt."

In a manner neither Guyot nor I anticipated, he settled my internal debate. Not long after our conversation, Guyot left with Luvaugn Brown, another Jackson activist, to join Sam Block (from Cleveland, Mississippi, a small town in the heart of the Delta) in Greenwood to begin SNCC's first Delta voter registration effort. While I was at the ***"freedom house"*** *(714 Rose Street)*, where civil rights workers lived, the telephone rang. It was Sam, calling from Greenwood to say that a white mob downstairs was beginning to attack their second-story office and that the FBI, whose staff were locals, had refused to help. If anything happens, the agents had told them, "call us back." Sam abruptly hung up the tele-

"Fix It for Free"

A huge area worthy of exploration is what happens with the convergence of younger people with older people within the context of civil rights struggle. It is an important and overlooked dimension of the movement, yet part of the key to its success. Unita Blackwell, who ultimately became the mayor of tiny Mayersville, in Issaquena County, Mississippi, still has vivid memories of the impact of the organizer who came to her town.

"Muriel [Tillinghast] came on down here to Issaquena County and stayed in the the summer of 1964. I'm sittin down watching her with this big hankerchief tied around her head . . . blue. It was a cottonfield hankerchief. You know, the kind you stuck it in the back of your pocket. She walked different than we did. Wasn't no fear we could see. And she was lookin white people in the eyes—you know, we didn't do that down here. And I'm thinking, 'Lord, that child gonna get herself killed; get us all killed.'

"We had never quite seen anybody this unafraid and yet she also recognized, now that I look back on it, the danger that she was in. She was the teacher. She explained to us what voting was. We started having meetings in our churches.

"Muriel was something. I planned to carry her to church one Sunday and I explained to her that she had to have her hair fixed. It wasn't ironed under that bandana. And she says, 'I will do that.' But when Sunday come the hair was in the same shape and the blue bandana was tied around her head and she was dressed up nicely and out she went to the church with the hair. Well, it took over the church. The women was lookin' and the men, too. I was trying to figure this out. The women were sayin we're going to have to do something with this child. And I agreed, and one woman said, 'Well, she's at your house. You tell her that I'll fix her hair.' Louise, she's on the board of supervisors now, used to fix hair at her house. I told Louise, 'You tell her you'll fix it for free.' She said, 'I'll get it done next week.' Next week has been thirty or forty some years. Last time I saw Muriel she still has not got her hair fixed."

—UNITA BLACKWELL TO CHARLIE COBB

On the 1966 James Meredith March Against Fear, Stokely and I keep concerned eyes on a band of young whites gathering nearby. CORE's newly elected director, Floyd McKissick, wearing sunglasses and a straw hat, is next to Stokely.

phone, and we didn't know what had happened. Bob Moses, then SNCC's Mississippi project director, who had been planning to begin a second Delta voter-registration campaign in Sunflower County, decided to rush up to the county with Charles McLaurin and Landy McNair, the two students who had committed to the Sunflower campaign. On the way Moses would investigate what had happened in Greenwood. I decided to go with them into The Delta. There simply was no way I could have gone on to Houston without knowing what had happened to Guyot.

As it turned out, the three Greenwood organizers had scrambled out through a back window, slid down a television antenna, and escaped. I never completed my journey to Houston.

The Mississippi I encountered that summer was a far more complex place than I had imagined it would be. The state was not, as most of us living outside it thought, simply an oppressive place where blacks were ground into total submission. And while it is certainly true that during most of its history Mississippi led the way in crafting repressive antiblack legislation and engaging in violence intended immediately to crush any civil rights effort, Mississippi blacks have also led the way in signaling that no matter how grinding and cruel the oppression, Afro-Americans would find a way to resist. Numbers have always helped that determination. When I arrived, 40 percent of the state was black; in the cotton-growing "Delta" counties, two-thirds of the population was black.

Between 1810 and 1860 a quarter million slaves were brought into Mississippi. For a brief, hopeful moment after the Civil War, the state began to reflect considerable black political power. Hiram Revels, an Afro-American AME minister born in Fayetteville, North Carolina, was elected to fill Jefferson Davis's Senate seat. He was the first Afro-American ever to serve in the U.S. Congress. Blanche K. Bruce, once a slave in Prince Edward County, Virginia, served a full term as a Mississippi senator (1875–81), and he was the last Afro-American to serve in the Senate until Edward Brooke of Massachusetts was elected in 1966. Throughout Mississippi after the Civil War, blacks were elected to local offices. (The state seemed promising enough to attract my great-grandfather, Samuel Kendrick, who had been born into slavery in Wetumpka, Alabama. He migrated to Mississippi and made his way into the Delta, which, despite the existence of some large plantations, was still largely raw frontier—a fertile but alligator-infested floodplain where bears roamed and mosquitoes brought malaria or yellow fever. There, in 1888, Sam Kendrick and other former slaves created a farming community called **New Africa**. Small black-owned farms remain in that community just off Highway 61 near Duncan, but residents have little knowledge of New Africa's roots.)

Such progress did not last. The new state constitution of 1890 imposed a literacy test that, along with the poll tax, took the vote away from blacks: Anyone seeking to register to vote was required to read any section of Mississippi's state constitution to the satisfaction of the circuit clerk in county courthouses (changed in 1954 to read *and* interpret). New Jim Crow laws began to segregate the state at every level. A "breach of the peace" law that carried a $1,000 fine and a six-month jail term stifled protest. Two months after the 1954 Supreme Court decision, the White Citizens Council was born in Indianola, Mississippi; and in 1956 a State Sovereignty Commission was created to investigate people and infiltrate organizations deemed to be subverting states' rights. The commission also had the vague mandate of protecting Mississippi from federal government "encroachment" on its sovereignty.

Despite this, blacks persevered and fought back. School desegregation suits were filed around the state. Also in the 1950s, huge civil rights rallies were held in the Delta. Black

Clarksdale pharmacist Aaron "Doc" Henry at a political rally on the Hinds County Courthouse steps in Jackson. He was running for governor on the Mississippi Freedom Democratic Party ticket. Tougaloo College chaplain Ed King (in clerical collar), who ran for lieutenant governor on the ticket, is to Doc's right.

World War II veterans such as Medgar Evers, Amzie Moore, and Aaron Henry formed a core group that led much of this black resistance to white supremacy. Medgar Evers built the NAACP youth chapters out of which would come many of the young people who worked with SNCC and CORE. Amzie Moore, president of the NAACP in Cleveland, Mississippi, put the idea of voter registration in SNCC's field of vision. Says Bob Moses, who would lead SNCC's campaign in the state, "I had been [hearing] about oppression behind the *iron* curtain and the meaning of the vote for freedom all through my college years, [but until I heard Amzie talk about this] I had not made the connection to the denial of the right to vote behind the *cotton* curtain." And like Amzie Moore, Clarksdale pharmacist Aaron Henry, who was state president of the NAACP, embraced the youthful cadres of SNCC and CORE despite misgivings from his national headquarters in New York City. The influence of "Doc," as Aaron Henry was known to us, was the key factor in reanimating a group that he and other black leaders in Mississippi had created in 1961, the Council of Federated Organizations (COFO). This organization would act as an umbrella under which all the civil rights organizations worked in Mississippi. "This was a major development," says Bob Moses. "Established local groups were conferring a kind of formal legitimacy on us by opening up to the young people of SNCC and CORE networks they had built up over years of struggle." Most of COFO's staff was made up of somewhat unruly organizers from SNCC and CORE who were in their early twenties or younger and had been involved in the sit-in movement. "Doc made us respectable," says David Dennis, who was CORE's Mississippi director. "We couldn't have done it by ourselves; we had to be introduced to these communities, and we were introduced by people carrying NAACP cards."

❧ JACKSON ❧

Under COFO's banner, SNCC, CORE, SCLC, and the NAACP all maintained offices in Jackson, the state's capital. But while Jackson may have been the capital of both a state government and a news media hostile to civil rights, it was also a city of much black strength. In 1960 Campbell College students led by student-body president Charles Jones organized an Easter boycott of Jackson's downtown white businesses, giving as the reason for the boycott "blacks' unwillingness to exist as people not yet free."

So we start right downtown, just a few blocks away from the old Greyhound bus station, at the *Mississippi State Capitol (400 High Street)*. This "new" capitol was completed in 1903, and in those early years of the twentieth century, Mississippi's legislature wrote the laws that entrenched Jim Crow in the state. The *Mississippi State Sovereignty Commission* coordinated its statewide operations of surveillance and destabilization from here before moving to the *Woolfolk building (on West Street)*. The

James Meredith March Against Fear ended here June 26, 1966, with a rally of some twenty thousand persons on the north side of the capitol.

The "old" capitol is now the **Old Capitol Museum** (*100 South State Street*). Stately magnolia trees rise from its wide front lawn; the building itself is vaguely reminiscent of the U.S. Capitol, but it was in this old capitol that Mississippi's legislature defeated passage of the 13th Amendment ending slavery, and created the Black Codes that effectively ushered in a legal form of slavery. Ironically, in 1984 the first floor of this building became the first permanent civil rights exhibit in the United States.

The **State Fairgrounds** (*Jefferson and Amite Streets*) are a few blocks to the east behind the old capitol. For decades "white" and "colored" fairs were held separately there. At the "colored" fair in 1963, members of the NAACP Youth Council protested, holding signs that read NO JIM CROW FAIR FOR US. Police arrested seven of the protesters. As civil rights demonstrations in Jackson grew during the spring of 1963, hundreds were imprisoned in two converted livestock-exhibition pavilions, surrounded with a barbed-wire fence. Jackson Mayor Allen Thompson boasted that he could handle ten thousand black protesters on these grounds. In 1965 supporters of the MFDP, marching on the Mississippi legislature to protest racial discrimination in the state's electoral process, were arrested and held at the fairground, too.

Hollis Watkins and Alverina Adams, both Tougaloo College students, sing Freedom Songs. Watkins now heads one of the most significant community organizing efforts in Mississippi: Southern Echo.

Also on State Street, at the former **Jackson Municipal Public Library** *(301 North State Street; now city administrative offices)*, the first sit-in in Jackson took place on March 27, 1961, when nine students from **Tougaloo College** *(500 West County Road)*, Mississippi's first accredited black college, sat down, began reading books, and were arrested by police for "disturbing the peace." The embarkation site for the protest was **Woodworth Chapel** *(on Tougaloo's campus)*, which for the next two years was the primary springboard for campus-planned protests aimed at downtown Jackson. A range of influential speakers, including Dr. Martin Luther King, Attorney General Robert Kennedy, George Washington Carver, and even Booker T. Washington have stood behind its pulpit. The **Tougaloo College Archives** contain personal papers, NAACP records, oral histories, photographs, and other memorabilia of people and events involved with Mississippi's civil rights struggle.

The arrest of the "Tougaloo Nine" for their library sit-in sparked a fury of protest. Students from Jackson State College (now Jackson State University) marched to the **City Jail and Municipal Court Building** *(327 East Pascagoula Street)*, where the Tougaloo students were being held. The March 29 trial of the nine was a protest demonstration in itself. The "colored" section at the Municipal Court filled up early that day, and supporters of the students spilled onto the courthouse steps. When the nine arrived, the crowd erupted into cheers and applause. Policemen moved in with clubs, dogs, and tear gas. Medgar Evers, one of those in the crowd, was battered to the ground. But the movement appeared unstoppable now. Students began challenging segregation at the city zoo and at city parks. Three Jackson State students boarded a bus at Lamar and Capitol Streets and sat in the white section, challenging segregation in public transportation. By the end of the summer of 1961 there had been more than three hundred arrests.

When the Freedom Riders arrived in 1961, they were arrested on charges of trespassing and breach of the peace. They were held at the **Hinds County Detention Center** *(407 East Pascagoula Street)* and tried at the **Hinds County**

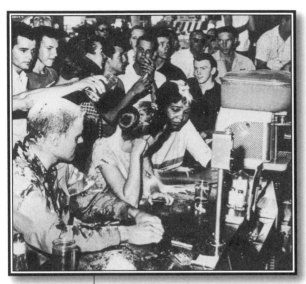

Tougaloo College students sit in at a Woolworth lunch counter in Jackson and are assaulted by a gang of young whites. Left to right: *John Salter, Joan Trumpauer, and Anne Moody, who later authored* Coming of Age in Mississippi.

Courthouse there. The **Hinds County Jail** is here, too. Several of those detained riders were already emerging as important civil rights leaders: Stokely Carmichael, Ruby Doris Smith, Bernard Lafayette, James Bevel, and John Lewis among them. Overcrowding resulted in some Freedom Riders' being sent to the Hinds County prison farm in Raymond, including SCLC's C. T. Vivian, who was beaten there for refusing to say "sir." In 1964, Byron De La Beckwith, who assassinated Medgar Evers in 1963, was tried in the county courthouse.

Throughout the early 1960s there was unrelenting local pressure to end racial segregation in Jackson. In 1962 the NAACP North Jackson Youth Council announced a Christmas boycott of downtown Jackson stores, and students went from door to door, passing out leaflets urging support for it. Although city officials attempted to dismiss the boycott's impact, after six months it was clear that Jackson's businesses were hurting. Meanwhile, almost simultaneously with the start of the boycott, students from Tougaloo College began picketing the *F. W. Woolworth store* on Capitol Street *(124 East Capitol Street; now a welcoming downtown city "green space" with the address One Jackson Place)*. A few months later Tougaloo students attempted a sit-in at the department store. On May 28, 1963, after entering Woolworth's through the back door, three Tougaloo students, Anne Moody, Pearlena Lewis, and Memphis Norman, sat down at the lunch counter and asked for service. They were ordered to go to the Negro section and refused. Word of this unprecedented action spread, and white students from nearby Central High School went to Woolworth's and attacked the Tougaloo group, kicking and pounding them to the floor. When white supporters on Tougaloo's campus joined the sit-in, the violence escalated. All of this was ignored by the police, who stood outside watching. Finally the store closed; the Tougaloo protesters were arrested and taken to jail. Photographs of this assault were used to design the sit-in display at the National Civil Rights Museum in Memphis.

Just off Lynch Street, the **Pearl Street AME Church** *(925 West Pearl Street)* gave active support to the Tougaloo students as soon as they began their Woolworth's sit-in. And it was here, at a huge mass meeting the night after her husband's assassination, that Medgar Evers's widow, Myrlie Evers, called on black Jackson to continue her husband's struggle. "I come to you tonight with a broken heart. I come to make a plea that all of you here and those of you who are not here, will, by his death, be able to draw some of his strength, some of his courage, and some of his determination to finish this fight."

One last stop in downtown Jackson takes us to **WLBT television station** *(715 South Jefferson Street)*, which was known for broadcasting messages of segregation and white supremacy. On April 15, 1965, the United Church of Christ asked the Federal Communications Commission not to renew the broadcast license of the station's owners, Lamar Life Insurance Company. Their petition argued that the station, whose viewing audience was 40 percent Afro-American, discriminated in news and programming content and overall failed to serve Jackson's black community. Lamar Life eventually lost its license and in June 1971, in what must be considered the significant turning of a page in Mississippi, Communications Improvement, Inc., a company with 91 percent Afro-American ownership, began operating the station.

Farish Street, which takes you right into Jackson's historic black business district, takes its name from Walter Farish, a former slave who settled on what is now the northeast corner of Davis and Farish Streets. Although this is part of a 125-acre **Historical District** *(roughly bounded by Amite,*

Mourners in Jackson, including Martin Luther King and Roy Wilkins (on King's left), parade from the Masonic Temple, where services for Medgar Evers had been held, to the Collins Funeral Home across town, in a procession honoring the murdered NAACP state field secretary.

Mill, Fortification, and Lamar Streets), and the black neighborhood is listed on the National Register of Historic Places, the buildings on Farish Street are now dilapidated and sagging, hardly reflecting the former vibrancy of the area. Between 1890 and 1930, skilled black craftsmen built many of the now shuttered buildings. Clubs, churches, restaurants, and small businesses along the street provided vital support to Jackson's and greater Mississippi's civil rights movement. Above **Big Johns** *(507½ Farish)*—known for pig ear sandwiches—Medgar and Myrlie Evers opened their NAACP office. Later the Mississippi Freedom Democratic Party and the Medical Committee for Human Rights (MCHR) maintained offices in the building. In the 1940s and 1950s the **Alamo Theater** *(333 North Farish Street)* showed first-run movies and was also the venue for great performers such as Nat King Cole.

At the beginning of the 1960s, only three Afro-American attorneys were licensed to practice law in the state: The offices of Carsie Hall, R. Jess Brown, and Jack Young were all on Farish Street. So were the editorial and business offices of the **Mississippi Free Press** *(538 Farish Street),* a movement alternative to Jackson's racist newspapers. The *Free Press* was actually published in Holmes County by feisty newspaperwoman Hazel Brannon Smith, who sent it down to Jackson every week. Though she did not openly support integration, Mrs. Smith felt the newspaper she owned in Holmes County, the Lexington *Advertiser*, should tackle injustice and corruption, which meant fighting the establishment. "The laws of America are for everyone—rich and poor, strong and weak, black and white," she wrote in a front-page editorial denouncing the county sheriff for brutalizing a black man. She was the first woman to receive the Pulitzer Prize for editorial writing. "Ours is the only paper in the county," she told an interviewer in 1964, "and I just cannot permit [White] Citizens' Councils to tell me how to run my newspaper." Her editorial offices were firebombed that year. Later, Henry Kirksey, who in 1979 became one of the first blacks elected to the state senate since Reconstruction, published and edited the *Free Press*.

The urban anger that had appeared in Birmingham earlier in 1963 and would erupt with rioting in city after city above the Mason-Dixon line in the late 1960s, appeared in Jackson the day of Medgar Evers's funeral: June 15, 1963. Thousands had followed the white hearse from the Masonic Temple on Lynch Street to the **Collins Funeral Home** *(415 Farish Street)*. Jackson's mayor had approved the march to the funeral home as long as it was silent. But after reaching the funeral home, hundreds of mostly young marchers continued down Farish Street, clapping their hands and singing movement songs. At the **intersection of Farish and Capitol Streets**, they encountered police barricades and tried to break through. They were forced back by police, who also brought up fire trucks, and the firemen began unrolling hoses. "We want the killers!" some in the crowd began shouting. Out of eyesight, police beat whomever they could grab and made about thirty arrests. Soon rocks and bottles were being hurled at the police, and it seemed that a full-blown riot was about to erupt. Then, seemingly appearing from nowhere, Justice Department attorney John Doar stepped between the police and the marchers, arms raised, gesturing for calm. "My name is John Doar. I'm from the Justice Department and anyone around here knows I stand for what is right. Go home. Medgar wouldn't want this; let's not have a riot." The crowd actually calmed down. For their part, the Jackson police were not likely to shoot down a well-known agent of the federal government. CORE's David Dennis then began organizing organizers to take bottles out of the hands of the angry youths as they dispersed.

The *Smith Robertson Museum and Cultural Center (528 Bloom Street)* pays particular attention to the Farish Street historical district. It exhibits artifacts from Mississippi's civil rights movement and also offers displays that highlight the contributions of southern blacks to all facets of life. The museum building was the first public school for Afro-American children in Jackson, and it, too, is the site of an early civil rights challenge. In 1948 Gladys Noel Bates, a science teacher at the school, sued the state of Mississippi to equalize white and black teachers' salaries. She and her husband, John M. Bates, were fired, but Mrs. Bates ultimately won her case. Mrs. Bates's father was one of the founding members of the Jackson NAACP, and in 1961 her parents provided housing for Freedom Riders in their home. The museum continues an education program today, with workshops and ongoing research that includes collecting the oral histories of participants in Mississippi's movement.

Lynch Street is the other significant civil rights corridor in Jackson. The street is named for John Roy Lynch, who was a three-term black congressman during Reconstruction. It is anchored by historically black *Jackson State University (1400 Lynch Street)*. Unlike Tougaloo, Jackson State was a state-funded school, and there was no overt, publicly expressed support for challenges to segregation from the administration. (Tougaloo president Dr. A. D. Beittel had visited the Tougaloo Nine in jail; Freedom Riders were housed in Tougaloo dorms.) Still, Jackson State students regularly defied the college's administration by engaging in protests. Shortly after the arrest of the Tougaloo Nine, hundreds of Jackson State students held a prayer vigil of solidarity with them in front of their own library. Today the school is home base for the **Fannie Lou Hamer Institute** *(1400 Lynch Street)*, which sponsors monthly lectures and other programs focused on grassroots efforts to strengthen democracy.

COFO headquarters *(1017 Lynch Street)* even then was a rather nondescript cement-block structure with peeling paint. This building, which had once housed a black radio station, was the nerve center of the 1964 Mississippi Summer Project, which brought nearly a thousand volunteers into the state to help the campaign for civil rights. From here, voter-registration projects, freedom schools, security, publicity, and direct-action protests were tracked with the assistance of a WATS (Wide Area Telephone Service) line that allowed unlimited calls throughout the state at a flat rate. Discussions about using the facility as an archive are under way with Jackson State.

Medgar Evers

Just up the street is the **Masonic Temple** *(1072 Lynch Street)*, where Medgar Evers ultimately chose to headquarter the NAACP in Jackson. There is some history to this. In 1954 Jackson's Masons had invited Thurgood Marshall to speak, planning to use the auditorium of Jackson State, which was then the largest assembly hall for blacks in the city. But the state and city vetoed the plan, so the Masons accelerated plans to build their own auditorium. Marshall inaugurated the new hall on May 30, 1955, marking it as a civil rights center. Evers's office was upstairs, in room ten. From this office base, Evers crisscrossed Mississippi, reconstructing and reinforcing NAACP chapters that were under constant assault by then-new white organizations such as the White Citizens Council. Racial killing was on the rise. Of particular importance to SNCC and CORE later on, Evers gave a great deal of attention to building NAACP youth chapters.

SNCC and CORE used the Masonic Temple for nonviolent workshops, and on August 6, 1964, while preparing to challenge the seating of the all-white Mississippi Democratic Party at the Democratic Party's national convention in Atlantic City later that month, the MFDP held its state convention to make the final selection of delegates here. Almost a year earlier, in October 1963, COFO had met here and decided to conduct a "freedom vote" among unregistered blacks to disprove the notion that apathy was the cause of their low voter-registration numbers.

The temple was a natural place for Medgar Evers's funeral, and some four thousand mourners attended in stifling heat. A few steps from the open casket, Martin Luther King, Roy Wilkins, and other civil rights leaders praised the NAACP leader's efforts in Mississippi. The NAACP is still headquartered at the Masonic Temple.

There is a Medgar Evers Boulevard in Jackson now, and on it you will find a bronze life-size **Medgar Evers Statue** *(4215 Medgar Evers Boulevard)* designed and cast in 1991 by T. Jay Warren, a white Mississippian from Rolling Fork who supported the movement. Evers stands relaxed and confident, one hand resting on his right thigh; his eyes seem to be gazing unalarmed into the future. The inscription reads "Dedicated to everyone who believes in peace, love and nonviolence. Let's keep the torch burning." The statue stands in front of the **Medgar Evers Library**, which has a permanent display detailing Evers's life and his role in Mississippi's civil rights struggle.

The **Medgar Evers House Museum** *(2332 Margaret Walker Alexander Drive, northwest of downtown)* is on a street named for Margaret Walker, the great Birmingham-born writer, who taught at Jackson State for years. Like Martin Luther King's parsonage in Montgomery, this humble home in a neighborhood of modest homes is moving for the access it gives to its owner's personal life. Because of Evers's work, abusive and threatening telephone calls constantly harassed the Evers family here, and the children were taught to stay away from the windows and dive to the floor at any out-of-the-ordinary sound. On June 12,

1963, returning home late from an NAACP meeting—a night on which his family had stayed up to listen to a civil rights speech by John F. Kennedy—two gunshots rang out as Evers stepped out of his car. One hit him in the back, tore through his chest, and finally lodged in a kitchen cabinet inside the house. Evers, bleeding profusely, crumpled, dropping the armful of "Jim Crow Must Go" T-shirts he was carrying, and lay facedown in his own blood. He died an hour later. Byron De La Beckwith had shot Evers with his deer rifle from behind the bushes across the street. He was not convicted of the murder until 1994; two all-white juries had deadlocked in 1964. After the first of those trials, Governor Ross Barnett stood at De La Beckwith's side and shook his hand.

The city is now served by the Jackson-Evers International Airport.

ᔐ PHILADELPHIA ᔐ

The story of Philadelphia, Mississippi (from Jackson, Interstate 20 east to Meridian, then south on Highway 19), is deeply imprinted on the national consciousness of civil rights struggle. On June 21, 1964, CORE field secretary Michael "Mickey" Schwerner, summer volunteer Andy Goodman, both white, and James Earl Chaney, a young black organizer from Meridian, left the **COFO/CORE office** (2505½ Fifth Street) to investigate the destruction of Mount Zion Baptist Church. The church had stood on its plot in the **community of Longdale** since 1899, and for the civil rights organizers Mount Zion represented a significant new toehold in Neshoba County, where there was widespread support for the Ku Klux Klan. Two months before, twelve KKK crosses had been burned around the

The burned blue Ford station wagon in which James Chaney, Michael Schwerner, and Andrew Goodman were traveling on the evening of June 21, 1964, when Neshoba County deputy sheriff Cecil Price stopped them and then jailed them in Philadelphia. Suddenly released around 10 P.M., the three disappeared shortly after driving off. On August 4 the FBI found their bodies on Olen Burrage's Old Jolly Farm, six miles southwest of Philadelphia.

county. Fear was thickening with the expectation of more white violence in response to the nascent Summer Project, which would bring hundreds of volunteers to the state to campaign for civil rights. Andy Goodman was one of these volunteers, an early arrival. In May Chaney and Schwerner had spoken at Mount Zion and the members had agreed that the church could be used as a freedom school site. Soon the church was under attack. On June 16 church officers leaving a routine business meeting were assaulted by the Ku Klux Klan; after savagely beating three of them, the Klansmen set a kerosene fire that burned the church down. Only the old bell used to signal the start of services survived. Chaney, Schwerner, and Goodman planned to get written statements about this violence. But they never made it to the church. Around 4 P.M. Deputy Sheriff Cecil Price pulled them over for speeding. All three were taken to the **Neshoba County Jail** *(422 Myrtle Street)* and held there until about 10:30 that night, then suddenly released. Price followed their blue station wagon out of town and stopped them again in the **House Community** *(on Highway 492 going toward Union)* and handed them over to a convoy of waiting Klan members who murdered the three on what is known as **Rock Cut Road** *(the intersection of County Roads 515 and 284).*

With these killings people across the nation recognized for the first time that Mississippi's racial oppression threatened their own children. The outrage and uproar were loud and instantaneous because of all the young people from around the country slated to begin working for civil rights in Mississippi that summer. Their parents, friends, and relatives were now shocked and fearful, and parents began demanding federal protection, which had been unavailable to local civil rights activists and organizers. They also pressed for a real investigation into the murders of Chaney, Schwerner, and Goodman. Mississippi authorities had been saying that the disappearance of the three was a hoax designed to generate publicity and sympathy for the just beginning Summer Project. Soon Neshoba County was flooded with FBI investigators and national press. There were movement investigators as well, staying with local families and waiting until the dead of night before making their own searches. On August 4, following up on the tip of a paid informant, FBI agents finally found the young civil rights workers' bodies buried in an earthen dam at *Old Jolly Farm* (*Highway 21 south, near the Neshoba County Fairgrounds*) about six miles from Philadelphia. Schwerner and Goodman had been shot once; Chaney, twice in the head and once in the chest. There is a NO TRESPASSING sign at the unmarked site today.

In Philadelphia I find myself wrestling with my feelings again. Some of this is personal. I knew Mickey Schwerner and James—"J. E.," as he was most often called—Chaney. And while the town and county seemed to be sincerely struggling to face up to their terrible and shameful past, it was the climate created by state, town, and county authorities that led to the murders in the first place, making it almost physically painful to hold in my hands a county-produced "Neshoba County African American Heritage Driving Tour" brochure which has written at the bottom of its cover "Roots of Struggle Rewards of Sacrifice." The text concludes in the "Rewards of Sacrifice" section, "Neshoba County discovered that the cancer of racism infects each person it touches . . . Although the ravages of this illness found a face in this community . . . today, Neshoba County has begun to heal." I know I am supposed to applaud this, but in all honesty, I still have unresolved emotions lodged in anger here, even though the brochure is useful and sends visitors where I would send them.

In February 1966 the rebuilt *Mount Zion United*

Methodist Church (*County Line Road; from downtown Philadelphia drive eight miles east on Highway 16E, south on County Line 747 for 2.2 miles*), the site of the 1964 beatings and burning that brought Chaney, Schwerner, and Goodman to Neshoba County, was rededicated. A granite plaque near the front of the church pays tribute to the three civil rights workers. Also in front of the church, hanging from a metal frame, is the bell that survived the torching.

Mount Nebo Missionary Baptist Church (*257 Carver Avenue*) was the first church in the county to give civil rights organizers from CORE a facility to use for mass meetings, and in 1966 Mount Nebo was the headquarters of a county-wide boycott in protest of police brutality. Here also is a monument to the three slain civil rights workers. Two years after the murders, when Martin Luther King held a memorial service here followed by a march to the *County Courthouse* (*401 Beacon Street*) in downtown Philadelphia, he found himself speaking while Deputy Sheriff Price and Sheriff Lawrence Rainey, who were await-

"Sick and Tired"

"I am not here to memorialize James Chaney, I am not here to pay tribute—I am too sick and tired. Do you hear me, I am sick and tired. I have attended too many memorials, too many funerals. This has got to stop. Charles Parker, Medgar Evers, Herbert Lee, Louis Allen, Emmett Till, four little girls in Birmingham, a thirteen-year-old boy in Birmingham, and the list goes on and on. I have attended these funerals and memorials and I am sick and tired. But the trouble is that you are not sick and tired and for that reason you, yes you, are to blame, every one of your damn souls. And if you are going to let this continue now then you are to blame yes YOU . . . Your work is just beginning. If you go back home and take what these white men in Mississippi are doing to us . . . if you take it and don't do something about it . . . then God Damn your souls!"

—DAVE DENNIS, AUGUST 7, 1964,
MEMORIAL TO JAMES CHANEY

ing trial on charges of violating the civil rights of Chaney, Schwerner, and Goodman, stood near him in the crowd of white onlookers. "I believe in my heart that the murderers are somewhere around me at the moment," King said, although I do not think he recognized Price and Rainey. "They're right behind you," yelled out someone among the hostile whites, who threw bricks and bottles at King as he made his way back to the church. Aided by the 1965 Voting Right Act, seven hundred fifty new black registered voters were on the rolls when King spoke; three hundred fifty had registered at the courthouse, another four hundred by a special federal registration center at the post office.

Practically next door to Mount Nebo, Lillie "Aunt Lil" Jones used to sit in a rocking chair on her front porch, offering encouragement to movement workers. From there she also kept a watchful eye on the cars coming up the street. **The Jones House** *(241 Carver Avenue in the section known as "The Hill")* was directly across the street from the **COFO office** *(242–244 Carver Avenue)*, which was established by Ralph Featherstone and others a week after the burial of James Chaney (the same Ralph Featherstone who was killed by a car bomb on the way to Cambridge, Maryland, in 1970). A large COFO sign with linked black and white hands hanging on the front of the building gave the office a highly visible presence as an island of defiance in a town used to seeing blacks cowed by white power. That sign is now at the Old Capitol Museum in Jackson. At the COFO office, living quarters were upstairs; downstairs was meeting and workshop space. Amos McCelland, one of the leading black businessmen in Philadelphia, owned the building. Across the street, **McCelland's Cafe** *(245 Carver Avenue)* fed movement workers; the cafe is still open.

James Chaney is buried just outside of Meredian, at the **Okatibbee Baptist Church Cemetery** *(from Interstate 59/20 take Exit 151 at Valley Road to Fish Lodge Road; cemetery is less than a mile down, on the right)*. For a time, vandals attempted to pull his gravestone out of the ground; it is now braced by steel supports. Nearby, an eternal flame burns. Schwerner and Goodman are buried in New York.

⭞ McCOMB ⭟

L ike the 1951 student walkout at Moton School in Prince Edward County, Virginia, the 1961 high-school-student–initiated protests in McComb are far too often overlooked. These protests reshaped civil rights struggle in Mississippi for a good part of the 1960s. They began quietly, as momentous events often do. Robert "Bob" Moses, a young New York City schoolteacher who grew up in Harlem, had arrived in McComb by bus from the Mississippi Delta in July. He was now a SNCC field secretary. McComb's NAACP leader, Curtis Conway "C. C." Bryant, had read a story in *Jet* magazine about a planned SNCC drive in the Delta, the "Move on Mississippi," and contacted his NAACP colleague in the Delta, Amzie Moore, to see if some of those people could be sent to McComb. Moore sent Moses, SNCC's only worker in the state.

In this small southwest Mississippi city, Bryant wanted Moses to help him organize a voter-registration drive. The New Yorker soon began that work, by August conducting voter-education workshops on the second floor of the **Masonic Hall** *(630 Warren Street)*. The first floor of the hall was actually the **Burgland Super Market**, a grocery store owned by Pete Lewis, who was already a registered voter. The building is unused today.

Years later Moses would remember that as he began his voter-registration effort in McComb, he really had not calculated the impact of Freedom Rides, sit-ins, and other direct-action protests. They were tapping a wellspring of youthful discontent in places like Mississippi where failing to say yessir to a white man was considered protest. Moses was a "Freedom Rider" to many young people in McComb, and they were waiting for him to lead them into direct-action protests.

Moses had not been in McComb long before four young men came to the city looking for him. They were from a rural community about three miles north of McComb. "We were actually coming from Lincoln County," says Hollis Watkins, who was nineteen years old at the time, "a little place called Chisholm or sometimes Chisholm Mission because that was the name of the AME church out there. The mail came to the Pike County post office at Summit, though." Also in this group was Curtis Hayes, who, along with Watkins, would figure prominently in Mississippi's movement in coming years. The four were hoping to meet the South's most famous civil rights leader. "A friend-girl told me she heard Martin Luther King was in McComb,"

said Hollis, and after approaching Bob Moses, he asked him:

March for voting rights in McComb

"Are you Martin Luther King?"

"No," Moses replied.

"Well, we heard he was here in McComb."

"I'm not him. I'm here to teach Negroes how to vote. I'm C. C. Bryant's voter-registration man."

Watkins and Hayes committed to the effort and began working with Moses. Two other SNCC organizers, Reggie Robinson from Baltimore's movement and John Hardy from Nashville's student movement, also joined Moses, and the five men formed a core group, traversing new ground in some respects by attempting to mobilize the entire community around voter registration rather than just concentrating on McComb's tiny black middle class.

Moses's work put McComb on SNCC's radar screen, and soon direct-action activists (among them future Washington, D.C., mayor Marion Barry) began holding nonviolent workshops there. These workshops generated great excitement among the young people working with

Bob Moses addressing a Jackson mass meeting

Moses, most of whom were too young to vote, themselves. They not only admired the heroes and heroines of sit-ins and Freedom Rides, but also wanted to emulate them. It wasn't long before the students decided that while they might not be able to vote, sit-ins were another story, and a new organization that had grown out of the workshops, the Pike County Nonviolent Action Movement (Hollis was president; Curtis was vice president), began planning one. Twenty-two students agreed to sit in at the public library. But when the day for action arrived, only Curtis and Hollis showed up. Nevertheless, the two teenagers headed for the library. When they got there, however, it was closed. "We decided this was the day we were supposed to get arrested and go to jail," says Hollis, "so we went to the ***Woolworth's (205 South Main Street)*** and sat down at the lunch counter there." When the police asked them to leave, they did not and wound up in jail. Their action encouraged another sit-in: notably, on August 31 fifteen-year-old Brenda Travis and two other people sat in at the ***Greyhound bus terminal** (206 Canal Street)* and were jailed.

Brenda Travis remained in jail until October 3. When she was finally released, she was not allowed back into ***Burgland High School** (1000 Elmwood Street)*, and more than one hundred students walked out. They decided to march to the county courthouse to protest, not only the situation at Burgland School, but also the denial of voting rights and the recent assassination of Herbert Lee, an NAACP leader in neighboring Amite County who had been working with Bob Moses. However, recalled Hollis, "The county seat was in Magnolia and we didn't know that was eight miles from McComb. When we found out, we decided to march on the City Hall in McComb instead." And so they set out, stopping at the SNCC office and marching up the stairs to tell the surprised organizers their plans. SNCC's staff, mostly there for voter registration and worried that such street protest might alienate the adults who had invited them into McComb, felt they had no choice but to accompany the students. "I thought about Gandhi when he saw his people massed for protest," says former SNCC chairman Chuck McDew, who was in McComb at the time.

"Leave and Go Back Where?"

"I was going from door-to-door talking with people in the community, trying to get them to register to vote, and there were a number of other young people doing the same thing with me. And this lady, she said to me: 'Son, you just don't know how these whites folks is down here. You young folks from out of town come down here and ya'll don't know about these white folks. When ya'll leave and go back, we're going to have all kinds of trouble.'

"'Leave and go back where?' I asked her.

"'When ya'll go back up north.'

"And I said, 'I'm not from up north; I'm from out in Chissum Mission. You probably know my family 'cause I got relatives that live in McComb and relatives that live in Summit. My family is the Watkins who do a lot of singing around.'

"'You mean you John Watkins' son?'

"And I say, 'Yes. That's my daddy.'

"And she says, 'Boy, you out here with all these young folks from up north.'

"And I say, 'All these other young folks that you see are from McComb and Summit too.' I called them over and she got so excited.

"'I can't believe that young folks from around here are out doing this,' she said. 'I'm gonna have to see how I can help ya'll. And I'm going to tell all my other friends 'cause we thought you folks was from somewhere out of Mississippi and didn't know nothin' about what was happening down here.'"

—HOLLIS WATKINS TO CHARLIE COBB

"'There go our people,' Gandhi said. 'We have to hurry and catch up with them for we are their leaders.'"

On the city hall steps, a Burgland student knelt in prayer and was arrested; then Curtis and Hollis; finally everyone. Attracting special hostility and brutality was SNCC's one white field secretary, Bob Zellner from South Alabama, whose father had once been a member of the Klan. Enraged whites kicked him in the face, gouged his eyes, pummeled him mercilessly as a traitor to the white race before Chuck McDew and Bob Moses were finally able to reach him and shield him as they pushed their way inside City Hall, where the building itself could offer some protection, since the police were not providing any.

Everyone was bailed out of jail in a few days, but when the students returned to school they were told they would be allowed back only if they signed a statement promising not to participate in any more protests. Their parents, too, would have to sign a promise pledging that they would not permit their children to participate in protests. Furthermore, the students were told they would have to accept a reduction in grade. Again about one hundred students immediately walked out of school. The next day they returned, handed in their books, and left. SNCC's organizers opened "Nonviolent High Schools" at scattered sites. One of these sites was **Saint Paul United Methodist Church** (*711 Warren Street*). This church was the site of the first civil rights movement mass meetings in McComb, and also where regular voter-registration workshops were held. The Nonviolent High School ended when Moses, McDew, Zellner, Hayes, Watkins, and seven other organizers who were not minors were sentenced to four months in the **Pike County Jail** (*in Magnolia*) for contributing to the delinquency of minors.

McComb's movement would not have been possible without support from an older generation. But at first there was not great enthusiasm for sit-ins from movement elders such as C. C. Bryant, who told Bob Moses this was *not* why he had brought him to McComb. Many parents were angry, too. But as significant parental support for the student move-

McComb high-school students campaigning for the right to vote

ment became apparent, Bryant soon changed his mind. As he declared at one mass meeting, "Where the students lead we will follow." Says Hollis, "I didn't know what [my father's] position was. I hadn't told him I was going to sit in, get arrested, and go to jail that first time; if he had said no, that would have been it. You weren't going to buck that. So I said I was going to spend the night with some friends—not exactly a lie. I found out much later—years later—that after we were arrested at City Hall he came to the mass meeting that night and spoke in our support. It was the only meeting he ever came to." This was important adult tolerance and support of student action, especially C. C. Bryant's voiced support. The *C. C. Bryant home (1533 Venable Street)* was a civil rights center. In his front yard he cut hair and maintained a small library of black books, newspapers, and magazines. It was a natural place for intense but informal discussion and planning. In fact, after the arrests at city hall, Bryant was arrested, too, because authorities believed that he must have had a hand in the protests. His house was bombed in 1964.

C. C. Bryant was (and still is, at this writing) a deacon at the *Society Hill Missionary Baptist Church (4098*

Highway 51 south). The original wood-frame sanctuary was firebombed and destroyed in 1964. For greater safety it was rebuilt with brick and now stands farther back from the highway.

Strong support for Bob Moses and the fledgling movement in McComb was provided by Biloxi-born Alyene Quin. Her cafe, ***South of the Border*** *(500 Summit Street),* which has since closed, fed movement workers and provided meeting space. When her white landlord demanded that she either stop feeding movement people in the cafe or be evicted, she began feeding people from her home.

One especially significant meeting occurred at Mrs.

I am writing this note from the drunk tank of the county jail in Magnolia, Mississippi. Twelve of us are here, sprawled out along the concrete bunker: . . .

Later on Hollis will lead out with a clear tenor into a freedom song. Talbert and Lewis will supply jokes, and McDew will discourse on the history of the black man and the Jew. McDew, a black by birth, a jew by choice, and a revolutionary by necessity, has taken the deep hates and loves of America, and the world, reserved for those who dare to stand in a strong sun and cast a sharp shadow.

In the words of Judge Brumfield, who sentenced us, we are "cold calculators" who design to disrupt the racial harmony (harmonious since 1619) of McComb into racial strife and rioting; we, he said, are the leaders who are causing young children to be led like sheep to the pen to be slaughtered (in a legal manner). "Robert," he was addressing me, "haven't some of the people from your school been able to go down and register without violence here in Pike County?" I thought to myself that Southerners are exposed the most when they boast.

It's mealtime now: we have rice and gravy in a flat pan, dry bread and a "big town cake"; we lack eating and drinking utensils. Water comes from a faucet and goes into a hole.

This is Mississippi, the middle of the iceberg. Hollis leading off with his tenor, "Michael row the boat ashore, Alleluia; Christian brothers don't be slow, Alleluia: Mississippi next to go, Alleluia." This is a tremor in the middle of the iceberg—from a stone that the builders rejected.

—BOB MOSES, NOVEMBER 1, 1961

Quin's cafe in August 1964, at the height of a spate of bombings that gained McComb the title "bombing capital of the world." At that meeting, black business leaders pledged fifty dollars each to the construction of a community center *(now the **Martin Luther King Memorial Center**, 601 Martin Luther King Drive)*, which would serve as headquarters of McComb's movement. They also formed food and housing committees to assist COFO staff and the summer volunteers. What was becoming apparent—and threatening—to the white power establishment in McComb was that the local black establishment had gotten beyond its initial fear and was now supporting the work of the COFO organizers. Attendance at mass meetings grew; Klan violence, mostly bombings, grew, too. During the summer of 1964, SNCC's old headquarters, the **Burgland Supermarket** *(see page 282)* building, was bombed. Two days later, armed with a warrant to search for illegal liquor, the police conducted a midnight raid of the COFO freedom house. Then, on September 20, 1964, Klansmen threw dynamite onto Alyene Quin's front porch, injuring her two youngest children when the front wall and roof collapsed where they were sleeping. Local authorities accused Mrs. Quin of bombing her own home. The bombs were "COFO plants" said the sheriff, who charged Quin and twenty-three others with "criminal syndicalism," a serious charge made possible by a law the state legislature passed just before the start of the Summer Project. It empowered local authorities to redefine organized civil rights struggle (or labor union organizing) as "terrorism" with ten years' imprisonment possible for any person who "by word of mouth or written words or personal conduct advocates, instigates, suggests, teaches or aids and abets criminal syndicalism or the duty, necessity, propriety or expediency of committing crime, criminal syndicalism, sabotage, violence or any other unlawful method of terrorism as a means of accomplishing or effecting a change in agricultural or industrial ownership or control or effecting any political or social change."

Media stories generated pressure on the FBI for serious investigation of the bombing of Mrs. Quin's home: first

Alyene Quin holding a protest sign. After the bombing of her home, the county sheriff accused her of doing it herself in an effort to gain sympathy. Quin responded: "Do you think I would work all these years to keep a house and then plant a bomb under it while two of my children were in it?"

an article by the powerful Washington, D.C.–based newspaper columnist Drew Pearson, then an editorial in the *New York Times*. These pieces reinforced the mounting anger in McComb's black community, and the idea grew that an armed response to white violence was needed. The White House threatened to impose martial law, and a week after the blast, nine white men were arrested and pleaded guilty to the crime. They received a suspended sentence, however. Remarking that the bombers "came from good families," County Judge W. H. Watkins said that they had been "unduly provoked" by civil rights workers and "deserve a second chance."

Brenda Travis had received much harsher treatment three years earlier. The City Hall protest in McComb was her second arrest, and that was the reason used to send her to reform school for a year. Later she finished her education in California.

McComb's movement slowed until it was reanimated by the Mississippi Summer Project of 1964. SNCC DONE SNUCK, read a sign in the Burgland Supermarket upstairs headquarters after its organizers seemed to have vanished. Still, SNCC had learned something about organizing and would keep trying to organize in Mississippi. As Bob Moses put it in *Radical Equations*, "I had thought after first meeting and talking with Amzie that a voter registration campaign would require the importation of SNCC workers. Now, young Mississippians who would spread across the state seemed the logical and most likely nucleus. Furthermore, 'direct action' had taken on a new character in Mississippi. We did not know yet how far we could go with it, but if McComb was any indicator, young people were prepared to try to go as far as they could."

The site where COFO's wood-frame 1964 ***"Freedom House"** (702 Wall Street)* stood is now an empty lot. It was bombed on July 8, two days after a visit by Congressman

Don Edwards, whose son was a 1964 Summer Project volunteer. Although the Department of Justice still refused to intervene, even after the murders of Chaney, Goodman, and Schwerner on the other side of the state, a Justice Department official in Washington urged Cong. Edwards not to stay in McComb overnight lest he come to harm. The hostility of those days is almost unimaginable now, but here is a reminder: Speaking to a relatively new white extremist organization called the Association for the Preservation of the White Race (APWR), Pike County Sheriff R. R. Warren told them that if his lawmen could not handle COFO, he would "recruit some of you."

✖ GREENWOOD ✖ AND RULEVILLE

After McComb, civil rights work in the Delta took center stage. "The most southern place on earth," writer James C. Cobb (no relation) dubbed the vast expanse stretching from Vicksburg, Mississippi, to Memphis, Tennessee—a fertile floodplain of eighteen counties enriched by the Mississippi, Yazoo, and Sunflower Rivers. Major clearing of delta swamp and forest began during Reconstruction; then came railroad lines and finally the levee to hold back and regulate the Mississippi River. Even in the mid-twentieth century you felt as though you had stepped back into the antebellum South; and it is no exaggeration to say that with its sagging sharecropper shacks and the long rows of cotton picked or chopped by people who can only be described as serfs, the region still seemed a feudal land not far removed from chattel slavery.

As plantations turned the land into a great white ocean of cotton, thousands, then tens of thousands of black share-croppers moved in to work the fields. The blues sank their deepest roots here and were part of the ritual of daily life: songs to ease labor for next to no pay, and often no pay at all; songs communicating longing for something better. Songs of escape. Often painful songs—life did not permit many illusions. You can see that in the Delta plantation houses, which tried to imitate grace but often failed. Up in the Delta, life was just hard: not enough rain or too much rain; floods; boll weevils chewing up all the cotton; banks calling in loans; lynchings; total white domination in a land that was two-thirds black. Although whites were out-numbered (perhaps *because* they were outnumbered), their constant fear of Afro-American political potential engen-dered resistance—often violent resistance—whenever there was the slightest sign of challenge or change. The White Citizens Council was born in the Mississippi Delta.

On the other hand, the state president of the NAACP, a pharmacist by the name of Aaron Henry, made his home in the Delta. He was a native son of one of the Delta's queen cities, Clarksdale. In 1959 when "Doc" Henry took over its leadership, the NAACP was still an underground organi-zation in many respects. Even in the 1960s, in small Delta towns a black person might ease up to you, reach into his pocket, surreptitiously pull out a card, and whisper, "See, I'm in the NAACP." Life could be dangerous for any black person seeking the rights of full citizenship. Yet despite the risks, heroic efforts aimed at that goal had been under way well before SNCC, CORE, or COFO came to be.

In late 1951 Dr. Theodore Roosevelt Mason Howard, a surgeon and Kentucky native, founded the Regional Council of Negro Leadership (RCNL) in the Delta town of Cleveland. RCNL open-air rallies in the 1950s attracted thousands. When Thurgood Marshall spoke at one of these large-scale events, ten thousand people turned out, and thousands attended a voter registration rally at which black

Detroit congressman Charles Diggs spoke. Dr. Howard organized a boycott of gas stations that refused to have bathrooms for blacks, distributing bumper stickers that read DON'T BUY GAS WHERE YOU CAN'T USE THE REST ROOM. During the Emmett Till murder investigation, Dr. Howard was instrumental in uncovering evidence and finding witnesses.

With the 1954 *Brown v. Board of Education* decision, violence and harassment directed at Howard and NAACP leaders across the state escalated. By October 1954 Mississippi's twenty-five-thousand-member White Citizens Council had the complete support of the state political establishment. In this climate the Ku Klux Klan flourished and stepped up its activities. Violence and intimidation grew, and voting-registration laws were revised to permit trick questions in the name of determining literacy. A school desegregation drive had begun in several communities, but Klan and Citizens Council pressure brought it to a halt. Dr. Clinton Battle, in Indianola, and Dr. Maurice Mackel, the founder of the Natchez NAACP chapter, along with scores of others, were driven from the state. In Belzoni, grocer Gus Courts was shot and wounded in front of his store, and fiery preacher and voter registration activist Reverend George Lee was ambushed and killed. Nothing at **Rev. Lee's gravesite** *(602 Church Street)* offers any hint of the brave role this pastor played, but it is worth a stop for reflection. Responding to NAACP demands for an investigation of the Lee murder, Governor Hugh L. White said he never responded to NAACP requests.

Dr. Howard was also a key target. Rumor had it that there was a $1,000 price on his head, and Dr. Howard felt he had to leave the state. He went to Chicago, where he established a medical practice. "I feel I can do more alive in the battle for Negro rights in the North than dead in a weed-grown grave in Dixie," he was quoted as saying.

Not everyone fled, however. Among those who chose to remain was farmer and NAACP leader Vernon Dahmer in Hattiesburg; he was assassinated in 1966. Doc Henry in Clarksdale, C. C. Bryant in McComb, and E. W. Steptoe in

Amite County, down in the far southwest corner of the state, were all survivors. They were vital mentors when SNCC and CORE moved into Mississippi. Perhaps none of these brave men was more important than Amzie Moore, president of the Cleveland, Mississippi, NAACP. Moore, a World War II veteran, worked in the post office and also owned a gas station. This gave him some independence. He had registered to vote in 1936, and at his gas station on Highway 61, then the main artery between Memphis and New Orleans, he had refused to put up WHITE and COLORED signs segregating his bathrooms. There was a restaurant, attached to the gas station, that was open to anyone. This outraged whites, who attempted to mount a boycott of his businesses, but in two-thirds-black Bolivar County, it was unsuccessful.

Moore was frustrated, however. Important NAACP colleagues had been killed or driven from the state, but his national headquarters seemed reluctant to take on Mississippi. He had watched the sit-ins with admiration, and by the summer of 1960, when SNCC's Bob Moses sat down in **Amzie Moore's home** *(614 Chrisman Avenue, Cleveland)*, Moore had decided that he wanted to tap into that young energy and use it. He was not interested in sit-ins, however; he wanted a voter-registration campaign, and that is what he got. As SNCC began working in the Delta, Moore's home was its central headquarters. The house was an orientation center, a place for breakfast of scrambled eggs or for a spaghetti dinner; it provided telephone connections and was always full of conversation, as well as Amzie's sometimes grim, sometimes funny stories of Delta life and earlier civil rights struggle. Floodlights washed his backyard because he was certain that one night Klansmen or white terrorists of some sort would attack his home. Often Amzie, who had

Amzie Moore

fought the Nazis overseas, after all, sat in the bay window of his living room with rifles and pistols, waiting to repel an attack. He died on February 1, 1982, the twenty-second anniversary of the Greensboro student sit-in. The headstone at the **Amzie Moore gravesite** (*Westlawn Memorial Gardens, Mullins Road between Chrisman Avenue and Winnie Drive*) has a portrait of Moore on it; the inscription reads MY SOUL IS AT REST.

GREENWOOD

The White Citizens Council was headquartered in Greenwood, and the city's mayor was a member. Greenwood was also the hometown of circuit judge Tom Brady, whose polemical and racist text, *Black Monday*, was White Citizens Council gospel.

Amzie Moore suggested Greenwood as a starting place for a Delta voter registration campaign and, from his own NAACP network, even provided an organizer who would try to open up that small Delta city: twenty-three-year-old Cleveland native Sam Block. When Block arrived in 1962, Greenwood was a cotton processing center that shipped out some eight hundred thousand bales of cotton annually. The **Cottonlandia Museum** (*1608 Highway 82 West*) offers the history and role of agriculture and cotton in the Delta; glimpses of black life in the Delta are integrated throughout the presentations.

Almost two thirds of Greenwood's twenty thousand residents were black; a little over two hundred were registered to vote. Sam Block was able to conduct two workshops at the **Elks Hall** (*Scott Street and Avenue F*), but then was asked to find another meeting place because of Citizens Council pressure. That pressure also resulted in his eviction from the home of Mrs. E. H. McNease, a school principal, where he was boarding, and Block wound up sleeping near a junkyard in his car. Finally Rev. Aaron Johnson opened up **First Christian Church** (*100 East Percy Street; now East Percy*

"Where You From?"

W e went up to register and it was the first time visiting the courthouse in Greenwood, Mississippi, and the sheriff came up to me and he asked me, he said, "Nigger where you from?" I told him, "Well I'm a native Mississippian." He said, "Yeh, yeh, I know that, but where you from? I don't know where you from." I said, "Well, around some counties." He said, "Well I know that, I know you ain't from here 'cause I know every nigger and his mammy." I said, "You know all the niggers, do you know any colored people?" He got angry. He spat in my face and he walked away. So he came back and turned around and told me, "I don't want to see you in town any more. The best thing you better do is pack your clothes and get out and don't never come back no more." I said, "Well, sheriff, if you don't want to see me here, I think the best thing for you to do is pack your clothes and leave, get out of town, 'cause I'm here to stay, I came here to do a job and this is my intention. I'm going to do this job . . . "

—FIELD REPORT FROM SAM BLOCK, LATE SUMMER 1962

Street Christian Church) to movement meetings. Despite a rapid and dramatic decrease in his congregation as a result, Reverend Johnson kept the doors of his church open to the movement, and the first mass meetings were held here. By late July Block had secured office space, and this second-floor **SNCC/COFO office** *(616 Avenue I between St. Charles and Broad streets)*, owned by local black photographer Robert Burns, who also put him up, was where Block, Lawrence Guyot, and Luvaugn Brown made their narrow escape.

Block next found space above a dry-cleaning shop, and Willie Peacock (now Wazir), a native of neighboring Tallahatchie County, soon joined the Block-Guyot-Brown team. At one point they went canvassing in the countryside outside Greenwood with a mule, in an attempt to blend into the life of the rural Delta landscape. Though they only persuaded a handful of people to attempt to register to vote, their not having been run out of town or killed could be counted a sign of success. Local people took note that the men stayed and continued to do their work.

Then something unexpected happened. The winter of 1963 was exceptionally cold, and it had been a poor year for sharecroppers. Owners used fewer field hands and paid even less money than usual. Dependency on commodities distributed by county government (a federal surplus-food distribution program that began in 1957, predating food stamps) was absolutely crucial for survival. But in reprisal for the voter registration effort, the county's board of supervisors halted commodity distribution. At the same time, after protesting the burning of four buildings near the COFO office, Sam Block was arrested for the seventh time in Greenwood. But at this trial, the courtroom filled with black people, many from rural Leflore County, who were angry about the commodity cutoff. As Bob Moses puts it, people were now seeing the "connection between political participation and food on their table." Rev. Johnson addressed a mass meeting at his church the night after Block's trial, and almost two hundred people tried to register to vote two days later. COFO workers now organized their own food-distribution program, using supplies collected by northern supporters. Comedian Dick Gregory flew to Greenwood with a chartered planeload of food and clothes several times that winter. COFO's office became a distribution center, and as word spread that the civil rights organization had food and clothing, people came in growing numbers and were given voter registration forms as well as commodities.

With the link to the distribution of food and clothing, Greenwood's voter registration movement accelerated. Suddenly and unexpectedly hundreds attempted to register to vote. In Atlanta, Georgia, the Voter Education Project (VEP), administered by the Southern

Bob Dylan with civil rights workers on the back porch of the COFO office in Greenwood, 1963. Bernice Johnson (in profile, facing Dylan), who later founded Sweet Honey in the Rock, listens intently.

Picketing for voter registration rights in front of Leflore County Courthouse in Greenwood, March 24, 1964

Regional Council and providing significant funding for COFO's efforts in Mississippi, sent Randolph Blackwell to look at this surprising turn of events, and he was almost killed. Blackwell was returning from the Greenwood COFO office to his hotel in Greenville with Bob Moses and COFO organizer Jimmy Travis. Gunfire suddenly erupted and bullets began spraying the vehicle. Travis was shot in the shoulder and neck and narrowly escaped death; Moses and Blackwell were unhurt. Furious, VEP director Wiley Branton declared that "Leflore County has elected itself the testing ground of democracy." He pledged an all-out campaign. COFO called staff from around the state to Greenwood. New, more spacious COFO headquarters were established in the **Sanders Building** *(708 Avenue N).*

    Wesley United Methodist Church *(800 Howard Street)* and **Turner Chapel** *(717 Walthall Street)* were starting points for voter registration marches. When Turner Chapel's young minister, Reverend David L. Tucker, led about one hundred people to **City Hall** *(Church and Main Streets)* with the intention of demanding to see the mayor, he was bitten in the leg by a police dog. Greenwood ministers rallied and publicly declared support for the voter registration campaign. Thirty-one black preachers signed a manifesto that read in part: "We do hereby endorse the Freedom Movement one-hundred percent and urge our members and friends of Leflore County and the state of Mississippi to register and become first-class citizens." However, even this broad backing did not slow efforts to intimidate. As part of the continuing effort to crush Greenwood's movement, ten of COFO's staff, including Moses, Willie Peacock, and Guyot, were arrested and held in the Leflore County Jail. But the Delta cotton capital was now making national headlines. Martin Luther King promised his support, and national press began to pour in. A team of Justice Department attorneys led by John Doar arrived but, under instructions from the White House, backed away from offering federal protection to blacks attempting to register.

By 1968 three quarters of black eligible voters in Leflore County were registered to vote. Media and most everyone else had lost interest in Greenwood by then. After the tumultuous winter and spring of 1963, the only moment of renewed national interest in Greenwood came on the night of June 16, 1966, when just after being released from jail, Stokely Carmichael spoke to a mass meeting at the **Broad Street Park** *(Broad Street between Avenues M and N)*. The park is near the old Avenue N SNCC/COFO office where, two years before, Carmichael had operated as SNCC's Delta project director. Now Carmichael and other civil rights leaders, including Martin Luther King, were continuing a "march against fear" begun by James Meredith, who had been shot shortly after beginning it. "This is the twenty-seventh time I been to jail," Carmichael told the large crowd in the park. "I ain't going to jail no more ... We been saying freedom for six years and we ain't got nothin! What we gonna start saying now is Black Power!" he roared, to amens, clapping, and stomping feet. He stood,

Continuing James Meredith's March Against Fear. Andrew Young is just behind Rev. King and to his right. Floyd McKissick is to King's left.

Willie Ricks agitating on an Atlanta Street. It was Ricks who really led the Greenwood mass meeting in the chant of "black power"—a phrase he had been using ever since joining the Meredith march.

eyes blazing, his left hand clenching a microphone and one right-hand finger pointing, looking like a wrathful prophet straight from the pages of the Old Testament as Willie Ricks, a SNCC organizer, leapt to the platform. "BLACK POWER!" Ricks began chanting, "BLACK POWER! What do you want?" "BLACK POWER!" the crowd responded, with a force that startled a press corps expecting to hear the tones of "We Shall Overcome." And Stokely Carmichael exploded into the national consciousness as yet another unexpected black leader. The events that night almost certainly marked the end of an era.

RULEVILLE

The Delta can seem one vast museum of rural grassroots civil rights struggle against enormous odds, and you cannot help but expect every county to have a story. Sometimes town names alone make you think "Something must have happened here" and you want to go there: Midnight, Yazoo City, Rolling Fork, Silver City, Alligator, Panther Burn, and Sunflower. How about a trip to It, Mississippi?

A country store in Money, Mississippi, **Bryant's Grocery and Meat Market**, was where young Emmett Till was said to have insulted owner Roy Bryant's young wife. The building sags now, empty and forlorn in a town that seems completely desiccated. The **Tallahatchie County Courthouse**, in the town square of the nearby county seat, Sumner, is where Roy Bryant and his half-brother, J. W. Milam, were tried in 1955 for the Till murder. All five lawyers in town offered to defend them. In court, Bryant's wife was addressed as Mrs. Bryant, Till's mother as Mamie. It took the all-white jury just sixty-seven minutes to acquit the two men. The judge had pulled the jurors' names from a straw hat. Since there were no black registered voters in this majority-black county, no blacks were eligible for jury duty.

There is a different Delta story in Clarksdale, where Aaron Henry had his drugstore. Most visitors come to the city for its **Blues Museum** (*Old Freight Depot, 1 Blues Alley*) and to honor the Delta's blues tradition; there are also several sites that represent Mississippi's civil rights tradition. Doc Henry's **Fourth Street Drug Store** (*213 Martin Luther King Street*), now a vacant lot, was a site of civil rights planning for decades. It was bombed in March 1963, and shortly thereafter Henry's home was set ablaze. That summer he led the picketing of city buildings, protesting the city's refusal to listen to and consider the grievances of the black community, and he was arrested, jailed, and assigned to garbage detail. **Haven United Methodist Church** (*corner of Martin Luther King and Yazoo Streets*) was the church of Henry and his wife, Noelle; until his death, all NAACP meetings were held here.

For the group of 12 Negro newsmen who covered the trial, it was a bitter, at times frustrating experience. As soon as we arrived in Sumner, Sheriff H. C. Strider laid down the law; there was to be no mixing with white reporters and any violation meant ejection from the courtroom and town. The day before the trial opened, our *Jet-Ebony* crew ran into a truckload of gun-bearing whites on a truck near Money, Mississippi, which brought it home to us that our assignment was no good neighbor get-together. The Sheriff's edict further restricted our movement. As a result, we stayed to ourselves in the far corner of the courtroom as the antagonistic Exhibit A of Northern Negro reporters who were capitalizing on low-rating the South.

—SIMEON BOOKER ON COVERING THE TILL MURDER TRIAL

He telephoned and said, "Baby, I'm in jail at midnight."

"But, Bob, it's 6 in the morning."

"No, Midnight, Mississippi. It's the name of a town. There's a little box on the side of the road they use for a jail and they're trying to put me in it."

—MARILYN LOWEN TO CHARLIE COBB

Not far away were **Henry's campaign headquarters** and the **NAACP office** (*Martin Luther King and Harrison Streets*). He ran for governor as an MFDP candidate, and from 1979 until 1986 he was a member of the Mississippi State Legislature.

Going south from Clarksdale, you come to Holmes County. It is not on many civil rights maps, but as COFO's work in the Delta expanded it became a strong center, partly because of its concentration of independent black farmers like Hartman Turnbow. No other county in the Delta had as many independent black farmers as Holmes County. In the 1960s Afro-Americans comprised 75 percent of the population and owned 73 percent of the land. This is one of the counties where McComb's Hollis Watkins wound up as an organizer: A three-person delegation (Hartman Turnbow, Ozell Mitchell, and his sister, Alma Mitchell Carnegie), attracted by the movement in Greenwood thirty miles to the north, came to COFO headquarters and urged civil rights workers to organize in their county. Hollis arrived in March 1963, and shortly thereafter the first mass meeting in the county was held at the **Sanctified Church** in Mileston. Less than a month later, Turnbow and thirteen others left **Ozell and Annie Bell Mitchell's farm** (*off Highway 49 between Mileston and Tchula*) and drove the twenty miles to the county courthouse in Lexington, where they made the first attempt at registering by black voters in more than one hundred years. Shortly afterward, when night riders attempted to burn down Turnbow's house, he drove them away using one of the numerous firearms he kept. The next morning he told civil rights organizers who arrived to investigate the attack, "I wasn't being non-nonviolent, I was just protecting my family." The **Mileston Community Center** (*just off Highway 49 outside of Mileston*), built by a 1964 summer volunteer, is still there but overgrown with foliage and weeds.

Highway 61, the "Blues Highway" that roughly follows the Mississippi River to Memphis, has now been canonized as part of essential U.S. culture; *Highway 49*, also connecting Jackson and Memphis, is one of the great roads of civil rights history. It is a narrow ribbon of highway that penetrates the heart of Sunflower County and also takes you to Greenwood and Clarksdale. This is classic Delta landscape: flat, wide, and still. It's as if you can see all the way to the ends of the earth. In the old days you always felt exposed to danger, but also safe in a way because you could see who was approaching from a distance.

Indianola, the county seat of Sunflower County, was where the White Citizens Council was born two months after the 1954 Supreme Court decision, making the county an important symbol for civil rights challenge the way Greenwood, the planter capital, was. Indianola saw much violence. The May 1, 1965, bombing of the home of movement activist **Irene Magruder** *(corner of Byas and Front Street Extended)* resulted in its complete destruction. There is a historical marker stating that "she was the first African American to open her home to civil rights workers during the Freedom Summer of 1964." That same day, the **Giles Penny Savers Store** *(100 block of Church Street)* was firebombed because owners Oscar and Alice Giles were active in the MFDP; there is a marker here, too. The **Freedom School building** *(just east of Carver Elementary School on Jefferson Street)* was destroyed by arson.

Also in Sunflower County, Parchman Penitentiary, the notorious plantation prison, was the grandfather of the plantation system in the state. And Sunflower was the home county of Senator James O. Eastland, who owned a two-thousand-acre plantation near Doddsville. Two thirds of the county's population was black, but only a handful were registered to vote.

In 1962 COFO work began in tiny Ruleville, a town of fewer than one thousand people near where Highway 8 meets Highway 49, about twenty-three miles north of Indianola. We did not know it at the time, but this is historic cultural territory. The huge **Dockery plantation** (*between Ruleville and Cleveland on Highway 8*), established in 1895, was central to the blues. Charley Patton, arguably the first of the great bluesmen, lived on the plantation, and he mentored Howlin' Wolf here. Bluesman Robert Johnson, one of the ancestors of rock and roll, was a frequent visitor, and so was another Delta blues great, Son House. The Staple Singers also lived there. The plantation was the center of major musical exchange, and a local railroad, the celebrated Pea Vine, sung of by Patton in his "Pea Vine Blues," carried musicians from the Dockery plantation to juke joints in neighboring Bolivar County. Many of the bluesmen coming on and off the Dockery plantation and from elsewhere performed at **Mack's Colored Cafe** (*Front Street*). The club was still there on August 19, 1962, when Amzie Moore deposited Charles McLaurin, Landy McNair, and me in Ruleville. It is still there, now called Mack's Cafe.

We stayed with **Joe and Rebecca McDonald** (*909 Reden Street*), a tough elderly couple who had managed to register to vote in the 1950s and were part of Amzie Moore's network. That Ruleville network made the people we encountered in the black community more welcoming of us than those in Greenwood had been of Sam Block. Whites were hostile, of course, and quickly made it known. On our second day, when we were walking down a dusty road (all streets in the black community were unpaved) near the McDonalds' house, a car suddenly roared to a stop next to us. Ruleville's mayor, Charles Durrough, jumped out. (He was also the justice of the peace and owned the town's hardware store.)

"I know y'all ain't from here," he said, waving a pistol. "And you're here to cause trouble. Best you get out of town!"

We began holding meetings at **Williams Chapel Missionary Baptist Church** (*O. B. Avenue at Lafayette Street*). In the fearful, politically hysterical climate generated by state and local authorities because of the pending admission of James Meredith to the University of Mississippi, only a few people participated. Nonetheless, McLaurin brought three people to the old **Sunflower County Courthouse** (it

October 1, 1962, James Meredith is escorted by federal marshals onto the grounds of the all-white University of Mississippi in Oxford for his first day of class. The Justice Department's John Doar is to Meredith's right.

has since been replaced), a formidable-looking structure right next to City Hall, within a week of our arrival. Indianola's reputation as a center of white terrorism makes it all the more remarkable that within two weeks eighteen people were willing to try to register to vote. In this group was a woman who would come to be the voice of black grassroots Mississippi: Fannie Lou Hamer.

She was not much noticed at first as the group boarded an ancient school bus that was usually used to haul workers to cotton fields for the eighteen-mile trip from Ruleville to Indianola. Everyone was nervous. Anything could happen at the county courthouse—or anywhere in this tough, notoriously racist county. Then a strong voice from the back of the bus began singing church songs, and those songs seemed to strengthen the group. It was Mrs. Hamer. She sang all the way to Indianola, and at one point Bob Moses commented, "She must know every church song in the world." Nothing much happened at the courthouse until afterward. The bus was stopped by police on the edge of town, and because it was an old black and yellow school bus, the driver was arrested on a frivolous charge: driving a bus of the wrong color. It was getting late now, no time to be on the road and identified with civil rights. When the police said the driver could be released after paying a one-hundred-dollar fine, fear became palpable because there was nothing close to one hundred dollars among the entire group. Then again as people milled about the bus, Mrs. Hamer's voice in song sliced through the fear; this time she was singing freedom songs: "This Little Light of Mine," "Ain't Gonna Let Nobody Turn Me Round," and her favorite, "Go Tell It on the Mountain." As before, her voice calmed and empowered. A member of the group explained to the police that they only had about fifty dollars; if this was not enough, perhaps they'd better take the entire busload of us to jail. The police accepted the money. Mrs. Hamer had emerged as a new leader.

The rest of the story is better known. Mrs. Fannie Lou Hamer was a timekeeper and sharecropper on the **B. D. Marlow plantation** just outside of Ruleville. When she returned from Indianola that night, Marlow demanded that she withdraw her registration application. She refused. "I didn't go down there to register for you; I went down there to register for myself." He threw her off the plantation that same night, and she found refuge in the **home of Mr. and Mrs. Robert Tucker** *(626 East Lafayette Street; it is now a vacant lot owned by William's Chapel; a large pecan tree stands on the property)*. Before the year was out, she became a SNCC field secretary—at forty-six years old, perhaps SNCC's oldest field secretary. She also became a powerful and nationally known movement voice. Her televised testimony before the national Democratic committee as an MFDP delegate during the 1964 challenge to the all-white "regular" Mississippi delegation was so compelling that President Lyndon Johnson himself interrupted it lest the powerful sympathy it created for the MFDP disrupt a national convention he had carefully staged. And, feeling betrayed by Hubert Humphrey's role in the denial of the MFDP challenge, she told the senator, shaking her head sadly and bringing him to tears, "Senator Humphrey, I been praying about you, and I been thinking about you, and you're a good man. The trouble is, you're afraid to do what you know is right."

White supremacists did not stop with the firing and harassment of Mrs. Hamer. The local newspaper published the names of everyone who went to Indianola with her. Some black businesses were closed down for minor legal violations. There was also violence. Night riders in a speeding car fired into the McDonald home and the Tucker home where Mrs. Hamer was staying. No one was hurt. They were not so fortunate just down the street from the McDonalds', at the **home of Herman and Hattie Sisson** *(Byron Street and L. F. Packer Drive)* that night. Their niece and another girl who happened to be visiting were wounded: Marylene Burks was shot in the head; her friend Vivian Hiller was wounded in the arm and leg. A few weeks later Mayor Durrough canceled the tax-exempt status of Williams Chapel. And as in Greenwood, the commodities program was canceled. For months, no one tried to register to vote, but what had begun could not be stopped. And today Ruleville has an Afro-American mayor.

A sign on Highway 49 as you enter Ruleville proclaims HOME OF FANNIE LOU HAMER, and the town's post office was named for her in 1994. Mrs. Hamer died April 14, 1971, from cancer and, I believe, the debilitating effects of a brutal 1963 beating by state and local policemen while she was in the Montgomery County jail in Winona, Mississippi. She had been taken off a Trailways bus and arrested after several of her movement traveling companions entered the white side of the bus station seeking food. The beating caused permanent damage to her kidneys. Mrs. Hamer is buried with her husband, "Pap," at the **Fannie Lou Hamer Gravesite** *(U.S. 49 west, turn east on Bryon, go to end; site on left).* Her headstone quotes a phrase that she made famous, and is an answer to the wonderment of Mamie Chinn that started us on the civil rights trail in this state: I AM SICK AND TIRED OF BEING SICK AND TIRED.

Mrs. Fannie Lou Hamer speaking outside the U.S. Capitol to disappointed and angry supporters after the House of Representatives rejected an MFDP challenge to the seating of five Mississippi congressmen who claimed victory in the 1964 election. "We'll come back year after year until we are allowed our rights as citizens," she said.

"I Question America"

M r. Chairman, and the Credentials Committee, my name is Mrs. Fannie Lou Hamer, and I live at 626 East Lafayette Street, Ruleville, Mississippi, Sunflower County, the home of Senator James O. Eastland, and Senator Stennis.

It was the 31st of August in 1962 that 18 of us traveled 26 miles to the country courthouse in Indianola to try to register to try to become first-class citizens.

We was met in Indianola by Mississippi men, Highway Patrolmens and they only allowed two of us in to take the literacy test at the time. After we had taken this test and started back to Ruleville, we was held up by the City Police and the State Highway Patrolmen and carried back to Indianola where the bus driver was charged that day with driving a bus the wrong color.

After we paid the fine among us, we continued on to Ruleville, and Reverend Jeff Sunny carried me four miles in the rural area where I had worked as a timekeeper and sharecropper for 18 years. I was met there by my children, who told me that the plantation owner was angry because I had gone down to try to register.

After they told me, my husband came, and said that the plantation owner was raising cain because I had tired to register, and before he quit talking the plantation owner came, and said, "Fannie Lou, do you know—did Pap tell you what I said?"

And I said, "Yes, sir."

He said, "I mean that." He said, "If you don't go down and withdraw your registration, you will have to leave," he said. "Then if you go down and with-draw," he said, "you will—you might have to go because we are not ready for that in Mississippi."

And I addressed him and told him and said, "I didn't try to register for you. I tried to register for myself."

I had to leave that same night.

On the 10th of September 1962, 16 bullets was fired into the home of Mr. and Mrs. Robert Tucker for me. That same night two girls were shot in Ruleville, Mississippi. Also Mr. Joe McDonald's house was shot in.

And in June the 9th, 1963, I had attended a voter registration workshop, was returning back to Mississippi. Ten of us was traveling by the Continental Trailway bus. When we got to Winona, Mississippi, which is in Montgomery

County, four of the people got off to use the washroom, and two of the people—to use the restaurant—two of the people wanted to use the washroom.

The four people that had gone in to use the restaurant was ordered out. During this time I was on the bus. But when I looked through the window and saw they had rushed out I got off of the bus to see what had happened, and one of the ladies said, "It was a State Highway Patrolman and a Chief of Police ordered us out."

I got back on the bus and one of the persons had used the washroom got back on the bus, too.

As soon as I was seated on the bus, I saw when they began to get the four people in a highway patrolman's car, I stepped off of the bus to see what was happening and somebody screamed from the car that the four workers was in and said, "Get that one there," and when I went to get in the car, when the man told me I was under arrest, he kicked me.

I was carried to the county jail, and put in the booking room. They left some of the people in the booking room and began to place us in cells. I was placed in a cell with a young woman called Miss Ivesta Simpson. After I was placed in the cell I began to hear the sound of kicks and horrible screams, and I could hear somebody say, "Can you say, yes, sir, nigger? Can you say yes, sir?"

And they would say other horrible names.

She would say, "Yes, I can say yes, sir."

"So say it."

She says, "I don't know you well enough."

They beat her, I don't know how long, and after a while she began to pray, and asked God to have mercy on those people.

And it wasn't too long before three white men came to my cell. One of these men was a State Highway Patrolman and he asked me where I was from, and I told him Ruleville, he said, "We are going to check this."

And they left my cell and it wasn't too long before they came back. He said, "You are from Ruleville all right," and he used a curse word, and he said, "We are going to make you wish you was dead."

I was carried out of that cell into another cell where they had two Negro prisoners. The State Highway Patrolmen ordered the first Negro to take the blackjack.

The first Negro prisoner ordered me, by orders from the State Highway Patrolman for me, to lay down on a bunk bed on my face, and I laid on my face.

The first Negro began to beat, and I was beat by the first Negro until he was exhausted, and I was holding my hands behind me at that time on my left side because I suffered from polio when I was six years old.

After the first Negro had beat until he was exhausted the State Highway Patrolman ordered the second Negro to take the blackjack.

The second Negro began to beat and I began to work my feet, and the State Highway Patrolman ordered the first Negro who had beat me to sit upon my feet to keep me from working my feet. I began to scream and one white man got up and began to beat me on my head and told me to hush.

One white man—since my dress had worked up high, walked over and pulled my dress down and he pulled my dress back, back up.

I was in jail when Medgar Evers was murdered.

All of this is on account of us wanting to register, to become first-class citizens, and if the Freedom Democratic Party is not seated now, I question America, is this America, the land of the free and the home of the brave where we have to sleep with our telephones off of the hooks because our lives be threatened daily because we want to live as decent human beings, in America?

Thank you.

—TESTIMONY OF FANNIE LOU HAMER
BEFORE THE CREDENTIAL COMMITTEE AT
THE DEMOCRATIC NATIONAL CONVENTION,
JULY 22, 1964

CHAPTER NINE

FULL CIRCLE

Nashville, Knoxville, and Memphis, Tennessee

66 *. . . and we just went on before the dogs and we would look at them; and we'd go on before the water hoses and we would look at it, and we'd just go on singing "Over my head I see freedom in the air." And then we would be thrown in the paddy wagons, and sometimes we were stacked in there like sardines in a can. And they would throw us in, and old Bull would say, "Take them off," and they did; and we would just go in the paddy wagon singing "We Shall Overcome." And every now and then we'd get in the jail, and we'd see the jailers looking through the windows being moved by our prayers, and being moved by our words and our songs. And there was a power there which Bull Connor couldn't adjust to; and so we ended up transforming Bull into a steer, and we won our struggle in Birmingham.* 99

—MARTIN LUTHER KING JR., 1968

It is odd, I think, that the state of Tennessee receives so little focus. After all, Nashville represents one of the high points of the civil rights movement; Memphis represents what certainly must be considered the low point. The student movement in Nashville, and its disciplined leadership so committed to nonviolence, may have been the most admired in the South; then again, Martin Luther King Jr. was murdered in Memphis. Furthermore, Knoxville was home for years to the Highlander Center led by Myles Horton, a secular "church" of civil rights struggle as important as the famed Ebenezer and Dexter Avenue churches pastored by Martin Luther King Jr. Going further back in history, newspaperwoman Ida B. Wells, perhaps the most militant advocate of civil rights in the late nineteenth and early twentieth centuries, was driven from Memphis because of her antilynching crusade. And finally, it is certainly necessary to note that the Ku Klux Klan was born in Pulaski, a small town near the Alabama border. The original organization was founded on Christmas Eve in 1865 around a fireplace in what was then the ***Law Office of Judge Thomas M. Jones*** *(209 Madison Street)*. The building is still standing, and a bronze plaque placed there by the Daughters of the Confederacy lists the names of the six Confederate Army veterans who were its founders (John C. Lester, James R. Crowe, John D. Kennedy, Calvin Jones, Richard R. Reed, Frank O. McCord). The building's owner has turned the marker's face to the wall. All of this, yet these days Tennessee hardly comes to mind when the words *civil rights struggle* are uttered.

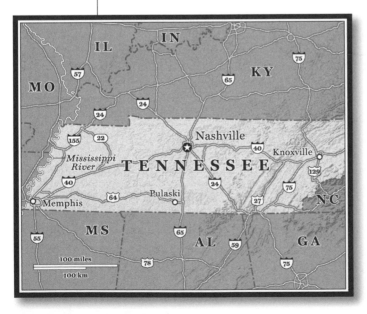

DO NOT:

1. Strike back nor curse if abused.

2. Laugh out.

3. Hold conversations with floor walker.

4. Leave your seat until your leader has given you permission to do so.

5. Block entrances to stores outside nor the aisles inside.

DO:

1. Show yourself friendly and courteous at all times.

2. Sit straight; always face the counter.

3. Report all serious incidents to your leader.

4. Refer information seekers to your leader in a polite manner.

5. Remember the teachings of Jesus Christ, Mahatma Gandhi and Martin Luther King. Love and nonviolence is the way.

—THE NONVIOLENT SIT-IN RULES CRAFTED BY JOHN LEWIS AND BERNARD LAFAYETTE IN NASHVILLE, TENNESSEE, AS RESULT OF THE WORKSHOPS LED BY JAMES LAWSON IN 1959–60

NASHVILLE

Although North Carolina's Greensboro students sat in "first" (on February 1, 1960), by then a group of students in Nashville, greatly influenced by divinity student James Lawson, had been planning sit-in action for almost a year. In fact, in the fall of 1959 they had already begun testing segregation by sending integrated teams to downtown department stores, where they purchased a few items, then took seats at the store lunch counters. When they were refused service, they asked why and then requested to see the store manager for discussion. These were reconnaissance missions into Nashville's segregated territory to determine precisely what they were up against. They were on an irreversible path toward sit-ins in which they would refuse to leave when ordered. The only question was when, and they had decided they would begin after the Christmas break, sometime in February.

Lawson, the organizer and mentor of this budding group of young activists, had been jailed in 1951 as a conscientious objector to the Korean war. He was paroled and for three years was a Methodist missionary in Nagpur, India, where he intensified his studies of nonviolent resistance and the philosophy of Mohandas Gandhi. He returned home via Africa in the spring of 1956 and visited Montgomery for discussions with Martin Luther King. In 1958 Lawson enrolled in Vanderbilt University's divinity school, becoming the second Afro-American ever admitted—he was also expelled in 1960 for his sit-in activities—and he began conducting nonviolent workshops in the basement of **Clark Memorial United Methodist Church** (*1014 Fourth Avenue North*), a few blocks away from Nashville's historically black colleges and universities.

Occasionally he led workshops at **First Baptist Church** (*then on "Capitol Hill" at 319 Eighth Avenue North*), and this church would also be the primary staging area for waves of sit-ins during February and March of 1960. A historical marker on the southwest corner of the church's old site commemorates the Nashville sit-in movement. First Baptist's pastor, Reverend Kelly Miller Smith, and other young ministers had organized an SCLC affiliate, the Nashville Christian Leadership Conference (NCLC) at **Capers Memorial Christian Methodist Episcopal (CME) Church** (*315 15th Avenue North*), in 1958. In a sense, Nashville was more receptive to a planned campaign of nonviolent direct action than were many southern cities.

Employees of Nashville's Tic Toc restaurant block the doorway to keep demonstrators from entering and sitting down. The owner had already been arrested and charged with disorderly conduct for spraying a fire extinguisher at protesters.

In once-a-week workshops on Tuesday or Thursday nights, Lawson taught the theory of nonviolence and explored the prospects for nonviolent action in Nashville. There was role-playing in which some took on the parts of sitters-in at a lunch counter or restaurant while others played hostile whites, screaming racial epithets and engaging in actual physical assault. They learned how to curl into a protective fetal position when knocked to the ground and viciously kicked; they learned how to protect others with their bodies. Nonviolent discipline was constantly stressed, with much discussion of the feelings that surfaced during the workshop insults and assaults. As Howard Thurman had written and taught, Lawson taught, too, that they were going to be not simply protesters but *teachers* as well, showing that love was the greatest power; that, like Jesus or like Gandhi, they were obligated to try to change the hearts and minds of their tormentors; that the enemy was not those *people*, but rather their belief in racial segregation was the enemy. All participants understood that the training they were undergoing was for actual sit-ins in downtown Nashville. Not surprisingly, these workshops did not attract huge numbers (fewer than twenty people), but several of them would become renowned in civil rights struggle: Diane Nash, John Lewis, James Bevel, Bernard Lafayette, Marion Barry, Cordell Reagon.

Nashville, known as the "Athens of the South" (an exact

"I Didn't Think Nonviolence Would Work"

"I'm from Chicago. I knew that the South was segregated, but the fall of 1959 when I went to Fisk was the first time I experienced segregation signs and that level of discrimination. I felt outraged. If you were downtown at lunch time, blacks were eating lunch on the curb or near an alley because the places that would serve them wouldn't seat them. Instead, they had to go to carry-out windows or take-out counters. It all made me very angry and I began looking for an organization that was fighting this. And I was looking for people who wanted to fight this. I asked students. I asked teachers and others; so many said no, I was feeling pretty discouraged. When I asked Paul LaPrad, he told me about Jim Lawson. Paul was an exchange student from Indiana and a member of the Church of the Bretheren, sort of like the Quakers, and a church that believed in nonviolence. Paul told me that Jim had decided to begin holding nonviolent workshops; he was going and I could go with him.

"I did. There were community people there—we called them 'the adults'; a few students—John Lewis was one of them; C. T. Vivian was there. Jim would take a different topic every week. And he gave us homework assignments. One time he asked us to write our definition of love for discussion the following week. I remember being fascinated about how many different definitions of love we all had, and they all had validity, too. It was so interest-

replica of the Parthenon stands in the city's Centennial Park), might seem an unlikely place for one of the civil rights movement's most dramatic episodes, but like Atlanta and Charleston, its veneer of gentility did not mitigate the hard knot of racism and segregation at the core of city life. Despite Vanderbilt University's admission of Lawson, and, before him, James Joseph Jr., its first black divinity student, Chancellor Harvie Branscomb once said that when he saw black ROTC students from Ohio sharing barracks with white ROTC students from Vanderbilt, the sight of them had made him "fighting mad." Integration of Nashville's schools had begun in the fall of 1957 but proceeded at a snail's pace; and although the city patted itself on the back ing and you had to learn to think differently. Jim used to say, for instance, "'An eye for an eye, a tooth for a tooth' just leaves everybody blind and unable to eat.' Meeting violence with violence leads to a lot more violence and not a solution, was something else he used to say. This really requires a different orientation, but it was helping me find some answers. I understood what Jim was saying when he said that even though we have to struggle, we don't want to end up with victor and vanquished. We're trying to move toward reconciliation, Jim said, and that requires a different sort of action. We should try and love the person but shouldn't tolerate what they were doing, which was segregation. Jim really impressed me as being extremely calm and contemplative. He talked to us about Gandhi, and the idea that India had won its independence using nonviolence was a monumental revelation to me.

"But I didn't think nonviolence would work; I grew up in this violent society. But I kept going to the workshops because no other organization seemed to be even trying to do something. And I certainly didn't think I would be doing any nonviolent action. And going to jail . . . We were discussing going to jail one day and try as I would I just could not picture myself doing that! After that workshop I told folks I would type, take care of the telephones or something like that, but I was not going to any jail!

"So how is it that I wound up with SNCC and all those times in jail? Right place, right time, I guess. My life has certainly been different than I set out to make it. I'm better for it."

—DIANE NASH TO CHARLIE COBB

for even proceeding with desegregation, Nashville, like every other city in the South, dragged its feet on school desegregation. When it finally did begin, the process did not escape violence. On September 10, the **Hattie Cotton Elementary School** *(1033 West Greenwood Avenue)* was dynamited after admitting just one black child.

Nashville's historically black colleges and universities, or HBCUs (Fisk University, Tennessee State, Meharry Medical College, and American Baptist), were incubators of ideas and exchanges about making a better city and making a better world. An especially strong sense of the roots of this can be gained at the **Fisk University Library** *(17th Avenue North between Charlotte Avenue and*

Jefferson Street), where on the second floor a large collection of written material about African and Afro-American life is maintained. W. E. B. Du Bois taught at Fisk for a time, and writer Arna Bontemps, one of the founding fathers of the "Negro Renaissance," was Fisk's librarian from 1943 until 1965. The **Aaron Douglas Gallery** is on the third floor of the library and contains many of Douglas's famous Harlem Renaissance works and a large collection of African art. Douglas was the first chairman of the university's art department. Also on campus, the **Carl Van Vechten Gallery of Fine Arts** *(corner of Jackson Street and D. B. Todd Boulevard)* offers an outstanding collection of African-American art as well as works by Toulouse-Lautrec, Picasso, Renoir, and Cezanne. Dr. Charles S. Johnson, the great black sociologist and another important figure in the Negro Renaissance, was Fisk's first black president; the **Race Re-**

"Redemptive Suffering"

We talked a lot about "redemptive suffering," which from the first time Jim Lawson mentioned the phrase made me think of my mother. Often, when I was growing up, I would hear her groan and moan while she was praying. "The seeds of the righteous must never be forsaken . . . ," she would recite. I didn't know what she was talking about then, but now I was beginning to understand. What my mother was saying, in her Old Testament phrasing, was that we must honor our suffering, that there is something in the very essence of anguish that is liberating, cleansing, redemptive. I always understood the idea of the ultimate redeemer, Christ on the cross. But now I was beginning to see that this is something that is carried out in every one of us, that the purity of unearned suffering is a holy and affective thing. It affects not only ourselves, but it touches and changes those around us as well. It opens us and those around us to a force beyond ourselves, a force that is right and moral, the force of righteous truth that is at the basis of human conscience. Suffering puts us and those around us in touch with our consciences. It opens and touches our hearts. It makes us feel compassion where we need to and guilt if we must.

—FROM *WALKING WITH THE WIND*, BY JOHN LEWIS

Student sit-in leader Rodney Powell talking with two demonstrators at the lunch counter of Nashville's downtown Walgreen Drug Store

lations Institute *(1000 Seventeenth Avenue North)* that grew out of a series of seminars he conducted in 1942 continues. A three-hour tour of key civil rights sites is offered by the **Nashville Nonviolent Student Movement Legacy Association**, part of the city's **African-American Cultural Alliance** *(1215 Ninth Avenue North).*

The February 1, 1960, Greensboro sit-in accelerated the timetable for sit-ins in Nashville. On February 6, after Durham, North Carolina, minister Douglas Moore, telephoned his friend Lawson, the Nashville students held sympathy sit-ins at downtown stores. They followed with another sit-in on February 13 at **Walgreens** *(226 Fifth Avenue North)*, and at nearby Fifth Avenue stores *(**Woolworth's, S. H. Kress**, and **McClellan's Five-and-Dime**).* Only Walgreens remains today; it is part of a downtown historic district on Fifth Avenue that is marked with a sign listing some of the nonviolent rules of protest developed by the students. They sat in for about two hours and then left.

On February 18, hundreds more students targeted the same site, remaining for about half an hour. When protesters arrived at Walgreens two days later, they found the counter shut down, with trash cans, flower pots, lamp shades, and rugs atop it. Tension was mounting as merchants dug

"I Am Fortified by the Truth, Justice, and Christ"

I was put into the backseat of the police car between two policemen. Two others sat in front. During the thirteen-mile ride to town they called me every conceivable name and said anything they could think of to incite me to violence . . . When we reached Nashville, a number of policemen were lined up on both sides of the hallway down which I had to pass on my way to the captain's office. They tossed me from one to another like a volleyball. By the time I reached the office, the lining of my best coat was torn, and I was considerably rumpled. I straightened myself as best I could and went in. They had my bag, and went through it and my papers, finding much of interest, especially in the [magazines] *Christian Century* and *Fellowship*. Finally the captain said, "Come here nigger." I walked directly to him. "What can I do for you?" I asked. "Nigger," he said menacingly, "you're supposed to be scared when you come in here." "I am fortified by the truth, justice, and Christ," I said. "There's no need for me to fear." He was flabbergasted and, for a time, completely at a loss for words. Finally he said to another officer, "I believe the nigger's crazy!"

—FROM *TIME ON TWO CROSSES: THE COLLECTED WRITINGS OF BAYARD RUSTIN*

in their heels despite their dependence on black shoppers. Groups of belligerent white toughs, many of them teenagers, appeared on the scene. On February 27 the first arrests occurred, when some four hundred protesters showed up at McCellan's. A white exchange student from Manchester College in Indiana, by the name of Paul LaPrad, was singled out for special abuse by a hostile mob, who pummeled and spit on him until *he* was arrested for disorderly conduct. Other students were heckled and beaten. Eighty other protesters were arrested that day and, like LaPrad, charged with disorderly conduct. And here, for the first time with these arrests, "jail, no bail" was introduced. One by one the students were fined $100 for disorderly conduct by the judge. But when Diane Nash stood up, she told the judge that she and fourteen others, including John Lewis, would not pay the fine. "We feel that if we pay these fines we would be contributing to and supporting injustice and immoral practices that have been performed in the arrest and detention of the defendants." So the group went to jail.

The arrest and jailing of some of black Nashville's best and brightest inspired the city's Afro-American community, who had been at first wary of and worried by these student-driven protests, to rally around the students—"the children," as Reverend Kelly Miller Smith always called them. "The local white officialdom helped greatly," notes David Halberstam in his book *The Children*. Halberstam was a reporter for Nashville's *Tennessean* newspaper in 1960. "The more it lashed out at the students, the more arrests there were, the more united the community became."

Along with the sit-ins, a black boycott of downtown Nashville was squeezing white businesses. Nashville mayor Ben West released the students, promising a biracial committee to consider downtown desegregation in return for their promise not to demonstrate in downtown stores. But at the end of March that committee recommended that stores open one half of their counters as integrated eating areas and one half as segregated. Protests continued. White violence increased, too. Early in the morning of April 19, the **home of NAACP attorney Alexander Looby** (*2012 Meharry Boulevard*) was dynamited. From the beginning he had supported the sit-ins, and Looby had been the attorney for those arrested during the February 27 protest. The blast badly damaged both the Looby home and their next-door neighbor's house. It also knocked out some 140 of the windows of **Meharry Medical School** across the street.

Martin Luther King came to Nashville the next day, and at a mass meeting in the Fisk University gymnasium, he described Nashville's movement as "the best organized and the most disciplined in the Southland." A bomb scare in the middle of this rally caused an evacuation, but the crowd returned and King went on to say that he had come to Nashville "not to bring inspiration but to gain inspiration from the great movement that has taken place in this community."

May 16, 1960, students (from left) Matthew Walker, Peggy Alexander, Diane Nash, and Stanley Hemphill eating at the just-desegregated lunch counter of the Post House Restaurant in Nashville's Greyhound bus terminal. It was the first time blacks had been served at previously all-white counters anywhere in the city.

For the bombing was not the main reason King had come to Nashville; rather, he had come to the city because of an unexpected civil rights victory. When attorney Looby's house was bombed, a protest was quickly organized, and later that same morning, Diane Nash and Reverend C. T. Vivian led a long line of silent marchers—three thousand to four thousand people—into downtown Nashville. When they reached **City Hall** *(1 Public Square)*, Mayor West met them on the steps. Vivian, reading from a prepared statement, accused the mayor of a "failure of leadership." West heatedly responded, saying that he resented the accusation. Then West, calling Diane Nash "little lady," boasted of desegregating the airport seven years before. But Nash suddenly confronted him with a blunt, challenging direct question: "Do you recommend that the lunch counters be desegregated?"

The mayor blurted out, "Yes." Then, perhaps realizing what he had just said, tried to backpedal. "That's up to the store managers, of course."

Too late; the mayor's inadvertent concession turned a page in city life. The headline in the next day's *Tennessean* was: INTEGRATE COUNTERS—MAYOR. Today a plaque on city hall that commemorates this event, reads in part, "And the walls of segregation cracked."

All of the ten rules of conduct for the sit-ins written by John Lewis and Bernard Lafayette can be read in the **Nashville Public Library Civil Rights Room** *(615 Church Street)*, which opened in December 2003. These rules became the model for protest groups throughout the South. Over the doorway of this room is a quote attributed to John Lewis that is actually from the Jewish Talmud: "If not us, then who; if not now, then when?" The room's central focus is a circular counter symbolic of the department-store lunch counters that were so often sit-in targets. While sitting on stools at this symbolic lunch counter, you can read the countertop, which describes more than one hundred significant events in civil rights movement history. Timelines accompanied by photographs wrap around a display above the countertop. Large photographs on the walls depict the beginning of school desegregation in 1957, the sit-in movement of 1960, attorney Alexander Looby's bombed home, the confrontation with Mayor West, and Dr. King's visit to Nashville. As I walked around in 2003 making notes, my twelve-year-old daughter, Zora, and her good friend Arabia Tillery settled comfortably and interestedly in an enclosed audio/video area where visitors can view a selection of eight documentary films. This is one of only a few sites devoted to the civil rights movement where you can actually see (on film) workshops on nonviolent protest.

Grace McKinley escorts her daughter, Linda Gail McKinley, and a friend to Nashville's Fehr Elementary School, September 9, 1957. Segregationists surrounding them carry picket signs and taunt them as their children watch.

KNOXVILLE

" . . . *I have had the fortunate experience of being part of two movements: the industrial union movement in its early days and the civil rights movement. I saw something in these two movements which helped me understand that you don't have to work out your problems alone, one by one. When people get involved in a movement they must take sides, and in struggle, individual problems became less important or disappear altogether.*

". . . For example, good people had been working for years on race relations, trying to change the antiblack feelings of white folks by changing their attitudes. Highlander's program was a social equality experience based on the belief that only action would change people's attitude toward one another. Then, when the civil rights movement came along, these white people who were struggling with their souls got their souls right in a hurry. When a black person said to whites, 'I'm not a nigger any longer and you are not going to treat me this way anymore,' those whites had to act differently all at once and without the benefit of a long-drawn out attitudinal change.

". . . [So when] Blacks started moving . . . they saved not only their own souls but some of ours as well. **"**

—MYLES HORTON, *The Long Haul*

Something else happened at the City Hall protest in Nashville, although its significance was not recognized at the time. As Mayor West stood before the still-silent crowd that had just marched there, a young man near the front of the marchers, a singer named Guy Carawan, began strumming his guitar and singing softly, "We shall overcome; we shall overcome some day. Oh deep in my heart, I do believe, we shall overcome someday." Protest leaders, including Nash, Bernard Lafayette, and James Bevel, quickly joined in singing, for unlike most in the crowd, they had heard the song before and in fact had played an important role in reworking the original with Carawan at a workshop at the Highlander Center in Knoxville. Rooted as it is in black church-song tradition, the crowd found it easy to join in the singing, too.

"Keep Your Eyes on the Prize"

"Guy [Carawan] . . . was a musician deeply interested in traditional culture. He joined the Highlander staff in 1959 to carry on the work of Zilphia Horton. He also became Septima Clark's driver as she traveled around the Gullah islands and often contributed music to her citizenship school classes. He knew many songs from the labor movement, including the song 'Keep You Hand on the Plow, Hold On.'

"A woman named Alice Wine was learning to read. In fact, she was the first person on Johns Island who asked for classes so that she would be able to vote. When she heard Guy sing 'Keep Your Hands on the Plow,' she told him, 'Young man, I know a different echo to that song. We sing "keep your eyes on the prize."' Guy loved that version and began using it at Highlander workshops. He taught it to gatherings of young freedom workers, including to students at the founding meeting of SNCC in the spring of 1960.

"Later on as Guy visited in the Sea Islands, Mrs. Wine told him that she could not believe that her words had gone all over the South and around the country. And she did become a registered voter and a first-class citizen, joining others who helped change the political structure in the islands."

—CANDIE CARAWAN TO CHARLIE COBB

Left to right: *Local schoolteacher and children's book writer May Justice, Septima Clark, and Highlander founder Myles Horton at Monteagle*

As we talk at the **Highlander Research and Education Center** *(1959 Highlander Way, New Market)*, Guy Carawan strums his guitar, playing and singing "We Shall Overcome" as he first heard it. Some of the Nashville students had first heard this version of the song while attending a workshop at Highlander that Septima Clark had put together in 1960. At that meeting there was much discussion about nonviolence, whether to stay in jail without bail, and civil rights struggle beyond sit-ins. Says Guy Carawan, "Sometimes a few of us would just go off into another room to sing, to jam—Bernard Lafayette, Jim Bevel, a few others. They even liked hillbilly music! Sometimes I'd introduce them to some song I'd learned, and 'We Shall Overcome' was one of them. They really didn't much care for this version," says Guy laughing. "And they kind of put their own rhythm to it. They fooled around with it and it came out 'We Shall Overcome' the way it's sung now. Then they took it into the movement."

As appropriate as it was that the song had emerged into public view during a protest, it was equally appropriate that the song should have been shaped at Highlander. When Myles Horton founded the Highlander Folk School (now the Highlander Center) on the top of Monteagle Mountain near Chattanooga in 1932, his primary concern was with workers' rights, especially the rights of

Appalachian coal miners and farmers. It was in the 1950s that Horton began focusing on civil rights. Highlander was one of the few places in the South where blacks and whites could meet and discuss subjects freely, and it was under constant attack as "Communist." Four months before

T he workshop opened Friday evening with reports from students who have been active in sit-in lunchroom demonstrations in the South. Reports related to the spontaneous origin of the demonstrations; the way leadership was used in each college group; the philosophy and purposes of the movement as understood by the students; and the ways in which demonstration groups have related to their wider communities.

The students differed considerably about the desirability of cooperation with the adult communities, Negro and white. Nashville students spoke appreciatively of support they have had from the Nashville community, but some were uncertain about the wisdom of seeking to work directly with community agencies, or with adults, Negro or white. Some from other areas than Tennessee felt there was need to confine the movement to college groups.

On Saturday morning Dr. Herman Long [of Fisk University], commenting on the impact of demonstrations on the southern scene, pointed out that the movement, essentially student inspired and student led, represented the kind of "direct action against immediate injustices of discrimination" which the average adult would find it difficult to undertake himself, regardless of how sympathetic he might be with the movement.

"The adults in those communities where the demonstrations took place, would probably not have taken action of this kind even if they had seen the possibilities in it," he said. "They would probably have had prestige positions and economic interests, or job interests, to protect. Furthermore adults are essentially conservative. Mass demonstration is not impossible for them, and some do participate in it, but it is not the method the adult community seems at present to believe is the final strategy for attack on discrimination.

"In this sense this is a unique movement, especially suited to students."

—Excerpt from the Report of the 7th Annual
Highlander Folk School College Workshop,
April 1–3, 1960 (written by Septima Clark)

Mrs. Parks refused to surrender her bus seat in Montgomery, she had participated in workshops at Highlander. In 1959 Highlander was raided by Tennessee lawmen on the basis of a trumped-up charge of bootlegging. After this raid the Tennessee legislature launched an investigation into the school's "subversive" activities, and in 1960 it revoked Highlander's charter because of its racially integrated workshops. The government confiscated the property and auctioned it off, but in 1961 the school relocated to a two-story house (1625 Riverside Drive) in Knoxville. The school was renamed the **Highlander Research and Education Center.**

Martin Luther King, Rosa Parks, Ralph Abernathy, and other civil rights leaders had participated in workshops at the Monteagle site. A photograph of King taken at the twenty-fifth-anniversary celebration of Highlander reappeared throughout the 1960s on billboards across the South with huge letters that charged: MARTIN LUTHER KING AT COMMUNIST TRAINING SCHOOL. And it was here that SNCC's fierce internal debate over what would be its primary mission—direct-action protests or voter registration—was resolved when Ella Baker suggested that the organization establish two wings, one addressing each issue.

In 1972 Highlander moved to its present hundred-acre site about twenty-five miles east of Knoxville in New Market and, in a way, returned to its roots by again pursuing environmental concerns and issues related to mine labor and mountain poverty. It has also been working with Latino immigrants, a new labor force in the region. Myles Horton died in January of 1990 and is buried with his family on the original Highlander site in Monteagle. Most of the acreage has been sold to private developers, but the Hortons' log cabin

An integrated workshop at Highlander

"As a White"

I n the first place, I knew I wasn't black. So, my relation to blacks was as a white who was concerned with problems of all people, and as a person who felt that the problems caused by whites were affecting whites as well as blacks. I believed that anything I wanted for myself, I must want for other people.

I didn't have any problem with saying to blacks, "All of us have problems that whites caused, but blacks will have to take the lead if the problems are to be dealt with. I will put Highlander at your disposal, and not try to share in making decisions. You've got to make the decisions, and if it doesn't violate our principles, we'll go along."

That way we had an honest basis of relating . . .

When we told black people we would put ourselves at their disposal they took it seriously, because by that time we'd had black labor-union students at Highlander. They knew we had demonstrated our belief and practice in social equality.

You have to be careful not to think that you're somebody else . . . I have to say to myself, "Look, Horton . . . , black people can't say they are col-or-blind. Whites and white-controlled institutions always remind them that they're black, so you've got to recognize color." This doesn't mean that you feel superior, it's just that you can never fully walk in other people's shoes . . . , that you have a different role to play.

You can't be accepted by people if you're trying to be what you're not. You've got to be genuinely what you are, but from what you are you've got to have empathy with and understanding of people and their situations."

—FROM *THE LONG HAUL*, BY MYLES HORTON

house, where Martin Luther King stayed when visiting, remains.

Knoxville's **Belk Cultural Exchange Center** *(1927 Dandridge Street)*, a small museum, library, and art gallery, is another stop on our civil rights trail. With its collection of more than thirty-thousand oral histories, photographs, documents, and African-American newspapers from 1840 to the present, the center educates about the black history of the city and greater east Tennessee. To sit down with Avon

Rollins, who directs the center, is to have direct access to valuable history. Rollins, who was a leader of Knoxville's student movement, participated in SNCC's founding meeting; was one of SNCC's organizers in Danville, Virginia; and has been jailed across the South some thirty times. The museum, which was originally in the luxurious home once occupied by prominent Knoxville blacks James and Ethel Beck, has undergone a $1.2 million expansion in recent years.

A site that does not want "tourist" visitors, but contributes to Knoxville's importance as a stop on the civil rights trail, lies about twenty-five miles north of the city. This is the **Alex Haley Farm** *(Old Highway 61 between Clinton and Norris)*. In February 1992, at the age of seventy, Haley, the Pulitzer Prize–winning author of *Roots*, died of a heart attack. Two years later the 127-acre farm, which he used as a retreat, was bought by the **Children's Defense Fund (CDF)**, which uses it for meetings and workshops, especially for its "Freedom School" leadership-training programs, which attract hundreds of students from all over the country. Architect Maya Lin, best known for the Vietnam Veteran's Memorial in Washington, D.C., and the Civil Rights Memorial in Montgomery, has designed two buildings on this site: the striking nondenominational Riggio-Lynch Chapel (named for strong CDF supporters Leonard Riggio, chairman of Barnes & Noble, and William Lynch, a former deputy mayor of New York) and the Langston Hughes Library. The Defense Fund's founder, Bennettsville, South Carolina, native Marian Wright Edelman, was one of the leaders of the sit-in movement while she studied at Spellman College in Atlanta. As a young attorney she was deeply involved with Mississippi's struggle. The message and mission of the CDF, worth repeating here, can be said to have roots in the southern civil rights movement: ". . . to Leave No Child Behind and to ensure every child a Healthy Start, a Head Start, a Fair Start, and a Moral Start in life."

~ MEMPHIS ~

---

66 *Well, I don't know what will happen now. We've got some difficult days ahead. But it doesn't matter with me now. Because I've been to the mountaintop. And I don't mind. Like anybody, I would like to live a long life. Longevity has its place. But I'm not concerned about that now. I just want to do God's will. And He's allowed me to go up to the mountain. And I've looked over. And I've seen the promised land. I may not get there with you. But I want you to know tonight, that we, as a people, will get to the promised land. And I'm happy, tonight. I'm not worried about anything. I'm not fearing any man. Mine eyes have seen the glory of the coming of the Lord.* **99**

—MARTIN LUTHER KING JR., APRIL 3, 1968

Inevitably, our journey takes us to Memphis and a kind of conclusion, where our civil rights trail ends with Martin Luther King's last public words. At **Mason Temple** (*930 Mason Street*), where he spoke those words the night before his assassination, Rev. King stood in a different relationship with the black community, the nation, and the world than he had in previous years. He was no longer unquestionably revered. His opposition to the Vietnam war had angered President Lyndon Johnson's White House, which despite King's Nobel Peace Prize slammed various doors in his face. The slogan "Black Power" and a kind of angry black nationalism by young people, especially in urban areas, seemed to be supplanting efforts to create the "beloved community" idealized by the Gandhian philosophy that had emerged with the Montgomery movement and the Nashville sit-ins.

The 1965 drive in Selma had been a success, but the following year SCLC-led demonstrations targeting discrimination in housing, employment, and schools in Chicago had been a disaster. The economic plight of the black community, the connection between jobs and freedom, had moved to the front and center of Dr. King's thinking and rhetoric, but the battle he wanted to wage in this arena (which was still taking shape in his mind) threatened to pit him against some of his former allies and even against some members of his own organization. Two decades of full-time movement experience had radicalized him.

Memphis, though, was an improbable place for the murder of Martin Luther King, despite its long history of lynching, segregation, job discrimination, and police brutality. By 1958 the once all-white Memphis State University was admitting black students. And under pressure from the city's powerful NAACP, other city-owned facilities—parks, buses, the river docks—were being desegregated. By 1962 restaurants and theaters were also desegregating, and public schools began admitting blacks. Memphis's movement even had a bank, the black-owned *Tri-State Bank* (*180 South Main Street*). When credit and loan pressure were placed on black businessmen after the Supreme Court's *Brown* decision, the NAACP used the bank to create a loan program for them. Many local sit-ins were planned in the bank's board room, and bank officials sometimes kept the vault open at night to provide bail money for protesters.

Despite being a city of plantation culture, feelings in Memphis had always been mixed when it came to completely embracing the racial tenets of that culture. Blacks had the vote early here, but they were expected to vote for the white political machine of Edward Hull "Boss" Crump, for whom, in 1909, band leader W. C. Handy composed a campaign tune that is the first published blues song, "Mr. Crump" (published three years later as "Memphis Blues").

After the infamous riot of 1866, Memphis leaders sought to avoid racial violence, and even as far back as the eve of the Civil War, city leaders were to a certain extent uneasy about seceding from the Union. The city's cotton trade, and thus much of its money, was very much tied to the North by buyers, and traders did not want to jeopardize that profitable relationship. On the other hand, the plantation owners in Mississippi, who also sold to the buyers, were dependent on slave labor and the slave system. And there was no significant trade with the North without cotton. Notwithstanding this tension caused by the pull of competing interests among some of the city's ruling elite, the white population's sympathies lay with the Confederacy, and young men joined the Army of the South to fight for it. Unlike Atlanta, Vicksburg, and Richmond, however, Memphis suffered no significant destruction in the war. For a time the city was the headquarters city of Union general Ulysses S. Grant. He resided at what is now a luxury bed and breakfast, the **Hunt-Phelan Estate** *(533 Beale Street)*. Nathan Bedford Forrest is buried on Union Street, in a park named for him, and **Confederate Park**, in downtown Memphis, is still presided over by a statue of Confederate president Jefferson Davis, who spent his later years in this city. In **Elmwood Cemetery** *(824 South Dudley Street)*, buried among the eighteen Confederate and two Union generals, there are prominent Afro-Americans, including singer Ma Rainey; Robert Church, the father of Mary Church Terrell and the South's first black millionaire; and A. W. Willis, the civil rights activist who in 1964 became the first black elected to the Tennessee State Legislature since 1887. Willis was the attorney of record in James Meredith's effort at desegregating the University of Mississippi.

Back in its antebellum days, paddle-wheel steamers coming up the Mississippi River docked in Memphis, where mountainous bales of cotton were unloaded by slaves, stacked along the riverbank, and stood awaiting other slaves to haul them into warehouses. The steamboats were long gone by the mid-twentieth century, but more than 40 percent of the nation's cotton crop was still being traded in Memphis. Essentially, Memphis was the great metropolitan depot of an agricultural region encompassing the cotton-growing floodplains of west Tennessee, northeast

Arkansas, and northwest Mississippi. *River Walk (inside Mud Island River Park, 125 North Front Street)* is an impressive five-block-long model of the Mississippi River, complete with flowing water. Visiting it is the best way to gain appreciation of both the river's awesome geography and its impact on the region, for you cannot understand the Mississippi Delta, especially the river that gives it its identity, without understanding the transportation of cotton.

Not much of Memphis's prosperity from cotton reached its Afro-American population. Despite the existence of a small black middle class, the stupefying inequality between black and white that defined The Delta was also present in this urban cotton capital. The city's manufacturing sector grew during World War II: from a little more than twenty-seven thousand before the war, the workforce grew to nearly forty-nine thousand jobs in two years; but most of those jobs in the expanding defense industry were denied to blacks. In the river-fed Delta cotton fields abutting the city, you were as likely to find a Memphis city dweller as you were to find a plantation-based sharecropper. Thousands of black men and women were bused daily from their Memphis homes to the rural plantations in Tennessee and Mississippi counties, where they tried as best they could to eke out a living picking cotton.

Dr. King's best friend and closest associate, Reverend Ralph David Abernathy, recalled that SCLC's road to Memphis actually began in one of the most impoverished parts of The Delta, Quitman County, Mississippi, while the two were visiting a school in the town of Marks. A teacher they had been talking to excused herself. "It's lunchtime; I need to feed the children," she explained.

"We watched as she brought out a box of crackers and a brown bag filled with apples," Abernathy wrote in his autobiography, *And the Walls Came Tumbling Down.*

"Then she went around to each desk and gave each child a stack of four or five crackers and a quarter of an apple."

Abernathy nudged King. "'That's all they get,' I whispered."

King turned to his friend, nodding his head. "And I saw that his eyes were full of tears."

Later, according to Abernathy, King told him that he had not known that there were starving children in America. And out of King's somewhat surprising acknowledgment of this blind spot was born the idea of a "Poor People's Campaign"—a caravan of the poor to Washington, D.C., that would bring their plight to the nation's attention. In this effort we see the outlines of the new direction King wanted to take. For the first time, instead of working with, and at the invitation of, local civil rights organizations, King sought to build a national movement, trying to bring together blacks, Hispanics, Native Americans, and poor whites, all of whom were trapped in poverty.

Work began on this new campaign in the fall of 1967, and it was within this context that King became engaged with the sanitation workers' strike that broke out in Memphis on February 12, 1968. The immediate cause of the strike was the death of two sanitation workers, who were crushed while sitting in a compacter in the back of a garbage truck; they had sought refuge from a cold rain

Sanitation workers picketing in downtown Memphis

there. Long-standing grievances included abysmally low wages ($1.80 an hour on average), no pension, no vacation pay, and ancient equipment. The men worked in their own clothing, often without gloves or masks. Black sanitation workers were called "walking buzzards" because at the end of a shift they were so foul smelling. Memphis mayor Henry Loeb dismissed these concerns and conditions and refused to talk to the workers, declaring their union, and later their strike, illegal.

For King, Memphis was impossible to ignore even though he was in the midst of planning the Poor People's Campaign. On February 22 some seven hundred sanitation workers had jammed into a City Council public works committee meeting and refused to leave. By the end of the month, more than a strike was under way. Various black civic and church leaders had allied themselves with the union effort under an umbrella organization called the Community On the Move for Equality (COME), which was headed by James Lawson of Nashville renown. Since June 1962 Lawson had been pastor of Memphis's **Centenary**

National guardsmen have blocked off Beale Street while armored vehicles remain at the ready as sanitation workers and supporters from the American Federation of State, County and Municipal Workers picket peacefully.

United Methodist Church *(584 East McLemore Avenue).* On March 18, at Lawson's invitation, King spoke before a large crowd and called for a general strike aimed at shutting the city down; he also promised to come back and lead a nonviolent march of striking workers. True to his word, ten days later, he led a march from ***Clayborn AME Temple*** *(294 Hernando Street)* toward City Hall. But some of the younger marchers abandoned nonviolent discipline, breaking the plate-glass windows of stores and looting; a distressed Dr. King was forced to flee. This may have been the first time King ever lost control of a protest—another sign of changing times. The police moved in, using force and violence that resulted in almost three hundred arrests and one death (sixteen-year-old Larry Payne). The next day, some three hundred members of the American Federation of State, County and Municipal Workers Union, carrying picket signs that read I AM A MAN, marched in peaceful protest with National Guard protection. Even after King's assassination barely a week later, marches from Clayborn Temple continued, including one led by Coretta Scott King on April 8, the day before her husband was to be buried in Atlanta. On April 16 the City Council finally agreed to a strike settlement.

    Mason Temple *(930 Mason Street),* where an exhausted Martin Luther King spoke his last public words, is headquarters of the Church of God in Christ, whose extensive membership—only the Baptists have more black congregants—made its support for the strike and civil rights struggle crucial. The temple can seat 7,500, and mass meetings were always packed. COME had been formed at the temple on February 24, and it was there that the Memphis strike went national with a March 14 appearance (just four days before King spoke in this city for the first time) by Bayard Rustin and the NAACP's Roy Wilkins. Brand-new garbage cans were used to take up a collection.

    It is King's last words at Mason Temple that continue to haunt: "I may not get there with you. But I want you to know tonight that we as a people will get to the Promised Land." For a moment after speaking he almost seemed to have lost control of himself as he collapsed into his seat. There is a welded corton steel **Martin Luther King Memorial** *(Poplar Avenue and North Main Street; walking distance from the famous Beale Street)* by the prominent Afro-American sculptor Richard Hunt. It offers the words "I have Been to the Mountain," taken from King's last speech.

The **National Civil Rights Museum** *(450 Mulberry Street)* will without a doubt be the primary stop for any visitor to Memphis who follows a civil rights trail. This is partly because the museum encompasses the Lorraine Motel, where Martin Luther King was assassinated. The museum is really a huge monument to the courage of ordinary people, and visitors can walk through virtually the entire history of civil rights struggle in the United States, beginning with the importation of the first African slaves in 1619. Galleries encompass the Civil War, the black migration, Jim Crow laws, the sit-ins, and the Montgomery bus boycott, as well as Birmingham and Memphis. You can listen to taped telephone calls between President John F. Kennedy and Mississippi governor Ross Barnett, as well Alabama governor George Wallace arguing with Kennedy. You can sit in a Greyhound bus like the one ridden by 1961 Freedom Riders, and at a replica of a lunch counter you can almost feel the torment of the sit-in students.

The tour ends, as does this book, in room 306 of the Lorraine Motel, the room King checked into on April 3, 1968—the day before his assassination. I am hostile to death and have seen too much of it, so I am willing only to peek in briefly. I already know much of the detail anyway. April 4 was a cool, somewhat wet day. King had a light, almost relaxing schedule. He was feeling playful and teased staffers, even engaging them in a pillow fight. Adding to his upbeat mood, during an afternoon meeting word had come that the court was about to approve a march. King's good friend Reverend Billy Kyles had invited him to a home-cooked dinner and arrived at 5:30 to pick him up. Mrs Kyles was planning to serve roast beef, asparagus, cauliflower, candied yams, pig feet, and chitlins; King, stretched out on the bed, was already licking his lips in anticipation. Ralph Abernathy,

who was planning to join him, had just finished a bath, so King stepped out onto the balcony to wait for him.

The room, I am told, is pretty much the way it was when Rev. King was assassinated. One of the two double beds is unmade and rumpled, generating a weird kind of metaphor in my mind for civil rights struggle. A soundtrack plays "Precious Lord Take My Hand." King had leaned over the balcony and asked Ben Branch, leader of the Operation Breadbasket band of Chicago, to play the song at the mass meeting he planned to attend later that evening. "Play it pretty," he told Branch. King was smoking a cigarette. The 1968 Cadillac a local funeral home always provided for King's use while he was in town is still parked in the parking lot where Branch stood. Movement comrades Andy Young, Jesse Jackson, Hosea Williams, and James Orange were in various spots nearby. Across the street a black detective from the Memphis police department was keeping a watchful eye.

James Earl Ray was also across the street. He waited at **Mrs. Brewer's Boardinghouse** *(418–22½ Main Street; now part of the Civil Rights Museum)* for his opportunity to

Martin Luther King, accompanied by Ralph Abernathy, walking across the balcony of the Lorraine Motel shortly after checking in on April 3.

shoot. Ray watched King from his second-floor room (2B), then set up in the bathroom. Around 6:30 P.M. he fired the single shot that killed King and fled down the back stairs. He dropped his Remington rifle, which was wrapped in a bedspread, in the doorway of a used-record store called **Canipe's Amusement Company** *(424 South Main Street)* and raced away in his Ford Mustang. Ray's fingerprints were on the rifle and he confessed to the crime, but he later retracted his confession. The exhibit in this part of the museum documents King's assassination in considerable detail, examining the State of Tennessee's investigative materials and exploring theories that hold that Ray could not have committed this act alone. Coretta King called for a "Truth and Reconciliation Commission," reflecting the King family's belief that Ray was a pawn. In an extraordinary March 27, 1997, meeting, King's youngest son, Dexter, visited Ray at the River Bend prison in Nashville and told Ray he believed he was innocent. In this part of the museum there is also a strong exhibit on guns and the people killed by them.

It is easy—even tempting—to say that the civil rights movement died as King fell and bled on the balcony of the Lorraine Motel, but let's recognize, at this bitter moment, the one lesson that emerges with clarity at the end of our civil rights trail: No matter how ugly and soul shattering the violence, nothing has ever been able to kill the civil rights movement. In the phrase activists after King's murder borrowed from Mozambique's struggle to liberate itself from Portugal: *a luta contínua*—"the struggle continues." However, it is probably accurate to say that the nonviolent movement that had defined civil rights struggle for over a decade fell to the ground that evening.

We go on, though. As Rev. King might say even today, while we cannot foresee every detail, what we're going to be still lies ahead and it still has to do with securing freedom.

" *If I were standing at the beginning of time, with the possibility of general and panoramic view of the whole human history up to now, and the Almighty said to me, 'Martin Luther King, which age would you like to live in?'— I would take my mental flight by Egypt through, or rather across the Red Sea, through the wilderness on toward the Promised Land. And in spite of its magnificence, I wouldn't stop there. I would move on by Greece, and take my mind to Mount Olympus. And I*

"I have been to the mountain top."

would see Plato, Aristotle, Socrates, Euripides and Aristophanes assembled around the Parthenon as they discussed the great and eternal issues of reality.

But I wouldn't stop there. I would go on, even to the great heyday of the Roman Empire. And I would see developments around there, through various emperors and leaders. But I wouldn't stop there. I would even come up to the day of the Renaissance, and get a quick picture of all that the Renaissance did for the cultural and esthetic life of man. But I wouldn't stop there. I would even go by the way that the man for whom I'm named had his habitat. And I would watch Martin Luther as he tacked his ninety-five theses on the door at the church in Wittenberg.

But I wouldn't stop there. I would come on up even to 1863, and watch a vacillating president by the name of Abraham Lincoln finally come to the conclusion that he had to sign the Emancipation

Proclamation. But I wouldn't stop there. I would even come up to the early thirties, and see a man grappling with the problems of the bankruptcy of his nation. And come with an eloquent cry that we have nothing to fear but fear itself.

But I wouldn't stop there. Strangely enough, I would turn to the Almighty, and say, 'If you allow me to live just a few years in the second half of the twentieth century, I will be happy.' Now that's a strange statement to make, because the world is all messed up. The nation is sick. Trouble is in the land. Confusion all around. That's a strange statement. But I know, somehow, that only when it is dark enough, can you see the stars. And I see God working in this period of the twentieth century in a way that men, in some strange way, are responding—something is happening in our world. The masses of people are rising up. And wherever they are assembled today, whether they are in Johannesburg, South Africa; Nairobi, Kenya; Accra, Ghana; New York City; Atlanta, Georgia; Jackson, Mississippi; or Memphis, Tennessee—the cry is always the same—'We want to be free.' **"**

—MARTIN LUTHER KING, APRIL 3, 1968

EPILOGUE

The struggle continues—it is worth repeating and neatly encapsulates the basic fact that one, two, three, or even ten decades of struggle are neither beginning nor at an end. This may seem obvious to anyone looking at all the unsolved problems in the United States today, or at what often seems like an increasingly chaotic world. And that I have not addressed these problems in what is primarily a travel guide is surely easily understood. Less clear, however, may be why important civil rights struggles and civil rights sites in some states are not chronicled in these pages. There is really no perfectly satisfactory explanation I can offer except to say that this book in part reflects *my* journey and the sites that most directly affected me as a participant in the southern civil rights movement.

The book could easily be twice its current size and still not contain every civil rights battlefield even of the 1960s alone. I have given that some thought while struggling toward some sort of conclusion, and while it will be barely adequate, in the next few pages, let me depart somewhat from the format that structures the preceding chapters by pointing you to a few sites that are not in the main narrative but have to be acknowledged.

LITTLE ROCK, ARKANSAS

The nine students braving white mobs to desegregate *Central High School* (*2125 West Fourteenth Street; now Central High School National Historic Site*) in

Sixteen-year-old Elizabeth Eckford braves a jeering mob organized by the governor as she enters Central High School in Little Rock.

1957 seemed like "us." Far more easily in Springfield, Massachusetts, I was beginning my first year at a mostly white high school, and despite Arkansas's distance, the first imprint of student civil rights struggle was left on my mind by these nine. The tumultuous and terrible events surrounding their effort dramatically illustrates that racist hostility and violence was (and is) often caused by the cynical manipulation of ambitious politicians. Governor Orval E. Faubus, the man at the center of white resistance to federal court-ordered school desegregation in Arkansas's capital, entered politics as a reform-minded "liberal" with Afro-American support. But his first race for the governor's office had been bitter, and Faubus had been forced to defend his attendance at Commonwealth College, a school once associated with the Southern Tenant Farmers Union and Highlander Folk School. Furthermore, Faubus's father, Sam, had been a state leader of the Socialist Party of America. Once he won the governorship, whipping up racist hysteria was the path Faubus chose to secure his political career, and Central High School was his testing ground for the effectiveness of this choice.

On September 2, 1957, he called out the Arkansas National Guard to prevent the entrance of the "Little Rock Nine," calling the action a "test of authority." He organized a "Mothers League" to gather at the school to harass and jeer the nine students. One of the most unforgettable scenes ever photographed is of the young Elizabeth Eckford making her way through these screaming women, some of whom spit at her. On September 20 Faubus suddenly withdrew the National Guard, thus permitting unrestrained white rioting at the school. Faubus's defiance forced a showdown with an angered, and until then silent, President Dwight D. Eisenhower, who called in the U.S. Army's 101st Airborne and nationalized the state's National Guard. Without this action the nine students may very well have been killed. Faubus, invoking his power as governor, ordered Little Rock high schools closed, and they stayed closed for a year (although the white Central High football team continued to play its regular schedule). Faubus's segregationist strategy to gain and keep political office worked; he served six terms as Arkansas's governor. In what was once a Mobile gas station across the street from the school, there is now a **Visitor's Center** *(2125 Daisy L. Gatson Bates Drive)*. The street is named for Daisy Bates, publisher of the *Arkansas State Press* newspaper and the primary adviser to the Little Rock Wire.

"A little-known political victory ended the school crisis. After segregationist school-board members voted on May 5, 1959, not to renew the contracts of forty-four teachers they accused of supporting school desegregation, an organization of businessmen and a women's group called the Women's Emergency Committee to Open Our Schools (WEC) combined to form a group called Stop This Outrageous Purge (STOP). On May 25 STOP won a recall election that resulted in the removal of three segregationist members from the school board, and the public schools reopened on August 12. Across from the Visitor's Center, ten marble benches—one for each of the Little Rock Nine and one in honor of past, present, and future students— are in a commemorative garden, where photographs of the Nine have been placed in large arches.

❧ ST. AUGUSTINE, ❧ FLORIDA

Florida may be the state that is most ignored in discussion and assessment of the southern civil rights movement, although significant events unfolded in the "Sunshine State." The color barrier in major league baseball was shattered in Daytona Beach when in 1946 Jackie Robinson began spring training with the Montreal Royals, a farm club of the Brooklyn Dodgers. The city's *Jackie Robinson Ballpark and Monument (105 East Orange Street)*, once called the Daytona City Island Ballpark, is a national historic site today.

Mary McLeod Bethune was also from Daytona Beach, as was Howard Thurman. And not far away, near Titusville and Cape Canaveral, rural Mims may be where the first assassination of a modern civil rights leader occurred when, on Christmas Eve 1951, Klansmen blew up the *home of NAACP state director Harry T. Moore (2180 Freedom Avenue)*, killing not only Moore but also his wife, Harriette. It is now the site of the *Harry T. and Harriette V. Moore Memorial Park and Cultural Center.*

With Native Americans, Caribbean Islanders, South Americans, black Seminoles, settlement by Spanish, and even the alligators, Florida's diversity and history have in some ways made it seem an exotic part of America, outside the cultural mainstream. South Florida—Miami in partic-

> "The NAACP in Miami . . . is perfectly willing to listen to sweet reason in the demands for equality and to work with responsible organizations toward a sensible approach to racial problems—up to a point. . . . We'll appeal to your reason, but when that fails, we'll appeal to your hide."
>
> —NAACP MIAMI PRESIDENT THEODORE R. GIBSON, QUOTED IN THE *MIAMI NEWS*, DECEMBER 13, 1959

ular, with its Cubans, Haitians, New York City retirees, and South Miami Beach fashion shoots—is not often thought of as "southern." But one of the earliest direct-action protests in the South took place in Miami when, on May 9, 1945, Father Theodore R. Gibson of Coconut Grove's Christ Church led a group of nine blacks in a swim-in at whites-only **Haulover Beach** *(10800 Collins Avenue)*. A sustained sit-in campaign for desegregation downtown began in March 1960 when seven black ministers attempted to enter the lunchroom of **Burdines Department Store** *(22 East Flagler Street)*; police blocked the door. Within months, as more sit-ins took place and under the threat of a boycott of downtown shops, a desegregation agreement was reached. Downtown stores opened to all in August.

Despite significant challenges to segregation that took place in Saint Augustine, Jacksonville, and Tallahassee, north Florida is also a forgotten part of the civil rights story. America's oldest city, **Saint Augustine**, established in 1565, was where the first Africans in America lived. Saint Augustine was also sanctuary for runaway slaves fleeing British colonies. They helped build San Marco Fort, the first line of defense against British attack, and so in 1693 the king of Spain, in gratitude as well as recognition that he had useful allies in the ex-slaves who had fled to Spanish territory, declared "Liberty to all." About two miles north of San Marco, the first settlement of free blacks in America was established in 1738, Gracia Real de Santa Teresa de Mose, usually shortened *to* **Fort Mose** *(pronounced moh-SAY; Saratoga Boulevard off U.S. 1)*. But twenty-five years later, the British took over the colony and, along with the Spanish, most of the blacks fled to Cuba. Slavery and segregation took root. The slave market, now called **Market House** *(Plaza de la Constitucion)*, still remains in this historic city.

Just after the Civil War a black community was established called **Africa**, then **Lincolnville**; it is now the **Lincolnville Historic District** *(bordered by King and Bridge Streets on the north, Washington Street and the banks of Maria Sanchez Lake on the east, and the San Sebastian River along the southern tip and to the west)*. Few U.S. cities

Wade-in violence in St. Augustine

contain as many historic structures as Saint Augustine—twelve hundred—and no one knows how many artifacts may be buried here; yet few cities do so little to preserve history. However, a local group, ACCORD (www.accordfreedomtrail .org), has begun to mark civil rights sites.

Sit-ins began in Saint Augustine in 1960, when Hank Thomas, who the following year would be a Freedom Rider, sat in at **Woolworth's** *(33 King Street; now the site of a T-shirt shop)*. Thomas was arrested, and city authorities, thinking that he must be insane, tried to have him committed to a mental institution.

Others were supposed to join Hank Thomas, but larger-scale actions did not begin until June 1963 when the NAACP Youth Council began picketing and sit-ins. One of the targets of their picket lines was the **Tourist Center** *(10 Castillo Drive, opposite the Castillo de San Marcos National Monument)*; tourism is this historic city's primary business. Their signs read AMERICA'S OLDEST CITY UNFAIR TO NEGRO CITIZENS. Klan activity steadily increased with these protests. In September 1963 Klan members kidnapped Dr. Robert B. Hayling, the local dentist and civil rights leader who had organized the protests, and three other black activists. They escaped with their lives when the sheriff, though hostile to civil rights, rescued them. Then in February 1964 the homes of two black families seeking to enroll their children in all-white public schools were bombed. Dr. Hayling was now writing to President Lyndon Johnson and the Justice Department,

Awaiting jail under police and canine guard, young St. Augustine demonstrators find strength in song and remain defiant.

seeking, without success, federal marshals to protect black citizens.

Finally, Hayling asked Martin Luther King for help. With the arrival of Hosea Williams, protest demonstrations were ratcheted up. There were almost nightly mass meetings at **Saint Mary's Missionary Baptist Church** *(69 Washington Street)*, which was also a launch pad for protest marches into the town square. The **Lincolnville Public Library** *(156 Martin Luther King Avenue)* as well as the **Elks Lodge** *(100 Washington Street)*, which was also SCLC headquarters, are where students trained in techniques of nonviolent protest. The Saint Augustine campaign, says Andy Young, who was beaten during a march, "turned out to be SCLC's most violent and bloody campaign." Martin Luther King said of Saint Augustine, "Of all the cities we have worked in, we have never worked in one as violent as this." Following a wade-in on the morning of June 24, in which groups of whites attacked the protesters, a Klan mob rushed other protesters at **Plaza de la Constitution** *(Martin Luther King Street and Cathedral Place)*, attacking them with bricks. There was serious concern for Martin Luther King's safety when he came to town, and he shuttled between two homes *(81 and 83 Bridge Street)*; there are markers at both houses. King was arrested at the **Monson Motor Lodge** *(32 Avenida Menendez, a site now occupied by the Hilton Garden Inn)*. It was here that the lodge's manager was photographed pouring muriatic acid into the motel's whites-only swimming pool after civil rights activists had jumped into it. Those pictures, which appeared in newspapers around the world, increased pressure on the city government.

After two months of lunch-counter sit-ins, beach wade-ins, marches, picketing, an influx of northern supporters, plus a boycott, the city finally gave in and began the process of desegregation. This highly visible campaign—during which both Mrs. Mary Peabody, the seventy-two-year-old mother of Massachusetts governor Endicott Peabody, and Mrs. John Burgess, wife of the Episcopal Bishop of Massachusetts, were arrested while sitting in with Dr. Hayling and other Afro-Americans in a restaurant at the **Ponce de Leon Motor Lodge** *(U.S. 1 north; now torn down)*—may have given the 1964 Civil Rights Act the final nudge needed for passage.

As in so many southern civil rights efforts, St. Augustine also had its own Rosa Parks: Mrs. Katherine "Kat" Twine, who was arrested so many times that whenever she thought she would be arrested, she wore a large-brimmed hat, which she called her "freedom hat," in order to have some shade from the sun in the stockade of the old **City Jail** *(167 San Marco Avenue)* where protesters were held. The hat had FREE-DOM NOW printed on it and a button from the 1963 March on Washington. (On encountering Mrs. Peabody in prison, Mrs. Twine told her, "You look just like Eleanor Roosevelt." To which Mrs. Peabody replied, "We are cousins.")

❧ JACKSONVILLE, ❧ FLORIDA

I n nearby Jacksonville, which often seems an extension of south Georgia, extreme violence was directed at civil rights activists. On Saturday, August 27, 1960, members of the NAACP Youth Council who had targeted downtown

"Lift Every Voice and Sing"

Lift every voice and sing, till earth and Heaven ring,
Ring with the harmonies of Liberty;
Let our rejoicing rise high as the listening skies,
Let it resound loud as the rolling sea.
Sing a song full of the faith that the dark past has taught us,
Sing a song full of the hope that the present has brought us;
Facing the rising sun of our new day begun,
Let us march on till victory is won.

Stony the road we trod, bitter the chastening rod,
Felt in the days when hope unborn had died;
Yet with a steady beat, have not our weary feet
Come to the place for which our fathers sighed?
We have come over a way that with tears has been watered,
We have come, treading our path through the blood of the slaughtered,
Out from the gloomy past, till now we stand at last
Where the white gleam of our bright star is cast.

God of our weary years, God of our silent tears,
Thou Who hast brought us thus far on the way;
Thou Who hast by Thy might led us into the light;
Keep us forever in the path, we pray.
Lest our feet stray from the places, our God, where we met Thee,
Lest, our hearts drunk with the wine of the world, we forget Thee;
Shadowed beneath Thy hand, may we forever stand,
True to our God, true to our native land.

—JAMES WELDON JOHNSON & JOHN ROSAMOND JOHNSON

lunch counters for sit-ins were assaulted by one hundred fifty ax handle–wielding Ku Klux Klansmen. Fifty people were injured. It might have been worse if a black street gang, the Boomerangs, hadn't moved in to protect the protesters from the mob. There is an **"Ax Handle Saturday" Memorial** (*downtown in Heming Park, on its southwest corner at Hogan Street*).

There is a great deal of significant black history in this city, and with the growing interest in black cultural tourism, you might expect Jacksonville to be a prime stop. Not much of this kind of traffic occurs, though, undoubtedly because so little is immediately visible here. Still, it is worthwhile visiting the city. With limited resources, the **Ritz Theater and LaVilla Museum** (*829 North Davis Street*) preserves as much as it can, offering, among other things, comprehensive exhibits of the city's civil rights movement and Jacksonville's black community. Here I learned that way back in 1901 and 1905, Jacksonville's Afro-American community organized boycotts that forced the city to back down from attempts to segregate streetcars (the state government finally imposed segregation); these may have been the earliest of such antisegregation boycotts.

The museum itself is almost all that remains of the LaVilla community that once upon a time helped make Jacksonville known as the Harlem of the South. Interstate highways and urban "renewal" have completely erased this historic neighborhood and also, it seems, awareness among both blacks and whites that Jacksonville has much of which it should be proud and committed to preserving. A. Philip Randolph grew up in Jacksonville, and the city was hometown to the NAACP's James Weldon Johnson, who, along with his brother, John Rosamond, composed "Lift Every Voice and Sing," a song now known as the Negro national anthem. A **James Weldon Johnson Memorial Park** (*West Church and North Broad Streets*) is being developed very near the **old Stanton School** (*West Ashley and Broad Streets*) where he taught, and which once helped make Jacksonville renowned for having one of the best-educated black populations in the United States.

Baseball, too, forms an important part of local Afro-American history—perhaps not surprising, for this is Florida, after all. The **home stadium of the Negro National League** (*Seventh and Myrtle Streets*) was in this city. The league no longer exists, but in 2006 a bronze life-size statue of a black baseball player was unveiled here, dedicated to the league and specifically to John Jordan "Buck" O'Neil, who played ball for years with the league's Kansas City Monarchs. In 1962 O'Neil became the first Afro-American coach of a major-league team, the Chicago Cubs.

Now within the corporate limits of Jacksonville, the **Kingsley Plantation** *(11676 Palmetto Avenue; off A1A/ Heckscher Drive, ½ mile north of the St. Johns River Ferry Landing, on Fort George Island)* offers a close-up view of slavery from a fascinating and unusual perspective. Zephaniah Kingsley, who bought the property in 1814, married one of his slaves, a woman from West Africa's Wolof country (now part of Senegal) named Anta Majigeen Njaay, who was called Anna in Florida. She helped manage the plantation and also acquired her own land and slaves. A few years later, when Spain ceded Florida to the United States in 1821, the territory's relatively less restrictive policies (slaves could sue their owners in court, for example) ended. As increasingly oppressive laws were enacted, to escape what Zephaniah Kingsley called "a spirit of intolerant prejudice," the family, with about fifty slaves whom he and his wife now freed, fled to Haiti, a nation he called "the purest republic."

Anta Kingsley returned to Jacksonville after her husband's death in 1843 and had to battle in the courts to claim the land her husband had willed to her and their children. She ultimately won, becoming owner of the Kingsley Plantation and one of the most influential of free blacks in north Florida. The plantation site is now managed by the National Park Service and is the best-preserved example of the old plantation system in Florida.

Seven generations later, one of Anta and Zephaniah Kingsley's descendants, MaVynne Betsch, became known as the "Beach Lady" of American Beach, where for thirty years—literally until the day she died, September 5, 2005— she passionately fought for environmental protection of the historic black resort area.

Just a few miles north of Jacksonville is **American Beach** *(Highway A1A between Fernandina Beach and the Amelia Island resort community)*. Established in 1933 and once the premier southern resort for blacks, it continues to resist the dollars being dangled by developers despite having fallen into steep decline since segregation ended and other nearby resorts opened their doors to blacks. At one time, Afro-Americans from all over the South came to splash in the ocean, eat out in restaurants, and jam into clubs to enjoy Duke Ellington and Billy Eckstine and other great musicians. There are few amenities today, but the beach is uncrowded—and beautiful. And whenever I walk along its shores, I am reminded that despite all the odds against it in a land of slavery and segregation, we not only survived, but also, whenever possible, seized opportunity and thrived—as the old saying goes, "made a way out of no way."

TALLAHASSEE, FLORIDA

Spontaneity as well as carefully planned strategy could kick off significant civil rights action. That is part of the lesson in Montgomery and Greensboro, and also what we learn once more in Tallahassee. On May 26, 1956, two students attending historically black Florida A&M University refused to give up their "white" seats on a city bus and were arrested for inciting a riot. Here, too, the protagonists were women: Carrie Patterson and Wilhelmina Jakes. A boycott was launched, and it met with as much white resistance as the one in Montgomery—perhaps more. The boycott was led by Reverend Charles Kenzie Steele, and there is a **Steele Memorial** *(111 West Tennessee Street).*

Military Bans

On the eve of America's entry into the war, civil rights groups such as the NAACP and the National Urban League, along with the Negro press and black college officials, campaigned to break down the barriers that kept the Army Air Corps from accepting black pilots. The War Department believed blacks incapable of flying aircraft. One report claimed

Seven airmen at the Tuskegee Army Air Field

that the "colored race does not have the technical nor the flying background for the creation of a bombardment-type unit." Nevertheless, persistent pressure and the negative publicity tarnishing the nation's democratic war aims led the War Department in 1941 to agree to train African-American pilots. The black fighter squadron remained segregated from white pilots, prompting criticism from the NAACP and the black press, which favored the cessation of racial criteria in the military. The *Pittsburgh Courier* blasted the Jim Crow policy as "a citadel to the theory that there can be segregation without discrimination." Yet by the end of the war, the exploits of the Tuskegee Airmen had made African Americans swell with pride. Stationed at Tuskegee Army Airfield in Alabama, on the grounds of an abandoned graveyard, black pilots eventually took to the skies over Europe and proved their skills in fighting the Nazis.

—FROM "CIVIL RIGHTS IN AMERICA THEME STUDY: RACIAL DESEGREGATION OF PUBLIC ACCOMMODATIONS," BY THE NATIONAL PARK SERVICE, DRAFT, FEBRUARY 2004

TUSKEGEE, ALABAMA

L astly, few places associated with black life are as famed as *Tuskegee, Alabama*. Part of its story is well known: Tuskegee Institute and Booker T. Washington; George Washington Carver and what seems like the million-and-one things he did with the peanut; and the famed Tuskegee Airmen whose bravery and skill as fighter pilots in World War II was probably the single most important factor in ending segregation in the U.S. military, all contribute to this small Alabama city's importance to civil rights. The *Tuskegee Airmen National Historic Site (U.S. 81 and 1616 Chappy James Drive)*, the *Tuskegee Human and Civil Rights Multicultural Center (104 South Elm Street)*, and the *Tuskegee Institute National Historic Site (1212 Old Montgomery Road off U.S. 80)* are all valuable sites for understanding these stories. The criminal "Tuskegee experiment" from 1932 to July 1972, in which 399 Afro-Americans were deliberately and systematically infected with syphilis by the U.S. Public Health Service for testing purposes, has also become fairly well known.

Less known is the story of 1950s and 1960s protest in Tuskegee. Following a decision by Alabama's state legislature to gerrymander city boundaries, placing Tuskegee Institute and most of the black population outside city limits, three thousand black residents crowded into and around *Butler Chapel AME Zion Church (1002 N. Church Street; there is a museum inside the church)* on the night of June 25, 1957, and launched a boycott: a "Trade with Friends" campaign against white downtown merchants who backed this move against black political power. "We are going to buy goods and services from those who help us, from those who make no effort to hinder us, from those who recognize us as first-class citizens," declared Tuskegee Institute sociologist Professor Charles Gomillion, a leader of the Tuskegee Civic Association. The boycott did not end until 1961 when, in response to a suit filed by the civic association, the U.S. Supreme Court ruled against gerrymandering aimed at reducing the power of black votes. But segregation remained in place, and this victory did not end protest. Shortly after the Selma-to-Montgomery march, students on the campus of Tuskegee Institute, led by student-body president Gwen Patton, began a campaign of sit-ins and picketing to end segregation. On January 3, 1966, the murder of Tuskegee student Samuel Younge Jr. triggered another round of protest; he was shot to death attempting to use the white bathroom at a gas station. It was the killing of Younge, just twenty-one years old and a navy veteran, that led to SNCC's statement of opposition to the Vietnam war.

There is, of course, more, much more. But let me offer this, my way of saying not only *a luta continua*, but that it *must* continue—there are not only more trails to follow but more trails to blaze. I am never very far from song when I think of the civil rights movement, and another song we sang, one that seems appropriate to past and future alike, comes to mind now as I conclude:

One man's hands can't tear a prison down
Two man's hands can't tear a prison down
But if two and two and fifty make a million
We'll see that day come 'round.

NOTES

ONE: MY COUNTRY 'TIS OF THEE—WASHINGTON, D.C.

2 *was arrested while picketing the U.S. Capitol*
While Pauli Murray's Little Palace sit-in (and others she conducted) is well known, hardly anyone pictures professorial Dr. Kenneth Clark as a direct action-ist and campus agitator. But Dr. Clark refers to his Capitol protest in a 1976 interview he gave for Columbia University, which can be found in the Notable New Yorkers Columbia University Libraries Oral History Research Office.

4 *angel of my redemption*
Ossie Davis interview with Ken Paulson recorded by the First Amendment Center November 28, 2000, http://www.firstamendmentcenter.org.

7 *sidebar "U.S. Capitol Artwork"*
"African-Americans in Capitol Artwork: A Glimpse of American History," by Erin Michaela Bendiner, U.S. Capitol Historic Society volunteer.

9 *Why should not armed Liberty wear a helmet?*
William C. Allen, *History of the United States Capitol: A Chronicle of Design, Construction and Politics* (University Press of the Pacific), chapter 7.

10 *who managed to escape*
Sandra Fitzpatrick and Maria R. Goodwin, *The Guide to Black Washington* (Hippocrene Books), 40.

14 *sidebar "The Spirit of Flight"*
Papers of the Kendrick-Brooks family, Library of Congress manuscript division.

14 *foreshadowing the civil rights struggles later in the century*
Peter Perl, "Race Riot of 1919 Gave Glimpse of Future Struggles," *Washington Post*, March 1, 1999.

20 *first elected mayor in 1974*
Walter Washington was first appointed mayor in 1968 by President Lyndon Johnson, and many viewed him as little more than a puppet controlled by the White House and Congress. But Washington soon proved stronger than expected. During the height of the 1968 riots, FBI director J. Edgar Hoover summoned Washington to bureau headquarters. "Start shooting looters," demanded the FBI chieftain. Washington refused. "Well, this conversation is over!" said Hoover. "That's all right," Washington shot back. "I was leaving anyway."

21 *That's millions, should you wonder*
Simeon Booker, "Testimonial Nets Final 5 mil. Pays Off on National Council of Negro Women Building," *Jet*, April 8, 2002.

23 *prominent role in civil rights struggle*
Stokely Carmichael (Kwame Ture), *Ready for Revolution* (Scribner), chapters 6 and 7; the book provides a valuable feel of those campus days. Also, Cleveland Sellers, *The River of No Return* (University Press of Mississippi), 57–66.

27 *the Alliance's tactic of combining boycotts, picketing and court action*
The full, fascinating story can be found in *Washington History*, Spring–Summer 1994, published by the Washington Historical Society. "'Don't Buy Where You Can't Work': The New Negro Alliance of Washington," by Michele F. Pacifico, 66–88.

29 *Bishop had long been running afoul of the District's race laws*
Bishop's story and all the other stories leading up to the 1954 *Brown* decision are told in *Simple Justice: The History of* Brown v. Board of Education by Richard Kluger (Vintage Books).

TWO: UP SOUTH—MARYLAND

34 *closely connected to Washington*
As in the District and Virginia, the trading and export of slaves was big business in Maryland. Quoting educator and abolitionist Horace Mann, in her book *The Pearl: A Failed Slave Escape on the Potomac* (University of North Carolina Press), Josephine F. Pacheco points out that selling slaves, more than using them for labor, was where the real money was made. So, the trading of slaves within the United States lasted well past the official prohibition of transatlantic trafficking.

35 *with respect to yourselves*
The full text of Benjamin Banneker's lengthy and powerful letter can be found in volume one of historian Herbert Aptheker's *A Documentary History of the Negro People in the United States* (Citadel Press), 22–26.

38 *first man in the group to actually reach the North Pole*
This claim has been controversial, but Arlington National Cemetery says that it was Henson, the Afro-American explorer, who first reached the Pole and planted the American flag. In 1987 Henson was disinterred from his New York burial site and, with the okay of President Ronald Reagan, reburied in Arlington National Cemetery, where he now lies next to Admiral Peary.

43 *were refused service*
As far as most restaurateurs were concerned, the federal government needed to stay out of their affairs. "I built this place with my sweat. Now you come up here with your clean shirt and pressed pants and tell me how to run my business," Cottage Inn proprietor Clarence Rosier told the State Department when Nigeria filed a complaint after one of their diplomats was refused service in Rosier's establishment. "No Diplomatic Immunity: African Diplomats, the State Department, and Civil Rights, 1961–1964," written by Renee Romano and published in the September 2000 issue of the *Journal of American History*, is an illuminating article on the Kennedy administration's awkward effort to maintain good diplomatic relations with black- and brown-peopled nations in the face of their continued encounters with racism. Also see "Racism Toward Black African Diplomats During the Kennedy Administration," written by Calvin B. Holder and published in the September 1983 issue of *The Journal of Black Studies*, 31–48.

43 *They sent my grandfather's meal to his home by way of a police car*
Fred Powledge, *Free At Last?* (HarperPerennial edition), 524.

48 *Richardson simply does not exist in the city's official history*
Fortunately, several authors have addressed both the Cambridge civil rights movement and the complex resoluteness of Gloria Richardson. Peter Levey's *Civil War on Race Street: The Civil Rights Movement in Cambridge* (University of Florida) is a good source. The section of the chapter titled "We Can't Deal With Her," 278–83, in Lynne Olson's *Freedom's Daughters* (Scribner) shows Richardson as much more than the usual portrayal as inflexible militant as does

the Anita K. Foeman article "Breaking the Black Mold," in the *Journal of Black Studies* (May 1996): 604–15. *Generation on Fire* (University Press of Kentucky), a set of oral histories collected by Jeff Kisseloff, includes Richardson's riveting story in her own voice.

51   *national media voices of civil rights advocacy*
http://www.afro.com.

53   *drafted the constitutions of the decolonizing African nations of Ghana and Tanzania*
A biographical sketch of Marshall provided by the Thurgood Marshall College in La Jolla, California, notes, "Mr. Marshall was asked by the United Nations and the United Kingdom to help draft the constitutions of the emerging African nations of Ghana and what is now Tanzania. It was felt that the person who so successfully fought for the rights of America's oppressed minority would be the perfect person to ensure the rights of the white citizens in these two former European colonies."

54   *Naturally, there is a story*
The story can be found in "Estate of Mind" by Marion Meade, *Book Forum* (April/May 2006).

55   *were especially important in the emergence of the modern civil rights movement*
Lisa Krause, "Black Soldiers in World War II: Fighting Enemies at Home and Abroad," *National Geographic News*, February 15, 2001.

THREE: DON'T CARRY ME BACK—VIRGINIA

61   *a black history film can also be arranged*
Two other great ironies are associated with the American Revolution in colonial Virginia. During the Revolutionary War, Virginia's last royal governor, John Murray, Earl of Dunmore, issued the first Emancipation Proclamation in America on November 15, 1775. It offered freedom to any slave reaching British lines. This tipped the balance among undecided white settlers who were weighing where to place their support, and they committed to the American rebellion against British rule. For the slaves, however, the escalating Revoutionary War greatly increased opportunities for escape.

61   *first Afro-American child whose name is known*
Associated Press writer Helen O'Neill, "History and Faith: Tracing the First Black Family in America," in *SouthCoast Today* (Massachusetts), February 8, 1998.

63   *Sally Hemings, the Afro-American mother of at least one of Jefferson's children*
This remains a huge controversy, although it is widely acknowledged that slave owners fathering children with their slave women was hardly uncommon. In January 2000, the Thomas Jefferson Memorial Foundation issued a report cautiously concluding that "the weight of evidence suggests that Jefferson probably was the father of Eston Hemings and perhaps the father of all of Sally Hemings' children."

64   *Intense role-playing sessions—sociodramas*
James Farmer's autobiography, *Lay Bare the Heart* (Arbor House), 198.

66–67   *sidebar "Origin of the "Freedom Rides"*
The definitive work on the subject is Raymond Arsenault's *Freedom Riders* (Oxford University Press), in which pages 11–15 recount Irene Morgan's story. See Robin Washington, "Irene Morgan: Civil Rights Pioneer Finally Recognized," *Boston Herald*, August 6, 2000; and Judith Haynes, "Local Hero Gets Presidential Honor," *Newport News (VA) Daily Press*, January 9, 2001.

68   *sidebar "Our Last Supper"*
John Lewis and Michael Dorso, *Walking with the Wind* (Harcourt Brace), 135.

69   *Some 3,800 Afro-Americans*
http://www.arlingtoncemetery.org.

70   *asked Dr. Drew to head the nation's blood drive*
Society of Black Academic Surgeons, "Charles Drew: Black American Medical Pioneer," http://www.sbas.net.

71   *but ten thousand slaves went through here*
From Lavern J. Chatman to Charlie Cobb. Also see *African American Historic Places*, edited by Beth L. Savage (Preservation Press), 27.

72   *not improved conditions or even wages, but freedom*
Josephine F. Pacheco, *The Pearl: A Failed Slave Escape on the Potomac* (University of North Carolina Press), 48–50.

72   *divulged the route they planned to take*
There are actually several theories about how the runaways were discovered, Pacheco, *The Pearl*, 58–60.

77   *taking over the city of Richmond*
Charles Johnson and Patricia Smith, *Africans in America: America's Journey Through Slavery* (Harcourt Brace), 253–58; also, Vincent Harding, *There Is a River: The Black Struggle for Freedom in America* (Harcourt Brace) 54–59.

80   *also the first college to enroll Native Americans*
A complete list of the Native American students from 1878 to 1923 can be found at: http://www.twofrog.com.

86   *ordered the schools to reopen*
This entire dramatic story is well told in Richard Kluger, *Simple Justice* (Vintage Books), chapters 19 and 20, 451–507.

88   *secretary of defense Robert S. McNamara*
The story of the demonstrating GI comes from singer/songwriter/organizer Matthew Jones, who was one of SNCC's field secretaries in Danville; he even wrote a song about it, "Demonstrating G.I.," published in *Sing for Freedom: The Story of the Civil Rights Movement Through Its Songs* (Sing Out Publications). In introducing the song, Matt would say, "On July 11, 1963, there was a soldier boy that came home in Danville. He saw what was going on and he had on his uniform. The Secretary of Defense issued a statement: 'You can go overseas and fight in a uniform, but you can't come back over here picketing and demonstrating in your uniform. That's un-American.' So he got up at a mass meeting and said, 'I'm an American fighting man. I'm gonna defend my country as long as I can, and if I can defend my country overseas, why don't you set my people free?'" 136.

FOUR: MORE THAN A HAMBURGER—NORTH CAROLINA

91   *Defamer of White Womanhood escapes*
Beyond resentment of successful black enterprise and black political power of which his newspaper was an important part, the anger at Manley in particular erupted because he had written a sarcastic response to a speech by one of Georgia's leading feminists, Rebecca Felton, who said black rapists were the biggest problem facing white farmwomen. "If it requires lynching to protect women's dearest possession from ravening, drunken human beasts, then I say lynch a thousand negroes a week." An angry Manley wrote in response that many of the rape charges were made by white women to cover up their consensual sexual relations with black men: "Our experience among poor white people in the country teaches us that the women of that race are not any more particular in the manner of clandestine meetings with colored men than are the white men with colored women."

92–93   *sidebar "1898 Wilmington Race Riot"*
Angela Mack, "Over a Century Later, Facts of 1898 Race Riots Released," North Carolina *StarNewsOnline*, December 16, 2005.

95   *meet violence with violence*
The NAACP's leadership, headquartered in New York, might have tolerated some of Williams's angrily spoken words. Even understanding his fury, however, Williams's rage erupted in such a volcanic stream of molten political lava that the organization—committed to legal action and building support for such action—felt threatened: "We must be willing to kill if necessary. We cannot take these people who do us injustice to the court and it [has] become necessary to punish them ourselves. In the future we are going to have to try and convict these people on the spot. [These court decisions] open the way to real violence. We cannot rely on the law. We get no justice under the present system. If we feel that injustice is done, we must right then and there on the spot be prepared to inflict punishment on these people. I feel this is the only way of survival," James Forman, *The Making of Black Revolutionaries*, 176. See also *Negroes with Guns* (Wayne State University Press), written by Robert Williams himself.

98   *trying to take over*
Tom Dent, *Southern Journey: A Return to the Civil Rights Movement* (William Morrow), 18.

102   *brought tears to my eyes*
William H. Chafe, *Civilities and Civil Rights: Greensboro, North Carolina and the Black Struggle for Freedom* (Oxford University Press), 81.

105   *indigenous leadership across the South*
Forman, *The Making of Black Revolutionaries*, 217.

105   *not enough can be said about Ella Josephine Baker*
Charles Payne, *I've Got the Light of Freedom: The Organizing Tradition and the Mississippi Freedom Struggle* (University of California Press), 79–100; Barbara Ransby, *Ella Baker and the Black Freedom Movement: A Radical Democratic Vision* (University of North Carolina Press), 1–12.

105   *about two hundred came*
Howard Zinn, *SNCC: The New Abolitionists* (Beacon Press), 32–33.

108 *We did both.*
Ransby, *Ella Baker*, 346–52; Cleveland Sellers, *The River of No Return* (University Press of Mississippi), 193–203; Clayborne Carson, *In Struggle* (Harvard University Press), 287–90.

110 *within their means*
Robert P. Moses and Charles E. Cobb Jr., *Radical Equations: Civil Rights from Mississippi to the Algebra Project* (Beacon Press), 56.

111 *began discussing the idea of nonviolent struggle for civil rights*
Actually, Moore and King were in very different places politically. Moore was part of a "spiritual cell movement" of radical divinity students who engaged in direct-action protests, while King was a member of what Moore considered the far too "abstract" Dialectical Society, a weekly campus discussion group. His first impression of King, Moore told me once, was, "just another Baptist preacher." To Moore, King seemed timid when it came to considering or taking radical action, and their brief political conversations at Boston University went nowhere. Moore was very surprised and pleased by King's emergence as leader of the Montgomery bus boycott, and wrote him a letter of support, thus reestablishing a relationship.

112 *Let us not fear*
Durham Civil Rights Heritage Project, http://www.durhamcountylibrary.org.

FIVE: I'LL OVERCOME—SOUTH CAROLINA

118 *sidebar "The Anti-Communist Thing"*
Interview by Sam Sills August 8, 1993, American Social History Project, http://historymatters.gmu.edu.

124 *thought to be from Angola*
For African context of revolt, *Stono: Documenting and Interpreting a Southern Slave Revolt*, edited by Mark M. Smith (University of South Carolina Press), 75–78.

124 *promised land and freedom*
For a summary of South Carolina slave laws: http://www.slaveryinamerica.org/geography/slave_laws_SC.htm.

124 *Jemmy was apparently literate*
In another interesting and consequential response to the Stono revolt, Lieutenant Governor William Bull, in a letter dated October 5, 1741, suggested to Britain's Board of Trade that Native Americans be offered rewards as incentive to help catch runaway and rebellious slaves, "Report from William Bull re. Stono Rebellion," Africans in America, http://www.pbs.org.

126 *We shot them. We are not ashamed of it.*
Justin Simmons, "Tillman Legacy Part of Dark Past," *Daily Gamecock* (University of South Carolina), September 1, 2004.

130 *I predated it*
Coastal Community Foundation of South Carolina, "From Civil Rights Activist to Teacher to Lover of the Arts," http://www.ccfgives.org.

130 *advocate for civil rights*
David Shi, "Prominent White Charlestonian Played Crucial Role in Desegregation of South," *Greenville News*, February 23, 2002; *Women in the Civil Rights Movement*, edited by Vicki L. Crawford, Jacqueline Anne Rouse, and Barbara Woods (Indiana University Press), 109–10.

132 *daughter of a former slave*
Septima Poinsette Clark's father, Peter Poinsette, was named after his "master," Joel Poinsette, owner of a rice plantation and the first U.S. ambassador to Mexico. Upon his return, Joel Poinsette brought back with him the flowering plant commonly seen during the Christmas season now, the poinsettia.

133 *sidebar "Dorothy Cotton"*
Humphrey Institute (now the Center for Democracy and Citizenship) interview by Harry Byte, 1991, http://www.publicwork.org.

134 *discovering local community leaders*
Septima Clark, *Echo in My Soul* (E. P. Dutton), 187–89.

139 *on different, more violent terrain*
John Lewis and Michael Dorso, *Walking with the Wind: A Memoir of the Movement* (Harcourt Brace), 137–39.

142 *You learn the truth in prison*
Lecture/presentation April 28, 2001: "What have the Romans Ever Done for Us?" by Colin Barker, Manchester Metropolitan University, and Laurence Cox, National University of Ireland, Maynooth.

146 *reluctantly began to desegregate*
Long before the sit-ins of the 1960s, boycotts were an important civil rights weapon. Between 1900 and 1906 blacks in thirty-five southern cities boycotted segregated streetcars. For more on this, see "The Boycott Movement Against Jim Crow Street Cars in the South, 1900–1906," written by Professors August Meir and Elliot Rudwick, published in the *Journal of American History*, 51, March 1967. In *The Origins of the Civil Rights Movement* (Free Press), 48–49, Aldon D. Morris briefly discusses the mid-1950s Orangeburg boycott, placing it within the context of other modern civil rights boycott efforts.

148 *considered integration "an irrelevant issue"*
Cleveland Sellers, *The River of No Return* (University Press of Mississippi), 209–10.

151 *for your nigger children*
Richard Kluger, *Simple Justice* (Vintage), 4.

SIX: ... ON MY MIND—GEORGIA

156 *to 462,198 in 1860*
"Slavery in Antebellum Georgia," *The New Georgia Encyclopedia*, http://www.georgiaencyclopedia.org.

157 *torch never to be put out*
From "Reconstruction: The Second Civil War," a PBS documentary that aired on *The American Experience*, http://www.pbs.org.

160   *lynched in the United States*
These numbers vary from source to source. In a study submitted for presentation at the 2006 annual meeting of the Population Association of America, sociologists Stewart E. Tolnay and Amy Kate Baily put the number of blacks lynched in the southern states during the period 1880 to 1930 at 2,754. A June 2005 BBC report of the U.S. Senate's apology for lynching led with "Nearly 5,000 Americans—mostly black males—are documented as having been lynched between 1880 and 1960."

161   *sidebar "Was there a murder?"*
http://afroamhistory.about.com.

163   *the only one of nineteen candidates to actively seek Afro-American votes*
"Helen Douglas Mankin," *The New Georgia Encyclopedia*, http://www.georgiaencyclopedia.org/nge/Article.jsp?id=h-744; "Atlanta in the Civil Rights Movement," Atlanta Regional Council for Higher Education, http://www.atlantahighered.org/civilrights/essay_detail.asp?phase=1.

163   *We got segregation in the state of Georgia!*
Harry G. Lefever, *Undaunted by the Fight: Spelman College and the Civil Rights Movement 1957-1967* (Mercer University Press), 9.

174   *and dump them in his lap*
Harry G. Lefever remembers Daddy King taking this stance at a mass meeting rather than at a Sunday church service; nevertheless, the essential point remains true; more than any single thing, the student sit-in at Rich's, Martin King's imprisonment, and Daddy King's pledge and power gave John Kennedy victory in the 1960 presidential election. The Kennedys were not supporters of sit-ins and feared freedom rides, and neither Robert nor John had much inkling of black political power. So what moved Robert Kennedy to agree that his brother John should telephone Mrs. King when some campaign aides pressed him to do so? "It made me so damn angry to think of that bastard sentencing a citizen to four months of hard labor for a minor traffic offense," he told his biographer, Evan Thomas, years later: *Robert Kennedy: His Life* (Simon & Schuster), 102.

188   *I did research. I found his method was nonviolence.*
After tricking King out of jail with promises to the Albany Movement he failed to keep, Prichett jubilantly told reporters, "We met nonviolence with nonviolence," Juan Williams, *Eyes on the Prize* (Penguin), 170.

190   *sidebar "What did we win?"*
Sanford Wexler, *An Eyewitness History of the Civil Rights Movement* (Checkmark Books).

192   *an early Christmas present*
"Savannah," *The New Georgia Encyclopedia* http://www.georgiaencyclopedia.org.

196   *sidebar "I'm going to do . . ."*
"Hosea Williams in His Own Words," http://www.gpb.org.

196   *the most integrated city in the South*
SCLC's Andy Young, almost the complete opposite of Hosea Williams in personality, more than once was in sharp disagreement with Williams. He nonetheless respected this man he called "perplexing." Young also is one of the few who have written about Williams with insight; see *An Easy Burden* (Perennial), 258–63. John Lewis says, in a right-on-the-mark short take on Williams: [Hosea] was always the

one who would throw up his hands and say people were just talking something to death here. What are we going to *do*? That's what Hosea always wanted to know," John Lewis and Michael Dorso, *Walking with the Wind* (Harcourt Brace), 319.

SEVEN: LOOK BACKWARD, MOVE FORWARD—ALABAMA

204   *demonized Afro-American workers in particular and the Afro-American community in general*
Henry M. McKiven Jr., *Iron and Steel: Class, Race and Community in Birmingham Alabama, 1875–1920* (University of North Carolina Press), introduction, 7–8. See also Brian Kelly, *Race, Class and Power in the Alabama Coalfields* (University of Illinois Press), 17–19.

207   *I want those seats*
Special fiftieth-anniversary *Montgomery Advertiser* edition, "Voices of the Boycott," by Jannell McGrew, December 1, 2005.

207   *I had my orders*
James F. Blake obituary, *Guardian* (London), March 27, 2002.

211   *sidebar "The Women's Political Council . . ."*
Vicki L. Crawford, Jacqueline Anne Rouse, and Barbara Woods, eds., *Women in the Civil Rights Movement: Trailblazers and Torchbearers, 1941–1965* (Indiana University Press).

213   *sidebar "The Woods of Vernon Johns"*
http://www.vernonjohns.org.

218   *guns have always been an integral part of that way of life*
Clayborne Carson, director of the King Papers Project at Stanford University, in the January 17, 1996, *Campus Report*, writes that at the time King's house was bombed, he "was seeking a gun permit, and he was protected by armed bodyguards." The presence of guns in Reverend King's house is also noted in the excellent biographical film on Bayard Rustin titled *Brother Outsider*. Rustin takes credit for moving King to a complete commitment to nonviolence.

228   *led Confederate cavalry against Wilson's troops*
Virginia Van der Veer Hamilton and Jacqueline A. Matte, *Seeing Historic Alabama* (University of Alabama Press), 151–52.

230   *has become known as "Bloody Sunday"*
Roy Reed, "Alabama Police Use Gas and Clubs to Rout Negroes," *New York Times*, March 8, 1965.

235   *It's part of the story of civil rights*
Gustav Niebuhr, "A Civil Rights Martyr Remembered," *New York Times*, April 8, 2000.

243   *sidebar "Things Happened So Fast"*
http://www.veteransofhope.org.

243   *Coleman was aquitted by an all-white jury*
Stokely Carmichael, *Ready For Revolution* (Scribner), 467–70.

248   *a roll call of freedom fighters*
Andrew Young, *An Easy Burden* (Perennial), 353.

249 *love songs to white women*
For a detailed description of the attack, see "Interrupted Melody: The 1956 Attack on Nat "King Cole" by Gary S. Sprayberry and published in the winter 2004 issue of *Alabama Heritage*. This article places the attack against the backdrop of increased pressure for civil rights and a cultural fear of the "corrupting" influence of rock and roll and rhythm and blues on white young people.

252 *most frustrating and bewildering hours I have lived*
Clayborne Carson *The Autobiography of Martin Luther King Jr.* (Warner Books).

257 *sidebar "I don't think I was scared"*
Hank Thomas to the *New York Post*, 1961.

EIGHT: DON'T KNOW HOW WE WERE SO BRAVE—MISSISSIPPI

264 *I never completed my journey to Houston*
See Lawrence Guyot's description of the white mob's attack in Howell Raines, *My Soul is Rested* (G. P. Putnam's Sons), footnote 244–45.

268 *were arrested by police for disturbing the peace*
John Dittmer, *Local People: The Struggle for Civil Rights in Mississippi* (University of Illinois Press), 86–89.

273 *the laws of America are for everyone*
"I'm no lady, I'm a newspaperwoman," Mrs. Smith used to say. In answer to a question by Henry Mitchell about the effect of a boycott whites tried to mount against her, she responded, "Oh, a handful of people cancelled their subscriptions during the civil rights years, but they sent their cooks down to buy the paper, issue by issue," *Washington Post*, May 4, 1973.

274 *out of the hands of the angry youths as they dispersed*
I distinctly remember the turnaround moment being when Doar stepped forward and alone placed himself between the crowd—some of whom were throwing bottles, and the heavily armed police. Some of the youthful anger was born of frustration that had found no outlet when the NAACP shut down; there was also anger at what seemed to be the use of Evers's death to raise funds. "The most important thing you can do for Medgar right now is make a contribution to the NAACP," said NAACP deputy director Roy Wilkins at one point. "That just pisses me off," said one Jackson activist standing next to me, who then stomped out of the Masonic Temple.

275 *Evers gave a great deal of attention to building NAACP youth chapters*
The NAACP's New York chiefs were reluctant to give Medgar the position, reflecting in part the organization's view that Deep South states like Mississippi were too difficult, too dangerous, and too expensive to challenge directly. Thurgood Marshall and Gloster Current argued over the issue of providing resources for Mississippi, with Marshall pressing for more, *Local People*, 31–33. With new southern activist organizations forming, organizational rivalry was another factor. In fact, when Medgar Evers began serving as assistant secretary of the newly formed SCLC on February 14, 1957, Current told him that was in conflict with his NAACP obligations; and when Evers asked Roy Wilkins for his opinion, Wilkins suggested he resign from SCLC, and on August 20, Evers did. One effect of this distancing was to make frustrated Mississippi NAACP leaders more welcoming of young SNCC and CORE field secretaries, who found in

the state a great pool of young activists from the NAACP Youth Councils that Evers had organized.

277   *two all-white juries had deadlocked in 1964*
Beckwith was confident that he would not be convicted, waving to friends and even offering cigars to the prosecutor, Charles Payne, *I've Got the Light of Freedom: The Organizing Tradition and the Mississippi Freedom Struggle* (University of California Press), 189.

281   *They're right behind you*
David J. Garrow, *Bearing the Cross* (Vintage Books) 483; Christine Gibson, "A Shooting—And the Civil Rights Movement Changes Course," *American Heritage* (June 2006).

286   *for contributing to the delinquency of minors*
Among the actual bone-chilling words of Judge Robert W. Brumfield during sentencing were: "Some of you are local residents, some of you are outsiders. Those of you who are local residents are like sheep being led to slaughter. If you continue to follow the advice of outside agitators you will be like sheep and slaughtered." Robert P. Moses and Charles E. Cobb Jr., *Radical Equations* (Beacon Press), 34.

288   *sidebar "I am writing"*
James Forman, *The Making of Black Revolutionaries* (University of Washington Press), 233.

292   *well before SNCC, CORE, or COFO came to be*
Aaron Henry, *Aaron Henry: The Fire Ever Burning* (University Press of Mississippi), 79–84.

293   *I feel I can do more alive*
Local People, 47–48, 70.

299   *backed away from offering federal protection to blacks attempting to register*
The reluctance of the federal government to offer protection was an issue that plagued voter registration efforts and still-uncounted deaths were the inevitable consequence. There was much greater federal concern about Communists allegedly influencing the movement, and greater effort to discover them.

304   *to juke joints in neighboring Bolivar county*
Robert Palmer, *Deep Blues: A Musical and Cultural History of the Mississippi Delta* (Penguin Books), 48–57.

306   *you're afraid to do what you know is right*
Chana Kai Lee, *For Freedom's Sake: The Life of Fannie Lou Hamer* (University of Illinois Press), 93.

NINE: FULL CIRCLE— TENNESSEE

314   *philosophy of Mohandas Gandhi*
Lawson, too, had made his way to nonviolence and Gandhi, at least in part, via theologian Howard Thurman. In college he had learned of the meeting between Gandhi and Thurman at which the Indian leader told Thurman that the United States was engaged in domestic colonial oppression. He regretted, Gandhi said, that he had not been successful in making the possibility of nonviolent struggle

more visible; a black American leader might. David Halberstam, *The Children* (Random House), 12.

315   *Athens of the South*
So named because of its large number of institutions of higher education, Nashville was also the first southern city to establish a public school system (1852).

318   *sidebar "Redemptive Suffering"*
John Lewis and Michael Dorso, *Walking with the Wind: A Memoir of the Movement* (Harcourt Brace).

321   *the great movement that has taken place in this community*
By the time of the April 1960 meeting in Raleigh that led to the formation of SNCC, the Nashville student movement was arguably the most influential of the student sit-in groups. The size of its delegation was rivaled only by that of the Atlanta delegation. Marion Barry, one of the Nashville student leaders (years later mayor of Washington, D.C.) became SNCC's first chairman; it might have been Diane Nash if she had not been a woman, although her inclination was to resist making herself the central leader lest a personality cult develop around her. And it was the mentor of the Nashville group, Jim Lawson, who along with Ella Baker seized the political imagination of the gathering. Lawson insisted that the issues underlying the student protests were spiritual and moral. Lawson also blasted the NAACP as being the voice of the black bourgeoisie and mainly concerned with fundraising and court cases instead of direct challenges to "racial evil." This was targeted more at the NAACP's national leaders than its local leaders. During the peak of Nashville's sit-ins, recalls John Lewis, Thurgood Marshall spoke at Fisk University and criticized the decision to refuse bail. "You've made your point," said Marshall. "If someone offers to get you out, man, get out." A year later, on a panel with Lewis, Marshall argued that continuing Freedom Rides into dangerous places such as Montgomery and Birmingham was wrong. "Thurgood Marshall was a good man, a historic figure, but watching him speak on that April evening in Nashville convinced me more than ever that our revolt was as much against this nation's traditional black leadership structure as it was against racial segregation and discrimination." Lewis and Dorso, *Walking with the Wind*, 107.

334   *I need to feed the children*
Ralph David Abernathy, *And the Walls Came Tumbling Down* (HarperCollins), 412–13.

EPILOGUE

345   *his attendance at Commonwealth College*
During this first campaign, Arkansas's attorney general requested an FBI investigation of Faubus's association with Commonwealth College; those files are in the University of Arkansas Special Collections.

345–46   *organized a "Mothers League"*
National Park Service, "All the World Is Watching Us: Little Rock Central High School and the 1957 Desegregation Crisis, http://www.nps.gov.

354   *environmental protection of the historic black resort area*
John-Thor Dahlburg, "Beach Lady" Triumphed Over the Tide of Development," *Los Angeles Times*, September 28, 2005, A14.

PERMISSIONS AND CREDITS

TEXT

"Youth," from *The Collected Poems of Langston Hughes* by Langston Hughes, edited by Arnold Rampersad and David Roessel, associate editor, copyright © 1994 by the estate of Langston Hughes. Used by permission of Alfred A. Knopf, a division of Random House, Inc.

"So much power and glory," from *Keep A-Inchin' Along: Selected Writings of Carl Van Vechten about Black Art and Letters*, Bruce Kellner, editor. Westport CT: Greenwood Press, 1979. Courtesy of the Carl Van Vechten Trust.

"U.S. Slavery Museum Takes Uncensored Look," by Heather Gehlert, reprinted with the permission of the *Los Angeles Times*. Copyright © the *Los Angeles Times* 2006.

"Willa Player, 94, Black Educator Dies," "South Carolina State Remembers 'Forgotten Protest,'" and "Groups Pay Homage to Hosea Williams," used with the permission of the Associated Press. Copyright © 2007. All rights reserved.

"The Second Battle of Fort Sumter" and Rutha Harris singing at Shiloh in Albany, Georgia, excerpted and reprinted with the permission of Simon & Shuster Adult Publishing Group from *Parting the Waters: America in the King Years, 1954–63* by Taylor Branch. Copyright © 1988 by Taylor Branch.

Excerpts from *The Long Haul* by Myles Horton © 1998 by Herbert Kohl, Judith Kohl, Charis Horton, and Thorsten Horton. Reprinted with the permission of Herbert and Judith Kohl.

"Wives Were Key in Civil Rights Struggle," by Bill Torpy, © 2006 the *Atlanta Journal-Constitution*. Reprinted with permission from the *Atlanta Journal-Constitution*.

"NAACP Appears Ready to Relocate to D.C.," by Nikita Stewart, December 19, 2006, reprinted with permission of the *Washington Post*; copyright © 2006 the *Washington Post*.

"I Am Fortified by the Truth, Justice, and Christ" sidebar. Excerpt from *Time on Two Crosses: The Collected Writings of Bayard Rustin*, edited by Devon W. Carbado and Donald Weise. Published by Cleis Press of San Francisco, 2003. Reprinted with permission.

PHOTOGRAPHS

Chapter One: My Country 'Tis of Thee—Washington, D.C.
Page 3: AP/Wide World Photos. **Pages 4, 12, 15, 16, 19, 31:** Library of Congress. **Pages 5, 28:** Getty Images/Hulton Archive. **Page 22:** Cecil Williams.

Chapter Two: Up South—Maryland
Pages 35, 38, 45, 46: Bettmann/Corbis. **Pages 36, 47, 48, 53:** Library of Congress. **Page 37:** Bob Adelman. **Page 42:** Fred Ward/Black Star. **Page 57:** Danny Lyon/Magnum Photos.

Chapter Three: Don't Carry Me Back—Virginia
Pages 61, 66, 81: Library of Congress. **Page 62:** University of Virginia, Special Collections. **Pages 63, 70:** Bettmann/Corbis. **Pages 65, 88:** Danny Lyon/ Magnum Photos. **Page 71:** Alfred Eisenstaedt/Time Life Pictures/Getty Images. **Pages 73, 79, 84, 85, 86:** *Richmond Times-Dispatch.* **Pages 74, 78:** Anderson Collection, Valentine Richmond History Center. **Page 75:** Matt Herron/Take Stock. **Page 82:** National Archives and Records Administration. **Page 87:** Library of Virginia.

Chapter Four: More Than a Hamburger—North Carolina
Pages 91, 97: Library of Congress (page 91, Frank Delano). **Pages 98, 99:** *Greensboro News and Record.* **Page 104:** George Ballis/Take Stock. **Page 112:** *Durham Herald Sun.*

Chapter Five: I'll Overcome—South Carolina
Pages 116, 117: Highlander Research and Education Center. **Page 120:** Granger Collection. **Pages 125, 132:** Library of Congress. **Pages 127, 143, 146, 152:** Cecil Williams. **Page 136:** Eve Arnold/Magnum Photos. **Page 138:** South Caroliniana Library, University of South Carolina. **Pages 139, 140:** *Rock Hill (SC) Herald.* **Page 148:** AP/Wide World Photos.

Chapter Six: . . . On My Mind—Georgia
Pages 155, 156, 160: Library of Congress. **Page 162:** Special Collections Department, Pullen Library, Georgia State University. **Page 166, 172, 176, 180, 183, 185, 189, 195:** Danny Lyon/Magnum Photos. **Pages 169, 171:** Courtesy of the Atlanta History Center. **Pages 173, 174, 187, 188, 197:** AP/Wide World Photos. **Page 178:** Julius Lester.

Chapter Seven: Look Backward, Move Forward—Alabama
Pages 203, 206, 220, 222, 231, 248, 251, 252, 256, 257: AP/Wide World Photos. **Pages 209, 218, 254:** Charles Moore/Black Star. **Page 210:** Bruce Davidson/Magnum Photos. **Pages 234, 237:** Danny Lyon/Magnum Photos. **Pages 229, 241:** Library of Congress. **Pages 230, 233, 250:** Matt Herron/Take Stock. **Pages 242, 244:** Bettmann/Corbis. **Page 255:** Bob Adelman/Magnum Photos.

Chapter Eight: Don't Know How We Were So Brave—Mississippi
Page 261: Getty/Hulton Archive. **Pages 262, 275:** Library of Congress. **Page 264:** Maria Varela. **Pages 266, 268, 284, 290, 299:** Matt Herron/Take Stock. **Pages 270, 287:** Wisconsin Historical Society. **Pages 278, 298, 305, 307:** AP/ Wide World Photos. **Page 272:** Flip Schulke/Corbis. **Page 283:** McCain Library and Archives, University of Southern Mississippi. **Page 294:** Harvey Richards Film Archive/Estuary Press. **Pages 297, 300:** Danny Lyon/Magnum Photos.

Chapter Nine: Full Circle—Tennessee
Pages 314, 336, 339, 341: AP/Wide World Photos. **Page 315:** Vic Cooley/ Nashville Public Library. **Pages 319, 322:** *Tennessean* (page 319, Jimmy Ellis; page 322 Gerald Holly). **Page 323:** Nashville Public Library. **Pages 326, 328:** Highlander Research and Education Center. **Page 335:** Vernon Matthews/ *Memphis Commercial Appeal.*

Epilogue
Page 345: Arkansas History Commission. **Pages 349, 350:** AP/Wide World Photos. **Page 356:** Library of Congress.

INDEX